An Introduction to
Language Policy

Language and Social Change

Series Editors:

Jennifer Coates, Roehampton University
Jenny Cheshire, Queen Mary, University of London
Euan Reid, Institute of Education, University of London

The series explores the relationships between language, society and social change, and encompasses both theoretical and applied aspects of language use. Books in the series draw on naturally occurring language data from a wide variety of social contexts. The series takes a broad view of the relationship between language and social change. It includes work on groups that are socially marginalized and that were previously neglected by sociolinguists. It also includes books that focus primarily on wider social issues concerning language, such as language ecology. The series takes a critical approach to sociolinguistics. It challenges current orthodoxies not only by dealing with familiar topics in new and radical ways, but also by making use of the results of empirical research which alter our current understanding of the relationship between language and social change. Above all, language will be viewed as constitutive of, as well as reflective of, cultures and societies.

1. *An Introduction to Language Policy: Theory and Method*
   Edited by Thomas Ricento

An Introduction to
Language Policy
Theory and Method

Edited by **Thomas Ricento**

Blackwell
Publishing

© 2006 by Blackwell Publishing Ltd

BLACKWELL PUBLISHING
350 Main Street, Malden, MA 02148-5020, USA
9600 Garsington Road, Oxford OX4 2DQ, UK
550 Swanston Street, Carlton, Victoria 3053, Australia

The right of Thomas Ricento to be identified as the Author of the
Editorial Material in this work has been asserted in accordance
with the UK Copyright, Designs, and Patents Act 1988.

First published 2006 by Blackwell Publishing Ltd

4   2009

Library of Congress Cataloging-in-Publication Data

An introduction to language policy : theory and method / edited by
Thomas Ricento
    p. cm. — (Language and social change ; 1)
    Includes bibliographical references and index.
    ISBN 978-1-4051-1497-4 (hard cover : alk. paper)
    ISBN 978-1-4051-1498-1 (pbk. : alk. paper)
    1. Language Policy.   I. Ricento, Thomas.   II. Series.

    P119.3.I577   2006
    306.449—dc22

                                            2005009260

A catalogue record for this title is available from the British Library.

Set in 10/12.5pt Palatino
by Graphicraft Limited, Hong Kong

The publisher's policy is to use permanent paper from mills that operate
a sustainable forestry policy, and which has been manufactured from
pulp processed using acid-free and elementary chlorine-free practices.
Furthermore, the publisher ensures that the text paper and cover board
used have met acceptable environmental accreditation standards.

For further information on
Blackwell Publishing, visit our website:
www.blackwellpublishing.com

Contents

Contributors

Colin Baker
University of Wales, Bangor, UK

Jan Blommaert
Ghent University, Belgium

Suresh Canagarajah
Baruch College of the City University of New York, USA

Don Cartwright
University of Western Ontario, Canada

Joshua A. Fishman
Yeshiva University, New York, USA

François Grin
University of Geneva, Switzerland

Kai Heidemann
University of Pittsburgh, USA

Nancy H. Hornberger
University of Pennsylvania, USA

Stephen May
University of Waikato, New Zealand

Christina Bratt Paulston
University of Pittsburgh, USA

Alastair Pennycook
University of Technology, Sydney, Australia

Robert Phillipson
Copenhagen Business School, Denmark

Timothy Reagan
Roger Williams University, USA

Thomas Ricento
University of Texas, San Antonio, USA

Harold Schiffman
University of Pennsylvania, USA

Ronald Schmidt, Sr
California State University, Long Beach, USA

Tove Skutnabb-Kangas
Roskilde University, Denmark

James W. Tollefson
International Christian University, Japan

Terrence G. Wiley
Arizona State University, USA

Ruth Wodak
Lancaster University, UK

Preface

This book is designed to provide the reader with a thorough introduction to the principal theories and methods which are used in current research in language policy. The book aims to be accessible to non-specialists from a variety of fields in the social sciences, and to position language policy as an area of research within sociolinguistics and, more broadly, within the social sciences and humanities. The common element to all of the chapters in this book is language and its role in social life. If there is any "argument" that I wish to put forward it is that in order to understand how and why language is imbricated in all aspects of social life, we need to avail ourselves of a variety of perspectives from core social science disciplines: ethnography, geography, historiography, linguistics, political science, psychology, and sociology. The theories and methods described in this book provide frames (or lenses) through which we can examine the role(s) of language in social life; readers will be able to ascertain the relative usefulness of these theories and methods for their own research interests in language policy.

A logical question at this point is: what topics fall within the purview of language policy? Some examples are provided in part III, "Topical Areas in Language Policy"; these were chosen because they have been the focus of research in recent years, because they can be studied in diverse contexts, and because they have tended to generate controversies (and social science research often gravitates toward controversy). As with any academic field, a complex set of factors is involved in choices about what is studied and how it is studied. This is especially true in the social sciences, in which major developments have often been motivated in large measure by the desire to change the social system, to validate existing social policies and practices, or to counteract hegemonic beliefs about human nature. For example, in recent years research in language policy has been motivated, at least in part, by concerns about the accelerating loss of languages worldwide. This has led to theorizing about how language policies are connected to economic, political, and social structures and processes, and to examination of the effects of ideologies about language and society on language behavior and policies. Policies (and policy approaches) are then proposed and/or evaluated on the basis of their relevance in slowing or even reversing language loss and shift (see chapters 14, 15, 17, and 19 for some examples). This desire to effect social change is what drives the research agenda, rather than theory-building for its own sake. Theories and models have heuristic value as tools to advance our understanding of language behavior in diverse contexts. This interplay between theory and practice is what provides language policy research with a certain vitality, unpredictability, and attractiveness as an area of research for persons who wish to combine theoretical/methodological rigor with social advocacy. This book provides a starting point for those who wish to begin these sorts of investigations.

Any book of this scope and ambition is a collaborative effort. I first want to extend my sincere gratitude to the contributors who have made this volume possible. I feel fortunate that such eminent scholars from a range of academic disciplines were committed from the start to producing authoritative, yet accessible, essays in their areas of expertise. All of the essays were written expressly for this volume and for the purpose of engaging the interest of persons wishing to investigate how and why language matters so much in human society. Each of the chapter authors has compiled an annotated bibliography of major works in their area of expertise; these are followed by discussion questions, which can be used by instructors or individuals interested in applying the ideas presented in the chapter to real-world problems or to hypothetical situations. All of the contributors were genuinely interested in learning what their colleagues were covering in their chapters so that they could avoid duplication while also referring to each other's work.

My thinking on language policy has been influenced by literally hundreds of scholars in the social sciences and humanities, especially from critical theory, linguistics, philosophy, political science, and sociology. Certainly, the work of the contributors to this book has had a large impact on my development over the years. Also influential has been the work of pioneers in the field, including Charles Ferguson, Einar Haugen, Heinz Kloss, and Joan Rubin, among many others too numerous to mention. Bernard Spolsky, Robert Kaplan, and Richard Baldauf have written authoritative books on language policy in recent years, and have also founded and edit the journals *Language Policy* and *Current Issues in Language Planning*, respectively. Sue Wright has also made a significant contribution to the field, especially with regard to Europe. The work of these and many other scholars has helped put language policy on the map as a serious scholarly endeavor.

I would like to thank Blackwell Publishing for inviting me to do this book in the first place. It has been a pleasure to work, first, with Tami Kaplan and, later, with Sarah Coleman; they have been supportive and accessible from the beginning of this project. I would also like to thank Jennifer Coates, Jenny Cheshire, and Euan Reid for developing the Language and Social Change series in which this book appears.

Very special thanks are owed to Kelly Lynne Graham, a (now former) graduate assistant in the Division of Bicultural-Bilingual Studies at the University of Texas, San Antonio. Without her tireless and meticulous attention to detail, including keeping track of changes, attending to consistency in documentation, contacting authors, looking up facts and references, and countless other chores, this book would not have been possible. These tasks were handled flawlessly and without complaint for the better part of a year; thanks for all of your great work, Kelly!

Finally, I want to thank the University of Texas, San Antonio, for support I received through a mini-grant from the College of Education and Human Development, and a Faculty Development Leave, 2004, to complete writing of the overview essays and introductory chapter. I would also like to thank the doctoral students who participated in my advanced topics in language policy seminar, fall, 2002, for their spirited engagement, probing questions, and commitment to scholarly inquiry.

T. R.
San Antonio, Texas

PART I

Theoretical Perspectives in Language Policy

Theoretical Perspectives in Language Policy: An Overview

Thomas Ricento

To begin, the word "theory," as Ronald Schmidt informs us in his chapter, traces it roots to the Greek philosophers of the classical era, especially Plato and Aristotle. It comes from the Greek word *theoria*, which means "seeing," as in "a place for seeing" or being a "spectator." A theory, then, is a statement, or series of statements, proposed by an individual or group of individuals, about a position on an understanding of the world (where "world" encompasses the material and non-material), or some aspect of it. Theories can be focused on a particular domain of human experience or ability (for example, the theory that the capacity for human language is an innate and highly specified faculty localized in the brain; cf. Chomsky), or it can be more abstract and general (for example, the theory that truth is constructed and reproduced in the discourses of the powerful; cf. Foucault). These examples suggest something of the range of theories about language (e.g., what it is, where it is "located," its role in social life) that inform research in the field of language policy and planning (LPP). Let us briefly rehearse some of these theories of, or about, language as reflected in the chapters in this part of the book and consider the implications for policy.

The assumption underlying most of the theoretical work described in these chapters is that a language is a code with various forms (written, spoken, standard, non-standard, etc.), functions (usually expressed in terms of domains and relative status within a polity), and value (as a medium of exchange, with particular material and non-material qualities). Postmodern characterizations of language problematize the idea that a language is a fixed code. Linguist Paul Hopper (1998) (cited by Alastair Pennycook in chapter 4), argues "there is no natural fixed structure to language. Rather, speakers borrow heavily from their previous experiences of communication in similar circumstances, on similar topics, and with similar interlocutors. System-aticity, in this view, is an illusion produced by the partial settling or *sedimentation* of frequently used forms into temporary subsystems" (pp. 157–8). This theory of language – namely that it is not *languages* that exist so much as *discourses*, which may be shared by various overlapping communities of speakers – has important consequences for research in LPP. One effect of this theory is that grand narratives, for example, about the role of "big" languages – such as English – in killing other languages (a position identified with linguistic imperialism; see Robert Phillipson, chapter 19, and Thomas Ricento, chapter 1), based on conceptions of English as a discrete code shared by millions of individuals and speech communities, are viewed as simplistic and deterministic. Rather than "English," under this view (or theory) of language, it is more appropriate (and accurate) to discuss "Englishes" as hybrids reflecting complex processes of borrowing, mixing, and styling with other language varieties (or discourses). Relatedly, "English" serves a variety of symbolic and practical functions in the diverse settings where it is used; it does not adhere to any particular cultural or socioeconomic perspective. Therefore, within this theory of language – that is, as having multiple and numerous discourses, functions, and statuses – it is not possible to assume or predict a particular, or even necessary, relation between a given language (or language variety) and the role(s) it might play in a given setting, whether local or national/supranational. Thus, while evidence does exist that speakers of local languages (and especially minority languages) may shift to a majority language, and that subsequent generations may no longer speak the original (local) language, or may use it only in certain domains as a result of the promotion of former colonial languages, for example, in Africa, it is also the case that a former colonial language, English, was adopted by the African National Congress (ANC) in the successful struggle against apartheid in South Africa. The evaluation of these two possible outcomes of language contact (i.e., language shift, leading to domain loss, and language adoption/adaptation in the service of social change) as relatively "good/desirable" or "bad/undesirable" will be based largely on extra-linguistic factors related to theories of what constitutes the social "good," including minimal criteria necessary to facilitate socioeconomic equality and fairness (discussed later in this overview; see also James Tollefson, chapter 3). Furthermore, language change is an inevitable consequence of prolonged language contact, seen for example in the thousands of English words from hip-hop, technology, and advertising that have found their way into the discourses of hundreds of language varieties world-wide, just as English varieties have incorporated tens of thousands of words from French, German, Spanish, Portuguese, Greek, Latin, Italian, and many other languages over the centuries.

This view of language has implications for conceptualizations of language status. Status is widely understood within LPP as the perceived relative value of a named language, usually related to its social utility, which encompasses its so-called market value as a mode of communication, as well as more subjective features rooted in what Harold Schiffman (chapter 7) calls a society's linguistic culture. The value(s) attached to or associated with a language, therefore, do not depend exclusively, or even necessarily, on any official or legal status conferred by a state through its executive, legislative, or judicial branches. For example, as Schiffman (chapter 7) notes, French became the national language of France not because it was given any special legal or official status (such status, Schiffman points out, was at best minimal), but because of powerful mythologies about both the language and the policy. Schiffman's research reveals, for example, that the French populace and even some French scholars who have written on language policy believe that legal provisions regarding the use of French exist which in fact do not exist, and did not until certain laws, known collectively as *la loi Toubon*, were enacted in the 1990s (Schiffman, p. 117). Further, according to Schiffman, the tendency to control many details of life (*jacobinisme*) is part and parcel of French linguistic culture. From the time of the French Revolution, the idea has persisted that non-standard languages (*les patois, les idiomes, les jargons*) "were not just defective or inferior, but even worse, they contained undesirable qualities, even ideas or ideologies, that were a threat to the Revolution, and which had to be extirpated" (p. 120). Thus, mythology, aesthetics, and political ideology (among many other possibilities) are central elements in the ascription and achievement of language status; language-policy goals which seek to enhance or modify in some way the social role(s) and functions of language(s) cannot override the effects of what Schiffman calls a society's linguistic culture. Schiffman provides examples of the effects of linguistic culture in other contexts as well, including Tamil in India and German in the United States.

In addition to the role of ideology in the ascription and achievement of language status, as Nancy Hornberger (chapter 2) notes, language planning nearly always occurs in multilingual, multicultural settings in which planning for one language has repercussions on other languages and ethnolinguistic groups. Decisions about which languages will be planned for what purposes ultimately reflect power relations among different groups and sociopolitical and economic interests. Therefore, although as Cooper notes "we have as yet no generally accepted language planning theory, if by theory we mean a set of logically interrelated, empirically testable propositions" (Cooper, 1989, p. 41), we do know that theoretically adequate models or approaches need to consider (as Hornberger notes) ideology, ecology, and agency in explaining how and why things are the way they are, and also to evaluate whose interests and whose values are being served when language plans and policies are proposed, implemented, or evaluated.

There are a number of important implications which follow from this focus on ideology, ecology, and agency in LPP. First, received categories, such as "nation-state," need to be (re)considered in light of history and current arrangements. The eighteenth-century European conception of the "nation-state," popularized by Herder, Fichte, and others, is inadequate to characterize today's world of multinational states, newly born (and newly configured) states, dysfunctional states (see Jan Blommaert, chapter 13, for a discussion of Tanzania), and divided states, among other possible types. Further, the state system itself has undergone changes, especially with regard to the degree and rate of change in the economic and cultural realms, so that the functions and roles of states are changing in important ways, especially in connection with religious, economic, or political ideologies that become tied to nationalist and pan-nationalist movements. In cases in which states have little control over their populations or territory, cross-border influences and penetrations may dictate language policies in the absence of state control. For example, in Somalia, a country which lacks a functioning government, the only functioning schooling is financed by Arabs, which means that Arabic has replaced Somali – the national language – in school curricula (Farah, 2004). The consequences of these geopolitical changes on theories of the role of the state in LPP are not insignificant. For example, theories of linguistic imperialism, which conceive of states as primary actors in the control of populations under their jurisdiction (whether as "imperial" agents or supporters of ["authentic"] nationalism), need to be modified in the face of dramatic changes in global geopolitics, in which the power of states to make decisions is highly influenced and constrained by both internal and external pressures related to economic and cultural forces, as well as transnational migration, both regionally and globally.

Theoretical work by political scientists has provided some useful tools to help us better understand what is at stake in conflicts involving language. Ronald Schmidt (chapter 6) provides two examples of such work that have relevance for current controversies in language policy. The first deals with identity politics, which, Schmidt argues, lies at the core of most language-policy conflicts. Schmidt cites the work of Bonnie Honig (2001) on the role of immigrants "in maintaining and resurrecting central myths that sustain Americans' understanding of themselves as a nation" (p. 100), thereby helping to explain the existence of both xenophilia and xenophobia in contemporary attitudes toward ethnolinguistic groups, and why particular language policies (e.g., the move to declare English the official national language when it is under no threat from other languages) are so strongly supported.

Another example of research from political science that helps us better understand and explain what is at stake in controversies involving language concerns the concepts of "equality" and "inequality" as they are used in conflicts over language policies. In the US context, assimilationists believe that the key to equal opportunity for non-English speakers is a shift to English as rapidly as possible; therefore, according to assimilationists, policies that might encourage non-English speakers to continue to rely on their native languages, such as bilingual education, bilingual ballots, etc., are actually *hindering* their chances of achieving social equality. On the other hand, pluralists believe that the US has always been a multilingual society, even though English has always been the dominant language. For pluralists, the relation between language and social equality and mobility is less clear cut, and they argue that the achievement of equal opportunity should take into account the country's fundamental ethnolinguistic diversity. The work of political theorist Will Kymlicka on multicultural citizenship (cited in chapter 6) provides a detailed argument in support of the pluralist position in this controversy. For Kymlicka, the well-being of the individual self is the proper moral foundation for any just community, and this well-being must be defined by the individual (not, for example, by the state), which means that individuals need to be free to define for themselves what is meaningful and worthwhile in their own lives. Kymlicka believes that since individual choices are made within a cultural context, the individual self has a stake in the community in which it has developed, because that community's cultural structure provides the "context for choice" for "me" (Kymlicka, 1989, pp. 164–5). Therefore, according to Kymlicka, it is important to preserve the structure of cultural communities in order to preserve meaningful choices about "the good" for the individual. Since the state operates within a linguistic and cultural context, it cannot operate neutrally with respect to language and culture, as some believe it can with regard to religious diversity. Applying this approach to LPP, Schmidt concludes that:

> the implications of Kymlicka's arguments are powerful for ethnolinguistic groups that are basic components of a multilingual country. In order to give individuals fair equality of opportunity to realize their own conception of a good life, the state must try to provide equally effective support for the structures of each component ethnolinguistic community making up the country. This would seem to provide powerful and reasoned support for a language policy in support of multiple languages in a multilingual country.
>
> *(p. 106)*

Kymlicka distinguishes between multinational and multiethnic countries, arguing that the rights of national groups (those that were incorporated through conquest, annexation, or voluntary merger) have the greater claim to full cultural protections (including language) than those of ethnic groups that came voluntarily as immigrants. Kymlicka's theories and implications for LPP are also discussed by Stephen May (chapter 14).

As Schmidt notes, a key element in the support of majority languages, often at the expense of support for minority languages, is that majority languages facilitate social mobility, higher earnings, and integration into the dominant culture. Research in the economics of language (François Grin, chapter 5), dating back to the 1960s, has applied economic models and principles to operationalize these claims as testable hypotheses. Topics researched have included language and earnings, language dynamics, language and economic activity, and the economics of language-policy evaluation. One of the important conclusions from this research is that while mainstream economic models and analyses can provide useful data for policy-makers to help guide their decision-making, when it comes to arguments in support of language diversity, almost every type of "market failure" occurs. It is for this reason, according to Grin, that state intervention on behalf of language diversity is both justified and necessary.

To summarize this discussion of the contributions to theory in LPP research from a variety of disciplines, the following points can be made:

1   Language-policy debates are always about more than language. Insights from political, economic, and social theory can provide

scholars in LPP research with the tools to explain what is at stake, why it matters, and what effect particular policies or policy approaches might (or might not) have on such debates.

2   The way(s) in which LPP scholars and researchers define and use terms such as "language," "language policy," "the state," "equality," and so on have consequences for their analyses and recommendations on issues which involve language planning and/or language policies.

3   Ideologies about language generally and specific languages in particular have real effects on language policies and practices, and delimit to a large extent what is and is not possible in the realm of language planning and policy-making.

4   Research in LPP must be understood as both a *multidisciplinary* and an *interdisciplinary* activity, in that conceptual and methodological tools borrowed from various disciplines need to be *appropriately integrated* and applied to real-world problems and challenges involving language, which, by definition, are embedded in all aspects of society and social life.

REFERENCES

Cooper, R. L. (1989). *Language planning and social change*. New York: Cambridge University Press.

Farah, N. (2004). Another little piece of my heart. *New York Times*, August 2, A21.

Honig, B. (2001). *Democracy and the foreigner*. Princeton, NJ: Princeton University Press.

Hopper, P. (1998). Emergent grammar. In M. Tomasello (ed.), *The new psychology of language* (pp. 155–75). Mahwah, NJ: Lawrence Erlbaum.

Kymlicka, W. (1989). *Liberalism, community, and culture*. New York: Oxford University Press.

CHAPTER ONE

Language Policy: Theory and Practice – An Introduction

Thomas Ricento

My goal in this chapter is to locate language policy (LP) as a field of inquiry within the social sciences and humanities. I argue that the most useful way to approach the history of LP research is by a consideration of the domains of inquiry that have attracted attention, and how findings have stimulated critical reflection on the goals and methods of research, including the questioning of some basic assumptions about the role of such research in reaffirming or opposing social inequalities. Following this, I will consider how theory has influenced practice, and vice versa.

Theory in Language Policy Research

Before addressing these topics, I make some preliminary comments about theory in LP research. An important claim of this book is that there is no overarching theory of LP and planning, in large part because of the complexity of the issues which involve language in society. As researchers and policy analysts we ask basic and varied questions about events in the world: for example, why are standard languages considered to be "better" than dialects? Why do members of some immigrant groups maintain their languages across generations, while members of other groups lose their language after one or two generations? Does the global spread of English entail the marginalization and eventual loss of indigenous languages in developing countries? If so, is this a good or bad thing? In some cases, a theory or model may be proposed to account for a specific type of phenomenon, based on triangulation of a preponderance of the best available empirical evidence. An example of this is Fishman's famous

Graded Intergenerational Disruption Scale (GIDS) (Fishman, 1991), which lists eight stages of the relative strength of a regional or minority language in competition with another more dominant language, or languages, for survival. In other cases, researchers might focus on relationships between attitudes within various speech communities and patterns of language use. While the GIDS is one of the few models available in the field of LP which endeavors to predict the chances of the survival of a language on the basis of the evidence of actual cases, it has value only to the extent a minority language group and/or a society wishes to "reverse" language shift and loss, and to take action to "protect" the language through concrete policies. A theory of language acquisition, use, shift, revitalization, or loss has little value in and of itself as a tool to argue for the need for specific language policies; rather, in order to advocate specific policies or policy directions, scholars need to demonstrate *empirically* – as well as conceptually – the societal benefits, and costs, of such policies. The best way to achieve this is to bring together empirical data from a range of disciplinary perspectives (and those perspectives and examples of data are provided in this book) which support the value of particular policy recommendations, however such value might be defined. While the compiling of such evidence does not constitute an LP, or even provide a road map for devising or evaluating effective policy options (see Grin, 2003, on how to evaluate language policies), it is a necessary component in any serious attempt to influence public policy choices and desired outcomes.

While much of the research in this book and elsewhere suggests that language behavior and social policy are ideologically encumbered, simply exposing these ideological formations is insufficient to justify enactment of particular policies; the assumption, for example, that linguistic diversity is a tangible social "good" requires evidence beyond moral or "naturalness" arguments. After all, LP is not just an exercise in philosophical inquiry; it is interested in addressing social problems which often involve language, to one degree or another, and in proposing realistic remedies. Yet this search for answers does not begin in a theoretical or methodological vacuum; researchers begin with assumptions about "how the world works" and, in the optimal situation, engage reflexively with the topics they choose to investigate, questioning and examining their epistemological and theoretical assumptions on a range of matters as they try to understand phenomena of which they partake and by which their views are formed. The beginning of wisdom is the recognition that "scientific" detached objectivity in such research is not possible, since researchers always begin with particular experiences and positions on what the social "good" might be and what sorts of changes in social (including language) policy might advance a particular vision of that good. Despite this observation (which unfortunately is not always or often acknowledged by social scientists, including those working in LP), there is a great and recognizable difference between good and less good research, reflecting (1) relative degrees of clarity and coherence of theoretical and conceptual frameworks or approaches; (2) the representativeness, depth, and quality of data; (3) the relative degree to which the data and conclusions support the theoretical assumptions and hypotheses which follow from those assumptions; and (4) the relevance of the findings for particular LP goals. Good research may not lead to effective policies, but bad research weakens the legitimacy of good research by casting doubts on the field as a whole.

An important point of this discussion thus far is that "domain of inquiry" is a better way to approach the field than "theories of LP," since researchers tend to ask questions about particular issues, or domains, which involve language matters, rather than searching for data to prove some *a priori* theory. In a few cases (such as Fishman's GIDS, described above), aggregate data obtained from specific cases can lead to models or theories, which can then be put to the test in novel situations; however, this is usually not the primary goal of research. This suggests that a useful way to approach LP as a field is to ask the following question: what is it that scholars who specialize in LP study?

The best way to answer this question is to do some historical archeology on LP research over the past half century to see which topics have attracted attention, and to analyze how insights from the theories and methods outlined in this book have contributed to reformulations of the nature and purpose of research in LP. Although LP is an interdisciplinary field, it came into its own as a branch of sociolinguistics. During the 1950s and 1960s, Western-trained linguists were engaged by many of the new nations of Africa, South America, and Asia to develop grammars, writing systems, and dictionaries for indigenous languages. Scholars trained in descriptive linguistics were eager to gather data on hitherto understudied languages and advance current theories of language structure and use. Joshua Fishman (1968, p. 11), the seminal figure in the sociology of language, saw developing nations as providing an "indispensable and truly intriguing array of field-work locations for a new breed of genuine sociolinguists." This research was directly relevant to language planning, especially for many aspects of corpus planning (see chapter 2 for a discussion of corpus and status planning activities). Beyond benefits to linguistic theory, the activities of many sociolinguists were understood (by them) as beneficial to nation-building and national unification; the decision of which language (i.e., colonial or indigenous) would best serve these interests was often based on which language would provide access to advanced, that is, Western, technological and economic assistance. A consensus view, especially among Western sociolinguists, was that a major European language (usually French or English) should be used for formal and specialized domains while local languages could serve other functions (Ricento, 2000, p. 198). The result – stable diglossia – had the (perhaps unintended) effect of lowering the status and relegating the domains of indigenous languages to local uses, while elevating the status and extending the domains of the former colonial language to national political and elite educational sectors, helping to perpetuate the stratified, class-based structures of the colonial era.

Beginning in the late 1970s and continuing through the 1990s, scholars with an interest in understanding the role played by language in the reproduction of social and economic inequality, and influenced by critical and postmodern theories, began to question some of the assumptions which informed the early work in LP. For example, reflecting on the role of linguistics in language-planning activities in newly independent states, a number of scholars argued that rather than recording languages or providing neutral descriptions of socio-linguistic reality, linguists had helped create languages (Crowley, 1990). The notion of language as a discrete, finite entity defined by standard grammars was characterized by a number of critical scholars and linguists as a function of the methods, and values, of positivistic linguistics (e.g., Harris, 1981; Le Page, 1985; Mühlhäusler, 1990, 1996; Sankoff, 1988). Even the construct "diglossia," which was invoked as a description of the situation in many developing countries, was criticized as "an ideological naturalization of sociolinguistic arrangements" (Woolard & Schieffelin, 1994, p. 69), perpetuating linguistic and (related) societal inequalities. Well-accepted terms, such as "native speaker," "mother tongue," and "linguistic competence," all central to mainstream linguistic theories, were called into question and even abandoned by some scholars as inadequate in dealing with the complex multi-lingualism that existed in many language-contact settings throughout the world. Thus, linguistic theories adopted by language planners, rather than being neutral, objective, scientific tools, were viewed by critical scholars beginning in the 1980s as detrimental to the development of equitable language policies in complex multilingual settings. This realization led to a rather broad calling into question of received ideas about the nature of language itself, and of the degree to which scholars of language were perpetuating assumptions that had the effect of rationalizing the support of colonial languages, and concomitant economic interests, at the expense of indigenous languages and local economic development. This movement from a more positivistic to a more critical epistemological orientation was seen in the publication of a number of important articles and books beginning in the 1980s. For example, the papers in Wolfson and Manes (1985, p. ix) were concerned with the ways that "language use reflects and indeed influences social, economic or political inequality." In the preface to that volume, Dell Hymes (1985, p. vii) noted that:

> Were there no political domination or social stratification in the world, there would still be linguistic inequality . . . Allocation and hierarchy are intrinsic. Nor should the investments of many, perhaps even including ourselves, in some existing arrangements be underestimated. Effective change in the direction of greater equality will only partly be change in attitude, or removal of external domination; it will be inseparable in many cases from change of social system.

The view that socioeconomic equality in developing countries was somehow connected to the establishment (or imposition) of a national language, based on arguments of increased efficiency leading to greater unity, was called into question. Clearly, there were many obstacles to overcome in the case of the newly independent states of Africa in terms of economic development, and not all of the blame can be put on language policies. Yet these policies fit into a broader pattern in which Western-based ideologies about the requisites for national development, which included the ideology of monolingualism as necessary for social and economic equality, were imposed on new states comprised of multiple national (and linguistic) groups. In other words, Western-based academic language-planning and LP approaches in the 1950s and 1960s often subsumed a number of ideologies about (1) the nature of language – that is, as a finite, stable, standardized, rule-governed instrument for communication; (2) monolingualism and cultural homogeneity as necessary requirements for social and economic progress, modernization, and national unity (with stable diglossia as a fall-back, compromise position); and (3) language selection as a matter of "rational choice" in which all options are equally available to everyone, or could be made equally available. These basic assumptions were often consonant with the views of Western-based and Western-trained state planners and policy analysts engaged in national (re)-construction in developing countries during the 1950s and 1960s, and continue to be influential to the present day.

In addition to arguing that language policies favored majoritarian or dominant interests at the expense of minority and non-dominant interests, critical scholars such as Tollefson (1986, 1991) and Luke, McHoul, and Mey (1990), among others argued that these interests are often implicit and enmeshed in hegemonic ideologies (such as those mentioned above), which, in effect, have become widely accepted, commonsense ideas, especially in Western societies. The goal of critical scholars interested in promoting social and economic equality was to uncover these ideologies and associated policies in order to bring about social change. This move, then, aligned the research interests of many LP scholars with the emerging tradition of critical theory, which "investigates the processes by which social inequality is produced and sustained, and the struggle to reduce inequality to bring about greater forms of social justice" (chapter 3, pp. 43–4).

At this point, we can see a branching beginning to occur between mainstream sociolinguistic research dealing with language shift in language-contact situations, in which shift is analyzed using census data, interviews, and ethnographic methods (see, e.g., Fasold, 1984, pp. 213–45), and critical approaches, in which language shift is understood not as an incidental and natural outcome of language contact but rather a manifestation of asymmetrical power relations based on social structures and ideologies that position groups – and their languages – hierarchically within a society. Rather than language, per se, the emphasis in research shifted to discourses, with their attendant ideologies and as sites where social relations were reflected, reproduced, and contested (see chapters 3 and 4). Scholars also looked at sociolinguistic arrangements not as inevitable or logical, but rather as the result of political processes and ideologies of state-formation. In this view, societal multilingualism – not monolingualism – was seen as normal, and its recognition and acceptance were taken as an important requirement for the realization of meaningful democracy, since the constituent groups of the state are better positioned to participate as equals when their cultures and languages are respected and afforded legitimacy through institutional recognition and support.

The purpose of the preceding discussion has been to show some of the ways in which theories about language influence, and are influenced by, the study of language-contact situations in diverse settings. How we understand and conceptualize *language* has important consequences for how we might evaluate linguistic *arrangements* and the explicit and implicit policies which contribute to – or oppose – such arrangements. This approach to the study of LP favors a deeper and broader perspective on language conflicts, which are too often reduced in popular treatments to technical discussions about the pros and cons of learning or using language/language variety A over language/language variety B in a particular domain or sector.

Theory and Practice in Language Policy

As with any academic field, theory has played an important role in LP research. The chapters in part I of this book describe many important theories and how they have been influential in models proposed to explain the role of language and language policies in the shaping of societies around the world. A good example of such a model is linguistic imperialism (Phillipson, 1992), which attempts to explain how the languages of current and former empires, principally those of the US, England, and France, have been promoted in former colonies through a process of economic, political, social, cultural, and educational domination and exploitation, with devastating effects on indigenous languages. This provocative and controversial claim has generated a great deal of research and a great many publications, which seek to reaffirm, contest, or recast the original claims within emerging new paradigms.[1] While the validity of linguistic imperialism as a descriptive model accounting, in part, for language shift and loss in many countries is hotly debated, the claims made by Phillipson and others have had influence on a range of topics concerned with language teaching, learning, and use. For example, questions have been raised about the morality of teaching "big" languages, such as English, in developing countries and about the privileging of native speakers over non-native speakers in hiring decisions; Phillipson (2003) himself has argued that English poses threats not only to indigenous languages in developing countries, but to smaller European languages as well. Other research by applied linguists has shown that some of the stronger claims of linguistic imperialism are not supported by empirical research. For example, Pennycook (2003) provides evidence that the spread of English is *not* leading inevitably to the "homogenization of world culture"; he shows how language mixing in the lyrics of rap and hip-hop music is contributing to a global popular culture which transcends national boundaries and ideologies, while reflecting local cultural and linguistic forms. Other research demonstrates how English has been used – both symbolically and functionally – to oppose repressive colonial governments, as in South Africa (de Klerk, 2002), and ultra-nationalist ideologies, as in Sri Lanka (Canagarajah, 2000). Thus, the positing of the model has stimulated new ways of thinking – and doing research – about the effects of the spread of languages such as English and French over the past decades and centuries.

Phillipson's model of linguistic imperialism has also stimulated research and theorizing on ways to neutralize or minimize the purported negative effects of the spread of "big" languages on minority languages and their speakers world-wide. One such approach is what is variously referred to as language rights or linguistic human rights (see chapter 15). Skutnabb-Kangas and Phillipson both have argued that an individual's right to use and learn his or her native language is as basic a human right as that to the free exercise of religion, or the right of ethnic groups to maintain their cultures and beliefs. Stephen May (2001, and chapter 14), in part on the basis of the work of Kymlicka (1995), argues that the languages of national minorities (as opposed to those of immigrant minorities) merit explicit protection and promotion by the state, because these minorities are legitimate groups within the nation-state and no less worthy of such support than dominant groups.

While linguistic imperialism and linguistic human rights have been influential constructs in LP research in the past decade or so, they fit within a larger, evolving set of interrelated research interests and goals. It is not clear that these related interests and goals rise to the level of a paradigm in the traditional sense of some grand theory which explains patterns of language behavior in contact situations, or can predict the effects of specific language policies on language behavior. However, there is a growing body of research in LP which is concerned with the role of language – materially and discursively – in the production, exercise, and contestation of power at all levels of society, and the effects of power on language practices, from the daily interactions of ordinary people to the official policies of governments. What differentiates the various strands of research concerned with the nature and operation of power through and by language are the different sites on which the research focuses. For example, in postmodern research, texts and their discourses are investigated as the sites where power relations are reflected and reproduced in a variety of genres of speech and writing. In studies of national identity (e.g., Blommaert & Verschueren, 1998; Wodak et al., 1999), analysis of contemporary political speeches, legislation, newspaper reporting, and focus group discussions have been contextualized within a broader sociohistorical framework that goes well beyond the texts themselves. In geolinguistic research, patterns of migration and settlement within geographical contexts (e.g., countries, regions, cities, localities, etc.) are correlated with patterns of language use, shift, and loss within particular political, cultural, and economic historical contexts. What these and other research methods have in common is an awareness of and interest in the operation of power in decision-making relating to languages, whether on the part of individuals, families, groups, states, regions, or supranational bodies, such as the European Union.

We have said that theories have played an important role in the evolution of LP as an interdisciplinary field, stimulating research relevant to language matters in education, economics, political science, history, sociology, geography, and other fields, while insights from these same fields have contributed to the development of integrated models in LP, such as linguistic imperialism and linguistic human rights. What has not been much discussed is the practice of language planning, that is, the development, implementation, and evaluation of specific language policies. To be sure, this is an understudied facet of LP research,[2] a legacy no doubt of the focus on theory from the earliest days of the field (described previously in this chapter). Another reason for the lack of attention to the mechanisms of language planning is that most sociolinguists and applied linguists have little or no training in the policy sciences. There have been quite a few studies on the effects of language policies in Canada (see, e.g., various articles in Edwards, 1998) and on aspects of US language policies, especially on federal policies dealing with the education of language minorities (e.g., Cazden & Snow, 1990; Fernandez, 1987; Ricento, 1998a, 1998b), among many other studies and countries that could be cited; what have not been well developed are clearly articulated models for analyzing and comparing different policy approaches in defined contexts, and ways to evaluate the outcomes that can be applied in different settings. This is not an easy task because of the many variables that need to be considered in proposing (i.e., planning) policies, and because success or failure is not always easy to measure, given the diverse expectations of different constituencies.[3] Grin (2003) has provided the most detailed proposal for policy evaluation to date; perhaps his work will stimulate additional research in this very important area of LP and planning.

Conclusions

While LP as an organized field of study is a relatively recent development, the themes explored today in LP research have been treated in a wide range of scholarly disciplines in the social sciences and humanities over the years. My goal in this chapter has been to position LP as a field of research by considering the kinds of topics that are explored and the way in which theory interacts with practice, leading to the questioning of theoretical assumptions and the generating of new lines of research and models. Language policies are made, or are implicitly acknowledged and practiced, in all societal domains. I have focused on some of the areas that have received a great deal of attention by academics over the past half century, in part, because they typify the kinds of theoretical, methodological, and practical challenges that researchers in LP must confront and deal with as they try to understand the role of languages in social life. These challenges on the part of the researcher include: (1) having a clearly articulated view about the nature of language, and a broad understanding about language varieties and processes of language change; (2) having an understanding of how power is represented and reflected in various language policies at all levels of social structure and processes; (3) having a position on the role of the researcher as an "interested" participant in research; and (4) adhering to high standards of research, especially with regard to the representativeness, depth, and breadth of data and the degree to which the findings support – or disconfirm – clearly articulated theoretical assumptions.

While topics such as the protection of dying languages and the effects of the global spread of English get a lot of play in scholarly and popular media, decisions about language made by legislators, educational leaders, dictionary makers, businesses, and advertisers are probably more influential in shaping language attitudes and patterns of language use than the combined effects of all the measures designed to protect moribund languages. Of course, legislators, educators, and businesses are greatly influenced by "bottom-up" social changes and practices. For example, we have witnessed how social movements beginning in the 1960s have contributed to important changes in language use and attitudes in the US and elsewhere. The women's movement had a powerful influence on changing attitudes toward sexist usage in English and other languages, leading to massive changes at the lexical level. The Civil Rights movement in the US pointed out the disparities between the educational opportunities of racial and ethnic minorities and the majority group, leading (among other things) to the abolishment of English literacy as a requirement for voting in the South and the provision of bilingual ballots in voting precincts where more than 5 percent of the electorate could not vote in English. The movement also was an important factor in the passage of the Bilingual Education Act of 1968, which provided federal funding for the use of languages other than English in classroom instruction.

The advent of computers and the internet has had a profound effect on language choice, use, and structure around the world, which includes the intermixing of languages, the creation of hundreds, if not thousands, of new words and acronyms, and changes in communication patterns and styles. While attempts to "regulate" language on the internet would be seen by most people as futile, there are, nonetheless, many official bodies and organizations that exist for the purpose of safeguarding language from precisely the sort of "chaos" that occurs daily on the internet. Primary among these are the various national academies, many of them in Europe, such as the Académie Française (see chapter 7). Regardless of their inability to halt language change and maintain the "integrity" of the national language, academies, dictionaries, and language departments in universities contribute to the belief (or myth) that there *is* a standard, correct, "fixed," language (English or French or Spanish, etc.), and that students must go to school to "learn" their native language. The "language industry," especially in Western or Westernized countries, contributes to the gate-keeping function of social institutions – especially schools – whereby persons who command the "standard" variety of the national language have social advantage over those who speak "non-standard" varieties. This is an example of an implicit LP with tremendous consequences for millions of people in terms of their access to social mobility; yet it is a policy which is largely hidden from view because most citizens accept it as logical, natural, fair, and efficient when, in fact, it is none of those things, since *no one* speaks the (mythical) standard variety, and *everyone* speaks some variant of one or another language variety. Discrimination against speakers of varieties that have been stigmat-ized as "non-standard" occurs all the time, and the victims of such discrimination have no legal recourse because this LP is hegemonic (see Lippi-Green, 1997).

When we begin to think of language issues as *personal* rather than abstract and removed from daily concerns, we quickly see how we all have a stake in language policies, since they have a direct bearing on our place in society and what we might (or might not) be able to achieve. Schools, the workplace, the neighborhood, families – all are sites where language policies determine or influence what language(s) we will speak, whether our language is "good/acceptable" or "bad/ unacceptable" for particular purposes, including careers, marriage, social advancement, and so on. Language is something most of us take for granted most of the time; it is usually when we discover that our language (or language variety) is different from, and perhaps less valued than, the language of others, or that our options are somehow limited, either because we don't speak/understand a language or language variety, or use it inappropriately or ineffectively in a particular context, that we begin to pay attention to language. Research in LP can contribute to our understanding of how such differences are experienced in varied contexts, and how policies – explicit or implicit – may reinforce, or oppose, social and economic inequalities related to gendered, ethnic, racial, tribal, religious, cultural, regional, and political differences.

NOTES

1 For a recent example of scholarly treatment of the controversy, see the articles, reviews, and interactive discussion in the following issues of the *Journal of Language, Identity, and Education*: 1(3), 2002; 3(1), 2004; 3(2), 2004.
2 Although see Kaplan and Baldauf (1997) and the journal *Current Issues in Language Planning*.
3 See Kaplan and Baldauf (1997) for discussion of some of these problems.

REFERENCES

Blommaert, J. & Verschueren, J. (1998). *Debating diversity: Analysing the discourse of tolerance*. London: Routledge.

Canagarajah, A. S. (2000). Negotiating ideologies through English: Strategies from the periphery. In T. Ricento (ed.), *Ideology, politics and language policies: Focus on English* (pp. 121–32). Amsterdam: John Benjamins.

Cazden, C. B. & Snow, C. E. (eds.) (1990). English plus: Issues in bilingual education. *Annals of the American Academy of Political and Social Science 508*.

Crowley, T. (1990). That obscure object of desire: A science of language. In J. E. Joseph & T. J. Taylor (eds.), *Ideologies of language* (pp. 27–50). London: Routledge.

de Klerk, G. (2002). Mother-tongue education in South Africa: The weight of history. *International Journal of the Sociology of Language, 154,* 29–46.

Edwards, J. (ed.) (1998). *Language in Canada.* New York: Cambridge University Press.

Fasold, R. (1984). *The sociolinguistics of society.* Oxford: Blackwell.

Fernandez, R. R. (1987). Legislation, regulation, and litigation: The origins and evolution of public policy on bilingual education in the United States. In W. A. V. Horne (ed.), *Ethnicity and language. Vol. VI* (Ethnicity and Public Policy Series) (pp. 90–123). Milwaukee, WI: University of Wisconsin System.

Fishman, J. A. (1968). Sociolinguistics and the language problems of the developing countries. In J. A. Fishman, C. A. Ferguson, & J. Das Gupta (eds.), *Language problems of developing nations* (pp. 491–8). New York: John Wiley & Sons.

Fishman, J. A. (1991). *Reversing language shift: Theoretical and empirical foundations of assistance to threatened languages.* Clevedon: Multilingual Matters.

Grin, F. (2003). *Language policy evaluation and the European charter for regional or minority languages.* Houndmills: Palgrave Macmillan.

Harris, R. (1981). *The language myth.* London: Duckworth.

Hymes, D. (1985). Preface. In N. Wolfson & J. Manes (eds.), *Language of inequality* (pp. v–viii). Berlin: Mouton.

Kaplan, R. B. & Baldauf, R. B. (1997). *Language planning from practice to theory.* Clevedon: Multilingual Matters.

Kymlicka, W. (1995). *Multicultural citizenship: A liberal theory of minority rights.* Oxford: Clarendon Press.

Le Page, R. (1985). Language standardization problems of Malaysia set in context. *Southeast Asian Journal of Social Science, 13,* 29–39.

Lippi-Green, R. (1997). *English with an accent: Language, ideology, and discrimination in the United States.* London: Routledge.

Luke, A., McHoul, A., & Mey, J. (1990). On the limits of language planning: Class, state and power. In R. Baldauf & A. Luke (eds.), *Language planning and education in Australasia and the South Pacific* (pp. 25–44). Clevedon: Multilingual Matters.

May, S. (2001). *Language and minority rights: Ethnicity, nationalism and the politics of language.* London: Longman.

Mühlhäusler, P. (1990). "Reducing" Pacific languages to writings. In J. E. Joseph & T. J. Taylor (eds.), *Ideologies of language* (pp. 189–205). London: Routledge.

Mühlhäusler, P. (1996). *Linguistic ecology: Language change and linguistic imperialism in the Pacific region.* London: Routledge.

Pennycook, A. (2003). Global Englishes: Rip slyme and performativity. *Journal of Sociolinguistics, 7,* 513–33.

Phillipson, R. (1992). *Linguistic imperialism*. Oxford: Oxford University Press.

Phillipson, R. (2003). *English-only Europe? Challenging language policy*. London: Routledge.

Ricento, T. (1998a). National language policy in the United States. In T. Ricento & B. Burnaby (eds.), *Language and politics in the United States and Canada: Myths and realities* (pp. 85–112). Mahwah, NJ: Lawrence Erlbaum.

Ricento, T. (1998b). The courts, the legislature and society: The shaping of federal language policy in the United States. In D. Kibbee (ed.), *Language legislation and linguistic rights* (pp. 123–41). Amsterdam: John Benjamins.

Ricento, T. (2000). Historical and theoretical perspectives in language policy and planning. *Journal of Sociolinguistics, 4*, 196–213.

Sankoff, D. (1988). Sociolinguistics and syntactic variation. In F. J. Newmeyer (ed.), *Linguistics: The Cambridge Survey. Vol. IV: Language: The socio-cultural context* (pp. 140–61). Cambridge: Cambridge University Press.

Tollefson, J. W. (1986). Language policy and the radical left in the Philippines: The New People's Army and its antecedents. *Language Problems and Language Planning, 10*, 177–89.

Tollefson, J. W. (1991). *Planning language, planning inequality*. New York: Longman.

Wodak, R., de Cillia, R., Reisigl, M., & Liebhart, K. (1999). *The discursive construction of national identity* (trans. A. Hirsch & R. Mitten). Edinburgh: Edinburgh University Press.

Wolfson, N. & Manes, J. (eds.) (1985). *Language of inequality*. Berlin: Mouton.

Woolard, K. A. & Schieffelin, B. B. (1994). Language ideology. *Annual Review of Anthropology, 23*, 55–82.

CHAPTER TWO

Frameworks and Models in Language Policy and Planning

Nancy H. Hornberger

The decade leading up to the turn of the millennium brought a resurgence of interest in the field of language policy and planning (LPP), fueled in large part by the imperious spread of English and other global languages and, reciprocally, the alarming loss and endangerment of indigenous and small language communities world-wide. Language teaching and language revitalization initiatives constitute pressing real-world LPP concerns on an unprecedented scale. At the same time, critical and postmodern theoretical developments in the social sciences have found their way into LPP research, infusing new perspectives and emphases.

The 1990s saw a lively output of LPP overview books and review articles, many of them calling for or proposing new theoretical directions. Cooper (1989) and Tollefson (1991) were among the first and most enduring contributions at that time. Cooper's accounting framework, organized around the question "What *actors* attempt to influence what *behaviors* of which *people* for what *ends* under what *conditions* by what *means* through what *decision-making process* with what *effect*?" (Cooper, 1989, p. 98), summarized the state of LPP as a descriptive endeavor, while he also clearly enunciated the need for a theory of social change in order to move LPP forward. Tollefson sought to "contribute to a theory of language planning that locates the field within social theory" (Tollefson, 1991, p. 8).

Streams of work in language planning and language policy began to coalesce more fully in the 1990s in what is increasingly referred to as LPP, as for example in Grabe's (1994) *Annual Review of Applied Linguistics (ARAL)* theme issue on LPP, Hornberger and Ricento's (1996) *TESOL Quarterly* special issue on LPP and English-language teaching, Huebner and Davis's (1999) edited volume on LPP in the United States, and Ager's (2001) treatise on LPP motivations. Fettes (1997, p. 14) envisions the link between language planning and language policy thus:

> Language planning ... must be linked to the critical evaluation of language policy: the former providing standards of rationality and effectiveness, the latter testing these ideas against actual practice in order to promote the development of better ... language planning models. Such a field would be better described as "language policy and planning", LPP.

The truth is that the LPP designation is useful, not just as a reminder of how inextricably related language planning and language policy are (and in recognition of the important role of each), but also as a way around the lack of agreement on the exact nature of that relationship. Does planning subsume policy (Fettes, 1997, p. 14) or policy subsume planning (Ricento, 2000, p. 209; Schiffman, 1996, p. 4)? Is policy the output of planning? Not always – "a great deal of language policy-making goes on in a haphazard or uncoordinated way, far removed from the language planning ideal" (Fettes, 1997, p. 14). Does planning have policy as its intended outcome? Not necessarily – language planning is first and foremost about social change (Cooper, 1989; Rubin & Jernudd, 1971; Tollefson, 1991). Given these dissociations (Grabe, 1994, p. viii) and ambiguities, LPP offers a unified conceptual rubric under which to pursue fuller understanding of the complexity of the policy–planning relationship and in turn of its insertion in processes of social change.

In light of the resurgence of LPP beginning in the 1990s, this chapter traces the development of frameworks and models in LPP research, showing how recent work goes beyond, but is also solidly built upon, the foundation of earlier work.

Historical Development of Language Policy and Planning

While LPP as an activity has certainly been going on for centuries, the first use of the term "language planning" in the scholarly literature is usually attributed to Haugen's study of language standardization in Norway, in which he wrote:

> By language planning I understand the activity of preparing a normat-
> ive orthography, grammar, and dictionary for the guidance of writers
> and speakers in a non-homogeneous speech community. In this prac-
> tical application of linguistic knowledge we are proceeding beyond
> descriptive linguistics into an area where judgment must be exercised
> in the form of choices among available linguistic forms.
>
> *(Haugen, 1959, p. 8)*

The scope of LPP has since become broader than the orthographic, grammatical, and lexical codification highlighted in Haugen's original usage above, but the tension between theoretical and applied know-ledge (theory and practice), captured in his comment on going beyond describing to making choices, has maintained itself as an important continuing thread in the development of the field over the last half-century.

The field was rather easily identifiable in its early days because of a select series of well-defined conferences, projects, and publications. We have, for example, the 1968 *Language problems of developing nations* (Fishman, Ferguson, & Das Gupta), emanating from a 1966 Airlie House Conference in Virginia; *Can language be planned?* (Rubin & Jernudd, 1971), resulting from the Ford Foundation-funded International Re-search Project on Language Planning Processes carried out in the 1960s by Fishman, Das Gupta, Rubin, and Jernudd, each one focusing on a national LPP case – Israel, India, Indonesia, and Sweden, respectively; and *Language planning processes* (Rubin et al., 1977), produced from a 1969 meeting at the East–West Center in Honolulu, part of that same project (cf. Huebner, 1999, pp. 7–8; Paulston & Tucker, 2003, p. 409). These pub-lications have become classics in the field, providing accounts of early empirical efforts and descriptive explorations of national LPP cases.

Ricento (2000) characterizes LPP development in terms of three phases, roughly two decades each, typified by macro-sociopolitical processes and events, epistemological paradigms, and strategic ends within, by, and for which LPP research has been and is conducted. He characterizes the first two phases as primarily addressing practical language problems of new nations, at first with a sense of optimism and ideological neutrality, and later with an evolving awareness of the potential negative effects and inherent limitations of the modernization and development models within which early LPP efforts were situated (Ricento, 2000, pp. 197–203).

By the 1970s–1980s (Ricento's second phase), LPP scholars were vigorously critiquing and questioning the descriptive models they had developed, and were calling for more theoretically motivated LPP frameworks. In the 1983 volume optimistically titled *Progress in language planning* and edited by Cobarrubias and Fishman, Haugen revisited and expanded on his own (1966) fourfold model – selection, codification, implementation, evaluation – while noting he could not "claim that it amounts to a theory of language planning" (Haugen, 1983, p. 274). Cobarrubias himself discussed – at length – a series of ethical issues in status planning (1983), while Rubin (1983) problematized the so-called rational model of planning and suggested that language-status planning is an instance of a "wicked" planning problem (borrowing the term from city planners Rittel & Webber, 1973). Similarly, in the 1986 volume *Language planning* (Annamalai, Jernudd, & Rubin), reporting on a 1980 international LPP institute held at the Central Institute of Indian Languages, Rubin elaborated further on these points, and several others provided examples of complex multilingual national LPP cases (e.g., India, Thailand, Nepal, and others) which challenge the one-language-one-nation ideological tenet of modernization and development theory (Ricento, 2000, p. 198; also Hornberger, 2002; May, 2001).

There was widespread dissatisfaction and a sense that the field was stymied and in need of heavy injections of new theoretical and empirical perspectives in order to move forward. This was in fact what followed in the 1990s. For us to appreciate those developments and their significance, however, it is important to first understand and consolidate the concepts and models that had been developed in those first three or four decades. For this purpose, we turn to an integrative framework originally proposed in Hornberger (1994).

An Integrative LPP Framework[1]

In a memorable piece entitled "The curse of Babel," Einar Haugen argued eloquently that "language [diversity] is not a problem unless it is used as a basis for discrimination" (Haugen, 1973, p. 40). Twenty years later, Dell Hymes reminded us of the difference between actual and potential equality among languages – that while all languages are potentially equal, they are, for social reasons, not actually so (1992, pp. 2–10). For language planners and policy-makers in multilingual contexts, then, the question is not so much how to develop languages as which languages to develop for what purposes, and in particular, how and for what purposes to develop local, threatened languages in relation to global, spreading ones.[2] In order to set about answering such questions, we need a framework which outlines our options, which identifies different languages (and literacies) and their different goals and uses. The LPP field is rich in frameworks and typologies, which I attempted to review and synthesize in one integrative framework, as recapitulated here.[3]

LPP types and approaches

The two main axes of the framework (see figure 2.1) represent widely accepted conceptual distinctions proposed early in the LPP literature, namely LPP types and LPP approaches. The first use of the status-planning/corpus-planning typology was by Heinz Kloss (1969), while acquisition planning as a third type of language planning was introduced 20 years later (Cooper, 1989). We may think of status planning as those efforts directed toward the allocation of functions of languages/literacies in a given speech community; corpus planning as those efforts related to the adequacy of the form or structure of languages/literacies; and acquisition planning as efforts to influence the allocation of users or the distribution of languages/literacies, by means of creating or improving opportunity or incentive to learn them, or both. These three types comprise the vertical axis of the figure.

The horizontal axis presents another distinction made early in the language-planning literature, between policy and cultivation approaches to language planning (Neustupny, 1974). The policy approach, seen as attending to matters of society and nation, at the macroscopic level, emphasizing the distribution of languages/literacies, and mainly concerned with standard language, is often interpreted to be the same as the status-planning type, while the cultivation approach, seen as attending to matters of language/literacy, at the microscopic level, emphasizing ways of speaking/writing and their distribution, and mainly concerned with literary language, is often interpreted to be synonymous with corpus planning. Yet the match is not perfect, and Haugen offers a more finely tuned interpretation which maps these two binary distinctions (status/corpus and policy/cultivation) onto a fourfold matrix defined by society/language and form/function axes and comprising selection of norm, codification of norm, implementation of function, and elaboration of function as the four dimensions (1966, 1983). His is the interpretation I use here, with the

Types	Policy planning approach (on form)	Cultivation planning approach (on function)
Status planning (about uses of language)	**Officialization** **Nationalization** **Standardization of status** **Proscription**	**Revival** **Maintenance** **Spread** **Interlingual communication –** **international, intranational**
Acquisition planning (about users of language)	**Group** **Education/School** **Literary** **Religious** **Mass media** **Work**	**Reacquisition** **Maintenance** **Shift** **Foreign language/second** **language/literacy**
	Selection Language's formal role in society *Extra-linguistic aims*	Implementation Language's functional role in society *Extra-linguistic aims*
Corpus planning (about language)	**Standardization of corpus** **Standardization of** **auxiliary code** **Graphization**	**Modernization** (new functions) **Lexical** **Stylistic** **Renovation** (new forms, old functions) **Purification** **Reform** **Stylistic simplification** **Terminology unification**
	Codification Language's form *Linguistic aims*	Elaboration Language's functions *Semi-linguistic aims*

Figure 2.1 Language policy and planning goals: an integrative framework

Notes: LPP types are in plain typeface, approaches in *italics*, goals in **bold**.

The goals are shown in six cells. Haugen's (1983) fourfold matrix is indicated by shading, and interpretive comments on those four quadrants are placed below the dashed lines.

Additional interpretive comments are enclosed in parentheses throughout.

The figure incorporates the work of Cooper (1989); Ferguson (1968); Haugen (1983); Hornberger (1994); Kloss (1968); Nahir (1984); Neustupny (1974); Rabin (1971); Stewart (1968).

addition of acquisition planning as a third type, thus yielding six rather than four dimensions of language/literacy planning.

LPP goals

Language-planning types and approaches do not in and of themselves carry a political direction, however, and as LPP scholars became increasingly aware of the political nature of LPP, a concern with the goals which LPP types and approaches could serve emerged. It is the goals that are assigned to LPP activities that determine the direction of change envisioned (Hornberger, 1990, p. 21), and the figure therefore represents goals at the heart of LPP. The matrix of types and approaches defines the parameters, but the goals identify the range of choices available within those parameters. In the six cells of the framework are included nearly 30 goals upon which there seems to be some consensus in the literature; however, I make no claim that these are the only possible goals.

An early formulation of language-planning goals was Ferguson's (1968) discussion of standardization of corpus, graphization, and modernization, placed in the figure under corpus policy and corpus cultivation planning, respectively (Ferguson's cover term, language development, seems to correspond to corpus planning). Standardization of corpus, referring to the development of a literacy norm which overrides regional and social literacies, and graphization, referring to the provision of a writing system for a hitherto unwritten language, both attend to the formal aspects of languages/literacies (cf. Haugen's codification, 1983, pp. 271–2); while modernization, referring to the lexical and stylistic development of a language/literacy for its expansion into hitherto unused domains, attends to the cultivation of languages/literacies for particular functions.

In a pair of articles, Nahir (1977, 1984) identified 11 goals of language planning, 9 of which I interpret as representing cultivation planning, of the status and corpus types, respectively. Revival (and similarly, revitalization, renewal, and reversing language shift; see Hornberger & King, 1996, p. 428; King, 2001, pp. 23–6, for brief comparative discussion of these terms), maintenance, spread, and interlingual communication all exemplify status cultivation, or the cultivation of a language's status by increasing its functional uses (cf. Haugen's implementation, 1983, p. 272); lexical modernization, purification, reform, stylistic simplification, and terminology unification belong to corpus cultivation, that is, the cultivation of a language's form for additional functions (cf. Haugen's elaboration, 1983, pp. 273–6).

Note that while lexical modernization corresponds to Ferguson's (1968) original modernization (which included both lexical and stylistic modernization), the remaining four corpus cultivation goals (purification, reform, stylistic simplification, and terminological unification) do not. Cooper's (1989) addition of renovation, as a fourth corpus-planning goal, to Ferguson's original standardization, graphization, and modernization, provides the appropriate rubric for these latter four sub-goals. Indeed, as Cooper (1989, p. 154) points out, the distinction between modernization and renovation (both of which belong to corpus-cultivation planning in my framework) is that while modernization finds ways for existing language forms to serve new functions, renovation does the opposite, finding new forms to serve existing functions. It is to this latter goal, renovation, that the sub-goals purification, reform, stylistic simplification, and terminological unification all belong.

Nahir's remaining two goals, standardization and auxiliary-code standardization, bring us to a closer look at the term "standardization." In the language-planning literature, the term covers a broad spectrum of meanings, embracing both process and product (Nahir, 1984, pp. 303–4, vs. Tauli, 1974, p. 62); both language status and language corpus (Nahir vs. Tauli and also Ray, 1963, p. 70, cited by Karam, 1974, p. 114; cf. Ferguson, 1968, p. 31); and means ranging from recognizing or accepting an existing standard (Ferguson), to creating, selecting, or imposing one (Nahir, Ray, Tauli). In the framework, status standardization refers to language-planning activities that accept or impose a language as the standard, while corpus standardization refers to language-planning activities that codify the linguistic forms of that standard as a uniform norm. Related to the latter is auxiliary-code standardization, which seeks to establish uniform norms for auxiliary aspects of language such as "signs for the deaf, place names, and rules of transliteration and transcription, either to reduce ambiguity and thus improve communication or to meet changing social, political, or other needs or aspirations" (Nahir, 1984, p. 318).

Turning from corpus standardization back to status standardization, we enter the status-policy dimension of planning (cf. Haugen's selection, 1983, pp. 270–1); here figure 2.1 includes, along with status standardization, three goals, none of which appear in Ferguson's, Nahir's, or Cooper's typology, but which are nevertheless widely recognized language-planning activities: officialization (cf. Cooper,

1989, pp. 100–4, following Stewart, 1968), nationalization (cf. Heath, 1985), and proscription (cf. Kloss, 1968).

As noted above, Cooper introduces acquisition planning as a third planning type (1989, pp. 157–63), distinguished from status planning by being about the users rather than the uses of a language, but by the same token having more in common with status than with corpus planning. Acquisition planning can be classified, he suggests, according to its overt goal, for which he identifies the possibilities of: reacquisition, maintenance, foreign-language/second-language acquisition, and to which I add shift as a fourth possible goal, thus producing an exact correspondence with the four status cultivation goals (revival, maintenance, interlingual communication, and spread). As for acquisition-policy planning, the latter five of Stewart's functions, as discussed and amended by Cooper in his discussion of status planning, make up the six goals here, identified in terms of the domains in which users are targeted to receive opportunity and/or incentive to learn the given language: group, education/school, literature, religion, mass media, and work.

In presenting the framework as a tool for beginning to answer the question of how to develop which languages/literacies for which purposes, I suggested that beyond identifying possible goals for development of a particular language/literacy, the framework might also provide a reminder that, no matter what the goal, language/literacy planning proceeds best if goals are pursued along several dimensions at once, consistent with Fishman's observation that status and corpus planning "are usually (and most effectively) engaged in jointly" (Fishman, 1979, p. 12). To take a simple example: to declare a language the national official language, while providing neither incentive nor opportunity for it to be a school language nor a writing system and standardized grammar for it, will not go far toward achieving the stated goal. Similarly, to endow a national official language with a new writing system that makes it more compatible with certain regional first languages (reform), while providing neither incentive nor opportunity for it to be learned nor a cross-regional communicative purpose for its use, will also not go far toward achieving its goal. On the other hand, undertaking a planning activity that not only selects a national official language, but also seeks to extend its use into interlingual communication by providing opportunity and incentive for people to learn it as a second language through the domains of religion, work, and education, and as well ensures that its writing system is standardized and its lexicon modernized,

offers far greater promise of success. In sum, LPP will be most effectively carried out if all six dimensions depicted in the framework are
attended to.

What the framework did *not* show, I reflected, was that planning
for a given language never occurs in a vacuum with regard to other
languages (Hornberger, 1994, p. 83). For that dimension, I turned to
language ideology, specifically to Ruiz's notion of LP orientations
(1984), concluding that local languages will thrive alongside global
languages where multiple languages are seen as a resource, and
not a problem. I cited as an example of LPP for local languages the
case of indigenous Quechua mother-tongue readers and writers
as bottom-up agents of LPP. These comments hinted at emerging
emphases on ideology, ecology, and agency in LPP at the turn of
the millennium.

Conclusion

The integrative framework was proposed in the early 1990s, at a time
of resurgence of interest in LPP and an intensifying call for an LPP
that would move beyond the descriptive to become more theoretical,
predictive, and explanatory. Cooper had noted that "we have as yet
no generally accepted language planning theory, if by theory we mean
a set of logically interrelated, empirically testable propositions" (Cooper,
1989, p. 41). Even earlier, Haugen had suggested that an explanatory
theory of language planning would "surely have to be one that takes a
stand on value judgments" (Haugen, 1983, p. 276), thus foreshadow-
ing what came to be an overriding concern for critically and theoretically informed LPP perspectives. By the 1990s, there were several
articles and volumes pointing the way toward addressing these concerns, many of them authored by contributors to the present volume.
In addition to the LP and language-policy volumes mentioned above
in the introduction, articles included Wiley (1996), who emphasized
the need for critical awareness that, given the role played by language
in struggles for power and dominance between groups, language
planning is not merely a technical undertaking and can often result
in creating conflicts rather than solving them; Paulston (1997), who
argued for attention to language rights as language policy, using a
theoretically informed language-planning approach; and Corson, who
called for a critically real approach to language planning, which would

"devolv[e] its research and decision-making processes down as much as possible to the least of the stakeholders" (Corson, 1997, p. 177).

Emerging emphases in LPP: ideology, ecology, and agency

Ricento (2000) explores the contributions of critical scholars such as Phillipson and Tollefson and of scholars associated with postmodernism such as Pennycook and Canagarajah in elucidating the relations between language policies and ideologies of power; and goes on to suggest that "the synthesis of elements of critical theory with an ecology of languages approach has led to the formulation of a new paradigm" (Ricento, 2000, p. 206); and later, that "the key variable which separates the older, positivistic/technicist approaches from the newer critical/postmodern ones is agency, that is, the role(s) of individuals and collectivities in the processes of language use, attitudes, and ultimately policies" (Ricento, 2000, p. 208). He credits work in LPP ideology, ecology, and agency with moving LPP theory forward.

Indeed, since the 1990s, we have seen a rich profusion of work in all these areas. Ruiz's highly influential work on LPP orientations (1984) foreshadowed a growing interest in language ideology among LPP scholars, exemplified in the work of Jaffe (1999) on language ideologies enacted through policy and bilingual education on Corsica. In an era of heightened awareness of language endangerment (e.g., Grenoble & Whaley, 1998; Krauss, 1992; Nettle & Romaine, 2000) and intensified efforts at language revitalization (e.g., Hinton & Hale, 2001), language ecology (also linguistic ecology, the ecology of language, ecolinguistics) has become increasingly welcome as both metaphor and paradigm in LPP (e.g., Fill & Mühlhaüsler, 2001; Hornberger, 2002; Mühlhaüsler, 1996, 2000; Phillipson & Skutnabb-Kangas, 1996), though not uncritically so given the potential for it to be misunderstood as suggesting that languages are involved in a natural evolutionary struggle, thereby downplaying the role of human agency and linguistic creativity (Pennycook, 2003). Meanwhile, a series of contributions called for greater attention to the role of human agency, and in particular bottom-up agency, in LPP (e.g., Canagarajah, 2002; Davis, 1999; Freeman, 1998, 2004; Ricento & Hornberger, 1996). Taken together, these critical perspectives and emerging emphases on ideology, ecology, and agency are indeed rich resources for moving the LPP field forward in the new millennium.

Yet, while it is true that new theoretical perspectives have moved the LPP field forward, it is also true that LPP remains, crucially, a field poised perpetually between theory and practice, as enunciated in Haugen's original 1959 definition. Fettes reiterates this dual focus in suggesting the potential of a conception of LPP as a "set of theories and practices for managing linguistic ecosystems" (Fettes, 1997, p. 19, citing Mühlhaüsler, 1996). It is to be hoped that recent LPP frameworks which consider ideology, ecology, and agency – frameworks such as Fishman's (1991, 2001) Graded Intergenerational Disruption Scale (GIDS) framework for reversing language shift, Kaplan and Baldauf's (1997) model of forces at work in a linguistic ecosystem, and Hornberger's (2003) continua of biliteracy framework – will prove useful in addressing the exigencies of actual LPP practice. After all, it is the real-world demands of LPP practice that make the theoretical work worth doing.

Annotated Bibliography

Cooper, R. L. (1989). *Language planning and social change*. New York: Cambridge University Press.
Among the gems in this slim but densely packed reference and course textbook are: a clearly formulated and well-substantiated definition of LP, concise accounts of four classic and diverse LP cases, four models for the study of behavioral change (diffusion of innovation, marketing, politics, and decision-making), and a comprehensive LP accounting framework.

Fishman, J. A. (1991). *Reversing language shift: Theoretical and empirical foundations of assistance to threatened languages*. Clevedon: Multilingual Matters.
Fishman, J. A. (ed.) (2001). *Can threatened languages be saved? "Reversing language shift" revisited*. Clevedon: Multilingual Matters.
These two volumes, one authored and one edited by Fishman, introduce and revisit, respectively, the theory and practice of his eight-stage Graded Intergenerational Disruption Scale (GIDS) in cases of reversing language shift. Intended for local-language advocates, language-policy specialists working for national and international bodies, and academic researchers and their students, the volumes assess the current status and future prospects of about 20 endangered

languages world-wide in light of the GIDS framework, and vice versa.

Hornberger, N. H. (ed.) (2003). *Continua of biliteracy: An ecological framework for educational policy, research and practice in multilingual settings.* Clevedon: Multilingual Matters.
Premised on a view of multilingualism as a resource and on the metaphor of ecology of language, the continua of biliteracy framework offers a comprehensive yet flexible model to guide educators, researchers, and policy-makers in designing, carrying out, and evaluating educational programs for the development of bilingual and multilingual learners, each program adapted to its own specific context, media, and contents. This volume presents both conceptual discussion of the model and cases of its application in contexts around the world.

Kaplan, R. B. & Baldauf, R. B. (1997). *Language planning from practice to theory.* Clevedon: Multilingual Matters.
This volume reviews the definitions, goals, processes, and economics of LP. LP case studies relating to nationalism and language rights, language status and ethnic identity, and language for specific purposes such as science, technology, business, and higher education are discussed. The authors offer a schema of processes and policy types for language-in-education planning. In their concluding chapters, they propose and exemplify a model depicting the array of forces (or language change elements) at work in a linguistic ecosystem.

Tollefson, J. W. (1991). *Planning language, planning inequality: Language policy in the community.* London: Longman.
Well organized for teaching and highly engaged with critical social theory, this book takes up a series of specific LP issues in turn, exemplified by cases from around the world – mother-tongue education, English-language teaching, refugee-language education, choice of national language, language rights – each introduced from the perspective of individuals facing difficult linguistic choices within the constraints of state language policies. The author argues for a historical-structural approach to LP, emphasizing the social, political, and economic factors which constrain or impel changes to language structure and language use. Importantly for Tollefson, while LP reflects power relationships, it can also be used to transform them.

Discussion Questions

1 What might newer emphases on ideology and agency add to our knowledge about LPP?
2 Take a language-planning case/language policy that you know of and use the integrative framework to analyze it.
3 How can we distinguish between language plans and language policies? What are the distinguishing characteristics?
4 What might future LPP frameworks include? What should future LPP research deal with?
5 What types of research approaches lend themselves to the different areas of LPP research (e.g., ecology, processes, agency, etc.)?
6 What other fields of research does the study of LPP depend on (e.g., sociolinguistics) and how?
7 Who should be involved in creating language policy?
8 Does LPP matter for education? Why or why not?[4]

NOTES

1 Significant portions of this section, including the figure, are reprinted, with minor modifications, from Hornberger (1994) with permission from Multilingual Matters, Clevedon, England. The original article, or portions of it, have also been reprinted in Hornberger (1996); Paulston and Tucker (2003); Ricento and Hornberger (1996); Wagner, Venezky, and Street (1999).
2 In the 1994 paper, I had posed the question in terms of literacies, but pose it here more generally in terms of languages (inclusive of literacies). The 1994 paper specifically addressed literacy planning in conjunction with language planning and therefore made an explicit argument that a concern with literacy is always subsumed within a concern for language; here the implicit inclusion of literacy in language planning is taken for granted and not always stated.
3 The 1994 paper referred to language planning, whereas here I adopt the LPP usage.
4 I am grateful to David Cassels Johnson for developing these discussion questions, and for valuable critical comments on early drafts of this chapter.

REFERENCES

Ager, D. (2001). *Motivation in language planning and language policy*. Clevedon: Multilingual Matters.

Annamalai, E., Jernudd, B., & Rubin, J. (eds.) (1986). *Language planning: Proceedings of an institute*. Mysore: Central Institute of Indian Languages.

Canagarajah, S. (ed.) (2002). Celebrating local knowledge on language and education. (Special issue). *Journal of Language, Identity, and Education*, 1(4).

Cobarrubias, J. (1983). Ethical issues in status planning. In J. Cobarrubias & J. Fishman (eds.), *Progress in language planning: International perspectives* (pp. 41–86). Berlin: Mouton.

Cobarrubias, J. & Fishman, J. (eds.) (1983). *Progress in language planning: International perspectives*. Berlin: Mouton.

Cooper, R. L. (1989). *Language planning and social change*. New York: Cambridge University Press.

Corson, D. (1997). Critical realism: An emancipatory philosophy for applied linguistics? *Applied Linguistics*, 18, 166–88.

Davis, K. A. (1999). The sociopolitical dynamics of indigenous language maintenance and loss: A framework for language policy and planning. In T. Huebner & K. A. Davis (eds.), *Sociopolitical perspectives on language policy and planning in the USA* (pp. 67–97). Amsterdam: John Benjamins.

Ferguson, C. A. (1968). Language development. In J. Fishman, C. A. Ferguson, & J. Das Gupta (eds.), *Language problems of developing nations* (pp. 27–35). New York: John Wiley & Sons.

Fettes, M. (1997). Language planning and education. In R. Wodak & D. Corson (eds.), *Language policy and political issues in education* (pp. 13–22). Dordrecht: Kluwer Academic.

Fill, A. & Mühlhaüsler, P. (eds.) (2001). *The ecolinguistics reader: Language, ecology, and environment*. New York: Continuum.

Fishman, J. A. (1979). Bilingual education, language planning, and English. *English World-Wide*, 1, 11–24.

Fishman, J. A. (1991). *Reversing language shift: Theoretical and empirical foundations of assistance to threatened languages*. Clevedon: Multilingual Matters.

Fishman, J. A. (ed.) (2001). *Can threatened languages be saved? "Reversing language shift" revisited*. Clevedon: Multilingual Matters.

Fishman, J. A., Ferguson, C., & Das Gupta, J. (eds.) (1968). *Language problems of developing nations*. New York: John Wiley & Sons.

Freeman, R. D. (1998). *Bilingual education and social change*. Clevedon: Multilingual Matters.

Freeman, R. D. (2004). *Building on community bilingualism*. Philadelphia: Caslon.

Grabe, W. (1994). Language policy and planning. *Annual Review of Applied Linguistics*, 14.

Grenoble, L. A. & Whaley, L. J. (1998). *Endangered languages: Language loss and community response*. Cambridge: Cambridge University Press.

Haugen, E. (1959). Planning for a standard language in Norway. *Anthropological Linguistics*, 1(3), 8–21.

Haugen, E. (1966). Linguistics and language planning. In W. Bright (ed.), *Sociolinguistics* (pp. 50–71). The Hague: Mouton.

Haugen, E. (1973). The curse of Babel. In M. Bloomfield & E. Haugen (eds.), *Language as a human problem* (pp. 33–43). New York: W. W. Norton.

Haugen, E. (1983). The implementation of corpus planning: Theory and practice. In J. Cobarrubias & J. Fishman (eds.), *Progress in language planning: International perspectives* (pp. 269–90). Berlin: Mouton.

Heath, S. B. (1985). Bilingual education and a national language policy. In J. Alatis & J. Staczek (eds.), *Perspectives on bilingualism and bilingual education* (pp. 75–88). Washington, DC: Georgetown University Press.

Hinton, L. & Hale, K. (eds.) (2001). *The green book of language revitalization in practice.* San Diego, CA: Academic Press.

Hornberger, N. H. (1990). Bilingual education and English-only: A language planning framework. *Annals of the American Academy of Political and Social Science, 508,* 12–26.

Hornberger, N. H. (1994). Literacy and language planning. *Language and Education, 8,* 75–86.

Hornberger, N. H. (ed.) (1996). *Indigenous literacies in the Americas: Language planning from the bottom up.* Berlin: Mouton.

Hornberger, N. H. (2002). Multilingual language policies and the continua of biliteracy: An ecological approach. *Language Policy, 1,* 27–51.

Hornberger, N. H. (ed.) (2003). *Continua of biliteracy: An ecological framework for educational policy, research and practice in multilingual settings.* Clevedon: Multilingual Matters.

Hornberger, N. H. & King, K. A. (1996). Language revitalisation in the Andes: Can the schools reverse language shift? *Journal of Multilingual and Multicultural Development, 17,* 427–41.

Hornberger, N. H. & Ricento, T. K. (eds.) (1996). Language planning and policy. (Special issue.) *TESOL Quarterly, 30*(3).

Huebner, T. (1999). Sociopolitical perspectives on language policy, politics, and praxis. In T. Huebner & K. A. Davis (eds.), *Sociopolitical perspectives on language policy and planning in the USA* (pp. 1–15). Amsterdam: John Benjamins.

Huebner, T. & Davis, K. (eds.) (1999). *Sociopolitical perspectives on language planning and policy in the USA.* Amsterdam: John Benjamins.

Hymes, D. H. (1992). Inequality in language: Taking for granted. *Working Papers in Educational Linguistics, 8,* 1–30.

Jaffe, A. (1999). *Ideologies in action: Language politics on Corsica.* Berlin: Mouton.

Kaplan, R. B. & Baldauf, R. B. (1997). *Language planning from practice to theory.* Clevedon: Multilingual Matters.

Karam, F. (1974). Toward a definition of language planning. In J. Fishman (ed.), *Advances in language planning* (pp. 103–24). The Hague: Mouton.

King, K. A. (2001). *Language revitalization processes and prospects: Quichua in the Ecuadorian Andes.* Clevedon: Multilingual Matters.

Kloss, H. (1968). Notes concerning a language–nation typology. In J. Fishman, C. Ferguson, & J. Das Gupta (eds.), *Language problems of developing nations* (pp. 69–85). New York: John Wiley & Sons.

Kloss, H. (1969). *Research possibilities on group bilingualism: A report*. Quebec: International Center for Research on Bilingualism.

Krauss, M. (1992). The world's languages in crisis. *Language, 68*, 4–10.

May, S. (2001). *Language and minority rights: Ethnicity, nationalism and the politics of language*. Harlow: Pearson Education.

Mühlhaüsler, P. (1996). *Linguistic ecology: Language change and linguistic imperialism in the Pacific Region*. London: Routledge.

Mühlhäusler, P. (2000). Language planning and language ecology. *Current Issues in Language Planning, 1*, 306–67.

Nahir, M. (1977). The five aspects of language planning – a classification. *Language Problems and Language Planning, 1*, 107–22.

Nahir, M. (1984). Language planning goals: A classification. *Language Problems and Language Planning, 8*, 294–327.

Nettle, D. & Romaine, S. (2000). *Vanishing voices: The extinction of the world's languages*. New York: Oxford University Press.

Neustupny, J. V. (1974). Basic types of treatment of language problems. In J. Fishman (ed.), *Advances in language planning* (pp. 37–48). The Hague: Mouton.

Paulston, C. B. (1997). Language policies and language rights. *Annual Review of Anthropology, 26*, 73–85.

Paulston, C. B. & Tucker, G. R. (eds.) (2003). *Sociolinguistics: The essential readings*. Malden, MA: Blackwell.

Pennycook, A. (2003). The perils of language ecology. Paper presented at the International Conference on Language, Education, and Diversity, Waikato University, New Zealand.

Phillipson, R. & Skutnabb-Kangas, T. (1996). English only worldwide or language ecology? *TESOL Quarterly, 30*, 429–52.

Rabin, C. (1971). A tentative classification of language planning aims. In J. Rubin & B. Jernudd (eds.), *Can language be planned? Sociolinguistic theory and practice for developing nations* (pp. 277–9). Honolulu: East–West Center and University of Hawaii Press.

Ricento, T. (2000). Historical and theoretical perspectives in language policy and planning. *Journal of Sociolinguistics, 4*, 196–213.

Ricento, T. K. & Hornberger, N. H. (1996). Unpeeling the onion: Language planning and policy and the ELT professional. *TESOL Quarterly, 30*, 401–28.

Rittel, H. W. J. & Webber, M. M. (1973). Dilemmas in a general theory of planning. *Policy Sciences, 4*, 155–69.

Rubin, J. (1983). Evaluation status planning: What has the past decade accomplished? In J. Cobarrubias & J. Fishman (eds.), *Progress in language planning: International perspectives* (pp. 329–43). Berlin: Mouton.

Rubin, J. (1986). City planning and language planning. In E. Annamalai, B. Jernudd, & J. Rubin (eds.), *Language planning: Proceedings of an institute* (pp. 105–22). Mysore: Central Institute of Indian Languages.

Rubin, J. & Jernudd, B. (eds.) (1971). *Can language be planned? Sociolinguistic theory and practice for developing nations*. Honolulu: East–West Center and University of Hawaii Press.

Rubin, J., Fishman, J., Jernudd, B., Das Gupta, J., & Ferguson, C. A. (1977). *Language planning processes*. The Hague: Mouton.

Ruiz, R. (1984). Orientations in language planning. *NABE Journal, 8*(2), 15–34.

Schiffman, H. F. (1996). *Linguistic culture and language policy*. New York: Routledge.

Stewart, W. (1968). A sociolinguistic typology for describing national multilingualism. In J. Fishman (ed.), *Readings in the sociology of language* (pp. 531–45). The Hague: Mouton.

Tauli, V. (1974). The theory of language planning. In J. Fishman (ed.), *Advances in language planning* (pp. 49–67). The Hague: Mouton.

Tollefson, J. W. (1991). *Planning language, planning inequality: Language policy in the community*. London: Longman.

Wagner, D. A., Venezky, R. L., & Street, B. (eds.) (1999). *Literacy: An international handbook*. Boulder, CO: Westview Press.

Wiley, T. G. (1996). Language planning and policy. In S. L. McKay & N. H. Hornberger (eds.), *Sociolinguistics and language teaching* (pp. 103–47). New York: Cambridge University Press.

CHAPTER THREE

Critical Theory in Language Policy

James W. Tollefson

Critical language-policy (CLP) research is part of a growing field of critical applied linguistics that includes critical discourse analysis, critical literacy studies, and critical pedagogy (Pennycook, 2001). In language-policy research, the term "critical" has three interrelated meanings: (1) it refers to work that is critical of traditional, mainstream approaches to language policy research; (2) it includes research that is aimed at social change; and (3) it refers to research that is influenced by critical theory.

The first meaning of *critical* in CLP research is that it entails an implicit critique of traditional, mainstream approaches. The central criticism of traditional research is that it emphasizes apolitical analysis of technical issues such as terminology development rather than underlying social and political forces affecting language policy. Traditional research (called the "neoclassical approach" by Tollefson, 1991) is characterized by the assumption that language policies are usually adopted to solve problems of communication in multilingual settings and to increase social and economic opportunities for linguistic minorities (e.g., Eastman, 1983). Traditional research first emerged in the 1960s and 1970s in order to aid programs of "modernization" in "developing" countries. This early work in language policy was seen as having practical value for newly independent, multilingual and multiethnic states facing the problems of national unity and socio-economic development. The traditional approach was extended to developed countries, where language policies were believed to be useful for integrating linguistic minorities into mainstream socio-economic systems. In contrast to this optimistic traditional research, a critical approach acknowledges that policies often create and sustain various forms of social inequality, and that policy-makers usually promote the interests of dominant social groups. Early critical research on South Africa was especially important in leading to disillusionment with traditional language-policy research.[1]

A second meaning of critical is that it refers to research aimed at social change. This research examines the role of language policies in social, political, and economic inequality, with the aim of developing policies that reduce various forms of inequality. For instance, prominent researchers (e.g., Cummins, 2000), academic journals (e.g., the *Bilingual Research Journal*), and professional associations (e.g., the National Association for Bilingual Education) in the sub-discipline of bilingual education are committed to policies promoting the maintenance and revitalization of indigenous and heritage languages as necessary for achieving social justice. Such research is fundamentally opposed to positivist approaches that emphasize the researcher's "objectivity" and distance from the "subjects" of research. In its concern for social change and social justice, CLP research highlights ethical questions of policy, as well as of research methodology.

A third meaning of critical is that it refers to work that is influenced by critical theory. Critical theory includes a broad range of work examining the processes by which systems of social inequality are created and sustained. Of particular interest is inequality that is largely invisible, due to ideological processes that make inequality seem to be the natural condition of human social systems. Critical theory highlights the concept of power, particularly in institutions, such as schools, involved in reproducing inequality.

These three meanings of "critical" are not mutually exclusive; indeed, most CLP research reflects all three uses of the term. Due to its particular importance in recent language-policy research, critical theory in CLP research will be the focus of the remainder of this chapter.

Critical Theory

Critical theory includes work by such thinkers as Bourdieu (1991), Foucault (1972, 1979), Gramsci (1988), Habermas (1979, 1985, 1987, 1988), and others. Much of this work involves a rethinking of Marxist theory, as well as of critiques of Marxist and neo-Marxist work. Although critical work varies considerably and significant areas of disagreement distinguish various critical thinkers (e.g., see Holt & Margonis, 1992), work in critical theory generally investigates the processes by which social inequality is produced and sustained, and the struggle to reduce inequality to bring about greater forms of social justice. In this sense, critical theory has a "practical intent" (Holt & Margonis, 1992, p. 5): to uncover systems of exploitation, particularly those hidden by ideology, and to find ways to overcome that exploitation.

Critical theory has influenced language-policy research in several important ways. In particular, two assumptions from critical theory are widely accepted in CLP research. The first assumption from critical theory is that structural categories – particularly class, race, and gender – are central explanatory factors in all social life. Initially, early CLP research (e.g., Tollefson, 1991) emphasized the neo-Marxist view that language policies should be viewed as one arena in which different classes are engaged in struggle over fundamentally antagonistic interests. Subsequently, CLP research was extended to focus on race and gender, and also on issues of culture and discourse (e.g., Pennycook, 1994, 1998; Tollefson, 2002d). For instance, CLP research on the Ebonics controversy in the United States examines (1) the role of school language policies in racist educational systems (Baugh, 2000), and (2) the impact of standard language ideology on attitudes toward African American Vernacular English and other stigmatized varieties (Lippi-Green, 1997). Gender has not received as much attention in CLP research as in critical pedagogy and other areas of applied linguistics; therefore gender deserves more intense investigation in language policy, perhaps along the lines of work by Norton (2000). Despite the trend in CLP research to move beyond class, it remains an important focus (e.g., Brutt-Griffler, 2002).

A second key assumption from critical theory that has become widely accepted in CLP research is that a critical examination of epistemology and research methodology is inseparable from ethical standards and political commitments to social justice. Partly upon the basis of the work of Habermas (1988), CLP researchers seek to develop a "critical method" that includes a self-reflective examination of their relationship with "Others" who are the focus of research. In a provocative indication of the gap between the perspectives of traditional researchers and indigenous communities, Smith (1999) asserts that "from the vantage point of the colonized . . . the term 'research' is inextricably linked to European imperialism and colonialism. The word itself, 'research,' is probably one of the dirtiest words in the indigenous world's vocabulary" (p. 1). A critical examination of research methodology raises several fundamental questions. First, how do different discourse communities, including language-policy researchers, establish and maintain their preferred forms of knowledge (Blommaert, 1996; Pederson, 2002; Ryon, 2002)? What "counts" as legitimate research questions, acceptable research methodologies, and persuasive forms of evidence (Gegeo, 1998; Watson-Gegeo & Gegeo, 1999; Williams & Morris, 2000)? What ethical responsibilities do researchers have in the research process (Smith, 1999)? CLP researchers also pose similar questions about ethnolinguistic communities: how are preferred forms of knowledge created and sustained among groups affected by language policies (Canagarajah, 2002)? What role should Others play in the research process, especially in evaluating research (Ryon, 2002)? Most CLP researchers accept the political principle that people who experience the consequences of language policy should have a major role in making policy decisions (e.g., Williams & Morris, 2000). This democratic principle of participation is a moral-political imperative based upon Habermas's (1986) conception of the social function of philosophy: "You put the responsibility for decisions on the shoulders of those who anyhow will suffer the consequences, and . . . at the same time you stimulate the participants who have to make up their minds in practical discourse to look around for information and ideas that can shed light on their situation" (p. 207). Extended to CLP research, this principle means that researchers should aggressively analyze the underlying ideologies of alternative policies and the links between language policies and social inequality, thereby contributing to the development of an informed and skeptical citizenry (Donahue, 2002).

Some of the most influential efforts to develop a critical method have been carried out by Canagarajah (1999) in Sri Lanka, Gegeo and Watson-Gegeo in the Solomon Islands (Gegeo, 1998; Watson-Gegeo & Gegeo, 1995), McCarty (2004) in the Southwestern United States, and Smith (1999) in Maori communities in New Zealand.

In addition to these two broad assumptions (the importance of structural categories and the need for ethical and political considerations in research), CLP research also incorporates a set of interrelated ideas from critical theory. Although they are not all necessarily implicit in every example of CLP research, together they define an approach to language-policy research that is increasingly influential.

Key ideas from critical theory

Power

In CLP research, power – which refers to the ability to control events in order to achieve one's aims – is seen as implicit in all social relationships. In investigating power, CLP research focuses on the dynamic relationship between social structure and individual agency, particularly in institutions, which constrain and provide meaning to individual actions (Pederson, 2002). In CLP research, power is implicit in the policy-making process, and language policies are seen as an important mechanism by which the state and other policy-making institutions seek to influence language behavior (Tollefson, 1991).

Struggle

Building on the Marxist notion that socioeconomic classes have fundamentally incompatible interests, many CLP researchers view the world as consisting of dominant groups, which usually control the state, and oppressed groups. Most language policies adopted by the state and other institutions controlled by dominant groups are viewed as serving the interests of the oppressors. For example, Pennycook (2002b) argues that mother-tongue education in some contexts may be part of efforts by dominant groups to sustain their system of privilege. Nevertheless, oppressed groups may seek to expand their power and further their interests through language policies. McCarty (2002a), for example, shows how some indigenous groups in the United States have revitalized their communities through language policies in education. In general, CLP researchers assume an adversarial model for social change, in which struggle is a prerequisite for social justice.

Colonization

CLP research examines the processes by which ethnocultural groups are impacted on by the policies of dominant institutions of the state (especially schools), as well as corporations, international agencies, and other powerful forces. This work is inspired by Habermas's *Legitimation crisis* (1975; also see Foucault, 1979). Habermas argues that the day-to-day communicative interactions of people living within identifiable cultural traditions (which he calls the "lifeworld"; also see Bourdieu, 1991, on *"habitus"*) are characterized by face-to-face inter-action in the family and other primary institutions; but these primary sources of identity are increasingly subject to encroachment by the market mechanisms and bureaucratic controls of capitalist societies – a process called "colonization" (Habermas, 1987, p. 355). The resulting loss of culture, identity, and socialization has enormous consequences, including the destruction of sources of meaning and a disillusioned and cynical citizenry (Donahue, 2002). CLP research examines the role of language policies in the process of colonization. For instance, in some CLP research, the spread of English is viewed not as a process in which individuals willingly learn a new language for their own well-being, but rather as a mechanism for the destruction of cultural identity and the imposition of an economic order that demands workers and consumers without ties to traditional institu-tions that might serve as a counter-balance to the state and the capitalist economy (Phillipson, 1992). Habermas identifies coloniza-tion – which takes place in part through language shift – as the major social problem of our age.

Hegemony and ideology

Gramsci (1988) defines hegemonic practices as institutional practices that ensure that power remains in the hands of the few. CLP research seeks to describe and explain hegemonic practices. For instance, Ramanathan (1999) explores how institutional practices in education in India keep English out of reach of low-income learners, despite a discourse of English opportunity in Indian schools. Similarly, Tollefson (1989) examines how "survival English" for refugees and immigrants contributes to their economic marginalization. CLP research pays par-ticular attention to such practices that have come to be invisible (that is, seen as common sense). The term "ideology" refers to unconscious beliefs and assumptions that are "naturalized" and thus contribute to hegemony. As hegemonic practices come to be built into the institu-tions of society, they tend to reinforce privilege and grant it legitimacy as a "natural" condition (Fairclough, 1989). In Bourdieu's terms, the cultural and linguistic capital of dominant and non-dominant groups is made unequal by the structure of social institutions (1991). The reproduction of such systems of inequality is the focus of CLP research that seeks to uncover the explicit and implicit policies contributing to hegemony.

Resistance

Building on work by Willis (1977), CLP research examines how ethnolinguistic minorities may undermine the basic logic of dominant social systems by sustaining alternative social systems. For instance, school-children's use of African American Vernacular English rather than standard English not only sustains their identity, but also constitutes a challenge to a social hierarchy in which individuals are expected to accept the need to acquire and use standard English in "appropriate" social contexts (Baugh, 2000). Similarly, language learners in some contexts may seek to acquire a dominant language but also resist its impact on their identities (Canagarajah, 1999). Thus, despite language policies favoring dominant groups, oppressed ethnolinguistic groups may exercise resistance by creating and sustaining alternative social hierarchies in which "non-standard" languages are crucial, and also by engaging in ongoing struggles to adopt alternative policies that lead to greater social justice.

Examples of Critical Approaches to CLP Research

Despite the use of concepts from critical theory in a rapidly expanding body of CLP research, a critical theory of language policy has yet to be developed. Indeed, theory remains relatively underdeveloped in the field of language policy generally (Williams, 1992). Nevertheless, CLP researchers have developed several distinct approaches to language-policy analysis. In this section, two of these approaches are summarized: the historical-structural approach and governmentality.

The historical-structural approach

The historical-structural approach to CLP research, first articulated by Street (1993) and Tollefson (1991), emphasizes the influence of social and historical factors on language policy and language use. Although not critical, seminal work on language policy in the 1960s also placed the field of language-policy research squarely within a broad social, political, and historical framework (e.g., Fishman, Ferguson, & Das Gupta, 1968). The historical-structural approach is distinguished from this earlier work by the influence of critical theory, particularly its emphasis upon the role of socioeconomic class in shaping language-policy alternatives, and its critique of ahistorical analyses that evaluate policies without regard to their role in systems of oppression and exploitation. For example, McCarty's (2004) "critical-historical" research on indigenous languages in the United States emphasizes efforts by the US government to eliminate indigenous languages and bring about language shift to English-only.

The historical-structural approach assumes that language-policy research is inescapably political, and that researchers should explicitly acknowledge their own role in shaping the discussion of policy alternatives. For example, Williams (1992) argues that many language-policy researchers lack an understanding of the political nature of language-policy processes and are unaware of relevant theoretical developments in political science and sociology. Williams calls for explicit analysis of the links between language policy and such sociohistorical processes as migration, state formation, and political conflict.

Street's (1993) contribution to the historical-structural approach is his insistence that literacy policy should be included in CLP research. Street's "ideological model" of literacy is critical of traditional research on literacy (which he terms "the autonomous model") for assuming that oral and written language are fundamentally different and that written literacy is more beneficial for cognitive development. Street argues instead that oral and written language are related to broad social practices, and are social acts whose meaning is defined within different social, historical, and cultural communities.

Since the early 1990s, the historical-structural approach has come to be widely used in CLP research. Nevertheless, alternative approaches focusing on other aspects of social systems have been proposed as well. One of the most promising is governmentality.

Governmentality

Drawing from Foucault's analysis of "governmentality" (Foucault, 1991), CLP researchers such as Moore (2002) and Pennycook (2002a, 2002b) shift attention from domination and exploitation by the state and capitalist market to the indirect acts of governing that shape individual and group language behavior. These researchers examine the techniques and practices of politicians, bureaucrats, educators, and other state authorities at the micro-level, as well as the rationales and strategies these authorities adopt. Thus these researchers argue that CLP research should not focus primarily on the historical and structural bases of state policy, but instead on "discourses, educational practices, and language use" – social processes involved in the formation of culture and knowledge (Pennycook, 2002a, p. 92). For example, Pennycook (2002a) argues that the policy on medium of instruction in colonial Hong Kong was not merely about selecting the language of education, but rather was part of a broad cultural policy aimed at creating a "docile" local population that would be politically passive and willing to cooperate in its own exploitation.

A governmentality approach may be extended beyond colonial contexts to contemporary liberal democracies, in which pluralist policies may appear to promote language rights, but in fact may be part of increased forms of government control over language use, particularly among linguistic minority groups. For example, drawing from work by Hindess (1997) as well as Foucault (1972, 1979, 1991), Moore (2002) examines the complex process by which the Australian government in the 1990s successfully defined the views of linguistic minorities and professional English-language educators as "factional" concerns, and thus marginal to policy-making dominated instead by government officials claiming to work in the "national" interest. Her analysis highlights the "art" of governing, whereby state authorities harness moral and cultural mythologies to shape public opinion and control the range of policy options seen as legitimate.

CLP research on governmentality offers great promise for extending research beyond static concepts of the state toward more dynamic theories that place analyses of interaction within historical and structural contexts. Especially promising is the potential for explicit links between political theory, CLP theory, and micro-sociolinguistics (see Dua, 1996; Williams, 1992).

Conclusion: Current Debates in CLP Research

Continuing CLP research focuses on four areas of concern. The first area is the relative importance of economic, political, cultural, and discourse factors. Tollefson (1991) argues that economic forces are central in most language processes; in contrast, Pennycook (1994, 1998) argues that an approach emphasizing cultural politics and discourse is more productive.

A similar debate focuses on the relative importance of the state in language policy. For example, May (2001) argues that the nation-state must be central to any analysis of policy issues facing linguistic minorities. Similarly, Tollefson (1991) argues that "the struggle to adopt minority languages within dominant [state] institutions such as education, the law, and government, as well as the struggle over language rights, constitute efforts to legitimize the minority group itself and to alter its relationship to the state" (p. 202). In contrast, Mazrui (2002) and Alidou (2004) point out that globalization has diminished the role of the state and given greater importance to international organizations such as the European Union and the World Bank and to multinational corporations. Future research in a wide range of settings should be aimed at developing more complex models of language policy that incorporate the full range of factors and institutions involved in it.

A second area of current concern is the value of language rights, particularly in education. Especially important is critical research that has questioned widely held assumptions about the right to mother-tongue education. While some researchers (e.g., Phillipson, 2000; Skutnabb-Kangas, 2000) support the right to education in the mother tongue, others argue that policies favoring mother-tongue education can be components in strategies to maintain the social, economic, and political advantages of dominant groups (see Ricento & Wiley, 2002). Particularly influential in this debate has been research in South Africa, where mother-tongue education was a central policy of apartheid (Blommaert, 1996; de Klerk, 2002). Clearly there is a need for additional analyses of mother-tongue policies that may be linked to social and political agendas unrelated to language rights, but instead to struggles for political power (see Tsui & Tollefson, 2004).

A third area of current concern is the possibility of language maintenance and revitalization. While there is general agreement that the family and local community are the crucial arena for language maintenance and revitalization, there is debate over the potential for schools to catalyze resistance to the intrusion of English and other dominant languages. For instance, Crawford (1995) is pessimistic about language revitalization in North America, due to the powerful political forces arrayed against such programs, while McCarty (2002b) argues that schools "*can* be constructed as a place where children are free to be indigenous in the indigenous language – in all of its multiple and ever-changing meanings and forms" (p. 304). A key agenda for CLP research is to develop better understanding of the factors contributing to successful language maintenance and revitalization programs, particularly the role of indigenous communities in shaping policies and programs (see Gegeo & Watson-Gegeo, 2002; May, 2001).

Implicit in this discussion is debate over why societies should invest resources in programs of language maintenance and revitalization. Some CLP researchers emphasize language rights (e.g., May, 2001; Skutnabb-Kangas, 2000), but others claim that arguments favoring language rights are essentially normative, and ultimately subjective and moral (Brutt-Griffler, 2002). A second approach is a focus on social justice. In this view, language maintenance and revitalization are essential components of programs that seek greater social, economic, and political equality for linguistic minorities. For example, Corson (1992) argues that schools are made inherently unequal for many children merely by the routine exercise of power by dominant groups, and thus assertive programs to support minority languages are essential if reasonable educational and economic opportunities are to be available to minority-language children. A third rationale for language maintenance and revitalization emphasizes the economic value of language diversity, which is seen as a social asset, like clean air. This perspective, which draws from ecological models of language, remains theoretically underdeveloped (see Grin, 2002; Grin & Vaillancourt, 2000).

Regardless of the approach to language maintenance and revitalization, with the rapid loss of languages world-wide, forms of resistance to language shift should continue to be the focus of CLP research. In this regard, work by May (2001), McCarty (2002a, 2002b), and Gegeo and Watson-Gegeo (2002) is particularly promising.

A fourth area of concern involves the question of how critical research can contribute to greater social justice (see Corson, 1992; Habermas, 1985). A key issue is whether – at a time of increasing domination by supranational structures of decision-making – more democratic forms of language policy-making can be developed, in which non-dominant ethnolinguistic groups can shape the language policies that affect them. Confronted with globalization and repressive measures such as official-languages laws, centralist policies that favor dominant languages, immigration restrictions, and military action, some ethnolinguistic minorities feel that they have no alternative but to demand autonomy in their home territories or turn to forms of ethnolinguistic nationalism, as in Yugoslavia and elsewhere (Tollefson, 2002c). CLP researchers should explore ways to develop policies that acknowledge the crucial importance of ethnolinguistic identity, and yet do not lead to new forms of inequality. One approach is a conception of citizenship in which principles for language use are central (Kymlicka, 1995; May,

2001; McGroarty, 2002). Another approach is to implement forms of pluralism that guarantee protection for a wide range of language varieties (Skutnabb-Kangas, 2000; Tollefson, 2002a). A third approach is to make explicit the ideology of alternative language policies in order to encourage the renewed participation of informed and skeptical citizens in all forms of policy-making (Donahue, 2002). Regardless of the approach used, CLP researchers agree that peace and social justice require greater attention to the complex interplay of language policies and language use in the full range of society's institutions, particularly the schools and the workplace.

Annotated Bibliography

Bourdieu, P. (1991). *Language and symbolic power*. Oxford: Polity.
In this influential work, Bourdieu presents his critical theory of language. Encapsulated in Bourdieu's concept of *habitus* are the dual forces of deterministic social structure and individual agency. Applied to language policy, the concept of *habitus* has influenced a broad range of work, including May's analysis of ethnicity (2001) and Tollefson's historical-structural approach (1991).

Foucault, M. (1991). Governmentality. In G. Burchell, C. Gordon, & P. Miller (eds.), *The Foucault effect: Studies in governmentality* (pp. 87–104). Chicago: University of Chicago Press.
Foucault's seminal analysis of governmentality has had an impact on CLP research, as well as other areas of the social sciences. Given the likelihood that additional scholars will adopt this perspective, it is important to understand its fundamental claims.

Habermas, J. (1975). *Legitimation crisis*. Boston: Beacon Press.
Habermas's classic analysis of the crisis facing contemporary societies has had a profound impact on critical theorists in a broad range of the social sciences. CLP researchers have followed up Habermas's work with an analysis of the ways in which language-policy processes and language use are "colonized," and thus serve the interests of the state and the capitalist economy rather than historical cultural communities.

Phillipson, R. (1992). *Linguistic imperialism*. Oxford: Oxford University Press.

Phillipson's important book summarizes his theory of linguistic imperialism. Although Phillipson's work is influenced mainly by development theory rather than critical theory, his focus on language and social inequality is consistent with critical approaches used by other CLP researchers.

Tollefson, J. W. (1991). *Planning language, planning inequality: Language policy in the community*. London: Longman.
This book presents the historical-structural approach to CLP research and contrasts it to the traditional neoclassical approach to language-policy analysis. Chapters include case studies of language policy in a variety of contexts, with a historical-structural analysis of policy alternatives in each context.

Tollefson, J. W. (ed.) (2002d). *Language policies in education: Critical issues*. Mahwah, NJ: Lawrence Erlbaum.
This book is a collection of case studies using critical approaches to language policy in education, including the historical-structural approach and governmentality. Included are contexts in which language policies create social inequality, as well as cases of critical pedagogy for social change, in which linguistic minorities successfully use language policies to resist domination by more powerful groups.

Williams, G. (1992). *Sociolinguistics: A sociological critique*. London: Routledge.
In this critique of sociolinguistics, Williams presents the case for an approach to language-policy research that is informed by critical sociology. Williams argues persuasively that sociolinguistic research is undertheorized, due to the failure of most sociolinguists to become familiar with recent theoretical developments in sociology and political science. Elsewhere, Williams applies his approach to language policy in Wales (Williams & Morris, 2000).

Discussion Questions

1 Some traditional (non-critical) language-policy research has failed to grasp the impact of language policies on social inequality. Consider the following quotation from an introductory textbook on language policy: "Modernization and preservation efforts are seemingly happening everywhere, to provide all people with

access to the modern world through technologically sophisticated languages and also to lend a sense of identity through encouraged use of their first languages (mother tongues)" (Eastman, 1983, p. 31). What assumptions about the goals of language policies are implicit in this quotation? What might the author mean by "technologically sophisticated languages"? Do "technologically sophisticated languages" provide access to the "modern world" while "mother tongues" provide a "sense of identity"?

2   One critical perspective toward social justice is that it may be measured "by the extent to which societies ensure that individuals may use their mother tongues for education and employment" (Tollefson, 1991, p. 210). After reading Corson's article on social justice and language policy (Corson, 1992), consider what you mean by "social justice." What is the role of language in your definition?

3   McGroarty (2002) examines the concept of "citizenship" and asks whether liberal democracies can adopt pluralist language policies in education. After reading McGroarty's article, consider whether citizenship should entail legal protection for language, as it does in many countries for gender, religion, speech, and race/ethnicity/national origin. Can language rights be protected, given the budgetary constraints facing educational systems in many countries?

4   Compare and contrast the historical-structural approach (e.g., McCarty, 2002b) with a governmentality perspective (e.g., Moore, 2002). What is the major focus of each? What are some differences in their views of state authority in language-policy-making? How are the two approaches similar?

5   McCarty (2002b) notes that her research "is not a disinterested or dispassionate account. It reflects my position as an invested outsider" (p. 286). One criticism of CLP research is that it confuses research with politics by inserting researchers' political views into what should be a scientific activity. For example, in his review of Phillipson's (1992) concept of linguicism, Davies (1996) argues that such personal involvement is incompatible with the research process. What is your view of the explicit political stance taken by many CLP researchers?

NOTE

1   For an account of the early history of language policy research, see Tollefson (2002b).

REFERENCES

Alidou, H. (2004). Medium of instruction in Sub-Saharan Africa. In J. W. Tollefson & A. B. M. Tsui (eds.), *Medium of instruction policies: Which agenda? Whose agenda?* (pp. 195–214). Mahwah, NJ: Lawrence Erlbaum.

Baugh, J. (2000). *Beyond Ebonics: Linguistic pride and racial prejudice.* Oxford: Oxford University Press.

Blommaert, J. (1996). Language planning as a discourse on language and society: The linguistic ideology of a scholarly tradition. *Language Problems and Language Planning, 20,* 199–222.

Bourdieu, P. (1991). *Language and symbolic power.* Oxford: Polity.

Brutt-Griffler, J. (2002). Class, ethnicity, and language rights: An analysis of British colonial policy in Lesotho and Sri Lanka and some implications for language policy. *Journal of Language, Identity, and Education, 1,* 207–34.

Canagarajah, A. S. (1999). *Resisting linguistic imperialism in English teaching.* Oxford: Oxford University Press.

Canagarajah, A. S. (2002). Reconstructing local knowledge. *Journal of Language, Identity, and Education, 1,* 243–59.

Corson, D. (1992). Social justice and minority language policy. *Educational Theory, 42,* 181–200.

Crawford, J. (1995). Endangered Native American languages: What is to be done, and why? *Bilingual Research Journal, 19*(1), 17–38.

Cummins, J. (2000). *Language, power, and pedagogy: Bilingual children in the crossfire.* Clevedon: Multilingual Matters.

Davies, A. (1996). Review article: Ironising the myth of linguicism. *Journal of Multilingual and Multicultural Development, 17*(6), 485–96.

de Klerk, G. (2002). Mother tongue education in South Africa: The weight of history. *International Journal of the Sociology of Language, 154,* 29–46.

Donahue, T. S. (2002). Language planning and the perils of ideological solipsism. In J. W. Tollefson (ed.), *Language policies in education: Critical issues* (pp. 137–62). Mahwah, NJ: Lawrence Erlbaum.

Dua, H. (1996). The politics of language conflict: Implications for language planning and political theory. *Language Problems and Language Planning, 20*(1), 1–17.

Eastman, C. (1983). *Language planning: An introduction.* San Francisco: Chandler and Sharp.

Fairclough, N. (1989). *Language and power.* London: Longman.

Fishman, J. A., Ferguson, C. A., & Das Gupta, J. (eds.) (1968). *Language problems of developing nations.* New York: John Wiley & Sons.

Foucault, M. (1972). *The archaeology of knowledge.* New York: Pantheon.

Foucault, M. (1979). *Discipline and punish.* Harmondsworth: Penguin.

Foucault, M. (1991). Governmentality. In G. Burchell, C. Gordon, & P. Miller (eds.), *The Foucault effect: Studies in governmentality* (pp. 87–104). Chicago: University of Chicago Press.

Gegeo, D. W. (1998). Indigenous knowledge and empowerment: Rural development examined from within. *Contemporary Pacific, 10,* 289–315.

Gegeo, D. W. & Watson-Gegeo, K. A. (2002). The critical villager: Transforming language and education in Solomon Islands. In J. W. Tollefson (ed.), *Language policies in education: Critical issues* (pp. 309–25). Mahwah, NJ: Lawrence Erlbaum.

Gramsci, A. (1988). *A Gramsci reader: Selected writings* (ed. D. Forgacs). London: Lawrence & Wishart.

Grin, F. (2002). [Review of the book *Language and minority rights*]. *Language Problems and Language Planning, 26*(1), 85–93.

Grin, F. & Vaillancourt, F. (2000). On the financing of language policies and distributive justice. In R. Phillipson (ed.), *Rights to language: Equity, power, and education* (pp. 102–10). Mahwah, NJ: Lawrence Erlbaum.

Habermas, J. (1975). *Legitimation crisis.* Boston: Beacon Press.

Habermas, J. (1979). *Communication and the evolution of society.* London: Heinemann.

Habermas, J. (1985). *The theory of communicative action* (vol. I). London: Polity.

Habermas, J. (1986). *Autonomy and solidarity.* London: Verso.

Habermas, J. (1987). *The theory of communicative action* (vol. II). Boston: Beacon Press.

Habermas, J. (1988). *On the logic of the social sciences.* Cambridge, MA: MIT Press.

Hindess, B. (1997). Politics and governmentality. *Economy and Society, 26*(2), 257–72.

Holt, L. & Margonis, F. (1992). Critical theory of a conservative stamp. *Educational Theory, 42,* 231–51.

Kymlicka, W. (1995). *Multicultural citizenship.* Oxford: Oxford University Press.

Lippi-Green, R. (1997). *English with an accent: Language, ideology, and discrimination in the United States.* London: Routledge.

May, S. (2001). *Language and minority rights: Ethnicity, nationalism, and the politics of language.* London: Longman.

Mazrui, A. M. (2002). The English language in African education: Dependency and colonization. In J. W. Tollefson (ed.), *Language policies in education: Critical issues* (pp. 267–82). Mahwah, NJ: Lawrence Erlbaum.

McCarty, T. L. (2002a). *A place to be Navajo: Rough Rock and the struggle for self-determination in indigenous schooling.* Mahwah, NJ: Lawrence Erlbaum.

McCarty, T. L. (2002b). Between possibility and constraint: Indigenous language education, planning, and policy in the United States. In J. W. Tollefson (ed.), *Language policies in education: Critical issues* (pp. 285–307). Mahwah, NJ: Lawrence Erlbaum.

McCarty, T. L. (2004). Dangerous difference: A critical-historical analysis of language education policies in the United States. In J. W. Tollefson & A. B. M. Tsui (eds.), *Medium of instruction policies: Which agenda? Whose agenda?* (pp. 71–93). Mahwah, NJ: Lawrence Erlbaum.

McGroarty, M. (2002). Evolving influences on educational language policies. In J. W. Tollefson (ed.), *Language policies in education: Critical issues* (pp. 17–36). Mahwah, NJ: Lawrence Erlbaum.

Moore, H. (2002). "Who will guard the guardians themselves?" National interest versus factional corruption in policymaking for ESL in Australia. In J. W. Tollefson (ed.), *Language policies in education: Critical issues* (pp. 111–35). Mahwah, NJ: Lawrence Erlbaum.

Norton, B. (2000). *Identity and language learning: Gender, ethnicity and educational change.* London: Longman.

Pederson, R. W. (2002). Language, culture, and power: Epistemology and agency in applied linguistics. Unpublished doctoral dissertation, Pennsylvania State University.

Pennycook, A. (1994). *The cultural politics of English as an international language.* London: Longman.

Pennycook, A. (1998). *English and the discourses of colonialism.* London: Routledge.

Pennycook, A. (2001). *Critical applied linguistics: A critical introduction.* Mahwah, NJ: Lawrence Erlbaum.

Pennycook, A. (2002a). Language policy and docile bodies: Hong Kong and governmentality. In J. W. Tollefson (ed.), *Language policies in education: Critical issues* (pp. 91–110). Mahwah, NJ: Lawrence Erlbaum.

Pennycook, A. (2002b). Mother tongue, governmentality, and protectionism. *International Journal of the Sociology of Language, 154,* 11–28.

Phillipson, R. (1992). *Linguistic imperialism.* Oxford: Oxford University Press.

Phillipson, R. (ed.) (2000). *Rights to language: Equity, power, and education.* Mahwah, NJ: Lawrence Erlbaum.

Ramanathan, V. (1999). "English is here to stay": A critical look at institutional and educational practices in India. *TESOL Quarterly, 33,* 211–31.

Ricento, T. & Wiley, T. G. (eds.) (2002). Revisiting the mother tongue question in language policy, planning, and politics. *International Journal of the Sociology of Language, 154.*

Ryon, D. (2002). Cajun French, sociolinguistic knowledge, and language loss in Louisiana. *Journal of Language, Identity, and Education, 1,* 279–93.

Skutnabb-Kangas, T. (2000). *Linguistic genocide in education – or worldwide diversity and human right?* Mahwah, NJ: Lawrence Erlbaum.

Smith, L. T. (1999). *Decolonizing methodologies: Research and indigenous peoples.* London: Zed Books.

Street, B. V. (ed.) (1993). *Cross-cultural approaches to literacy.* Cambridge: Cambridge University Press.

Tollefson, J. W. (1989). *Alien winds: The reeducation of America's Indochinese refugees.* New York: Praeger.

Tollefson, J. W. (1991). *Planning language, planning inequality: Language policy in the community.* London: Longman.

Tollefson, J. W. (2002a). Conclusion: Looking outward. In J. W. Tollefson (ed.), *Language policies in education: Critical issues* (pp. 327–37). Mahwah, NJ: Lawrence Erlbaum.

Tollefson, J. W. (2002b). Disadvantages of language policy and planning. In R. B. Kaplan (ed.), *The Oxford handbook of applied linguistics* (pp. 415–23). Oxford: Oxford University Press.

Tollefson, J. W. (2002c). Language rights and the destruction of Yugoslavia. In J. W. Tollefson (ed.), *Language policies in education: Critical issues* (pp. 179–99). Mahwah, NJ: Lawrence Erlbaum.

Tollefson, J. W. (ed.) (2002d). *Language policies in education: Critical issues.* Mahwah, NJ: Lawrence Erlbaum.

Tsui, A. B. M. & Tollefson, J. W. (2004). The centrality of medium of instruction policies in sociopolitical processes. In J. W. Tollefson & A. B. M. Tsui (eds.), *Medium of instruction policies: Which agenda? Whose agenda?* (pp. 1–18). Mahwah, NJ: Lawrence Erlbaum.

Watson-Gegeo, K. A. & Gegeo, D. W. (1995). Understanding language and power in the Solomon Islands: Methodological lessons for educational intervention. In J. W. Tollefson (ed.), *Power and inequality in language education* (pp. 59–72). Cambridge: Cambridge University Press.

Watson-Gegeo, K. A. & Gegeo, D. W. (1999). Culture, discourse, and indigenous epistemology: Transcending the current models in language policy and planning. In T. Huebner & K. A. Davis (eds.), *Sociopolitical perspectives on language policy and planning in the USA* (pp. 99–116). Amsterdam: John Benjamins.

Williams, G. (1992). *Sociolinguistics: A sociological critique.* London: Routledge.

Williams, G. & Morris, D. (2000). *Language planning and language use: Welsh in a global age.* Cardiff: University of Wales Press.

Willis, P. (1977). *Learning to labour.* Westmead: Saxon House.

CHAPTER FOUR

Postmodernism in Language Policy

Alastair Pennycook

Postmodernism might not appear a likely candidate to be linked to language policy. Used in popular discourse to mean anything from "contradictory" and "confusing" to "contemporary" or "pretentious," and employed to describe anything from architectural styles that combine modern and traditional elements to new forms of communication technology, the notion of the postmodern might seem too vague or too easily derided to be usable as a philosophical framework that can shed light on decisions about language use. And yet a reasonable case can nevertheless be made that there are sufficiently serious ideas within the discursive field of postmodernism to warrant a discussion of its implications for language policy.

Postmodernity and Postmodernism

First of all, it is important to make at least one very basic division within understandings of the notion of postmodernism. The first – sometimes distinguished as *postmodernity* (or *neomodernism*; see Alexander, 1995) – takes as its central argument a realist position that focuses on the state of the world under late capitalism. From this point of view, the interest is in changes to social structures, communication, culture, and so forth as a result of new conditions of work, economy, and political structure. Of principal concern for people in the domain of applied linguistics is how post-Fordist work practices, "new times," flattened work hierarchies, new technologies, and new media impact on issues such as literacy, leading to a call, for example, for multiliteracies (Cope & Kalantzis, 2000; Kress, 2003) to cope with the diverse skills of the new workplace. From a language-policy point of view, this position is principally concerned with the state of languages in the new millennium, with implications for the survival of many of the world's languages under current economic and political relations.

From this point of view, then, postmodern language policy is about mapping language policy against changing economic and political conditions. What are the causes and effects, for example, of the spread and promotion of major languages, such as English? How and why have language policies shifted from the colonial to neocolonial eras? (A similar distinction to the one between postmodernity and postmodernism can be made between neocolonialism/postcoloniality and postcolonialism.) Whose interests are served by the adoption of major international languages over local languages? Can a notion of language rights address the death of many languages (see, for example, Brutt-Griffler, 2002a; Kamwangamalu, 1997; Pennycook, 1994; Phillipson, 1992; Skutnabb-Kangas, 2000)? One of the principal challenges from this perspective is to combine sophisticated analyses of globalization with complex understandings of how new flows of language and literacy relate to new flows of capital, media, technology, people, and culture (see Appadurai, 1996), or to deal with Hardt and Negri's (2000) challenge to account for "the novelty of the structures and logics of power that order the contemporary world. Empire is not a weak echo of modern imperialisms but a fundamentally new form of rule" (p. 146). To date, too little work on language in the global context has adequately engaged with sufficiently complex conceptions of this postmodern condition.

It is not, however, with this version of postmodernity that I intend to deal here, both because it is discussed (at least implicitly) elsewhere in this book, and because it sits uncomfortably with an alternative understanding. To accept the idea that we live in postmodern times, and that linguistic and cultural concerns are a reflection of political and economic forces, is, from a different perspective, to remain within a modernist and structuralist epistemology, in which language reflects society, and superstructural concerns are a reflection of infrastructural relations (language, culture, discourse, and ideology are reflections or legitimations of more primal social, economic, and political goals). It is precisely such materialism and realism that a second understanding of postmodernism seeks to challenge, attempting either to invert this relationship or to collapse it all together (making language, discourse, ideology, and culture primary sites of how the world is organized and understood). This second meaning of postmodernism is principally concerned with questioning the assumptions of modernity, the so-called Enlightenment, the hegemony of Western thought in the world, and the tools and concepts that have been used to understand the world. From an applied linguistic or language-policy perspective, the principal concerns from this point of view have to do with questioning the very concepts of language, policy, mother tongues, language rights, and so forth that have been the staples of language policy and planning up to now. It is this understanding of postmodernism that I shall be pursuing in this chapter.

Postmodernism: a brief overview

I cannot here explore at length the many strands of postmodern theory. What I want to present, therefore, is a version of postmodernism as both an intellectual, cultural, and political crisis in the Euro-American project of modernity, and a political project that remains grounded in a concern for change. While many of the global trends discussed above were emerging over the last 50 years, so too was a fundamental disquiet that the arrogant European epistemologies of the so-called Enlightenment, far from comprising a version of development that could save the world from increasing horror and destruction, were, by contrast, part of the problem. Postmodern intellectual inquiry started to turn back on itself, to question how we come to think as we do, why we construct particular visions of reality, in whose interests supposed norms, values, and givens operate. Postmodernism, then, is a philosophical questioning of many of the foundational concepts of received canons of knowledge. Postmodern thought can generally be viewed as anti-essentialist, anti-foundationalist, and opposed to grand narratives. Thus, it calls into question any claims to overarching truths such as "human nature," "enlightenment," or "emancipation"; it makes us skeptical about talk of reality, truth, or universality. Postmodernism rejects unity, totalization, transcendental concepts, or a belief in disinterested knowledge. Put most simply, we can view postmodernism as "the restive problematization of the given" (Dean, 1994, p. 4).

Lest such a view appears to be little other than epistemological anarchy, however, several considerations are important. First, postmodernism should be understood not so much as a canon of thought, but rather as a way of thinking and doing, a skeptical view of the world that tries to take nothing for granted. In this sense postmodernism refers "more to a state of mind, a critical posture and style, a different way of seeing and working, than to a fixed position, however oppositional, or to an unchanging set of critical techniques" (Usher & Edwards, 1994, p. 17). Second, contrary to naïve critiques of post-modernism, it does not espouse a hopelessly relativistic stance; rather it challenges the relativist–universalist dichotomy, favoring instead a concept of situated knowledge (see Lather, 1992): "The relativism of modernity needs to be distinguished from the partiality and particularity of the postmodern moment" (Usher & Edwards, 1994, p. 223). Postmodernism, then, can help us think beyond polarities such as universalism and relativism, suggesting instead that knowledge, action, and value are always specifically located.

Third, while there are reasonable grounds for the critique that postmodernism (like postcolonialism) may lack a political stance (focusing endlessly backwards, and caught eternally in its own problem-atizing), Young's (1990) definition of postmodernism "as European culture's awareness that it is no longer the unquestioned and dominant centre of the world" (p. 19) locates postmodernism within a broader politics of knowledge. Thus, by focusing on how the West became the West (occidentalism: see Venn, 2000), and how things might look different (postoccidentalism: see Mignolo, 2000), postmodernist thought *is* politically engaged as part of an attempt to rethink the world. And finally, by acknowledging both the need to address very real dimensions of inequality (see McGee, 1995) and the need for an epistemology that can inform action, by adopting, as Scott (1999) suggests for postcolonial theory, both a politics of refusal and a skepticism about liberation (both Fanon and Foucault), postmodernism can reconnect with postmodernity, avoiding the former's tendency toward intellectual play without a politics, and the latter's political realism without intellectual skepticism.

The view of postmodernism I have been trying to establish here, then, may be summarized as a skepticism toward many cherished concepts and modes of thought. Taken-for-granted categories such as man, woman, class, race, ethnicity, nation, identity, awareness, emancipation, language, power, policy, or planning are seen as con-tingent, shifting, and produced in the particular, rather than having some prior ontological status. Such a position nevertheless needs to remain responsive to and engaged with questions of difference, dominion, disparity, and desire (and compare Janks, 2000): difference being concerned with the construction of and engagement with forms of social and cultural difference; dominion referring to the contingent effects and workings of power; disparity having to do with issues of access and disadvantage; and desire having to do with why people engage with particular social and cultural forms, and how to create possibilities for alternative futures.

Postmodernism and Language Policy

Postmodernism, then, suggests a number of significant concerns for language policy and planning: First, it raises important questions about how power operates in relationship to the nation-state, and in particular how governance is achieved through language; second, it urges us to rethink the ontology of language as a colonial/modernist construct; third, it raises questions about the grand narratives or sweeping epistemologies of imperialism, language rights, or language access; and fourth, it points toward local, situated, contextual, and contingent ways of understanding languages and language policies.

Governmentality

Language policy has always been about far more than choosing which language to use in government, education, or the law, making decisions about the medium of instruction in schools or the role of translators in courts and governments, or implementing rational state policy resolutions. Language policy has to do with the use of languages as part of *language governmentality*. The notion of governmentality, as developed by Foucault in his later work (e.g., 1991), focuses on how power operates at the micro-level of diverse practices, rather than in the macro-regulations of the state. Indeed, in the notion of governmentality these micro- and macro-relations are elided. As Dean (1994) explains, "Rather than a theory of the state, Foucault proposes to analyse the operation of governmental power, the techniques and practices by which it works, and the rationalities and strategies invested in it" (p. 179).

As Rose (1996) explains, governmentality is best understood as an "array of *technologies of government*," which can be analyzed in terms of the different strategies, techniques, and procedures by which programs of government are enacted. This is not, then,

a matter of the implementation of idealized schema in the real by an act
of will, but of the complex assemblage of diverse forces (legal, architectural, professional, administrative, financial, judgmental), techniques
(notation, computation, calculation, examination, evaluation), devices
(surveys and charts, systems of training, building forms) that promise to
regulate decisions and actions of individuals, groups and organizations
in relation to authoritative criteria.

(p. 42)

Language governmentality can therefore be understood in terms of
how decisions about languages and language forms across a diverse
range of institutions (law, education, medicine, printing) and through
a diverse range of instruments (books, regulations, exams, articles,
corrections) regulate the language use, thought, and action of different
people, groups, and organizations.

The notion of governmentality is significant for a number of
challenges it makes to the received canons of language policy and
planning: It moves an understanding of governance away from a focus
on the intentional and centralized strategies of government authorities
and focuses instead on the multiplicity of ways in which practices of
governance may be realized. In so doing, it moves us away from
a focus on the state as an intentional actor that seeks to impose its will
on the people, and instead draws our attention to much more localized
and often contradictory operations of power. It also suggests that in
order to understand how the regulation of domains of life may be
effected, we need to look not so much at laws, regulations, policing,
or dominant ideologies as at the operation of discourses, educational
practices, and language use. And finally, it sheds light on the ways
in which the move from supposedly more authoritarian to more
liberal government may be accompanied by increasing modes of
governmentality through a greater multiplicity of modes of surveillance.
Such a position can help us see that what may at one level look like
an enlightened state policy on bilingualism, for example, may, by dint
of a range of systems for monitoring bilingualism in educational and
other domains, also become an increased strategy of governmentality.
Of great significance here, then, is the challenge governmentality poses
to the normativity of what is often from a critical/liberal standpoint
seen as obviously good: policies that favor bilingualism, multilingualism, less-used languages, and so on. It is not so much that these
are not good policy goals as that governmentality asks us to reframe
the question in terms of the governmental effects of such policies.

Questioning language ontologies

If on the one hand a postmodern approach to understanding questions of politics and governance raises important concerns for the ways in which we conceive the operation of the state, power, and control, it also poses, on the other hand, significant challenges for many understandings of language. First of all, it suggests that the very notion of a language, as a product, or invention, of the colonial/ modernist state, is something that requires critical examination. As Errington (2001) explains, colonial authorities and missionaries "shared a territorial logic that was similarly inscribed in colonial linguistic work, presupposing mappings of monolithic languages onto demarcated boundaries . . . Within these bounded confines were conceived to be ethnolinguistically homogeneous groups that were localized, and naturalized, as 'tribes' or 'ethnicities'" (p. 24).

The idea that languages somehow exist as ontological entities, with their attendant structures, boundaries, grammars, and forms, has become an almost unquestioned given of both academic thought and more popular discourse on language. Yet, as Harris (1990) argues,

inguistics does not need to postulate the existence of languages as part of its theoretical apparatus. What is called in question, in other words, is whether the concept of "a language," as defined by orthodox modern linguistics, corresponds to any determinate or determinable object of analysis at all, whether social or individual, whether institutional or psychological. If there is no such object, it is difficult to evade the conclusion that modern linguistics has been based upon a myth.

(p. 45)

If we take such a proposition seriously, then the very notion of "language" in language planning is brought into question, with numerous consequences for both the exteriority and interiority of languages. On the one hand, according to Harris, we at least need to develop an integrationalist approach to language, in which languages are no longer seen as bounded entities but rather are relocated within a much broader system of multimodal semiotics. This position no longer isolates language from other social behaviors and semiotic systems, allowing for a broader approach to multimodality (see, for example, Kress, 2003) that includes other modes of representation (such as the body, music, dance, clothes) into an understanding of meaning. On the other hand, premises such as their being underlying grammatical systems in languages are also called into question. As Hopper (1998) argues, "there is no natural fixed structure to language. Rather, speakers borrow heavily from their previous experiences of communication in similar circumstances, on similar topics, and with similar interlocutors. Systematicity, in this view, is an illusion produced by the partial settling or *sedimentation* of frequently used forms into temporary subsystems" (pp. 157–8).

A postmodern (or postcolonial) approach to language policy, then, suggests we no longer need to maintain the pernicious myth that languages exist. Thus we can start to develop an anti-foundationalist view of language as an emergent property of social interaction and not a prior system tied to ethnicity, territory, birth, or nation. The very notion that languages can be planned, therefore, that we can choose between this language and that, that we can decide to have one, two, three, five, or eleven languages in a language policy becomes highly questionable. In their forceful critique of language policy and planning, Luke, McHoul, and Mey (1990) argued that while language can be planned, discourse cannot. Yet the questions I have raised here suggest that languages cannot in fact be planned either, since there is ultimately no good reason to continue to posit their existence. Of course, this is not to say that language policy has no effects but rather, as I suggested in the discussion of governmentality, to raise this question: if the languages that language policy claims to deal with cannot themselves claim ontological status, what then is language policy concerned with?

Questioning grand narratives

A postmodern approach to language policy turns a skeptical eye on the grand narratives of the field, whether these are seen as conservative or emancipatory discourses. The grandest critical narratives of recent times have been the juxtaposed positions on linguistic imperialism and language rights. On the one hand we have a totalizing view of an all-consuming English, killing other languages and homogenizing the world; a view that sees English as both linked to imperialism and an imperialist force in itself. As Phillipson (1999) describes this diffusion-of-English paradigm, based on Tsuda's (1994) work, the spread of English is tied to "an uncritical endorsement of capitalism, its science and technology, a modernization ideology, monolingualism as a norm, ideological globalization and internationalization, transnationalization, the Americanization and homogenization of world culture, linguistic, culture and media imperialism" (p. 274). On the other hand, we are presented with a universalizing concept of language rights (see for example Skutnabb-Kangas, 2000) intended to retain heterogeneity and diversity for the globe. These macro-frameworks for discussing language policy in the global context are discussed elsewhere (see, e.g., chapters 14 and 15), so I shall limit my discussion here to postmodern perspectives on these concepts.

Amongst the various problems with the notion of linguistic imperialism (see, for example, Canagarajah, 1999a), an important consideration, as Rajagopalan (1999) suggests, is that

> the very charges being pressed against the hegemony of the English language and its putative imperialist pretensions themselves bear the imprint of a way of thinking about language moulded in an intellectual climate of excessive nationalist fervour and organized marauding of the wealth of alien nations – an intellectual climate where identities were invariably thought of in all-or-nothing terms.
>
> *(p. 201)*

Parallel objections have been raised about the notion of language rights. Coulmas, for example, asks whether the notion that language shift is necessarily a catastrophe may be a passing ideological fashion, based as it is on a "nineteenth-century romantic idea that pegs human dignity as well as individual and collective identity to individual languages" (1998, p. 71). As May (2004) suggests, critiques of the linguistic human rights position (e.g., Blommaert, 2001; Brutt-Griffler, 2002b) have pointed to a "preservationist" (see Pennycook, 2002) and "romanticist" account of minority languages and their loss and the assumption of an ineluctable connection between language and ethnicity. May (2004) suggests that such a position is countered by a "constructivist/postmodernist rejection of any intrinsic link, even any *significant* link, between language and identity" (p. 35). Rassool (1998) further argues that the complex, interconnected nature of the modern world and the problematic claims to universality of rights discourse suggest the need to investigate other ways of looking at questions of language rights: "in the light of these dynamic changes taking place globally and nationally can the argument for a universalizing discourse on cultural and linguistic pluralism be sustained?" (p. 98; and see also Pennycook, 1998a).

Linguistic-imperialism and language-rights discourses thus construct their critical frameworks from within the same paradigm they wish to critique. Imperialism is seen as a neocolonial structure threatening the world with a hegemonic object, English, while universal language rights are seen as a global panacea for maintaining diversity. While the two concepts operate from different epistemological and political assumptions – the one being based on a Marxian-influenced political economy of global relations, the other on a liberal, universalist concept of shared humanity – both operate from within theories of economy, the state, humanity, and politics that have their origins in the grand modernist project. The challenge is to move away from this dichotomy between linguistic imperialism and language rights and to try to understand in more mobile, fluid, and contextual ways how language resources are mobilized for different ends. Thus, Blommaert (in press) talks of the need to understand "speech resources and mobility" within the context of globalization; Rampton (1999) focuses on crossing and styling; May (2001, 2004) has sought ways to rethink the relationship between language and ethnicity; Stroud (2001, 2004) has argued that a notion of linguistic citizenship can combine an understanding of language as a resource and the relationships between language and governance.

Disinvention, local contingencies, and the performative

A postmodern understanding of language policy and planning, therefore, urges us to rethink, to disinvent, and to reconstruct (Makoni & Pennycook, in press) the ways we think about language policy and planning. This view of language has major implications for many of the treasured icons of liberal-linguistic thought. Not only do the notions of language and languages become highly suspect, but so do many related concepts that are premised on a notion of discrete languages, such as language rights, mother tongues, multilingualism, or code-switching. It is common in both liberal and more critical approaches to issues in sociolinguistics to insist on plurality, sometimes strengthened by a concept of rights. Thus, there are strong arguments for mother-tongue education, for an understanding of multilingualism as the global norm, for understanding the prevalence of code-switching in bilingual and multilingual communities, and for the importance of language rights to provide a moral and legal framework for language policies. Although such arguments may be preferable to blinkered views that take monolingualism as the norm, they nevertheless remain caught within the same paradigm: They operate with a strategy of pluralization rather than a questioning of the inventions at the core of the whole discussion. Without strategies of disinvention, most discussions of language rights, mother-tongue education, or code-switching reproduce the same concept of language as underlies all mainstream linguistic thought.

One of the crucial connections that needs investigation here is the relationship between language and identity. As Williams (1992) and Cameron (1995, 1997) have observed, sociolinguistics has operated all too often with fixed and static categories of class, gender, and identity membership as if these were transparent givens onto which language can be mapped. Cameron argues that a more critical account suggests that "language is one of the things that *constitutes* my identity as a particular kind of subject" (1995, p. 16). This opens up the issue of performativity (see Pennycook, 2003, 2004), which emphasizes the point that language use is centrally an agentive act, an act of reconstruction rather than of reproduction (as an argument that languages have fixed structures that we repeat would suggest). Linking this notion to Le Page and Tabouret-Keller's (1985) argument that linguistic and cultural identities are constituted through the performance of *acts of identity*, we can suggest that language use is not so much the repetition of prior grammatical structure as it is a semiotic restructuring as a claim to a particular identity.

Just as recent thinking (e.g., Butler, 1990) has focused on gendered and other identities in a non-foundational light, so may language itself be seen as a product of performative acts. Butler (1999) argues that identities are a product of ritualized social performatives calling the subject into being and "sedimented through time" (p. 120); similarly, we may start to see language identifications as active and often transgressive modes of language use. Important here is work such as Rampton's (1995) on "crossing" – ways in which members of certain groups use forms of speech from other groups – or "styling the Other" – "ways in which people use language and dialect in discursive practice to appropriate, explore, reproduce or challenge influential images and stereotypes of groups that they *don't* themselves (straightforwardly) belong to" (Rampton, 1999, p. 421). Instead of focusing on a "linguistics of community," this work focuses more on a "linguistics of contact," "looking instead at the intricate ways in which people use language to index social group affiliations in situations where the acceptability and legitimacy of their doing so is open to question, incontrovertibly guaranteed neither by ties of inheritance, ingroup socialisation, nor by any other language ideology" (Rampton, 1999, p. 422). Significant too in this work has been the focus on popular culture, word play, and contextual interaction. As Hill suggests, the "kaleidoscopic, ludic, open flavor" of much of the language use described profoundly challenges the methods of mainstream sociolinguistics "by transgressing funda-mental ideas of 'speakerhood'" (1999, pp. 550–1). This work, then, looks at language and identity in much more contingent, shifting, and challenging ways, so that rather than assuming language identities to be linked to ethnic, territorial, or national boundaries, it focuses on identifications across and beyond languages.

Conclusion

If postmodernism is allowed to remain nothing but a strategy of deconstruction, a pulling apart of what are perceived to be grand narratives, essentialist categories, fundamentalist claims, and so forth, it leaves us only with fragmented knowledge claims. If, on the other hand, postmodernity continues only as a form of linguistic realpolitik, without questioning the terms and concepts that it employs, it leaves us only with political critique without epistemological critique. Canagarajah (1999b) makes a similar point when he warns of both the absolutism of notions such as linguistic imperialism and the pluralism and relativism of notions such as linguistic hybridity in world Englishes. While a reconciliation between the two positions is perhaps never possible, there is a need to keep them in constant confrontation. Fanon and Foucault: postmodernity and postmodernism.

Where, then, does this leave us? A postmodern approach to language policy and planning suggests a rethinking of our social, economic, and political categories in favor of a more localized understanding of modes of governmentality. It suggests that we may be missing the point if we limit our discussions of language policy simply to the use of certain codes called "languages," and especially if we do so within the grand narratives of modernity in terms of rights and imperialisms. Languages are not so much ontological systems that precede the utterance as the products of language use sedimented through acts of identity. As we perform identity with words (rather than reflect identities in language), we also perform languages with words. What we therefore have to understand is not how this "thing" called "language x" or "language y" does or does not do things to and for people, but rather the multiple investments people bring to their acts, desires, and performances around these language effects.

Annotated Bibliography

Mair, C. (ed.) (2003). *The politics of English as world language.* Amsterdam: Rodopi.
This is a large and excellent collection of papers that deal with language policies as well as postcolonial literature. A number of the issues discussed above can be found in the different contributions to this book. Another of its strong points is that it includes both language policy/sociolinguistic orientations and work in postcolonial literature, a connection that is rarely made. It also has wide coverage, including Australasia and the Pacific, the Caribbean, Africa, and South Asia.

Maurais, J. & Morris, M. (eds.) (2003). *Languages in a globalising world.* Cambridge: Cambridge University Press.
One of the advantages of this book is that, while there is little that might be seen as postmodern in its approach, it looks at languages other than English around the world in an attempt to give a picture of the current state of languages in a changing world.

Pennycook, A. (2001). *Critical applied linguistics: A critical introduction.* Mahwah, NJ: Lawrence Erlbaum.
This book is an attempt to provide an overview of the field of critical applied linguistics. Organized around themes such as the "politics of language" (of particular relevance here), the "politics of text," the "politics of pedagogy," and so on, it contrasts liberal, critical, and postmodern views on applied linguistics.

Ricento, T. (ed.) (2000). *Ideology, politics and language policies: Focus on English.* Amsterdam: John Benjamins.
This is a very useful collection of papers on language policy, with an introductory paper by Ricento that presents an overview to changing philosophies of language policy. This collection contains useful contrasts between different critical approaches to language policy.

Usher, R. & Edwards, R. (1994). *Postmodernism and education.* London: Routledge.
This readable and interesting book discusses education in relation to postmodernism. The discussion of postmodernism is clear and concise, and the implications for education – with a particular focus on adult education – are well laid out.

Discussion Questions

1 Consider discussions elsewhere of postmodernism. Are they concerned with postmodernism or postmodernity as discussed above?

2 Dealing with a context with which you are familiar, turn a skeptical eye on the concepts and definitions of language employed. How might things be looked at differently?

3 By arguing for contextual and contingent language relations, postmodernism approaches to language may run the danger of missing the "big picture." On the other hand, by focusing on macro-structures of the globe, postmodernity approaches may miss the importance of location. How can we reconcile such tensions?

4 Look at other chapters in this book. To what extent do they employ grand narratives of language or to what extent do they look at local, contingent language effects?

5 How can governmentality and local understandings of language be understood in relationship to language policy in a context with which you are concerned?

REFERENCES

Alexander, J. C. (1995). Modern, anti, post, neo. *New Left Review, 210,* 63–101.
Appadurai, A. (1996). *Modernity at large: Cultural dimensions of globalization.* Minneapolis: University of Minnesota Press.
Blommaert, J. (2001). The Asmara Declaration as a sociolinguistic problem: Notes in scholarship and linguistic rights. *Journal of Sociolinguistics, 5,* 131–42.
Blommaert, J. (in press). In and out of class, codes and control: Globalisation, discourse and mobility. In M. Baynham & A. De Fina (eds.), *Dislocations/relocations: Narratives of displacement.* Manchester: St Jerome.
Brutt-Griffler, J. (2002a). *World English: A study of its development.* Clevedon: Multilingual Matters.
Brutt-Griffler, J. (2002b). Class, ethnicity and language rights: An analysis of British colonial policy in Lesotho and Sri Lanka and some implications for language policy. *Journal of Language, Identity and Education, 1,* 207–34.
Butler, J. (1990). *Gender trouble: Feminism and the subversion of identity.* London: Routledge.
Butler, J. (1999). Performativity's social magic. In R. Shusterman (ed.), *Bourdieu: A critical reader* (pp. 113–28). Oxford: Blackwell.
Cameron, D. (1995). *Verbal hygiene.* London: Routledge.

Cameron, D. (1997). Performing gender identity: Young men's talk and the construction of heterosexual masculinity. In S. Johnson & U. H. Meinhof (eds.), *Language and masculinity* (pp. 47–64). Oxford: Blackwell.

Canagarajah, S. (1999a). *Resisting linguistic imperialism in English teaching.* Oxford: Oxford University Press.

Canagarajah, S. (1999b). On EFL teachers, awareness and agency. *ELT Journal, 53*, 207–14.

Cope, B. & Kalantzis, M. (eds.) (2000). *Multiliteracies: Literacy learning and the design of social futures.* London: Routledge.

Coulmas, F. (1998). Language rights – interests of state, language groups and the individual. *Language Sciences, 20*, 63–72.

Dean, M. (1994). *Critical and effective histories: Foucault's methods and historical sociology.* London: Routledge.

Errington, J. (2001). Colonial linguistics. *Annual Review of Anthropology, 30*, 19–39.

Foucault, M. (1991). Governmentality. In G. Burchell, C. Gordon, & P. Miller (eds.), *The Foucault effect: Studies in governmentality* (pp. 87–104). Hemel Hempstead: Harvester Wheatsheaf.

Hardt, M. & Negri, A. (2000). *Empire.* Cambridge, MA: Harvard University Press.

Harris, R. (1990). On redefining linguistics. In H. Davis & T. Taylor (eds.), *Redefining linguistics* (pp. 18–52). London: Routledge.

Hill, J. (1999). Styling locally, styling globally: What does it mean? *Journal of Sociolinguistics, 3*, 542–56.

Hopper, P. (1998). Emergent grammar. In M. Tomasello (ed.), *The new psychology of language* (pp. 155–75). Mahwah, NJ: Lawrence Erlbaum.

Janks, H. (2000). Domination, access, diversity and design: A synthesis for critical literacy education. *Educational Review, 52*, 175–86.

Kamwangamalu, N. M. (1997). The colonial legacy and language planning in Sub-Saharan Africa: The case of Zaire. *Applied Linguistics, 18*, 69–85.

Kress, G. (2003). *Literacy in the new media age.* London: Routledge.

Lather, P. (1992). Postmodernism and the human sciences. In S. Kvale (ed.), *Psychology and postmodernism* (pp. 88–109). London: Sage.

Le Page, R. & Tabouret-Keller, A. (1985). *Acts of identity: Creole-based approaches to language and ethnicity.* New York: Cambridge University Press.

Luke, A., McHoul, A., & Mey, J. L. (1990). On the limits of language planning: Class, state and power. In R. B. Baldauf, Jr, & A. Luke (eds.), *Language planning and education in Australasia and the South Pacific* (pp. 25–44). Clevedon: Multilingual Matters.

Makoni, S. & Pennycook, A. (eds.) (in press). *Disinventing language.* Clevedon: Multilingual Matters.

May, S. (2001). *Language and minority rights: Ethnicity, nationalism and the politics of language.* London: Longman.

May, S. (2004). Rethinking linguistic human rights: Answering questions of identity, essentialism and mobility. In D. Patrick & J. Freeland (eds.),

Language rights and language survival: A sociolinguistic exploration (pp. 35–53). Manchester: St Jerome.

McGee, T. G. (1995). Eurocentrism and geography: Reflections on Asian urbanization. In J. Crush (ed.), *Power of development* (pp. 192–207). London: Routledge.

Mignolo, W. (2000). *Local histories/global designs: Coloniality, subaltern knowledges, and border thinking.* Princeton, NJ: Princeton University Press.

Pennycook, A. (1994). *The cultural politics of English as an international language.* London: Longman.

Pennycook, A. (1998a). The right to language: Towards a situated ethics of language possibilities. *Language Sciences, 20,* 73–87.

Pennycook, A. (1998b). *English and the discourses of colonialism.* London: Routledge.

Pennycook, A. (2002). Mother tongues, literacy and colonial governmentality. *International Journal of the Sociology of Language, 154,* 11–28.

Pennycook, A. (2003). Global Englishes, Rip Slyme, and performativity. *Journal of Sociolinguistics, 7,* 513–33.

Pennycook, A. (2004). Language studies and performativity. *Critical Inquiry in Language Studies, 1,* 1–19.

Phillipson, R. (1992). *Linguistic imperialism.* Oxford: Oxford University Press.

Phillipson, R. (1999). Voice in global English: Unheard chords in Crystal loud and clear. [Review of the book *English as a global language* by David Crystal]. *Applied Linguistics, 20,* 265–76.

Rajagopalan, K. (1999). Of EFL teachers, conscience and cowardice. *ELT Journal, 53,* 200–6.

Rampton, B. (1995). *Crossing: Language and ethnicity among adolescents.* London: Longman.

Rampton, B. (1999). Styling the Other: Introduction. *Journal of Sociolinguistics, 3,* 421–7.

Rassool, N. (1998). Postmodernity, cultural pluralism and the nation-state: Problems of language rights, human rights, identity and power. *Language Sciences, 20,* 89–99.

Rose, N. (1996). Governing "advanced" liberal democracies. In A. Barry, T. Osborne, & N. Rose (eds.), *Foucault and political reason: Liberalism, neo-liberalism and rationalities of government* (pp. 37–64). London: UCL Press.

Scott, D. (1999). *Refashioning futures: Criticism after postcoloniality.* Princeton, NJ: Princeton University Press.

Skutnabb-Kangas, T. (2000). *Linguistic genocide in education – or worldwide diversity and human rights?* Mahwah, NJ: Lawrence Erlbaum.

Stroud, C. (2001). African mother-tongue programmes and the politics of language: Linguistic citizenship versus linguistic human rights. *Journal of Multilingual and Multicultural Development, 22,* 339–55.

Stroud, C. & Heugh, K. (2004). Language rights and language citizenship. In J. Freeland & D. Patrick (eds.), *Language rights and language survival: A sociolinguistic exploration* (pp. 191–218). Manchester: St Jerome.

Tsuda, Y. (1994). The diffusion of English: Its impact on culture and communication. *Keio Communication Review, 16*, 49–61.

Usher, R. & Edwards, R. (1994). *Postmodernism and education*. London: Routledge.

Venn, C. (2000). *Occidentalism: Modernity and subjectivity*. London: Sage.

Williams, G. (1992). *Sociolinguistics: A sociological critique*. London: Routledge.

Young, R. (1990). *White mythologies: Writing history and the West*. London: Routledge.

CHAPTER FIVE

Economic Considerations in Language Policy

François Grin

Economic considerations in language policy constitute a relatively new development. Traditionally, policy discourses about language have tended to rely on one of three main perspectives: a legal one, in which language policy often takes the form of the enunciation of language rights in given contexts; a culturalist one, in which languages are mostly seen as manifestations of culture, confining policy to a set of measures affecting corpus or, at best, support for literary creation or publication; and an educational one, focusing on language teaching.

By contrast, economics is not often thought of as a discipline relevant to language. This situation has changed in recent years, as a result of an evolution taking place on two distinct planes. On the one hand, a certain degree of interest in language matters has always existed in the economics profession, resulting in the progressive development of a small but exciting body of literature raising questions that practitioners of language generally omit. On the other hand, an increasing number of specialists in language issues have come to realize that the types of policies they often advocate have economic implications. These congruent (though not necessarily converging) concerns have so far led not to a unified economic theoretical perspective on language, but nonetheless to the development of a range of interrelated propositions on language policy. This chapter offers a critical review of this set of propositions.

The first section lays some of the conceptual groundwork by reviewing the field generally known as "language economics" or "economics of language." The second section presents the main strands of research in language economics. The following section turns to the economic approaches to language policy and argues that the latter must be seen as a form of public policy – just like transportation policy, environmental policy, etc. The final section highlights some key findings of language policy evaluation in economic perspective.

What is the Economics of Language?

Several authors trace the emergence of language economics back to the publication of Jacob Marschak's paper on "Economics of language" in *Behavioral Science* (Marschak, 1965). Surprisingly, relatively few scholars since then seem to have been concerned with proposing a formal definition of the field. Confining ourselves to edited books on language economics, we can quote Vaillancourt (1985, p. 13), who characterizes publications in the field as "writings by economists on language questions"; Breton (1998, p. iii), who talks about "topics related to the interconnections between languages . . . and the economy"; and finally, in his introduction to a collection of reprints of 20 papers by different authors, Lamberton (2002, p. xi), who eschews any definition, but starts out by stating that the field "merges with the economics of information."

Given the relative lack of formal definitions, I keep using one proposed elsewhere (Grin, 1996): "The economics of language refers to the paradigm of theoretical economics and uses the concepts and tools of economics in the study of relationships featuring linguistic variables; it focuses principally, but not exclusively, on those relationships in which economics variables also play a part" (p. 6). This definition points to the three main lines of inquiry in the economics of language, namely:

1   How do language variables affect economic variables (for example, do language skills influence earnings)?
2   How do economic variables affect linguistic variables (for example, do the relative prices of certain goods affect patterns of language use)?
3   How do essentially economic processes (such as constrained utility maximization) affect language processes such as language dynamics?

The very notion of an economic perspective on language raises a number of epistemological questions regarding the delimitation of academic disciplines, in relation to their application to language issues. For the purposes of this chapter, it will be enough to state the spirit in which economics is invoked here. No issue is, per se, "sociological," "linguistic," "political," or "economic"; rather, almost every issue presents sociological, linguistic, political, and economic dimensions. The corresponding disciplines offer complementary angles from which an issue can be looked at, and depending on the issue at hand, the contribution of any particular discipline can be major or minor. This also applies to economics, which can contribute to the study of language issues through insights or conceptual tools that other disciplines do not provide.

Let us also note that this chapter focuses on the contributions of mainstream economics. This merely reflects the absence of research work on language issues from the perspective of non-mainstream (e.g., Marxian) economics. Likewise, this definition does not cover the rather different area of "the language *of* economics" whether from an economic (McCloskey, 1990) or linguistic (Henderson, Dudley-Evans, & Backhouse, 1993) perspective.

The Main Lines of Research in Language Economics

A historical perspective

The economics of language, as an identifiable field of research rooted in economics but addressing language issues, dates back to the mid-1960s. Much of the early work in language economics is due to Canadian (particularly Québécois) economists, and their papers analyze the French–English language issue; likewise, most US studies equate, to this day, "the economics of language" with the econometric investigation of earnings differentials between Hispanics and Anglophones. This "embeddedness" of researchers in their social and political context probably explains the three important stages in the early development of language economics, which well into the 1980s focused on the effects of language on labor income (Grin & Vaillancourt, 1997, pp. 44–5). First, many of the earlier contributions emphasized the role of people's native language as an ethnic attribute affecting their earnings – thereby raising the question of possible language-based discrimination. A second wave of contributions analyzed language (generally, though not always, a *second* language) as a form of human capital: this approach underpins estimations of the rate of return, for Hispanics in the United States, on competence in English. In a third wave, opened by Vaillancourt (1980), language was treated both as an ethnic attribute and as an element of human capital.

Other avenues had of course been pursued in parallel, discussing for example the meaning of language as a medium of international trade (Carr, 1985) or as a criterion for the distribution of resources between groups (Breton, 1964; Breton & Mieszkowski, 1977), and by the early 1990s, the economics of language had also started to fan out in a broader range of topics, addressing for example language dynamics and minority-language promotion.

The main lines of research in language economics can be arranged in four main categories, three of which are briefly reviewed in the rest of this section. The fourth one, which is centered on language-policy evaluation, is discussed in a section of its own. A more extensive literature review can be found in Grin (2003c).

Language and earnings

This line of research, apart from being the oldest in language economics, remains the main one in terms of the number of publications. It focuses on the effect of language skills on labor income (or "earnings"). This mostly empirical tradition uses survey or census data on self-reported language skills (in the first language [L1], L2, L3, etc.) and self-reported earnings to see, in line with human-capital theory, whether the former are predictors of the latter, controlling for other determinants of income such as education, work experience, or (data permitting) type of work. Proper data sets remain, outside of Canada, remarkably few and far between; accordingly, the most detailed studies use Canadian or Québec data (see Vaillancourt, 1996, for an overview; or various contributions in Breton, 1998). Studies on other countries rely on survey data, including in particular on immigrant groups in the United States (e.g., Bloom & Grenier, 1996; Dávila & Mora, 2000), Australia, (e.g., Chiswick & Miller, 1995), Israel (e.g., Chiswick & Repetto, 2001), or Germany (Dustmann, 1994), sometimes in a comparative perspective, or on representative population samples (Grin, 1999, for Switzerland).

Far fewer are the papers venturing a theoretical explanation other than the human-capital model of the effect of language on earnings. Early models (Raynauld & Marion, 1972) invoke a deliberate strategy, by the capitalists in a dominant group, to channel the largest possible share of aggregate income to group members; Lang (1986) views unequal earnings as the result of cost-minimizing strategies by owners of capital (most of whom are assumed to belong to one group) employing workers from the other group.

Language dynamics

Research proposing explanations for the decline or spread of languages varies considerably. Some focuses on minority languages, generally assuming speakers to be bilingual and to also know a majority language (Grin, 2002); other research focuses on actors' interest in learning or not learning another language, taking account of the costs and benefits of this decision. This line of work (Church & King, 1993; Dalmazzone, 1999; Selten & Pool, 1997) stresses one aspect of language that, from an economic perspective, has crucial analytical importance and sets it apart from standard economic goods. The more people use it, the more valuable it becomes, *as a tool for communication*, to people who already use it. This goes beyond non-rival consumption – a standard feature of public goods – leading some authors to define language as a "super-public" or "hypercollective" good (De Swaan, 2001). The "hypercollective" nature of language opens up some of the most challenging research avenues in language economics, but it does contain numerous pitfalls. For example, it has been used by some to defend, on allegedly economic grounds, support for the teaching of *majority* languages (Jones, 2000). However, the validity of this proposition crucially rests on one assumption, namely, that language is *only* a tool for communication (sometimes relabeled a "communication technology"). Sociolinguists have known for a long time that this does not do justice to the complexity of language in human experience.

Language and economic activity

This somewhat heterogeneous category brings together research that studies the role of language in core economic activities like production, consumption, and exchange. For example, do people really prefer goods to be advertised and sold to them in their native language? Is productive efficiency affected by the choice and range of languages used in the company? Some argue that the relationship is positive, because linguistic diversity may allow for greater creativity, while others contend that diversity mostly gives rise to added communication costs. Many of the contributions in this category are case studies, too numerous to discuss here. However, there also exists some valuable (and regrettably neglected) theoretical work, such as Hocevar's (1975) examination of markets for language-specific goods, or

Sabourin's (1985) analysis of the "matching" process between the language profile of a job in a firm and the language profile of a worker.

It is important to point out that the production, consumption, and exchange of "language goods" (such as translation services, language learning materials, etc.) is not a core concern for language economics, because the economic processes operating are not necessarily different from those operating in the case of *any* standard good. Some commentators may dispute this point: for example, Lamberton's (2002) edited volume casts the net wide and includes a study on telephone interpreting services. Nonetheless, translation and interpretation can have profound meaning in language dynamics (Mélitz, 2000) and language policy (Pool, 1996).

Let us also observe that, alluring as it may seem, the analogy between language and money is liable to create confusion rather than fruitful analytical insight, because language has, analytically, very little in common with either goods or currency as the *object* being exchanged.

The Economics of Language Policy Evaluation

Economics and policy evaluation

The economics of language policy evaluation constitutes an additional and increasingly active line of research. In what follows, "policy" refers to *public* policy, initiated and carried out by the state or its surrogates, although some of the considerations developed below can carry over to corporate environments.

Economic perspectives on language policy blend in almost seamlessly with a distinct, yet closely related, disciplinary tradition, namely, policy analysis (Dunn, 1994), which is, in turn, solidly anchored in political science. The extent to which policy analysis is, or is not, wedded to the "rational-choice" perspective of political science is a matter that will not be explored further here; however, it is certainly concerned with increases in welfare – the definition of which admittedly raises problems of its own. The basics of the approach are straightforward: *ex ante*, several policy options regarding language can be envisaged; each carries advantages and drawbacks, which can sometimes be reinterpreted as "benefits" and "costs" (albeit in a broad sense: see below), and the policy option that should be chosen is the one that maximizes the difference between benefits and costs. *Ex post*, policies that have been implemented can be evaluated by identifying and measuring their benefits and costs, in order to assess which, out of a given set of policies, has proved most effective, least costly, or – combining both criteria – most cost-effective. Since this approach characterizes the economic- as well as the policy-analysis mindset, we shall, in this and the next section, use either phrase to denote the analytical underpinnings of studies in this area.

For the most part, these studies address issues of language status, while language corpus is largely ignored or taken for granted. This may be because the actual cost of coining new vocabulary or engaging in spelling reform is comparatively modest; by contrast, elevating a language to official status, or introducing another language as a medium of instruction in the education system, is likely to be a much costlier policy decision – and hence one that does deserve attention.

Language policy can be broken down according to its goals, as suggested by Kaplan and Baldauf (1997, p. 59 ff), who list 11 different categories. From the perspective of policy evaluation, such distinctions matter less than the principle sketched out above, namely, the weighing of the pros and cons of the options considered. Let us, somewhat roughly, define a linguistic environment as a set of demolinguistic, institutional, and sociolinguistic facts – all of which are facets of what Fishman calls (with hyphens), language-in-society. Language policy, ultimately, proposes movement from one given, existing "linguistic environment" to another, supposedly preferable linguistic environment. Therefore its object, instead of being a language in relation with others, may be linguistic diversity itself (Grin, 2003a).

The rationale for state intervention

To the extent that language policy is a form of public policy, another question that arises is why the state should intervene at all in language matters. One underlying assumption of mainstream economics and policy analysis is that the free interplay of market forces can be expected to result in the provision of an adequate amount of goods and services, at minimum average cost. There are, however, exceptions to this basic principle, and these exceptions, which give rise to what is known in the literature as "market failure," justify state intervention. Six main forms of market failure can be identified:

1 insufficient information preventing actors from making the best decisions;

2 transaction costs preventing actors from closing deals that would otherwise prove mutually advantageous;

3 the absence of markets for certain goods or services – for example, there is no market on which *future*, yet unborn generations could express their wish for a particular animal or vegetal species to be preserved;

4 the existence of "market imperfections" (typically, monopolies or oligopolies), resulting in a sub-optimal production level for some goods, usually with an excessive market price for these goods;

5 positive or negative *externalities*, that is, situations in which one person's (or group's) behavior affects other persons' welfare, without the loss or gain thus created giving rise to any form of compensation. For example, the fact that I drive a massive SUV causes pollution, which lowers the appeal and market value of houses located along the road; yet as a driver, I am not required to pay compensation to the people who live in and/or own these houses;

6 the existence of public goods, which can be consumed by one person without reducing the amount of the good available to another, and whose consumption cannot be restricted to those who actually pay for it; the standard textbook example is public lighting. In the presence of *super*-public or hypercollective goods (see preceding section), market failure is even more likely.

Linguistic environments exhibit many forms of market failure. For one, future generations cannot bid for the preservation of endangered languages. In a market mechanism, this absence from the bidding process means the same as if they did not care for these languages, which is quite a different matter. Externalities are also present, if, for example, a person's language learning (or non-learning) behavior affects the value of another person's language skills. In fact, it could be argued that almost every form of market failure occurs when it comes to the provision of linguistic diversity. However, it is enough to establish that only one type of failure is present to justify state intervention. Hence, from a policy-analysis standpoint, language policy *is* justified, and the policy-analysis perspective provides a rationale for intervention. This point, which may seem obvious to some readers, deserves to be made, since there is no lack of voices, in the political debate, claiming that languages should best be left to fend for themselves, going as far as to dismiss most language-policy interventions as harmful meddling.

Estimating language environments

The next problem is to select a policy among several options. In principle, policy analysts will have to identify and measure, for each of the options considered, different types of effects. The latter can also be defined as components of the net value of the linguistic environments that are expected to emerge as a result of choosing alternative policies. The conceptual and methodological difficulties of carrying out this evaluation in practice are, at this time, far from solved; nevertheless, the procedure can help to identify coherently distinct steps in an evaluation exercise.

The first and less arduous step is to estimate the net "private market" value of each policy option. This refers to effects that can be observed on a market and which accrue to identifiable individuals. For example, a policy requiring civil servants to be trilingual (instead of merely bilingual) will, all other things being equal, drive up the wage rate of trilinguals in society as a whole, at least in the short run. These gains, however, may imply costs (such as increases in taxes to cover the corresponding wage increases in the public sector, unless this effect has been compensated for by a drop in the wage rate accruing to monolingual and bilingual employees); such costs will have to be subtracted from the gains, in order to yield net private market value (which may *a priori* be positive or negative).

One should then attempt to move on to the estimation of social market value, which is the aggregate of private market values across all members of society. Unfortunately, aggregation will require a more complex operation than a simple sum, owing to the presence of externalities. If externalities are positive (or negative), social market benefits will exceed (or fall short of) the simple sum of private market benefits.

The steps just described for market value then need to be replicated for the much more complex non-market value – namely, the gains and losses associated with a change in the linguistic environment, but without these gains and losses being expressed through one or another explicit market. These effects, which can often be described as "symbolic," entail direct gains or losses in satisfaction (or, in economic parlance, in "utility"). There again, these effects must be estimated at the individual level, and then aggregated to obtain social non-market value.

Non-market benefits and costs are perfectly legitimate concerns for an economic evaluation because, as we have noted before, economic analysis is not confined to material or financial questions. The psychological loss experienced when one's language is (formally or not) downgraded to a secondary position is a relevant form of cost; likewise, the pride that may be associated with the visibility of one's minority language in prestige domains is a relevant benefit. Obviously, estimating these non-market benefits and costs is extremely difficult and, to my knowledge, this has not been formally attempted yet. The most promising methodologies are likely to be found in environmental economics, in which a considerable body of experience has been developed in the evaluation of complex, non-market commodities, such as clean air or water.

For each policy contemplated, one would then compute the sum of social market and social non-market benefits and costs, yielding the overall net value; the policy that promises to give rise to the highest overall net value should, *ceteris paribus*, be selected.

The distributive dimension

The procedure that enables us, in principle, to define a policy as the "best" relies on a measurement of aggregate (social) welfare, encompassing both market and non-market effects. This assessment focuses on resource allocation. However, moving from an existing to a presumably better linguistic environment also entails gains and losses, and the question arises of who gains, who loses, and how much, as a result of the implementation of language policy.

This distributive aspect of policy tends to be neglected in economic analysis, under the all too comfortable assumption that if a policy does give rise to a net welfare gain, then gainers *can* compensate the losers. The problem, however, is whether they actually do so of their own accord, or if a compulsory compensation mechanism has to be built into the policy design for such compensation to occur. At the same time, the form and amount of such compensation needs to be determined, on the basis of a reliable and transparent identification of the transfers that arise *without* a compensation mechanism.

In order to clarify matters, let us consider just one example of such transfers. In the case of the European Union, the progressive, though presently not official, drift toward the dominant, or even sole, use of English as a working language of European institutions amounts to a massive transfer in the direction of native speakers of English, paid for by everybody else. This transfer arises as a result of the fact that native speakers of English: (1) need not invest any time or money in learning other languages, since native speakers of other languages learn English; (2) may profitably invest the resources thus saved in other, growth-enhancing development strategies; (3) get a quasi-monopoly on the market for translation and interpretation into English, as well as on the market for English-language text editing and language teaching; (4) need not make any effort to make themselves understood in international settings; and (5) retain a decisive edge in negotiation and conflict, simply because it takes place in their own language, while others have to struggle in English – for them, a foreign language (Grin, 2004).

By comparison with a system resting on the hegemony of one of the Union's official languages, many alternative arrangements can prove superior from a public-policy perspective, even if they appear to be costlier in terms of resource allocation (Pool, 1996). This result arises because such alternative arrangements do not carry negative distributive implications. Alternatively, the transfers entailed by a system in which English enjoys a hegemonic position can be compensated for through various subsidy schemes from predominantly English-speaking members of the Union to all the others, in order to finance, for example, the latter's expenditure on English-language teaching (Pool, 1991; van Parijs, 2001).

The Practice of Language Policy Evaluation

Practical experience in language-policy evaluation remains relatively scattered and partial. However, it has been applied in recent years to an expanding range of cases (Chalmers, 2003; Grin & Vaillancourt, 1999; Grin et al., 2002), and in this closing section, I highlight some areas where this approach has yielded useful results.

Norms, outputs, and outcomes

As noted at the beginning of this chapter, much of the published literature assessing language policies is rooted in law or sociolinguistics. Therefore, policies have often been assessed in terms of the legal texts, that is, *norms* (for example on minority-language education) in which policies are enshrined, or in terms of the administrative measures taken, usually relying, for a measurement, on the *direct output* of these measures (for example, the number of new minority-language classes opened during a given calendar year). However, neither form of assessment tells us whether these legal norms or policy measures have been effective. Actual effectiveness can only be measured in terms of *outcomes* further down the line. For example, if a policy aims at minority-language revitalization through the education system, the proper criterion for assessing the policy must be an indicator of revitalization itself, such as increases in language competence among the target population, or in actual language use. Thinking in public-policy terms helps to focus attention on truly relevant evaluation criteria.

Cost evaluation

The costs of language policies are largely unknown, and are liable to be the stuff of wild fantasies – usually in the form of cataclysmic expectations of uncontrollable expenditure if diversity-preserving policy measures were adopted. Where figures exist, they yield a sobering picture. Although the lack of data often prevents precise calculations, cost ranges can be estimated (Grin, 2004). For example, the supposedly prohibitive cost of translation and interpretation in European institutions numbering 15 member states and 11 official languages amounted to €1.82 per resident per year; translation and interpretation represented 0.8 percent of the European Union budget (corresponding figures for the expanded EU are not yet available).

The concept of counterfactual

One of the single most important concepts in policy evaluation is that of counterfactual (Grin, 2003b). This term does not refer to anything that would be contrary to fact; rather, it refers to "what would occur in the absence of a policy," or, even more directly, to "the relevant alternative." For example, the added expenditure entailed by moving from a monolingual to a bilingual education system is much smaller than commonly believed. Where evaluations have been made, they point in the direction of a 3–4 percent range, because even if the education system were to remain monolingual, children would have to be schooled *anyway*. Therefore, only comparatively modest additional financial outlays need to be factored in. However, in line with the procedure sketched out in the preceding section, we should broaden the range of effects (both market and non-market) taken into consideration. This means that the assessment of both the policy measure and the counterfactual should take account, for example, of the differential effects they may have on school participation, graduation, and drop-out rates among the majority and the minority population. The true costs of the counterfactual (that is, in this example, of *not* engaging in a policy of bilingual education) can prove to be much higher than expected, thereby significantly heightening the attractiveness of the bilingual education policy (Vaillancourt & Grin, 2000).

Conclusion

Let us, in conclusion, recall that although language-policy evaluation as described here has an important role to play, its limits must not be forgotten. The economic approach to language policy, despite its relevance, is in no way meant to dictate policy decisions or to displace other approaches. I have stressed, earlier in this chapter, that different disciplines provide complementary perspectives. This is also true when the issue at hand is language policy. By definition, language policy is an expression of a set of choices that society makes. As such, it remains an inherently political matter. The main role of economic considerations in language-policy research, therefore, is to help social actors assess the pros and cons of different avenues open to them, and to make principled and transparent choices.

Annotated Bibliography

Church, J. & King, I. (1993). Bilingualism and network externalities. *Canadian Journal of Economics, 26*, 337–45.
A formal model of language as a "super-public" good whose communicational value increases with the number of users, suggesting that majority- (rather than minority-) language learning may need to be supported to maximize allocative efficiency – this result, however, requires the assumption that language is nothing but a tool for communication. The paper also offers a good introduction to the concept of externality.

Grin, F. (2003b). *Language policy evaluation and the European charter for regional or minority languages*. London: Palgrave Macmillan.

This book, which includes two invited chapters by R. Jensdóttir & D. Ó Riagáin, is entirely devoted to the evaluation of minority-language protection and promotion, from the standpoint of public-policy analysis. It focuses on the meaning of effectiveness and cost-effectiveness as criteria for policy selection and design, and it is primarily intended as a handbook for decision-makers in language policy when they need to formulate a structured policy approach.

Grin, F. & Vaillancourt, F. (1999). *The cost-effectiveness evaluation of minority language policies: Case studies on Wales, Ireland and the Basque Country. Monograph series, No. 2.* Flensburg: European Centre for Minority Issues.
This text contains a causal model that formally connects policy decisions, direct policy outputs, language behavior, and final policy outcomes in terms of language revitalization. The theoretical model is applied to cost-effectiveness evaluations illustrating different types of policy intervention.

Pool, J. (1996). Optimal language regimes for the European Union. *International Journal of the Sociology of Language, 121,* 159–79.
An exploration into six different models of language policy for multilingual organizations. Its main result is to show that, contrary to frequently held beliefs, there are no "obviously" superior solutions to this problem, and that the rank-ordering of solutions, even under appropriately identified costs and benefits, depends on priorities which have to be clearly enunciated – and adequately justified.

Vaillancourt, F. (ed.) (1985). *Économie et langue.* Québec: Conseil de la langue française.
The first volume ever published entirely devoted to language economics, this contains in particular essays by Carr (1985) and Sabourin (1985) on issues that, some 20 years on, remain insufficiently explored and have potentially important implications for language-policy evaluation.

van Parijs, P. (2001). Linguistic justice. *Politics, Philosophy and Economics, 1,* 59–74.
This careful exposition and theoretical discussion of the distributive consequences of linguistic dominance, under the assumption that language is chiefly a communication tool, implies that the drift toward the hegemony of one language is a natural process. Therefore the focus

of policy evaluation is shifted toward the relative appropriateness of alternative compensation schemes.

Discussion Questions

1 In what fundamental sense is language policy a form of public policy, just like policies affecting transportation, health, or the environment?

2 Critically assess the notion that "language economics merges with the economics of information."

3 Describe several instances of actual or potential language policy, and check for each case whether you can spot the presence of one (or many) forms of "market failure," thereby strengthening the case for state involvement.

4 Provide examples of the non-market benefits and costs of granting partial official recognition to immigrant languages in countries like Britain, France, or the Netherlands. Which of these benefits and costs would you take into account in a policy decision, and for what reasons? Are there some that you might deliberately choose to leave out of your calculation? Why?

5 Use the concept of counterfactual to develop a hypothetical policy case in favor of making Navajo an official language of some Southwestern states in the United States.

NOTE

The author thanks François Vaillancourt for helpful comments on an earlier version of this chapter. The usual disclaimer applies.

REFERENCES

Bloom, D. E. & Grenier, G. (1996). Language, employment and earnings in the United States: Spanish–English differentials from 1970 to 1990. *International Journal of the Sociology of Language, 121,* 45–68.

Breton, A. (1964). The economics of nationalism. *Journal of Political Economy, 62,* 376–86.

Breton, A. (ed.) (1998). *Economic approaches to language and bilingualism.* Ottawa: Canadian Heritage.

Breton, A. & Mieszkowski, P. (1977). The economics of bilingualism. In W. E. Oates (ed.), *The political economy of fiscal federalism* (pp. 261–73). Lexington, MA: Lexington Books.

Carr, J. (1985). Le bilinguisme au Canada: l'usage consacre-t-il l'anglais monopole naturel? In F. Vaillancourt (ed.), *Économie et langue* (pp. 27–37). Québec: Conseil de la langue française.

Chalmers, D. (2003). The economic impact of Gaelic arts and culture. Doctoral dissertation, Glasgow Caledonian University, Glasgow.

Chiswick, B. & Miller, P. (1995). The endogeneity between language and earnings: International analyses. *Journal of Labor Economics, 13,* 246–88.

Chiswick, B. & Repetto, G. (2001). Immigrant adjustment in Israel: The determinants of literacy and fluency in Hebrew and their effects on earnings. In S. Djajic (ed.), *International migration: Trends, policies and economic impact* (pp. 204–88). London: Routledge.

Church, J. & King, I. (1993). Bilingualism and network externalities. *Canadian Journal of Economics, 26,* 337–45.

Dalmazzone, S. (1999). Economics of language: A network externalities approach. In A. Breton (ed.), *Exploring the economics of language* (pp. 63–87). Ottawa: Canadian Heritage.

Dávila, A. & Mora, M. (2000). English fluency of recent Hispanic immigrants to the United States in 1980 and 1990. *Economic Development and Cultural Change, 48,* 369–89.

De Swaan, A. (2001). *Words of the world: The global language system.* Cambridge: Polity.

Dunn, W. N. (1994). *Public policy analysis. An introduction.* Englewood Cliffs, NJ: Simon & Schuster.

Dustmann, C. (1994). Speaking fluency, writing fluency and earnings of migrants. *Journal of Population Economics, 7,* 133–56.

Grin, F. (ed.) (1996). Economic approaches to language and language planning (Special issue). *International Journal of the Sociology of Language, 121.*

Grin, F. (1999). *Compétences et récompenses. La valeur des langues en Suisse.* Fribourg: Éditions Universitaires de Fribourg.

Grin, F. (2002). Towards a threshold of minority language survival. In D. Lamberton (ed.), *The ecomonic of language* (pp. 49–76). Cheltenham: Edward Elgar. (Reprinted from *Kyklos, 45,* 69–97, 1992.)

Grin, F. (2003a). Diversity as paradigm, analytical device, and policy goal. In W. Kymlicka & A. Patten (eds.), *Language rights and political theory* (pp. 169–88). New York: Oxford University Press.

Grin, F. (2003b). *Language policy evaluation and the European charter for regional or minority languages.* London: Palgrave Macmillan.

Grin, F. (2003c). Language planning and economics. *Current Issues in Language Planning, 4,* 1–66.

Grin, F. (2004). On the costs of linguistic diversity. In P. van Parijs (ed.), *Cultural diversity versus economic solidarity* (pp. 193–206). Brussels: De Boeck-Université.

Grin, F. & Vaillancourt, F. (1997). The economics of multilingualism: Overview and analytical framework. In W. Grabe (ed.), *Annual Review of Applied Linguistics*, vol. 17 (pp. 43–65). New York: Cambridge University Press.

Grin, F. & Vaillancourt, F. (1999). *The cost-effectiveness evaluation of minority language policies: Case studies on Wales, Ireland and the Basque Country. Monograph series, No. 2*. Flensburg: European Centre for Minority Issues.

Grin, F., Moring, T., Gorter, D., Häggman, J., Ó Riagáin, D., & Strubell, M. (2002). *Support for minority languages in Europe. Report to the European Commission* (2000 1288/001-001 EDU-MLCEV). Retrieved January 21, 2004, from http://europa.eu.int/comm/education/policies/lang/langmin/support.pdf.

Henderson, W., Dudley-Evans, T., & Backhouse, R. (eds.) (1993). *Economics and language*. London: Routledge.

Hocevar, T. (1975). Equilibria on linguistic minority markets, *Kyklos, 28*, 337–57.

Jones, E. (2000). The case for a shared world language. In M. Casson & A. Godley (eds.), *Cultural factors in economic growth* (pp. 210–35). Berlin: Springer.

Kaplan, R. & Baldauf, R. (1997). *Language planning. From practice to theory*. Clevedon: Multilingual Matters.

Lamberton, D. (ed.) (2002). *The economics of language*. Cheltenham: Edward Elgar.

Lang, K. (1986). A language theory of discrimination. *Quarterly Journal of Economics, 101*, 363–82.

Marschak, J. (1965). Economics of language. *Behavioral Science, 10*, 135–40.

McCloskey, D. N. (1990). *The rhetoric of economics*. Madison, WI: University of Wisconsin Press.

Mélitz, J. (2000). English-language dominance, literature and welfare. Unpublished manuscript, Institut d'études politiques, Paris.

Pool, J. (1991). The official language problem. *American Political Science Review, 85*, 495–514.

Pool, J. (1996). Optimal language regimes for the European Union. *International Journal of the Sociology of Language, 121*, 159–79.

Raynauld, A. & Marion, P. (1972). Une analyse économique de la disparité inter-ethnique des revenus. *Revue économique, 23*, 1–19.

Sabourin, C. (1985). La théorie des environnements linguistiques. In F. Vaillancourt (ed.), *Economie et langue* (pp. 59–82). Québec: Conseil de la langue française.

Selten, R. & Pool, J. (1997). Is it worth it to learn Esperanto? Introduction to game theory. In R. Selten (ed.), *The costs of European linguistic non integration* (pp. 114–49). Rome: Esperanto Radikala Asocio.

Vaillancourt, F. (1980). *Difference in earnings by language groups in Quebec, 1970. An economic analysis* (Publication B-90). Québec: Centre international de recherche sur le bilinguisme.

Vaillancourt, F. (ed.) (1985). *Économie et langue*. Québec: Conseil de la langue française.

Vaillancourt, F. (1996). Language and socioeconomic status in Quebec: Measurement, findings, determinants, and policy costs. *International Journal of the Sociology of Language, 121*, 69–92.

Vaillancourt, F. & Grin, F. (2000). *The choice of a language of instruction: The economic aspects. Distance learning course on language instruction in basic education*. Washington, DC: World Bank Institute.

van Parijs, P. (2001). Linguistic justice. *Politics, Philosophy and Economics, 1*, 59–74.

CHAPTER SIX

Political Theory and Language Policy

Ronald Schmidt, Sr

The discipline of political theory has much to offer students of language policy. This chapter aims to demonstrate this assertion through both discursive argument and example. I begin with a general discussion of the discipline of political theory and its potential contributions to our understanding of language-policy conflicts. This discussion is followed by brief but demonstrative examples drawing upon the literature of political theory to illuminate what is at stake in two inter-related controversial issues regarding language policy: the issue of identity politics in language-policy conflict, and the issue of realizing greater equality for language minorities.

Political Theory's Perspective

Most scholars of the subject concur that the discipline of political theory traces its Western intellectual roots to the Greek philosophers of the classical era, and especially to the writings of Plato and Aristotle. The term "theory" derives from the Greek word *theoria*, whose meaning originally centered on "seeing," as in "a place for seeing," or being a "spectator," etc. Thus, political theorists are those who try to *see* political life in a particular way. In casting its distinctive gaze on the political world, political theory occupies an unusual position in the academic world in that its characteristic methods of inquiry are derived mainly from the humanities, while its practitioners are overwhelmingly located in social science departments of political science.[1] Accordingly, it is useful to focus briefly on the types of *questions* that political theorists characteristically try to answer, particularly in contrast to those questions that typically preoccupy social and political *scientists*. A recent essay by Ruth Grant (2002) is helpful here. Grant argues that the central difference between political *science* and political *theory* is not the relative degree of rigor of their methods, or of their respective capacities for cumulating indisputable knowledge. Rather, what divides them is a deep difference in the types of questions each mode of study tries to answer. Modeling itself after the physical sciences, political *science*, she argues, tries to answer questions about *cause* and *effect*. Accordingly, political scientists try to explain *why* things are the way they are in the political world, and how and why the political world (dependent variable) changes in response to changing circumstances (independent variables). Some political scientists, moreover, aspire to go beyond explanation to prediction, hoping that cumulating knowledge of cause and effect will enable us to predict how political changes A or B will result in further changes X or Y.

More akin to practitioners of the humanities, on the other hand, political *theorists* are centrally preoccupied with questions of *significance* and *meaning*, rather than with cause and effect. At the heart of the political theorist's work the question is not "what will she or he do?" but "so what?" Why is it important to us, and what does it mean for us, that things are going this way and not that way? What is the significance for us of the facts as we know them, and how should our understanding of these facts inform our judgments about what we should do in response to this information? These are the kinds of questions that lie at the heart of the multiple discourses that constitute the discipline of political theory. The central perspective of political theory, then, is that of a political actor needing to make judgments about political matters. Ultimately, the political theorist tries to *envision* political life in ways that will sharpen, deepen, and extend the grounds for making good judgments about the meaning and significance of political events and actions. Inevitably interpretive, this work does not reject the political scientist's efforts at explaining cause and effect in political life, but uses the results of political science in its own efforts to understand what is at stake when political actors make the judgments that all political life entails.

Political Theory and Language Policy

How can political theory's distinctive perspective be useful to students of language policy? As several recent essays have emphasized (Patten, 2001; Patten & Kymlicka, 2003), political theorists have mostly neglected language policy as such, although a large number of political theorists have focused their attention in recent years on issues of close relevance to language policy (e.g., multicultural citizenship, identity politics, the politics of "difference," etc.). It is only very recently (see, e.g., Kymlicka & Patten, 2003), then, that political theorists have explicitly focused their analyses on language policy as such. Despite this relative inattention, I will argue that the discipline of political theory contains a treasure-trove of materials that can be usefully "mined" by scholars interested in questions of meaning and significance regarding language policy. More particularly, I will try to demonstrate that political theory can be quite helpful in enabling us to better understand just what is at stake when political conflicts erupt over issues of language policy.

Language policy involves the development of public policies that aim to use the authority of the state to affect various aspects of the status and use of languages by people under the state's jurisdiction. Language policy gets onto the political agenda when political actors believe that something important is at stake regarding the status and/ or use of languages in their society, and that these stakes call for intervention by the state. At the core of the politics of language, I argue, lies a form of *identity politics*, in which language policy partisans compete to shape public perceptions about the "we" that constitutes the relevant political community, and to embody their aims in the language policy of the state.[2]

Because the central issues in language policy conflict revolve around competing attempts to socially construct group and individual identities, disputed questions of *meaning* and *significance* abound in the politics of language. It is for this reason that we might imagine the writings of political theorists – stretching over 2,000 years in Western intellectual history – as offering helpful insights and reasoned critical thinking to students of language policy. Despite the fact that political theorists have only begun to systematically analyze language policy as such, I hope to demonstrate that political theorists' writings on related issues can be quite helpful in language-policy research aimed at discovering just what is at stake in political conflicts over language policy.

There is a wide range of important language-policy issues that could be illuminated using the methods of political theory, but space limitations make impossible even a cursory overview of these issues.[3] Rather, I will seek to demonstrate the potential utility of these methods by drawing on the writings of two contemporary political theorists to articulate the meaning and significance of two core issues in political conflicts over language policy: (1) identity politics in relation to language policy, and (2) the meanings and significance of equality in language-policy conflicts. The chapter, in short, aims to be illustrative and suggestive rather than comprehensive in its scope.

Language Policy and Identity Politics

It was suggested above that questions of identity politics lie at the core of most language-policy conflicts. I want to elaborate that assertion here and draw upon the work of a contemporary political theorist to help articulate what I believe to be one of the chief stakes in the politics of language in many parts of the world.

What is meant by the phrase "identity politics"? Identity politics derives from the perception that *who we are* matters in political life, and there is a variety of politically significant answers to the question "who are we?" Among the most salient have been answers marking persons' gender, family roles, profession, region, ethnicity, race, nation, religion, class, and language. How do such identities become important in *political* life, and why?

At its most basic level, all politics derives from the intersection of two realities of human existence: *difference* and *interdependence*. If we did not have "differences," if we were completely the same as all others, always in perfect harmony about everything, there would be no politics. Further, if we were totally autonomous individual beings, never needing others for anything, there would be no politics. But in combination the realities that we do have differences and yet we do need each other lead to *conflicts* that are dealt with in ways that we call political. This is especially the case when our differences and interdependencies exist on a community-wide basis. In the context of this understanding, identity politics involves the tensions and conflicts in political communities deriving from fault lines that center on identity markers such as those outlined in the preceding paragraph (and others as well). In one form or another, political theorists have been writing about these fault lines and their political implications for a long time. In the past several decades, however, political theorists have devoted an unprecedented amount of energy and writing to issues of identity politics.[4]

How can this outpouring of analysis and argument be helpful to students of language policy? As noted above, I believe that the writings of political theorists can help us *understand what is at stake* in language-policy conflict. For example, one of the most perplexing questions facing students of language-policy conflict in the United States is how to make sense of the emotional intensity often found among those who are active in the campaign to make English the sole official language of the country, and who seek to shut down bilingual education programs and/or to eliminate the Voting Rights Act provisions enabling certain non-English-speaking citizens to obtain election materials and ballots in a language in which they are literate. To many observers, the emotional intensity of the activists in this campaign is unexpected and difficult to explain. In the global competition among languages, after all, English appears to be winning handily, as people throughout the world scramble to acquire English literacy and fluency in truly astonishing numbers (see, e.g., Sonntag, 2003). Within the United States, moreover, study after study finds that non-English-speaking immigrants are eager to learn English and are doing so at unprecedented rates. And the children of immigrants are acculturating as English speakers more quickly and more effectively than did second-generation immigrant children during any previous period of high immigration (see, e.g., Portes & Rumbaut, 1996). Given these facts, why do advocates of "English-only" feel so strongly that it is necessary to make English the only "official" language of the United States, and to spend so much political (and financial) capital trying to eliminate all public usage of other languages? Given the emotional intensity displayed here, it is clear that these activists experience *something* as an important stake.

Official English advocacy groups (e.g., U.S. English, English First) provide several rationales for their language-policy campaigns. These groups express alarm deriving from their perceptions that the United States is undergoing significant and threatening changes that need to be corrected. These changes involve the combination of large increases in recent immigration and a perceived shift in public policy (as compared with previous periods of large-scale immigration) that encourages multiculturalism and multilingualism rather than linguistic and cultural assimilation among immigrants. As a consequence, they claim, "national unity" in the United States is being threatened, and particularly by immigrants from Latin America and the Spanish-speaking Caribbean. These groups are often singled out by assimilationists because Spanish-speakers make up more than half of all US residents who normally speak a non-English language in their homes, and because they are perceived as having established separatist enclaves throughout the country (for an overview of these claims, see Schmidt, 2000, chs 4–6).

Assimilationists believe, then, that rather than being encouraged by language policies to retain their non-English languages (via, e.g., bilingual education, "bilingual" ballots, etc.), immigrants need to be encouraged by public policy to become truly *American*, and that means making English their primary language. As proof of their concerns, spokespersons for these groups point to large enclaves in a number of US cities where residents (neighbors, shoppers, merchants, and others) routinely speak Spanish in the public spaces of civil society; where individuals can get their news from television, radio, papers, and magazines in Spanish; where, in the words of former Miami mayor Jose Ferrer, "you can go through life without having to speak English at all" (quoted by Lamm & Imhoff, 1985, p. 92).

There are many insightful ways in which this alarm and its resultant calls for language-policy reform might be understood and evaluated by researchers. Here, however, I'm going to use a recent book by political theorist Bonnie Honig, *Democracy and the foreigner* (2001), to illustrate the value of political theory's perspective on "the political." I will do so by suggesting that Honig's work can help us understand the underlying meaning and intensity of the above claims being made by US official English advocates. Honig's work can help us better understand certain tensions and themes central to long-standing political projects of American national identity-formation and, as such, to better understand the political context and stakes of language-policy conflict for some of its most active protagonists. As is true of many students of political identity, Honig assumes that national identities are socially constructed (and endlessly reconstructed) through discourses among competing political elites. Unlike many theorists, however, she argues as well that these discourses take place *within* our individual selves (elites and non-elites alike), as tensions or ambivalences in our perceptions, values, and beliefs, embedded in the complexities of the human psyche.

Within this context of national identity-formation in the United States, Honig argues that *immigrants* play a vital role in maintaining and resurrecting central myths that sustain Americans' understanding of themselves as a nation. In particular, Honig posits four key mythic themes of national revival in which immigrants play the central redemptive role. These themes are the "capitalist, communal, familial, [and] liberal" (Honig, 2001, p. 74). In the capitalist version of the American myth, first, "the immigrant functions to reassure workers of the possibility of upward mobility in an economy that rarely delivers on that promise, while also disciplining native-born poor, domestic minorities, and unsuccessful foreign laborers into believing that the economy fairly rewards dedication and hard work" (p. 74). Second, the "communitarian immigrant" myth "responds to the dissolution of family and community ties" generated by "a capitalist economy's unresisted need for a mobile labor force" (p. 74). Third, the "familial" myth portrays immigrants as "saviors of traditional patriarchal family arrangements that have been variously attenuated by capitalist mobility and materialism, liberal individualism, and feminism" (p. 74).

And finally (fourth), "liberal consent theorists" look to immigrants to solve the problem of legitimacy in a country in which government claims to be based on the "consent of the governed," but native-born citizens are rarely given opportunities to explicitly consent to be governed. As Rousseau understood, Honig (2001) states, "merely periodic practices such as voting do not position citizens to experience the law as their own" rather than as imposed by undemocratic authoritarian rulers (p. 74). Genuinely experienced consent of the governed, that is, requires more than occasional voting by a shrinking electorate and the "tacit consent" said by some liberal theorists to have been given by those of us who continue to live unexamined political lives in our country of birth. Under these conditions, Honig suggests, immigrants come to the rescue "through the agency of foreignness": "The regime's legitimacy is shored up by way of the explicit consent of those celebrated foreigners – immigrants – who, almost daily are sworn into citizenship in the nation's naturalization ceremonies" (Honig, 2001, p. 75).

These four themes of the positive, even redemptive, contributions made to American well-being by immigrants, Honig asserts, combine into an iconic "super-citizen" who

> somehow manages to have it all – work, family, community, and a consensual relation to a largely nonconsensual democracy – even though these very goods are experienced by the rest of us as contradictory or elusive: work in late modern capitalist economies often demands hours and mobilities that are in tension with family and community commitments; meaningful consent eludes the native born.
>
> *(2001, p. 78)*

While these images of iconic super-citizens help to revitalize Americans' faith in their nation's virtues and opportunities, the elusiveness of their achievement by the native-born at the same time reinforces a mirror-image *negative* symbol for each of the contributions made to American national identity by immigrants. Indeed, the real power of Honig's analysis is found in her insight that a Gothic tale of negative/positive, of constructivism/destructiveness, of contradictory yet deeply intertwined mirror-image symbols of nature and nurture lies at the very heart of the American self-understanding. Thus, xenophilia is intimately intertwined with xenophobia. The negative side of the economically upwardly mobile immigrant's super-citizen image, for example, is that of the foreigner who takes from the country's economy to enrich self and family without accepting and sharing the burdens of contributing to the well-being of the local or national community.

More directly related to the language-policy debate, the negative side of the communitarian super-citizen is the "clannish" immigrant who insists on living in ethnic "enclaves" where he or she continues to speak a "foreign" tongue and resists integration into the larger (individualistic, anomic) society. Similarly, the negative side of the politically "consenting" super-citizen is the foreigner, probably an "illegal" immigrant, who takes the government's services and tax-dollars without ever naturalizing as a citizen.[5]

Honig's point is that each of these intertwined images of immigrants, those generating both xenophilia and xenophobia, is a powerful symbol performing important work in shoring up the ambivalent and fragile hold on our psyches of our assumptions about American nationalism. It is through these powerful images – negative *and* positive – that we see the emotionally powerful stakes that Americans might have in the behavior of the immigrant. To restore and revive the health and vitality of their American national identities (particularly, the communal and the liberal), Americans *need* to see the immigrant choose to transform herself or himself into an "American," which is to actively replay the national mythic drama of Americanization, moving out of the ethnic enclave and adopting English as her or his only public language. In the absence of such recurring reinforcement, the grasping materialism, alienating and divisive decommunalization, and coercive manipulation experienced in the contemporary American political economy become all too evident. Failure of the immigrant to perform her or his "work" in the service of our national identity, accordingly, is experienced as ingratitude, rejection, and an opportunistic exploitation of "real" Americans.

The problem with this scenario, as Honig points out, is that it fails to capture important parts of the American national experience. Puerto Ricans living on the mainland, for example, are not immigrants at all, but US citizens whose origins lie in a Spanish-language-dominant Caribbean island that the United States forcibly took from Spain in 1898. Unlike immigrants, Puerto Ricans do not have to pass an English-language test to become US citizens; like other native-born Americans, they acquire their membership through birth and not through a voluntary (and self-transformative) act of "consent."

Similarly, Mexicans who migrate north to the Southwestern United States are "returning" to a land that was taken from their country by force (after the US military invaded Mexico City) in 1848, and from which their culture and language (as well as the people practicing them) have never been erased. In the historical context in which Mexican immigrants find themselves after arriving in the United States, "assimilation" as Americans need not imply substituting English for Spanish in their public lives, but might instead mean learning to live a bilingual, bicultural life both privately and publicly, as do many native-born Mexican-origin US citizens. Attending to *these* realities of the American experience would enable us to see other stakes in the language-policy debate that might have equally powerful emotional impacts leading in directions different from that of an "English-only" approach. Honig suggests that pursuing a *democratic* integration of the "foreigner," rather than a *nationalistic* one, would be far more satisfactory for both immigrants and the native-born.

There is not space to pursue the implications of this analysis here, but it is hoped that enough has been sketched out to illustrate the powerful insights possible from a political theorist's attentiveness to questions of meaning and significance in political life. What does it mean to be an "American"? Given the increasingly dominant role of English as the world's global language, why is it so important to the "English-only" activists that American nationality be officially *identified* with the country's dominant language? Alternatively, what is the significance of the fact that not all who are Americans became part of the country's people through individual and familial voluntary immigration? The distinctive sensibilities and modes of inquiry characteristic of skilled political theorists, I argue, can be very helpful to language-policy researchers in providing new insights and perspectives on these difficult questions of interpretation.

Language Policy, "Equality," and Political Theory

As noted above, another of the core issues that seems to crop up everywhere there is political conflict over language policy is that of how to achieve greater *equality* among ethnolinguistic groups. Advocates of many different approaches to language policy justify their proposals on the grounds that these will result in greater equality among ethnolinguistic groups. In the US conflict over language policy, for example, assimilationists argue that adopting a language policy that promotes language shift to English is the best way to ensure greater equality for US language minorities. In contrast, pluralists argue that an assimilative language policy promotes continued *in*equality for US language minorities, and that greater "equality" requires a language-policy approach that promotes bilingualism among the population. What is meant by "equality" and "inequality" in this discourse of conflict over language policy? Once again, political theorists can help us understand the meaning and significance of this protean concept.

Despite its highly complex meanings, equality as a legitimate political aim is widely understood in the United States to mean something like "equality of opportunity" for social mobility. Social inequality as such (e.g., inequalities of income, wealth, or social prestige) is not viewed as illegitimate by most Americans; nevertheless, certain obstacles to "equal opportunity" to advance up the social ladder *are* viewed as unfair and calling for public-policy intervention. Among the obstacles that have been attacked as illegitimate in recent decades have been those of discriminations based on race, religion, national origin, and gender. How does language fit into this framework of thinking?

US assimilationists begin from the assumption that the United States is an English-speaking society, and therefore it is very clear to them that non-English speakers in the country are being blocked (or are blocking themselves) from "equal opportunities" for social mobility if they are not learning the language in all haste. Assimilationists claim, therefore, that any public policies encouraging non-English speakers to retain reliance on their heritage languages are policies standing in the way of social equality for language minorities.

Pluralists, on the other hand, begin from the assumption that the United States has always been a multilingual society, albeit one in which English has been the dominant language since the country's origin. For pluralists, this results in a wholly different calculation of the obstacles to equal opportunity for social mobility. Since pluralists perceive the United States as having become multilingual through conquest, purchase, and annexation, as well as through voluntary immigration, they believe that our understanding of equal opportunity to achieve social mobility should take the country's fundamental ethnolinguistic diversity into account.

Political theorist Will Kymlicka's works on multicultural citizenship (1989, 1995), while not focused directly on language policy as such, provide among the most widely cited and fully developed arguments supportive of the pluralist position on this question. As a liberal, Kymlicka begins from the premise that the *individual self* is the proper moral foundation for any just political community. The well-being of individuals, each of whose lives has the same moral worth or value (the equality criterion), is the key to political justice. However, this well-being ("the good") must be defined by the individual herself ("from the inside"), which requires that she be free to define for herself what is meaningful and worthwhile in her own life. Since learning is always possible, moreover, she must be free to change her mind about that which is most meaningful and worthwhile.

Next, Kymlicka asserts that individual choices about which path leads to *my* "good" are necessarily made within a *cultural context*, so that "I" cannot be "me" apart from the culture I have inherited from my family and society. While I may come to reject or modify some of the values taught to me by my family and society, I cannot critically analyze, or even think, about my values and priorities without drawing upon my inherited culture (which includes, of course, my language). Thus my individual self has a stake in the cultural community in which I have developed because that community's cultural structure provides the "context for choice" for me (Kymlicka, 1989, pp. 164–5). This ontological reality leads Kymlicka to argue that preserving the structure of cultural communities is important to the preservation of meaningful choices about "the good" for individuals.

If I live in a country composed of two or more cultural communities, moreover, "equality of opportunity" for individual persons must take this reality into account. The criterion of individual equal worth requires the state to pursue policies enabling our individual choices about how to live our lives to begin from an "egalitarian plateau" (Kymlicka, 1989, p. 182), meaning that we are not penalized by disadvantages derived from circumstances over which we have had no control. Since the state cannot operate at all outside of a linguistic and cultural context, it cannot operate "neutrally" in respect of language and culture, as some believe it can with respect to religious diversity.

The implications of Kymlicka's arguments are powerful for ethnolinguistic groups that are basic components of a multilingual country. In order to give individuals fair equality of opportunity to realize their own conception of a good life, the state must try to provide equally effective support for the structures of each component ethnolinguistic community making up the country. This would seem to provide powerful and reasoned support for a language policy in support of multiple languages in a multilingual country.

The question that is unanswered in this discussion, of course, is how we define a "multilingual country." Kymlicka's call for equality of treatment is based on the premise that any inequalities that exist in our opportunities to realize "the good" must not be traced back to our own choices. When we make choices, we must assume responsibility for the consequences of those choices. An assimilationist might fairly respond to the above arguments, therefore, with the assertion that, since immigrants have freely chosen to come to this (English-speaking) country, they are obligated to learn its language. It is certainly not the country's obligation to provide equal support for the language of every immigrant group that freely chooses to come to the United States in search of better opportunities.

Kymlicka's own answer to this question relies on a distinction between "multinational" and "multiethnic" countries (Kymlicka, 1995), arguing that the former countries, brought together through the melding of two or more previously existing "national" groups (through, e.g., conquest and annexation or voluntary merger), have obligations to protect the rights of individuals that are different from those of multiethnic countries resulting from small-scale migrations based on individual choices. Thus, for example, if Puerto Ricans and Mexicans (as well as a multitude of indigenous groups) became part of the US population through the forcible annexation of their territories, they would seem to fit Kymlicka's definition of "national" rather than "ethnic" groups, and therefore the United States is obligated to provide support for their cultural structures in order to ensure fair equality of opportunity to members of these communities.

As noted, Kymlicka's analysis has become widely cited and discussed by political theorists and other scholars, but it remains quite controversial (see, e.g., Barry, 2001, for an in-depth critique). Once again, unfortunately, there is not space to pursue this controversy here, or to discuss its further implications for language policy in any particular country. Rather, it is hoped that this brief discussion has served to illustrate again the potential utility of the literature of political theory for the study of language policy. Kymlicka's analysis is rich in insight and provides multiple opportunities for critical thinking about the meaning and significance of the claims made on behalf of various language-policy proposals in the name of "equality."

Conclusion

This chapter has argued that the literature of political theory, with its characteristic ways of *seeing* the political, is a potentially valuable resource for students of language policy conflict. The chapter has argued that many language-policy conflicts center on issues of *meaning* and *significance* that are inherently contestable, and that, accordingly, are subject to multiple interpretations. In this context, I argue, political theory's methods of discourse are ideally suited for providing insights and reasoned interpretations of what is at stake in political conflicts over language policy.

In the chapter I have sought to demonstrate the validity of this argument with two (all too brief) illustrations: (1) Bonnie Honig's interpretation of the "work" performed by images of immigrants in the construction and maintenance of US national identity as a way of understanding the emotional intensity fueling the "official English" movement; and (2) Will Kymlicka's argument, based on liberal individualistic premises, for multicultural citizenship rights, as an analysis providing reasoned support for multilingual language policies as a way to realize equality of opportunity for language minorities. As these examples demonstrate, I hope, political theory will not put an end to political conflicts over language policy (or any other kind of policy), but it will enlarge our vision and sharpen our analytical tools for understanding what is at stake in such conflicts.

Annotated Bibliography

Grant, R. W. (2002). Political theory, political science, and politics. *Political Theory, 30,* 577–95.
This seminal article articulates the frame of reference of political theorists, in contrast to that of political scientists.

Kymlicka, W. & Patten, A. (eds.) (2003). *Language rights and political theory*. New York: Oxford University Press.
The first book-length collection of articles on language policy by political theorists, this is framed by a rights-centered, liberal approach.

Patten, A. (2001). Political theory and language policy. *Political Theory*, 29, 691–715.
This seminal article articulates the need for, and potential benefits deriving from, political theorists paying more explicit analytical attention to issues of language policy. It is framed by a liberal, rights-centered approach.

Discussion Questions

1 What are the central questions that contrast political *science* with political *theory*?
2 How can Honig's analysis of "democracy and the foreigner" be helpful to students of language policy? Can you think of some practical ways her analysis could influence policies on immigrant languages in both the public and private sectors?
3 Consider Kymlicka's analysis of the claims for "multicultural citizenship." What sorts of arguments have been used by politicians and policy-makers in your country to oppose (or support) such claims?
4 This chapter has argued that the literature of political theory can be useful in better understanding what is at stake in conflicts that involve language to one degree or another. Choose a contemporary context with which you are familiar (e.g., a particular country, region, city, or town) and discuss the underlying political theories or philosophies which inform particular language policies. To what degree are these theories or philosophies explicitly stated, to what degree are they assumed, and to what degree are they denied?

NOTES

An earlier version of this chapter was presented at the 2003 Annual Meeting of the American Political Science Association (August 29), in Philadelphia, PA. The author thanks Ronald Schmidt, Jr, and Anna Sampaio for helpful comments and suggestions on that earlier version.

1 According to Grant (2002), in the late 1990s more than 80 percent of academic political theorists were employed in departments of political science.
2 See Schmidt (2000, ch. 2) for an elaboration of the conditions under which language policy conflicts are most likely to emerge.
3 See Patten and Kymlicka (2003), however, for an excellent beginning overview.
4 For just a sampling, see Barry (2001); Benhabib (1996, 2002); Connolly (1991, 1995); Fraser (1997); Gutmann (2003); Honig (2001); Kymlicka (1989, 1995); Lash & Friedman (1992); Norton (1988); Parekh (2000); Taylor (1993, 1995); Taylor et al. (1994); Young (1990, 2000).
5 US naturalization, of course, involves taking an exam to demonstrate one's proficiency in one language, English, as well as renouncing one's former citizenship.

REFERENCES

Barry, B. (2001). *Culture and equality: An egalitarian critique of multiculturalism.* Cambridge, MA: Harvard University Press.
Benhabib, S. (ed.) (1996). *Democracy and difference: Contesting the boundaries of the political.* Princeton, NJ: Princeton University Press.
Benhabib, S. (2002). *The claims of culture: Equality and diversity in the global era.* Princeton, NJ: Princeton University Press.
Connolly, W. E. (1991). *Identity/difference: Democratic negotiations of political paradox.* Ithaca, NY: Cornell University Press.
Connolly, W. E. (1995). *The ethos of pluralization.* Minneapolis, MN: University of Minnesota Press.
Fraser, N. (1997). *Justice interruptus: Critical reflections on the "postsocialist" condition.* New York: Routledge.
Grant, R. W. (2002). Political theory, political science, and politics. *Political Theory, 30,* 577–95.
Gutmann, A. (2003). *Identity in democracy.* Princeton, NJ: Princeton University Press.
Honig, B. (2001). *Democracy and the foreigner.* Princeton, NJ: Princeton University Press.
Kymlicka, W. (1989). *Liberalism, community, and culture.* New York: Oxford University Press.
Kymlicka, W. (1995). *Multicultural citizenship: A liberal theory of minority politics.* New York: Oxford University Press.
Kymlicka, W. & Patten, A. (eds.) (2003). *Language rights and political theory.* New York: Oxford University Press.
Lamm, R. D. & Imhoff, G. (1985). *The immigration time bomb: The fragmenting of America.* New York: Truman Talley Books.

Lash, S. & Friedman, J. (eds.) (1992). *Modernity and identity*. Cambridge, MA: Blackwell.

Norton, A. (1988). *Reflections on political identity*. Baltimore, MD: Johns Hopkins University Press.

Parekh, B. C. (2000). *Rethinking multiculturalism: Cultural diversity and political theory*. Cambridge, MA: Harvard University Press.

Patten, A. (2001). Political theory and language policy. *Political Theory, 29,* 691–715.

Patten, A. & Kymlicka, W. (2003). Introduction: Language rights and political theory: Context, issues, and approaches. In W. Kymlicka & A. Patten (eds.), *Language rights and political theory* (pp. 1–51). New York: Oxford University Press.

Portes, A. & Rumbaut, R. G. (1996). *Immigrant America: A portrait* (2nd edn). Berkeley, CA: University of California Press.

Schmidt, R., Sr (2000). *Language policy and identity in the United States*. Philadelphia, PA: Temple University Press.

Sonntag, S. K. (2003). *The local politics of global English: Case studies in linguistic globalization*. Lanham, MD: Lexington Books.

Taylor, C. (1993). *Reconciling the solitudes: Essays on Canadian federalism and nationalism*. Montreal: McGill-Queen's University Press.

Taylor, C. (1995). *Philosophical arguments*. Cambridge, MA: Harvard University Press.

Taylor, C., Appiah, K. A., Habermas, J., Rockefeller, S. C., Walzer, M., & Wolf, S. (1994). *Multiculturalism: Examining the politics of recognition* (ed. A. Gutmann). Princeton, NJ: Princeton University Press.

Young, I. M. (1990). *Justice and the politics of difference*. Princeton, NJ: Princeton University Press.

Young, I. M. (2000). *Inclusion and democracy*. New York: Oxford University Press.

CHAPTER SEVEN

Language Policy and Linguistic Culture

Harold Schiffman

The notion of "linguistic culture" and its applicability to language policy is one that seems to be something I must take credit and/or blame for, since I cannot escape responsibility for connecting the two ideas, or attribute it to anyone else. When I began to use the term "linguistic culture," I assumed it was a term already in use, a commonplace, that is, something in need of no explanation. I thought of it as simply that part of culture (defined as "that which is *learned*") that has anything to do with language, just as we tend to speak, in common lay parlance, of *sports* culture, *business* culture, and so on. The idea that there was that part of culture that had to do with language seemed to me uncontestable, since there were already in the literature of sociolinguistics many studies that referred to such things as "folk linguistics" (Hoenigswald, 1971) "folk etymologies," or "myths about language" (Ferguson, 1968; Miller, 1982). Linguists and linguistic anthropologists had been writing about the connection between language and culture (Hymes, 1964) for decades, since Sapir (1949) at least, and I wanted a term that referred to all of the phenomena that could be subsumed under one rubric. It also seemed to me axiomatic that culture did not reside *in* language (more about this below), certainly not within language as most narrowly defined, that is, in the *code* or the grammar of the language, but somewhere in the consciousness (or memory, or shared knowledge, or imagination) of linguistic communities. So if there was a feature of language-and-culture that needed to be discussed, such as attitudes about a language, I wanted to be able to talk about it as being located in, or being part of, linguistic culture, rather than *in* a language.

I was surprised to learn somewhat later that there were scholars from other disciplines who were displeased with the idea of linguistic "culture" since they were, as it turned out, dissatisfied with the term "culture." These "culture-critics" disliked the term because they felt that it had been "misused" by other scholars, colonial authorities, or whatever, and therefore they wished to replace it with something else. What they planned to use instead never became clear to me, but my rejoinder was that simply because a term has been "misused" and abused by others does not make it useless. After all, the fact that some people misuse an automobile and cause someone's death in "vehicular homicide" does not render the automobile a useless tool that ought to be abolished.

The other group of scholars who were unhappy with the term were those who had espoused the notion that linguistic "ideology" (also known as "language ideology/ies") was the only way to explain the kinds of concepts I wished to embrace with the term "linguistic culture," and that since a large number of people had written about language "ideology,"[1] which was by then the dominant discourse, I should abandon my approach and join the larger school of thought.

I should perhaps first define what I mean by the term. In particular, I see language *policy* (roughly, "decision-making about language") as inextricably connected to *linguistic culture*, which I define as the sum totality of ideas, values, beliefs, attitudes, prejudices, myths, religious strictures, and all the other cultural "baggage" that speakers bring to their dealings with language from their culture. Linguistic culture also is concerned with the transmission and codification of language and has bearing also on the culture's notions of the value of literacy and the sanctity of texts. In other words, I think it is important to view language policy as not only the explicit, written, overt, *de jure*, official, and "top-down" decision-making about language, but also the implicit, unwritten, covert, *de facto*, grass-roots, and unofficial ideas and assumptions, which can influence the *outcomes* of policy-making just as emphatically and definitively as the more explicit decisions. It seemed to me that language policy had too often been defined as the explicit and the overt, while the cultural notions about language that influence the underlying ideas about language that are current in a particular culture (and which may also influence, sometimes rather profoundly, the *implementation* of language policies) are often ignored, or are treated as impediments that must be overcome. That is, policy-makers, if they are too confident that their explicit decisions are the correct ones, often see the implicit factors (which are more embedded in the "unconscious" linguistic culture) as *problematical*, thwarting the well-intentioned plans of the decision-makers, who of course are only trying to do the "right thing."

Evolution of this Concept

I first used the term "linguistic culture" in print in connection with my study of the shift from German to English in the United States (Schiffman, 1987). However, my thinking about language policy has been more deeply influenced by my experience working with Tamil, one of the major languages of India, which has the second-oldest literary tradition in India, after Sanskrit, and exhibits a number of sociocultural characteristics that are difficult to explain without some notion that there is a kind of Tamil "linguistic culture" that differs in some ways from that of other language groups in India, while also sharing many features with the larger South Asian linguistic culture.

My stay in India in 1965–6 to study this language and do research for a linguistics dissertation on a topic of Tamil syntax coincided with a year of political turmoil in India that had begun when the deadline for the replacement of English as India's official language, with Hindi, had come due. The Indian Constitution of 1950 specified that there should be a change-over from English to Hindi, but in order to allow for an orderly transition, a 15-year period of adaptation was specified. Little had been done to effectuate this transition (the old "implementation" bugaboo I mentioned above), but in early 1965, advocates of Hindi proclaimed that the time was up, and English should now cede its place. Speakers of other languages in India reacted with great emotion, and in some cases, violence.

The Tamils in particular, steeped in their own reverence for their language, its "purity," its unique ancient literature, and who had spent at least half a century attempting to revitalize the Tamil language, "purify" it of the foreign influences (Sanskrit and Hindi) that had "corrupted" it, were determined to resist the imposition of Hindi. Violent resistance ensued, and lives were lost; some Tamils immolated themselves by fire and others took poison, rather than give in to this "abomination" (Ramaswamy, 1997).

I arrived in Tamil Nadu (then Madras State) in September 1965, somewhat oblivious to the political turmoil that had closed down a number of universities for almost nine months, and not until I went to a conference in North India in January 1966 did I learn that the Tamils were perceived as "language *fanatics*."

Though I had studied Tamil for three years in America, and a number of other languages in my undergraduate years, I experienced for the first time what it meant to learn to use a language that had two distinct forms, one spoken and one primarily written. This condition, known as *diglossia* (Ferguson, 1959, 1991), had been identified for such diverse languages as Arabic, Swiss German, French Creole, modern Greek, and many of the languages of South Asia. In Tamil Nadu, I found that I was not only not expected as a foreigner to be able to speak the spoken variety, in fact it was deemed *inappropriate* that I try to learn the spoken language, and instead should only speak the formal literary form, even though all other members of Tamil society around me were communicating *only* in spoken Tamil to each other. My attempt to record speech samples was seen as somehow *contributing to the corruption* of the language, and when some members of the Dravida Munneetra Karakam (DMK) political movement learned of my activities, they visited me in my quarters and entreated me to cease and desist from this project. Why my study should have led to more degradation of Tamil than the daily speech habits of 60 million Tamils was not clear to me, but they seemed to be implying that I was *dignifying* a variety of language that was best ignored, and that this was inappropriate, especially for a *foreigner*.

Diglossia and Linguistic Culture

It was in this situation that I first began to think about how these powerful ideas regarding the Tamil language affected linguistic habits and behavior, and in particular, how the fact that diglossia, which can be a long and stable linguistic condition, but one that has come about without any overt planning or policy-making, can characterize a language, and influence people's speech habits. It was clear that the fact that Tamil is diglossic was a sort of *implicit policy* – nothing explicit had been done to make it come into existence, and nothing explicit could, or apparently ever would, be done to change it. I saw it (Schiffman, 1997) as a long-established way of thinking about language in the Indian subcontinent, since Sanskrit also exhibited diglossic features.

Tamil speakers all seemed to know when to use the spoken ("low" or "L" variety) forms and when to use the literary ("high" or "H") variety, and yet they were never explicitly taught what the contexts were in which the proper form was to be used, and no explicit rules about use seemed to exist. The idea that any change in this situation was necessary was anathema to almost every Tamil speaker I met. In fact, no Tamil term for diglossia exists, nor is the concept even overtly realized or discussed – if any discussion arose, it was that the "beautiful" literary version of the language was the *real* Tamil, and the spoken variants were corrupt, degraded, used primarily by children, the uneducated, and women, and best ignored and forgotten. Some Tamils even denied that they *ever* spoke vernacular versions of the language, and if observed doing so, would say that they simply had to use it to communicate with these lesser mortals, but that they weren't really *speaking* it – and it certainly wasn't their mother tongue.

In my book-length exposition of linguistic culture and its connection to language policy (Schiffman, 1996) I devote one chapter to the linguistic culture of South Asia in general and another to Tamil linguistic culture, so it is not necessary for me to recapitulate that discussion here. Suffice it to say that the notion that language policy is rooted in linguistic culture certainly grew out of my involvement with Tamil and Indian linguistic culture. It had been influenced too by my previous study of Russian, and of Soviet language policy, which also exhibited characteristics that exemplified the "covert" in conflict with the more overt policy. And, as mentioned above, I first used the term "linguistic culture" in the late 1970s in a study of the assimilation of German-Americans to English, at which point I thought of it not as a new idea or term, but simply as a description of that part of culture that has to do with language.

What I realized from my study of the shift from German to English among the large numbers of German-Americans who had settled in America primarily in the nineteenth century was that German policy-makers (those responsible for making policy about what language would be taught in German-American parochial schools, and used in church services) had both ignored and to some extent suppressed facts about spoken and written language in their zeal to preserve the German language in America. Imbued with a love of German (as the Tamils were with a love of Tamil), and with religious reverence for the language of Luther and his translation of the Bible, they could not conceive of anyone who was offered that "treasure" wanting to use the English language instead. But the kind of German taught in the schools of the German-American church was not the same as the usually non-standard dialect German brought to America by most immigrants, so a kind of diglossia similar to that of Tamil also prevailed, but was, like diglossia in India, ignored by policy-makers. German policy-makers apparently believed that enforcing the use of standard *Hochdeutsch* in German-American schools and churches would preserve this language for all generations, but they did not reckon with the possibility that American-born

Germans would adopt English as their spoken vernacular, and they certainly did not believe it would result in language shift.

Thus the German-American policy-makers were both blind to the effects of German diglossia and of the German–English diglossia that developed among American-born Germans, and failed to reckon with its consequences. Stonewalling demands for English services and English-speaking pastors, and faced with constantly increasing immigration from Germany, they overlooked the fact that they were losing members, especially among the linguistically assimilated. These and other conditions prevailing in the German-American immigrant community, and even in the literature about German-American immigration, which ignored internal documents and gave credence only to official pronouncements of the German-American church, concealed the aspects of language policy that I came to refer to as "covert." Overt policy in the German-American church gave the impression that it was the effects of World War I and anti-German legislation of that era that killed the German language in America, whereas internal documents of the church revealed demands for English as early as the 1880s that were not so obvious. It was therefore the combination of German diglossia, coupled with overt denial of demands for English, that led me to posit the notion of linguistic culture as being made up of both overt and covert aspects, since if one simply takes at face value what decision-makers and the "power elite" in a society say about language and language policy, the true picture of what is happening will not emerge.

Another instance of covert policy is that of the situation in schools in czarist-occupied Poland, the birthplace of Marie Skłodowska Curie. Her biography describes how schools in Poland (before 1918) secretly taught in Polish, but when the Russian inspectors arrived to visit, instruction would switch to Russian. As a bright student, Marie Skłodowska was usually called on to recite the lesson in Russian. The inspectors, pleased by what they saw, left, and instruction in Polish resumed. This seemed to me another kind of covert policy – a *subversive* and *resistant* policy, but one that succeeded in keeping the Polish language alive for a century, until independence after World War I. The Russian inspectors only believed what they observed, so were unaware of a covert policy that was more representative of actual practice than they could realize. The tendency to present one face to the world while keeping other linguistic activities "under cover" turned out not just to be a feature of language policy in czarist Russia and its dominions, but in post-czarist Soviet Russia as well, as we learned when the lid finally came off with the fall of the Berlin Wall, and long-suppressed animosities that had supposedly been eliminated by "enlightened" Soviet policy came bubbling to the surface. Soviet policy on language and ethnicity, in other words, as with Soviet policy on the environment and many other issues, turned out to be a sham.

Language policy in France

It is difficult, if not impossible, to characterize French language policy succinctly; books have been written about it, and I have also published on the subject (Schiffman, 1996, 2002). What I learned in France about language policy in general, and linguistic culture in particular, is that the strong beliefs the French have about their language policy are mainly based on what I call *mythologies* about both the language and the policy. My research for these chapters revealed that the French populace in general, and even some French scholars who have written about the policy, believe certain things very strongly, such as that certain legal provisions regarding use of the French language exist, which in fact *do not* exist, and did not, until certain laws, known collectively as *la loi Toubon*, were enacted in the 1990s. That is, the French believed so strongly that they had the most explicit and ancient language policy in the world (Balibar, 1985) that even though the provisions they thought existed did *not* exist, their belief in these supposed laws made for a policy that was quasi-legal, since everyone believed it.

As Balibar puts it,

> France is today the only nation in the world with legislation requiring (since 1794) the exclusive use of the national language in all public and private acts, from the drafting of laws to the language of commercial transactions and even a private citizen's last will and testament, etc. . . . France is the most extreme case [*le cas limite*] of a nation totally identified with one language, but which goes beyond this to defend the integrity of this linguistic personality in all aspects of social life against the claims and encroachments of any and all languages from inside or outside its borders . . . But French public opinion, perhaps anaesthetized by its poorly-understood monolingualism, is not sensitive to the urgency of language problems.
>
> *(Balibar, 1985, p. 9; translation mine)*

When I first read this statement, written by a French scholar of language policy, I resolved to seek out the legislation she was describing, but my search ended in a blind alley. The legislation she was referring to fell far short of specifying the exclusivity of French in all these domains, and the circumstances in which it was enacted were clearly shrouded in a subsequently developed myth that far exceeded the terms of the actual legislation. Yet French public opinion, as she says, "perhaps anaesthetized by its poorly-understood monolingualism" (and, I would add, by its poor understanding of the history of *language legislation* in France), believes something very different from the facts. This lack of understanding, I believe, is epitomized by the use of the term *le decret Barère* (the Barère Decree) instead of what should have been the official name of the law (*8 pluviose an II*). Barère is a person who became famous for his virulent denunciation of the non-standard forms of French, such that words he uttered have come to be taken as part of the *legislation* itself, when in fact the text of the law was much milder and weaker, and never took effect. But the myth of its power became the power of the myth, and leads ordinary people and scholars alike (e.g., Balibar) to believe something that never happened.

Barère acted as the spokesman of the Committee of Public Safety to the *Convention*, the representative body that was then the chief legislative organ in existence. Speaking for this committee to the delegates of the *Convention* on January 27, 1794 (which under the French revolutionary calendar was then the *8 pluviose*), he asserted that

> Federalism and superstition speak Breton; emigration and hate of the Republic speak German; the counter-revolution speaks Italian and fanaticism speaks Basque. Let us smash these faulty and harmful instruments. It is better to instruct than to translate; it is not up to us to maintain these barbarous jargons and crude dialects which can only be of further service to fanatics and counter-revolutionaries.[2]

Since this kind of rhetoric became part of revolutionary discourse, it is easy to see how the fiery denunciation of non-standard languages, which was much more interesting and memorable than the actual text of the law, could come to be remembered as the text, and, coupled with Barère's name, entered French linguistic culture as emblematic of what happened in 1794, rather than the actual legislative text, which was much tamer. Thus even scholars of the subject remember better what Barère said than what the law said.

What the Law of *8 pluviose an II* actually said was that "French shall be taught in every commune where the local people do not speak French." This rather mild and toothless proposal was based on the assumption that schools would have to be opened in such communes, and that bilingual teachers would have to be found; no one assumed that an immersion approach would do (teaching French to children who did not understand a word of it). But it was quickly discovered that there were no teachers who were perfectly bilingual in both the local languages and French, and anyone who was capable of teaching bilingually was already otherwise preoccupied. Few applicants applied for the positions specified, and the net result was that despite the best of intentions, the decree could not be implemented. As implementation is almost always the weakest link in language policies, we see here that fiery rhetoric was one thing, but carrying out the intention of the law was another.

So another solution was proposed: start an *école normale* or teacher training institute; this would be conducted in Paris, and the trainees would then be sent to the provinces to teach others. So the *école normale* was created by the decree of September 27, 1794 (6 *vendémiaire an III*). But again, poor planning: there were few candidates who showed up, and meanwhile the original old schools were closed with nothing to substitute for them. Plus, by now France was in the period known as the Reign of Terror, so what ensued was a *terreur linguistique*, with much persecution and bloodshed. The law that Balibar claims is responsible for implementing a rigorous and explicit language policy did no such thing, and was "dead on arrival."

One could go on at length, exposing the facts and how they contrast with the myths and misunderstandings, rampant in French linguistic culture, about the status of French, the explicitness and rigor of its putative language policy, but this would be extremely repetitive. As we have already noted, it was only in the mid-1990s that France finally realized that its supposedly explicit language policy was in fact largely unwritten. So the *loi Toubon* was enacted to make explicit and legal what had been largely unofficial and unwritten, and many French people could then breathe sighs of relief that French language policy was finally explicit (because without this, who could predict what might happen?).

My point in discussing all of this, of course, is to make it clear that France did not need an explicit language policy to make people understand that certain restrictions applied – the existence of a myth, deeply embedded in French linguistic culture, took care of that. As I put it in my 1996 study, the power of French language policy "rests in what people imagine it to consist of, rather than on actual statutes or rigid codes. In other words, it is not as explicit as French people think it is, but it is every bit as restrictive as they think it is, as long as they think it is" (Schiffman, 1996, p. 123). Perhaps we can better understand this dilemma by noting the difference in legal traditions: in Anglo-Saxon law, what is not explicitly forbidden is permitted. But in other legal traditions (including the French), the opposite assumption applies – what is not expressly permitted is forbidden, so that not making French official and other varieties unofficial is, in such legal traditions, downright dangerous. What this tradition fails to observe, however, is that even if there is no common-law tradition, there are still implicit assumptions that can be as strongly constitutive (of language policy, etc.) as explicit formulations can be.

Jacobinisme, dirigisme, monarchisme . . .

The tendency to decide things centrally and to control so many details of life is known, since the time of the French Revolution, as *jacobinisme*. It developed as an antidote to tendencies that were seen as counter-revolutionary, and has remained in force in French life as part of the way the French govern themselves. It is thus part and parcel of French linguistic culture as well, since linguistic *jacobinisme* is part of this culture of attempting to control things that Anglo-Saxons would not consider necessary, or even desirable, to control. The counter-revolutionary tendencies, as we have seen above, were most typically denounced in the words of Barère – the idea that non-standard languages (*les patois, les idiomes, les jargons*) were not just defective or inferior, but, even worse, they contained undesirable qualities, even ideas or ideologies, that were a threat to the Revolution, and which had to be extirpated. This notion persists to this day, and the threat from English, and from *le franglais*, is seen as similar; ideas inimical to French culture are perceived to be contained in, embodied in, the English language and the English loan-words that are flooding into France, and they must be eliminated, or French culture will be ruined.

Conclusion

To summarize, it seems clear that when it comes to language policy, things are not always "as they seem," and we must look more deeply than explicit policy to understand how policy works in practice.

To emphasize that language policy is embedded in culture also recognizes the role of language as the main vehicle for the construction, replication, and transmission of culture itself. And though language itself is a cultural construct, this does not imply that it can be deconstructed, changed, or radically altered by the application of particular theoretical frameworks, or political scrutinies of one sort or another. Language (and languages) mean different things to different people, and policy-formulation is often vague, ill-defined, or poorly understood. The best example of this is exhibited by language policy in the United States – we have no explicit language policy, but we have a linguistic culture that supports the use of English to the exclusion of almost all other languages, so that an explicit policy that would officialize English is not necessary, and probably never will be.

What might be the weaknesses of such a theory? For some, as I have already noted, the notion of "culture" and what constitutes it is poorly defined, and can be "misused." One might also find fault with the possibility that "culture" (and in particular "linguistic culture") could be circular, that is, that defining "linguistic culture" as that part of culture that is concerned with language could be tautological, or at best vague, with ill-defined borders. What I would answer is that we need a theory that can handle as many variables as in fact seem to be involved in language-policy formation (and this includes factors that are unforeseen when individual policies are formulated – the law of "unintended consequences" always seems to turn up new results that were not accounted for when a particular policy was initiated). Some theories would treat these "cultural" factors as pesky problems that pop up to thwart the plans of the planners, but I hold that if the data confounds the theory, then the theory needs to be fixed, not the data.

I also think it important to be able to differentiate between different kinds of ideas about language – myths, attitudes, religious beliefs, economic ideas – instead of lumping them all together into an undifferentiated, oversimplified, and reductionist one-size-fits-all rubric. Another fault I find with certain social-science approaches to the study of language policy is that they constantly treat language like some sort of "black box" with no internal factors or features that would make any difference to the grander scheme of a policy. Such approaches treat language as almost irrelevant, as if it would make no difference in, for example, France if the Japanese language were substituted for French. Clearly Japanese language policy and French language policy are different, and the languages are not interchangeable; but if we read Marxist language-policy theory carefully, we find that language is in the end *irrelevant*, and that when the state finally "withered away," differences between languages would also cease to exist. Fortunately, the Soviet Union collapsed before the "state withered away" and we did not have to wait for this eventuality.

Annotated Bibliography

Calvet, L.-J. (1987). *La Guerre des langues et les politiques linguistiques.* Paris: Payot.
This work focuses on the issues of language conflict as an outcome of language policy and planning. Calvet's title, *The war of languages and language policies*, focuses on the fact that languages have a birth, a life, and then a death, and because there are many languages spoken in the world, they come into conflict with each other, and some survive and some don't. He avoids proposing that those that die do so because they are somehow defective, but does look in some detail at the question of language planning, and whether the intervention of humans in the life of languages has a salutary effect, or whether the jury is still out on this question.

Hymes, D. (ed.) (1964). *Language in culture and society.* New York: Harper and Row.
This edited volume, a pioneering work on the relationship of language to culture, brings together studies from many different sub-fields of linguistics, anthropological linguistics, and the sociology of language. Of particular interest are part III, "World View and Grammatical Categories," and part VII, "Social Structure and Speech Community." The former deals with issues that later became categorized as "ideological," in particular whether grammar reflects thought; in the latter, treatments by Martin on speech levels in Japan and Korea, Ferguson's pioneering diglossia article, and Wolff's "Intelligibility and inter-ethnic attitudes" foreshadow later concerns with culture and language policy.

Miller, R. A. (1982). *Japan's modern myth: The language and beyond.* New York: Weatherhill.
One of the best treatments of language and "mythology" by a non-Japanese who knows Japan and Japanese intimately, Miller's work deals with attitudes the Japanese display toward their own language and to the learning of others. In particular, it deals with the mythology

surrounding the Japanese language and its supposed "special status" (i.e., "unrelated" to any other language in the world), which Miller holds are a way of holding on to some formerly racist ideas that could be attributed to the Japanese language, instead of Japanese culture or society.

Schieffelin, B., Woolard, K. A., & Kroskrity, P. V. (eds.) (1998). *Language ideologies: Practice and theory*. New York: Oxford University Press. This is an excellent overview and review of the subject of language and linguistic ideologies, which has now replaced the former "worldview" or "Weltanschauung" approach, known previously as the "Sapir–Whorf Hypothesis," in which cultural ideas about the world are supposedly reflected in the different grammatical structures of various languages. From this hypothesis, it is a mere hop-skip-and-a-jump to making claims about language influencing thought, how ideologies are (or can be) "built in" to language, and other ways in which cultural ideas can be found to be embedded in language.

Schiffman, H. F. (1996). *Linguistic culture and language policy*. London: Routledge.
The first full-length treatment of the notion of "linguistic culture" and its relationship to language policy, this study reviews a number of language-and-culture precursors, devotes considerable background to issues of religion, myth, and language, shows the difficulties inherent in typologizing language policies, and then illustrates various ways in which linguistic culture interacts with language policy in three multilingual "democracies": France, India, and the United States. One chapter is devoted to the overall picture of each polity, and then another focuses on one region of the polity – Alsace for France, Tamil Nadu for India, and California for the United States.

Discussion Questions

1 How important do you consider the historical and cultural background of a country in the evolution of a language policy? Can language policy be easily changed by legislators acting against the basic historical trends?

2 In what ways do religious ideas about language differ from other ideas, such as nationalist or racist ideas about language? How easy

would it be to go against these ideas, and implement a language policy that challenged them?

3 When it comes to language issues in your part of the world, in what ways does actual practice differ from policy as laid down from above? Is the policy on language use in licensing drivers different from actual practice?

4 Americans are often accused by people from other countries of being aggressively monolingual. Would you say that this is part of American "linguistic culture," or just laziness, or a recognition of pragmatic reality?

5 The English language has been accused of being "imperialistic" – aggressively asserting itself over other languages and seeking to annihilate them. Do you see this notion as having any validity?

NOTES

I am indebted to Ann Shepherd White for a careful reading of the final draft of this chapter, and for suggesting judicious editorial comments.

1 Cf. Woolard (1998) for an excellent overview of some of these approaches. Although I have many reservations about this school of thought, the multidisciplinary approach taken by van Dijk (1998) is more satisfying to me than some others.

2 "En somme, le fédéralisme et la superstition parlent bas-breton; l'émigration et la haine de la République parlent allemand; la contre-revolution parle italien et le fanatisme parle basque. Brisons ces instruments de dommage et d'erreur. Il vaut mieux instruire que faire traduire, comme si c'était à nous à maintenir ces jargons barbares et ces idiomes grossiers qui ne peuvent plus servir que les fanatiques et les contre-révolutionnaires" (translation mine).

REFERENCES

Balibar, R. (1985). *L'Institution du français: Essai sur le colinguisme des Carolingiens à la république*. Paris: Presses Universitaires de France.

Ferguson, C. F. (1959). Diglossia. *Word, 15*(2), 325–40.

Ferguson, C. F. (1968). Myths about Arabic. In J. A. Fishman (ed.), *Readings in the sociology of language* (pp. 375–81). The Hague: Mouton. (Reprinted from *Languages and Monograph Series. Vol. 12*, 1959 [pp. 75–82], Georgetown University. Reprinted 1972.)

Ferguson, C. F. (1991). Diglossia revisited. *Southwest Journal of Linguistics, 10*(1), 214–34.

Hoenigswald, H. (1971). A proposal for the study of folk-linguistics. In W. Bright (ed.), *Sociolinguistics* (pp. 16–26). The Hague: Mouton.

Hymes, D. (ed.) (1964). *Language in culture and society.* New York: Harper and Row.

Miller, R. A. (1982). *Japan's modern myth: The language and beyond.* New York: Weatherhill.

Ramaswamy, S. (1997). *Passions of the tongue: Language devotion in Tamil India, 1891–1970.* Berkeley, CA: University of California Press.

Sapir, E. (1949). *Selected writings of Edward Sapir in language, culture and personality* (ed. D. G. Mandelbaum). Berkeley, CA: University of California Press.

Schiffman, H. F. (1987). Losing the battle for balanced bilingualism: The German-American case. In J. Pool (ed.), *Linguistic inequality* (Special issue), *Language Problems and Language Planning,* 11(1), 66–81.

Schiffman, H. F. (1996). *Linguistic culture and language policy.* London: Routledge.

Schiffman, H. F. (1997). Diglossia as a sociolinguistic situation. In F. Coulmas (ed.), *The handbook of sociolinguistics* (pp. 205–16). Oxford: Blackwell.

Schiffman, H. F. (2002). French language policy: Centrism, Orwellian *dirigisme,* or economic determinism? In J. A. Fishman (series ed.) & L. Wei, J.-M. Dewaele, & A. Housen (vol. eds.), *Contributions to the sociology of language. Vol. 87: Opportunities and challenges of bilingualism* (pp. 89–104). Berlin: Mouton.

van Dijk, T. A. (1998). *Ideology: A multidisciplinary approach.* London: Sage.

Woolard, K. A. (1998). Introduction: Language ideology as a field of inquiry. In B. Schieffelin, K. A. Woolard, & P. V. Kroskrity (eds.), *Language ideologies: Practice and theory* (pp. 3–47). New York: Oxford University Press.

PART II

Methodological Perspectives in Language Policy

Methodological Perspectives in Language Policy: An Overview

Thomas Ricento

As James Paul Gee (1999, p. 5) notes, "any method always goes with a theory. Method and theory cannot be separated, despite the fact that methods are often taught as if they could stand alone." In this part of the book, historical, ethnographic, linguistic, geolinguistic, and psycho-sociological methods are clearly linked with (and at times critical of) extant theoretical approaches in various disciplinary literatures. Each of the chapters provides a state-of-the-art discussion of how theories and methods within that discipline have contributed to better understandings of issues addressed by scholars in the various sub-fields of language policy. While it is useful to examine methods and techniques available from different disciplinary perspectives, language policy and planning (LPP), as an interdisciplinary field, requires an understanding and use of multiple methods in exploring important questions about language status, language identity, language use, and other topics that fall within the purview of research.

History occupies an important position in most work in LPP, whether at the micro-level of interpersonal communication or the macro-level of state formation. Terrence Wiley (chapter 8) draws our attention to the many ways that the assumed superiority of Western civilization has informed attitudes and policies toward non-Western, non-Christian societies and states. Relatedly, Wiley notes that "in popular and scholarly discourse about language politics and policy, . . . specialists occasionally appeal to the *authority* of history to bolster their claims about how the past informs us about contemporary issues" (p. 136). Such appeals, Wiley notes, are based on the view that there is a correct, empirically based "true" story of what happened in the past. Wiley describes in some detail the work of historian Hayden White, who, "while believing the past at the factual level and our capacity to represent it with some accuracy, maintains that, nevertheless, historians do not discover *the* story. Instead we invent emplotments to explain the facts . . . [but] *we prefigure the past as history of a particular kind* . . . The stories we impose on the past are done so for reasons that are contemporary, cultural, linguistic, conceptual, discursive, ideological – for reasons that are epistemic" (Munslow, 2000, p. 18). In recognizing the strengths and limitations of both conventional and postmodernist perspectives on historical knowledge, Wiley argues that the choices for those who consider history in their work become: "*when to critique* products of historical work that acknowledges the ideologically driven trappings of grand narratives, and *whether* and *when to do historical investigation that attempts to provide alternatives to the limitations of dominant unitary models*" (pp. 139–40).

Another research approach useful for probing and questioning "grand narratives" or "objective models" accounting for the nature and/or effects of language policies or policy approaches is ethnography. As Suresh Canagarajah (chapter 9, p. 154) notes, "considerations of language allegiance, linguistic identity, and linguistic attitudes are not necessarily rational, pragmatic, or objective. They are ideological. As such, language relationships are difficult to predict or manage." Ethnography can provide insights about life at the grass-roots level and lead to better understanding of the role of language(s) in the lives of people directly affected by overt or covert language policies or regimes. In a number of studies cited in this chapter, evidence is provided on the ways in which individuals and communities resist such policies by constructing alternate practices, examples of "language planning from below." Canagarajah notes tensions between the goals and methods of ethnography and the requirements of doing language-policy research. Ethnographers may find that the requirement for "objective" results and recommendations imposed by funding agencies runs counter to their scholarly need for reflexive exploration of emerging hypotheses during the course of the research. Another dilemma is posed by the relativism of ethnography in which the views and interests of the community being researched are always right. Yet, as Canagarajah points out, "the community's perspective may be self-interested and partisan in a multilingual context, hampering inter-community relations" (p. 163). The community may also adopt positions that go against the "enlightened" or "disciplined" positions of scholars and policy-makers, such as the view that language maintenance is inherently "good" or necessary. To deal with such dilemmas, the ethnographer needs to move beyond passively listening to the local informant and engage in reflexive rethinking of his or her own and the informant's positions (Willis, 1997).

Like anthropological approaches to LPP, psycho-sociological methods (discussed by Colin Baker in chapter 12) aim to explore and evaluate the attitudes and beliefs of individuals and speech communities to better understand the effects of language policies, in part to develop more realistic and effective language-policy goals and planning strategies. However, as with ethnography, research on language attitudes has strengths and limitations, and the best research is that which uses an array of techniques and perspectives in order to achieve the most valid results possible. At a minimum, this suggests that, for example, in attitudinal research, both quantitative (e.g., Likert, the Semantic Differential Technique, and the Matched Guise technique) measures and qualitative analysis (e.g., document analysis, structured or open-ended interviews, and autobiographies) should be used. Another important source for information on language use is national census data. Baker points out the wide variation in language questions asked (or not asked) on national censuses and the many limitations of surveying language use by means of self-report. He cites recent censuses in Venezuela and Bolivia as noteworthy for their sophistication, especially compared to the censuses of Europe and North America.

One of the most promising techniques developed in recent years is social network analysis, which was employed in research conducted by the Commission of the European Union (1998) in Ireland, Catalonia, Wales, and Friesland. This technique (described in some detail by Baker) gives a more nuanced picture of the actual use of the minority language based on network size, average duration of acquaintance, network density, and density of minority-language usage in networks. Another important trend noted by Baker is "target language planning," which has come into vogue, for example, in Wales and the Basque Country. Target language planning, according to Baker, involves: (1) a clear overall conceptualization of language planning (e.g., status, corpus, acquisition, and opportunity/incentive planning), and (2) the setting of realizable and sustainable targets that are (3) prioritized and (4) monitored for their completion, effectiveness, and outcomes. Examples of various planning targets are provided.

While all of the methods and techniques discussed to this point involve the interpretation of texts and discourses, linguistic analyses (Ruth Wodak, chapter 10) can provide greater detail and specificity about how particular social beliefs, values, and ideologies are constructed and reproduced (often implicitly) in a variety of written and spoken genres in defined contexts. Of the methods described in this section, critical discourse analysis (CDA), and specifically the discourse-historical approach, may be the most comprehensive in analyzing texts debating, proposing, or criticizing language policies. In addition to employing a range of linguistic techniques in the analysis of written, oral, and visual texts, the discourse-historical approach "attempts to integrate a large quantity of available knowledge about the historical sources and the background of the social and political fields in which discursive 'events' are embedded. Further, it analyzes the historical dimension of discursive actions by exploring the ways in which particular genres of discourse are subject to diachronic change" (Wodak, p. 175). To avoid bias in its methods or interpretation of data, Wodak recommends that critical discourse analysts follow the principle of triangulation, which means working with different approaches and methods and a variety of empirical data and background information. The method of CDA described by Wodak has been used successfully in several research projects examining the discourses of language policies in the European Union. In her chapter, Wodak provides a detailed analysis of a group discussion demonstrating, in part, how certain concepts such as "national identity" or "linguistic hegemony" are co-constructed among speakers of different ethnolinguistic backgrounds. Using techniques from ethnography, history, sociology, political theory, and linguistic analysis, the discourse-historical approach offers a rich and complex range of methods and approaches in the study of language policies, from conversational analysis to political documents.

Don Cartwright (chapter 11) describes how practitioners of geolinguistic research have combined analysis of relationships between languages and their physical and human contexts with a focus on historical processes that have played a role in the development of patterns of contact and interaction between different culture groups. Unlike researchers in human geography, practitioners of geolinguistics offer "a more positive, practical appreciation of the role of geographic space, territory, and scale of analysis as additional elements that are employed in a more holistic, sociolinguistic approach to language communities" (Cartwright, p. 196). The relevance of this approach for research in LPP is demonstrated in this chapter through case studies of two types of communities: (1) a geographically peripheral and fragmented ethnolinguistic community, and (2) a more extensive and contiguous community. An important goal of geolinguistic research is to assess the relation between, and effects of, language policies and policy approaches and the relative degree of ethnolinguistic vitality of a group, where survival of group identity is dependent to varying degrees on inter-generational transmission of the mother tongue. The first community type is exemplified through the case of Welsh in Wales and the second through the Flemish (Dutch-speaking) and Walloons (French-speaking) in Belgium. In the first case (Welsh), Cartwright argues that "in peripheral ethnolinguistic communities, the settlement pattern of population tends to be fragmented; hence, the nationalists' objectives are mainly to reinforce and entrench key domains in which the minority language exists" (p. 199). Without such reinforcement of domains, a situation of subtractive bilingualism will occur, in which the mother tongue of the minority is gradually displaced in an increasing number of domains by the majority language. While there have been some advances in the revitalization of the Welsh language within targeted domains, according to Cartwright, "vigilance and language planning must be constant in the face of expanded economic opportunities within the European Union" (p. 199).

The second community type is illustrated in the case of the two dominant ethnolinguistic groups in Belgium, the Flemish and Walloons. Between 1830, when Belgium became an independent state, and 1932, the dominant Walloons resisted bilingual parity with the Dutch-speaking Flemish population. Finally, in 1932, efforts by the Flemish to achieve a bilingual country were abandoned and unilingual regions were created with the Flemish in the north and Walloons in the south, except for the capital and some areas along the linguistic frontier that remained bilingual. Fears of territorial encroachment by the Walloons on the part of the Flemish led to the official demarcation of Flanders and Wallonia in 1963 as permanently unilingual regions, in which use of language outside of the home would be legally determined by a person's place of residence and not by home language or personal preference. Brussels, the capital, remained officially bilingual. The case of Belgium, according to Cartwright, demonstrates the application of two principles for policy formation: the principle of territoriality and that of personality. The first principle was appropriate because there are two, clearly defined, unilingual areas: Flemish (Dutch) in the north and Walloons (French) in the south. Each group enjoys the right to protect its language within a contiguous territory. The situation in Brussels demonstrates the application of the principle of personality, in which every person is free to obtain services in the language of his or her choice. The evolving cosmopolitan nature of Brussels, aided by the establishment of international bodies, such as the European parliament, means that bilingualism is viewed as additive, not subtractive, since access to the other language neither threatens replacement of the mother tongue, nor diminishes the ethnolinguistic vitality of either group.

The determination of which methods are appropriate for a particular research topic is related, among other things, to:

(1) the goals of research;
(2) the existence and availability of various types of data (for example, census data, policy texts, historical records); informants (for example, policy-makers, community representatives, government officials);
(3) financial, human, and technological resources available for research.

The methods (and associated theories) described in this part of the book are frameworks within which are subsumed a variety of techniques. For example, if one were to do a linguistic analysis of various texts, it would be desirable to have familiarity with a variety of tools from specialized fields, such as pragmatics, rhetoric, discourse analysis, and conversational analysis, among other possibilities. In addition to such specialized tools, there are methods which can be applied to virtually any domain of investigation, such as content analysis and grounded theory (see Titscher et al., 2000, for extensive discussion of these and other methods).

REFERENCES

Gee, J. P. (1999). *An introduction to discourse analysis: Theory and method.* London: Routledge.

Munslow, A. (2000). *The Routledge companion to historical studies.* London: Routledge.

Titscher, S., Wodak, R., Meyer, M., & Vetter, E. (2000). *Methods of text and discourse analysis.* London: Sage.

Willis, P. (1977). *Learning to labour: How working class kids get working class jobs.* Manchester: Saxon House.

CHAPTER EIGHT

The Lessons of Historical Investigation: Implications for the Study of Language Policy and Planning

Terrence G. Wiley

A century ago, Max Weber addressed the issue of explaining the rise and dominance of the West. In his and most of Western scholarly thinking of the time, the historical fact of Western superiority was unquestioned. The social historian's task was to explain how and why that supremacy had been achieved. He posed the question thus: "A product of modern European civilization, studying any problem of universal history, is bound to ask himself to what combination of circumstances the fact should be attributed that in Western civilization, and in Western civilization only, cultural phenomena have appeared which (as we like to think) lie in a line of *universal* significance and value" (1992, p. 13; cited in Mignolo, 2000, p. 3).

With the rise of postcolonial states, many of their prescribed models for language planning and policy formation follow in the footsteps of successful Western nations and resemble universalistic models that assume a linear path to economic and national *development* (Rostow, 1960). Linguistic unification and dialect homogenization through the promotion of mass literacy are recipes from the nation-builder's cookbook that can be reduced to a step-by-step formula of status and corpus planning. The assumption that the historical experience of some Western states provides that universal path for emulation is deeply engrained not only in works of history, but in the social sciences and humanities as well. As Mignolo's words below note, the invention and continuous revision of the purported superiority of the West and the universalistic presumption that it serves as a model for the world are deeply embedded in its own construction of historical knowledge:

> If history and literature . . . became complicitous in imperial expansion after the eighteenth century, during the late Renaissance they had the encyclopedia and letter writing as companions. However, alphabetic writing (in connivance with Christianity) was the foundation not only of the massive transmission of information but also, and mainly, of its organization and evaluation. China, Islam, and the New World were all evaluated (in their organization and transmission of knowledge) with the yard stick of Renaissance discursive genres and their implicit epistemology.
>
> *(Mignolo, 1995, p. 169)*

Today, in popular and scholarly discourse about language politics and policy, demagogues, politicians, and even language-policy specialists occasionally appeal to the *authority* of history to bolster their claims about how the past informs us about contemporary issues. Such appeals to history are based on the assumption that there is a correct, empirically based, "true" story of what happened in the past.

Given the importance accorded to history, this chapter briefly discusses aspects and limitations of conventional historical explanation and imagination, as well as the challenges and paradoxes facing both so-called modernist and postmodernist thought with reference to historical work.[1] Next, Eurocentric universalistic models of history and the role of language and literacy ideologies therein are critiqued. Examples of the appropriation of Eurocentric historical modes in South Asian anti-colonial nationalist movements are noted briefly.

Limitations of Conventional History as the "True" Story of the Past

Underlying confidence that conventional history provides the correct story of the past is the belief that a "true" accounting of the past is produced from empirical investigations of primary sources, historical documents, records, artifacts, biographies, eye-witness accounts, and other texts, which, through inferential analysis by the historian, allows her or him to discover the "real" events that resulted from the choices of historical agents of the period under investigation.

In attempting to write the past-as-history, historians face a number of calculated choices. Like ethnographers, historians,

> must adopt an attitude toward both the society to be described and the informants who describe it; select a limited number of topics to cover, since no general description of a society can ever be complete, and choose the literary form to convey the results to a public. In each of these decisions, *models matter*. Few writers weave whole new tapestries of their own, rather, they make quilts from ready-made ingredients.
> **(Grafton et al., 1992, p. 42; emphasis added)**

As they undertake these decisions, conventional historians assume that their language, concepts, and categories are up to the task of recapturing and representing (re-presenting) the "real" essence of the past. This view presumes a *correspondence* between the past, the facts selected by the historian, and her or his narrative. Methodologically, the conventional historian relies on inferential analysis, *deduction*, and *induction* to portray actual past events and social reality, as well as ongoing critical reassessment of evidence (Munslow, 2000).

The past as constructed by historical imagination

In addition to inductive and deductive approaches, however, Munslow notes that there is a third aspect of historical inquiry that is *abductive*, which is "the characteristic feature of historical explanation and the historical imagination" (2000, p. 122). As Munslow notes, "Historians do tend to use 'the facts' to create their own meanings. If they did not, then history would be much less revisionist (re-vision) than it is" (p. 18). Since the mid-1970s, Hayden White has been one of the primary interrogators of the historical imagination. In his groundbreaking work, *Metahistory: The historical imagination in nineteenth-century Europe* (1975), White critiqued the nineteenth-century confidence in the autonomy of history and historical consciousness. *Metahistory* was followed by a number of works (e.g., White, 1987, 1998) that expanded his initial emphasis on the structure of historical narrative.

In *Metahistory*, White postulates four fundamental modes of historical consciousness: *metaphor, synecdoche, metonymy*, and *irony*, each of which "provides the basis for a distinctive linguistic protocol by which to *prefigure* the historical field" (p. xi), using specific strategies of historical interpretation that can be employed to *explain* it. Influenced by Valery,

Heidegger, Sartre, Lévi-Strauss, and Foucault, White stressed the *fictive* character of historical consciousness, and he set out to probe what he called the *deep structure* of historical imagination (1975). White distinguished among several levels of conceptualization, which he used to analyze the work of major historians: *chronicle; story; mode of emplotment; mode of argument;* and *mode of ideological implication.*

For White, chronicles and stories are produced through the "selection and arrangement of data from the *unprocessed historical record* in the interest of rendering that record more comprehensible to an *audience* of a particular kind" (1975, p. 5). Following Northrop Frye (1957), White sees historical text organized according to four modes of emplotment: *romance, tragedy, comedy, satire,* and a possible fifth, *epic.* Emplotment is enhanced by explanation through formal, explicit, or discursive argument. Using Stephen Pepper's *World hypotheses* (1966) framework, White differentiates four discursive "paradigms of form" (p. 21), or in Pepper's terms, four *root metaphors,* that underlie any historical or naturalistic account: *formist, organicist, mechanistic, contextualist.* Lastly, White adds the lens of ideological implication to the analysis of historical texts. He defines ideology as "a set of prescriptions for taking a position in the present world of social praxis and acting upon it" (p. 22). As Munslow observes,

> The big question, so forcefully put by Hayden White, is does the past-as-history correspond with *the* story that exists in the evidence? How can a historian's narrative discover *the* real narrative? . . . White, while believing the past at the factual level and our capacity to represent it with some accuracy, maintains that, nevertheless, historians do not discover *the* story. Instead we invent emplotments to explain the facts . . . [but] *we prefigure the past as history of a particular kind.* [See "tunnel history" below.] The stories we impose on the past are done so for reasons that are contemporary, cultural, linguistic, conceptual, discursive, ideological – for reasons that are epistemic.
>
> *(2000, p. 18)*

Modernist and Postmodernist Paradoxes

Derrida (1982) and Geertz (1983), among others, have extended the attack on the status of historical truth claims by attempting to expose the limits of "modernist" rational empiricist rigor (Iggers, 1997). As Munslow concludes, "The unavoidable Modernist paradox is that while historical discourse claims provide a truthful content (based on rules of evidence), it has to do it in the form of a knowing narrative" (2000, p. 77). In other words, the historian is "directly implicated in the process of knowing" (p. 122) by attempting to mediate the past.

The postmodernist perspective on historical knowledge, however, is not without its own paradox. Iggers observes, "the critics of historical realism who insisted on the autonomy of texts" have seldom gone "beyond theoretical states to confront a concrete historical subject matter" (1997, p. 10). Iggers concedes a number of points underscored in the postmodern critique, namely that a "unitary history" is not defensible; history has both "ruptures" as well as "continuity"; dominant ideological assumptions are embedded in historical discourses; and exaggerated claims of the authority of historical experts should be challenged. Nevertheless, postmodernist critics raise the specter of a nihilistic regress that can result in a morally irresponsible position. As Iggers concludes, if postmodernist critics remove

> not only the admittedly fluid border that lies between historical discourse, which always involves fictional elements, and fiction . . . but also that which lies between honest scholarship and propaganda, this blurring of borders . . . become[s] particularly troublesome in recent discussions on the Holocaust as a historical event. The contradictions of resolving history into purely imaginative literature become apparent in Hayden White's admission that from a moral perspective it is unacceptable to deny the reality of the Holocaust, yet it is impossible in a historical narrative to establish objectively that it happened.
>
> *(1997, p. 13)*

Should we, from a postmodernist perspective of the limitations of historical investigation, also fail to deal with the history of the American holocaust (see Stannard, 1992) that ensued with the conquest of the "New World" and the linguistic and cultural repression that followed in its wake? Iggers charges that postmodernists appear willing "to throw out the baby with the bathwater when they deny the possibility of any kind of rational historical discourse and with it historical falsity" (1997, p. 13), and thereby, do not attempt to do history at all.

Recognizing the paradoxes of both the conventional and postmodernist perspectives concerning the efficacy of historical knowledge, the choices for those who would consider history become: *when to critique* products of historical work that acknowledges the ideologically driven trappings of grand narratives, and *whether* and *when to do historical investigation that attempts to provide alternatives to the limitations of dominant unitary models.* The next section considers the need to critique grand narratives that wittingly or unwittingly falsify the writing of the past.

Critiquing Eurocentric Unitary Historical Models

From a global perspective, how are the "rise of the West" and its subsequent linguistic dominance to be explained? Over the past five centuries an ideology of the superiority of the West has been a major theme of historical emplotment – one that has been revised to fit the contemporary agendas of historians and other social scientists. New disciplines emerged, including *modern* and *romantic* historical linguistics (Kaiwar, 2003), along with attempts to explain and catalog the otherness of the "New World" and colonized regions of Africa, the Pacific islands, and South Asia (Willinsky, 2000). Allegedly superior Western cultural institutions, techniques, language and literacy practices, and moral values were positioned against the "subalternation" (Mignolo, 2000) of non-Western ones.

Blaut (2000) and Willinsky (2000) have undertaken content analyses of major works by prominent historians and common school history textbooks that reveal some striking commonalities regarding the purported uniqueness of Europe and the West's ultimate rise and continued dominance over the rest of the world. Although most of the overtly racist nineteenth-century arguments rationalizing the alleged superiority of the West have been dropped or muted, as Blaut and Willinsky demonstrate, notions of European superiority not only persist, but also prevail, in much of popular and scholarly discourse. Drawing from work ranging from that of Weber (1951) to that of more contemporary scholars (including Diamond, 1997; White, 1982), Blaut (2000) has cataloged 30 major arguments in the work of prominent historians which hold that Western dominance resulted from various geographical, technological, economic, class, and political advantages that allegedly led first to the rise of Europe, and then to the West's continued global dominance. Even though Blaut (1993, 2000) and others have refuted these as spurious arguments, they persist as elements of a hegemonic, epistemic grand narrative, which Blaut calls *the colonizer's model of the world*. This model assumes Europe or the West as the center from which all human inventions of value are diffused to a "less-developed/underdeveloped" periphery.

Blaut asserts "that a fundamental rather than explicit error has been made in our conventional past thinking about geography and history, and this error has distorted many fields of thought and action . . . It is in a sense folklore" (1993, p. 2). He notes that although the Eurocentric colonizer's model may be thought of as a prejudicial attitude like racism, sexism, or religious bigotry, "the really crucial part of Eurocentrism" is that it is "a matter of science, scholarly, and informed expert opinion . . . supported by facts" (p. 9).

Discipline-specific discourses across the social sciences and humanities often have common assumptions and features, thus creating the appearance of consensus across fields of study. Recalling Foucault's (1972) construct of *episteme*, which refers to interconnected knowledge across various domains of knowledge or fields of study in a given historical period, Munslow warns, the "concept of episteme . . . alerts us not only that all historical periods organize the acquisition and utilization of knowledge according to differing criteria and for distinct purposes," but that "the criteria for knowledge creation invariably revolve around the social distribution of power" (2000, p. 18). Ricento (2003, especially pp. 614–15) notes the differential power of elite discourse to shape public discourse and popular attitudes. Within the academy, discipline-specific discourses assume the status of "scientific" or at least "scholarly" authority. However, as Willinsky (2000) has demonstrated, many of the social sciences' emergence as fields of study coincided with the "Age of Discovery" (and conquest), and thus their epistemologies originated along with the agenda of cataloging and explicating of otherness.

The colonizer's model employs *prefiguration*, or what Blaut (1993, 2000) calls *tunnel history*, which rationalizes the outcomes of the past on the basis of the purposes of the present. As Munslow explains, "choices are made about how the-past-as-history is composed and configured, *because of the wished for ends*; for some it may be the need to discover the truth, while for others it is the wish to establish and promote a variety of intellectual, gender, ethical, cultural, economic or social programmes" (2000, pp. 18–19; emphasis added).

The colonizer's model also denies non-Western equivalencies to Western institutions and achievements. Hegel's work provides an unambiguous example of tunnel history as he depicts the Western nation-state as the end point of a history that moved geographically and temporarily to the West: "The history of the World travels from East to West, for Europe is absolutely the end of History" (Hegel, 1956, p. 103). While Hegel's and Weber's views could be dismissed as merely outdated Eurocentric triumphalism, the persistence of the West-as-center in the work of contemporary historians (see Blaut, 2000) and its lingering influence in school texts (see Willinsky, 2000) demonstrate the necessity to consider its relevance for contemporary social questions, including those related to language policy and planning.

For Blaut (1993) the major premises of the colonizer's model are that (1) most human communities are *uninventive*, (2) a minority of human communities, places, or cultures are *inventive*, and (3) these remain the *permanent* centers of cultural change and progress. *Eurocentric diffusionism* is based on a center–periphery model with Greater Europe (and its extensions, the US, Canada, Australia) as Inside and everywhere else (particularly colonized areas) as Outside. Furthermore, because the center invents, it changes, progresses, and therefore is historical. Conversely, the periphery is stagnant and unchanging, or at best sluggish, traditional, backward, without history. The basic elements of the center's progressivism are: special characteristics of the European mind, *spirit, character, rationality* (or *race* in older versions), which have allowed the inventions of literacy, and therefore, history, law, and high cultural institutions (Blaut, 1993, 2000). Another feature of the model is what Blaut (1993) calls *the myth of emptiness*. According to this myth, the periphery is devoid of basic cultural institutions that result from literacy and rationality. A non-European region, prior to settlement/colonization, is empty of essential institutions that allow people to be grounded and legitimized. History texts dealing with colonization and treaty periods often depict the non-Europeans as being mobile, nomadic, wanderers, or just passing through as migratory peoples. Thus, European "settlement" and the imposition of treaties are not depicted as violating any prior rights of political sovereignty, because the inhabitants have no concept of property and lack civilizing institutions that would govern it (Blaut, 1993).

To progress, develop, or modernize, the periphery must *receive* knowledge and techniques that are diffused from the center, rather than by its own inventiveness. But the gift of civilization is not received without cost. The colonial center drew out the resources and wealth of the colonies in exchange for knowledge and inventiveness; so too contemporary "nation-building" has a price tag. Thus, the expropriation of wealth from the colonies – which, by the way, helped to fuel the capitalization and further "modernization" of the West, and thereby guarantee its continued dominance in the postcolonial era, according to Blaut (1993, 2000) – has been rationalized in the grand narratives of Western and world history.

Privileged Languages and Literacies in the Colonizer's Model

How does this Eurocentric diffusionist perspective relate to the history of language politics, planning, and policy? Within the colonizer's model, a special status is accorded to issues of language and literacy, both as core ingredients of the rise of the West, and as recipes for its emulation in "underdeveloped" societies. Literacy, as it developed in the West, is seen as instrumental to the development of historical thinking itself as a key component of the rise of rationalism, which is held to have originated primarily in the West. All good things, including dominant languages, develop first in the West, and are then "diffused" to the periphery, based on Western models. Language planning itself has often been viewed as a form of social engineering that can be used to advance higher levels of educational achievement through mass literacy in "underdeveloped" countries, which in turn, is seen as furthering economic development and modernization. At a macro-level, this technocratic view of language planning typically perceives language diversity as a social deficiency that causes social and economic "backwardness." Thus linguistic unification and language standardization based on the nationalist models of the West are prescribed as panaceas for the socioeconomic ills of "modernizing" nations.

Alphabetic literacy and the great divide

Goody and Watt (1988) have argued that the invention of the alphabetic writing system resulted in salient intellectual changes and cognitive effects in ancient Western society that gradually led to developmental differences between non-literate and literate societies. Boone and Mignolo (1994) and Mignolo (1995, 2000) detail how notions of literate and linguistic superiority among Spaniards were used to provide an ideological justification for colonization and the subjugation of the indigenous peoples of the Americas five centuries ago. Around 1492 two events occurred in close proximity of time. First, the kingdoms of Aragon and Castile were united and, shortly thereafter, Columbus found his way to what would later be called the "Americas," even though he did not know where he was. In the same year, court scholar Antonio de Nebrija, through his publication of *Grammatica de castellana*, prescribed a standardized model of Castilian for the linguistic unification of the Iberian peninsula, thus linking nation-state with language, and deemed language as the "consort of empire" (Willinsky, 2000, p. 191; see also Ilich, 1979; Mignolo, 1995).

When the Spanish conquerors became colonizers of the peoples of the Americas, a fierce debate ensued regarding the humanity of the peoples there. Among the critical deficiencies noted was that these peoples did not have alphabetic literacy, and thereby lacked "history." But through the decree of the church it was determined that they at least had "souls" and thus could be converted and "saved" (Boone & Mignolo, 1994; Mignolo, 1995). From the conquerors' perspective, there were two major obstacles to saving them: their lack of alphabetic literacy and their heretical indigenous knowledge. The imperial agenda for linguistic unification was subverted by the pragmatic demands of communicating with converts in languages they understood. (How much of contemporary linguistic knowledge of the world's languages has resulted from the same motivation?) Thus, the missionaries who accompanied the conquerors acquired a great deal of information about local knowledge and non-alphabetic writing without words (Boone & Mignolo, 1994), even as they subordinated or subalternized it (see also Mignolo, 1995, 2000).

The colonizer's model has been particularly resilient over time as it pertains to Western notions of language and literacy. In its more recent manifestations, some historians and historical anthropologists have attempted to determine the cognitive and societal effects of literacy. Western standardized languages of literacy provide the models for corpus and status planning or intellectualization. Goody and Watt (1988), Havelock (1963, 1988), and others (e.g., Olson, 1977, 1988; Ong, 1982, 1992) have argued that literacy, particularly Western alphabetic literacy, produces individual cognitive and institutional advantages for literates. Goody (1987, 1999), Goody and Watt (1988), and Olson (1994, 1999) have subsequently qualified their conclusions. Nevertheless, the linking of linguistic standardization to nation-building serves as a model for the multilingual periphery.

Historically, the debate over the alleged cognitive great divide, as it relates to the invention of the alphabet and the diffusion of Western literacy more fundamentally, calls into question the ideological rationalizations for colonial subjugation on the basis of literate/non-literate statuses (Mignolo, 1995, 2000). The significant point here is that the original formulation of the great-divide theory was notable for not only its emphasis on a cognitive divide related to the development of literacy, but also for its intrinsic Eurocentrism (Mignolo,

1995, 2000; Street, 1984), in which the development of alphabetic literacy was presumed to be the means to both individual cognitive development and institutional advancement. Gough (1988) has refuted this claim by underscoring the development of literacy in India and China. Boone and Mignolo (1994) demonstrate the importance of studying the hieroglyphic, logographic, and mnemonic writing systems of Mesoamerica and the Andes as alternatives to alphabetic systems. The complexity and utility of these systems were initially denigrated by the Spanish conquerors. Following in that dismissive tradition, some contemporary scholars, such as Goody, write off counter-evidence as postmodernist attempts "to eliminate supposed developmental differences between cultures in an excess of relativism" (Goody, 1999, p. 30). Nevertheless, the comparable merits of various orthographies, alphabets, syllabaries, and logographs as optimal representational systems of oral language have largely nullified claims regarding the intrinsic exceptionality of alphabetic systems.[2]

The late Ivan Illich (1979) explored the promotion of nationally endorsed standardized languages of literacy and the role of schools in promoting those languages as a means of social control. He concluded that the sanction of the language of schooling precluded the development of common vernaculars and diminished the values associated with local common languages. As an example, he maintained that the imposition of literacy in standardized languages, such as Castilian, actually restricted the local vernacular functions of literacy in late fifteenth- and early sixteenth-century Spain. People would have to go to school to learn their "mother tongues" as artificially constructed "out of a jigsaw puzzle of local or regional dialects which constituted the non-literary languages as actually spoken" (Hobsbawm, 1987, p. 147). Historical variations in the dichotomized "great divide" views of standardized/schooled version of language and literacy are summarized in table 8.1.[3]

The Appropriation of Eurocentric Models of History

Although it is necessary to interrogate the colonizer's model and its contributing elements, such as the great divide, and while it is fashionable to tag the Enlightenment and modernism as the primary perpetrators of notions of superiority and inferiority, it is also necessary to consider how Eurocentric models have been appropriated. In the

Table 8.1 Variations on the purported cognitive great divide

Developed	Less developed/Underdeveloped
Original Eurocentric version:	
Alphabetic literacy	Non-literacy
	Non-alphabetic literacy
Western literacy	Orality (Western or non-Western)
Developed/intellectualized languages	Primitive or underdeveloped languages
Anglocentric version:	
Educated native speaker of English (presumes English literacy)	Limited English proficient English-language learner
Contemporary constructs in language acquisition and planning theory:	
Fully proficient	Limited proficiency
	"Non non" (alingual)[a]
Balanced bilingual	Partial bilingual
	Subtractive bilingual
CALP[b]	BICS[b]

Notes
[a] "Non non" refers to speakers who have no proficiency in two or more languages in which they are assessed. The classic case is a presumed Spanish speaker who lacks test proficiency in Spanish and English, but who in fact may speak another language or non-standard form of language missed in the assessment.
[b] BICS = Basic Interpersonal Communication Skills; CALP = Cognitive Academic Language Proficiency (Cummins 1981, 2000).

eighteenth century, for example, the founders of modern historical linguistics sought to connect the lineage of Western languages to those of their ancient ancestors, even as others were constructing lineages of racial ancestry. Kaiwar (2003) demonstrates how work on Sanskrit was appropriated by the Romantics to critique the rational empiricism of the Enlightenment and enshrine the authority of ancient Sanskrit texts, which were assumed to be the foundational texts of the Aryan race. Venkatachalapathy (2003) further demonstrates how the construction of orientalism was appropriated in South Asian contexts, and how notions of the purity of primal languages and sacred texts can be used to promote the contemporary agendas of anti-colonial nationalist movements. Thus, blanket neo-romantic prescriptions for mother-tongue promotion also need to be scrutinized within the historical contexts of struggles, where, for example, in South Africa, the former apartheid government's construction of mother tongues was used to divide those otherwise not so far linguistically removed (Alexander, 2002; de Klerk, 2002).

Conclusion

The pervasiveness of the colonizer's model and the great-divide theory makes it obvious that there is much history to critique, if history is to better inform language-policy formation. First we must disentangle and decolonize the web spun by the agendas of contemporary historians and eye-witness chroniclers of the past. Then we can learn from historical investigation that demonstrates the value of careful, cautious work; among the most promising is that being devoted to *local knowledge* and *border thinking*. The work of Mignolo, cited herein, and Canagarajah (2002) provide exemplary starting points.

Annotated Bibliography

Blaut, J. M. (1993). *The colonizer's model of the world: Geographical diffusionism and Eurocentric history.* New York: Guilford Press.
This work lays bare the many forms of Eurocentric diffusionism, the idea that progressive historical progress results from unique characteristics of the European "mind," culture, and/or "literate" institutions, which allegedly provide models for the development of the non-European world.

Blaut, J. M. (2000). *Eight Eurocentric historians.* New York: Guilford Press.
This analysis, the second in a trilogy being developed by Blaut, extends the author's original (1993) thesis as he takes aim at a diverse group of well-known modern and contemporary historians. Of particular value is his taxonomy of common Eurocentric arguments, which he refutes.

Boone, E. H. & Mignolo, W. D. (eds.) (1994). *Writing without words: Alternative literacies in Mesoamerica and the Andes.* Durham, NC: Duke University Press.

The development of the alphabet and Western language standardization are often taken as paradigms in language planning. This important historical work significantly challenges that orthodoxy. See also Mignolo (1995, 2000).

Kaiwar, V. & Mazumdar, S. (eds.) (2003). *Antinomies of modernity: Essays on race, Orient, and nation.* Durham, NC: Duke University Press.
This important collection interrogates both Eurocentric views of the relationship between race, language, and nation and their appropriation in postcolonial contexts.

White, H. (1975). *Metahistory: The historical imagination in nineteenth-century Europe.* Baltimore, MD: Johns Hopkins University Press.
Now a classic, White's groundbreaking work provides a structuralist framework for the analysis of historical discourse.

Willinsky, J. (2000). *Learning to divide the world: Education at empire's end.* Minneapolis: University of Minnesota.
Willinsky's award-wining work provides insights into the historical formation of the colonial legacy and demonstrates how it persists in contemporary education. His analysis of educational language policies is particularly relevant to this chapter.

Discussion Questions

1 Identify and discuss some of the inherent limitations of conventional historical inquiry.
2 What is the relevance of White's interrogation of the "historical imagination" for the study of history broadly and language policy specifically?
3 Discuss the postmodernist critique of doing conventional history.
4 What paradoxes do both conventional historians and postmodernist critics of history face?
5 Describe the components of the "colonizer's model."
6 Briefly discuss the implications of Eurocentric history and its appropriation in postcolonial contexts for the study of language planning and policy.

NOTES

1 The constraints of space allotted for discussion strongly affect the decisions I have made regarding the topics selected. Given this, my emphasis is less a systematic review of historical work in language politics, planning, and policy than a brief discussion of the implications of contemporary issues in historiography and historicism, and a critique of prevailing models of Eurocentric *unitary history* and the purported role of privileged languages and alphabetic literacy within it. Elsewhere (Wiley, 1996, 1998, 1999, 2000, 2003), I have provided examples of historical case-study research and addressed the need for extending the historical-structural approach in the analysis of language policies and ideologies (cf. Tollefson, 1991), so I will not reintroduce these topics here.

2 The ease of phonological processing may be weighed against additional criteria such as semantic processing (see Coulmas, 1989; Taylor & Taylor, 1995). Depending on the phonotactics, or permissible vowel and consonant sequences, of any particular language, a case may be made for syllabaries as optimal, rather than alphabetic systems, for many of the world's languages (see Daniels, 1992).

3 See: Street (1984) and Wiley (1996, ch. 3) for a discussion of the great divide; Wiley (1996, ch. 8) for elaboration on the relationship between Basic Interpersonal Communication Skills (BICS) and Cognitive Academic Language Proficiency (CALP) and the great divide; Cummins (2000, ch. 4) for a reply to Wiley and others; Valadez, MacSwan, and Martinez (2002) for a critique of "semilingualism" and "non-nonism"; and Willinsky (2000, ch. 8) for a review of the "native speaker" controversy.

REFERENCES

Alexander, N. (2002). *An ordinary country: Issues in the transition from apartheid to democracy in South Africa*. Pietermaritzburg: University of Natal Press.

Blaut, J. M. (1993). *The colonizer's model of the world: Geographical diffusionism and Eurocentric history*. New York: Guilford Press.

Blaut, J. M. (2000). *Eight Eurocentric historians*. New York: Guilford Press.

Boone, E. H. & Mignolo, W. D. (eds.) (1994). *Writing without words: Alternative literacies in Mesoamerica and the Andes*. Durham, NC: Duke University Press.

Canagarajah, S. (ed.) (2002). Celebrating local knowledge on language and education (Special issue). *Journal of Language, Identity, and Education, 1*.

Coulmas, F. (1989). *The writing systems of the world*. Oxford: Blackwell.

Cummins, J. (1981). The role of primary language development in promoting educational success for language minority students. In Office of Bilingual Education, California State Department of Education (ed.), *Schooling and language minority students: A theoretical framework* (pp. 3–49). Los Angeles: Evaluation, Dissemination and Assessment Center, CSULA.

Cummins, J. (2000). *Language, power and pedagogy: Bilingual children in the cross-fire*. Clevedon: Multilingual Matters.

Daniels, P. T. (1992). The syllabic origin of writing and the segmental origin of the alphabet. In P. Downing, S. D. Lima, & M. Noonan (eds.), *The linguistics of literacy* (pp. 83–110). Amsterdam: John Benjamins.

de Klerk, G. (2002). Mother-tongue education in South Africa: The weight of history. *International Journal of the Sociology of Language, 154*, 29–46.

Derrida, J. (1982). *Margins of philosophy* (trans. A. Bass). Chicago: University of Chicago Press.

Diamond, J. (1997). *Guns, germs, and steel: The faces of human societies*. New York: Norton.

Frye, N. (1957). *The anatomy of criticism*. Princeton, NJ: Princeton University Press.

Foucault, M. (1972). *The archeology of knowledge*. New York: Harper and Row.

Geertz, C. (1983). *Local knowledge: Further essays in interpretive anthropology*. New York: Basic Books.

Goody, J. (1987). *The interface between the written and the oral*. Cambridge: Cambridge University Press.

Goody, J. (1999). The implications of literacy. In D. A. Wagner, R. L. Venezky, & B. V. Street (eds.), *Literacy: An international handbook* (pp. 29–33). Boulder, CO: Westview Press.

Goody, J. & Watt, I. (1988). The consequences of literacy. In E. R. Kintgen, B. M. Kroll, & M. Rose (eds.), *Perspectives on literacy* (pp. 3–27). Carbondale, IL: Southern Illinois University Press. (Reprinted from *Comparative Studies in Society and History, 5*, 304–26, 1963.)

Gough, K. (1988). Implications of literacy in traditional China and India. In E. R. Kintgen, B. M. Kroll, & M. Rose (eds.), *Perspectives on literacy* (pp. 44–56). Carbondale, IL: Southern Illinois University Press.

Grafton, A., with Shelford, A., & Siraisi, N. (1992). *New worlds, ancient texts: The power of tradition and the shock of discovery*. Cambridge, MA: Belknap Press of Harvard University Press.

Havelock, E. A. (1963). *Preface to Plato*. Cambridge, MA: Belknap Press of Harvard University Press.

Havelock, E. A. (1988). The coming of literate communication to Western culture. In E. R. Kintgen, B. M. Kroll, & M. Rose (eds.), *Perspectives on literacy* (pp. 127–34). Carbondale, IL: Southern Illinois University Press.

Hegel, G. W. (1956). *The philosophy of history* (trans. J. Sibree). New York: Dover. (Original work published 1899.)

Hobsbawm, E. (1987). *The age of empire, 1875–1914*. London: Weidenfeld & Nicolson.

Iggers, G. G. (1997). *Historiography in the twentieth century: From scientific objectivity to the postmodern challenge*. Middletown, CN: Wesleyan University Press.

Illich, I. (1979). Vernacular values and education. *Teacher's College Record, 81*(1), 31–75.

Kaiwar, V. (2003). The Aryan model of history and the Oriental Renaissance: The politics of identity in an age of revolution, colonialism, and nationalism. In V. Kaiwar & S. Mazumdar (eds.), *Antinomies of modernity: Essays on race, Orient, and nation* (pp. 13–61). Durham, NC: Duke University Press.

Mignolo, W. D. (1995). *The darker side of the Renaissance: Literacy, territoriality, and colonization.* Ann Arbor: University of Michigan Press.

Mignolo, W. D. (2000). *Local histories/global designs: Coloniality, subaltern knowledges, and border thinking.* Princeton, NJ: Princeton University Press.

Munslow, A. (2000). *The Routledge companion to historical studies.* London: Routledge.

Olson, D. R. (1977). From utterance to text: The bias of language in speech and writing. *Harvard Educational Review, 47,* 257–81.

Olson, D. R. (1988). The bias of language in speech and writing. In E. R. Kintgen, B. M. Kroll, & M. Rose (eds.), *Perspectives on literacy* (pp. 175–89). Carbondale, IL: Southern Illinois University Press.

Olson, D. R. (1994). *The world on paper: The conceptual and cognitive implications of reading and writing.* Cambridge: Cambridge University Press.

Olson, D. R. (1999). Literacy and language development. In D. A. Wagner, R. L. Venezky, & B. V. Street (eds.), *Literacy: An international handbook* (pp. 132–6). Boulder, CO: Westview Press.

Ong, W. J. (1982). *Orality and literacy: The technologizing of the word.* London: Methuen.

Ong, W. J. (1992). Writing is a technology that restructures thought. In P. Downing, S. D. Lima, & M. Noonan. (eds.), *The linguistics of literacy* (pp. 293–319). Amsterdam: John Benjamins.

Pepper, S. C. (1966). *World hypotheses: A study in evidence.* Berkeley, CA, and Los Angeles: University of California Press.

Ricento, T. (2003). The discursive construction of Americanism. *Discourse and Society, 14,* 611–37.

Rostow, W. W. (1960). *The stages of economic growth: A non-Communist manifesto.* Cambridge: Cambridge University Press.

Stannard, D. E. (1992). *American holocaust: The conquest of the New World.* New York: Oxford University Press.

Street, B. (1984). *Literacy in theory and practice.* Cambridge: Cambridge University Press.

Taylor, I. & Taylor, M. M. (1995). *Writing and literacy in Chinese, Korean, and Japanese.* Amsterdam: John Benjamins.

Tollefson, J. (1991). *Planning language, planning inequality.* London: Longman.

Valadez, C., MacSwan, J., & Martinez, C. (2002). Toward a new view of low achieving bilinguals: A study of linguistic competence in designated "semilinguals." *Bilingual Review, 25,* 238–48.

Venkatachalapathy, A. R. (2003). Coining words: Language and politics in late colonial Tamilnadu. In V. Kaiwar & S. Mazumdar (eds.), *Antinomies of modernity: Essays on race, Orient, and nation* (pp. 126–45). Durham, NC: Duke University Press.

Weber, M. (1951). *The religion of China*. New York: Free Press.

Weber, M. (1992). *The Protestant ethics and the spirit of Capitalism* (ed. A. Giddens). New York: Routledge.

White, H. (1975). *Metahistory: The historical imagination in nineteenth-century Europe*. Baltimore, MD: Johns Hopkins University Press.

White, H. (1987). *The content of the form: Narrative discourse and historical representation*. Baltimore, MD: Johns Hopkins University Press.

White, H. (1998). *Figural realism: Studies in the mimesis effect*. Baltimore, MD: Johns Hopkins University Press.

White, L., Jr (1982). *Machina ex deo: Essays in the dynamism of Western culture*. Cambridge, MA: MIT Press.

Wiley, T. G. (1996). *Literacy and language diversity in the United States*. Washington, DC: Center for Applied Linguistics.

Wiley, T. G. (1998). The imposition of World War I era English-only policies and the fate of German in North America. In T. Ricento & B. Burnaby (eds.), *Language and politics in the United States and Canada: Myths and realities* (pp. 211–41). Mahwah, NJ: Lawrence Erlbaum.

Wiley, T. G. (1999). Comparative historical perspectives in the analysis of U.S. language polices. In T. Heubner & C. Davis (eds.), *Political perspectives on language planning and language policy* (pp. 17–37). Amsterdam: John Benjamins.

Wiley, T. G. (2000). Continuity and change in the function of language ideologies in the United States. In T. Ricento (ed.), *Ideology, politics, and language policies: Focus on English* (pp. 67–85). Mahwah, NJ: Lawrence Erlbaum.

Wiley, T. G. (2003). Learning from history. In R. N. Campbell & D. Christian (eds.), Directions in research: Intergenerational transmission of heritage languages, *Heritage Language Journal*, 1(1). Retrieved May 12, 2003 from www.heritagelanguages.org.

Willinsky, J. (2000). *Learning to divide the world: Education at empire's end*. Minneapolis: University of Minnesota.

CHAPTER NINE

Ethnographic Methods in Language Policy

Suresh Canagarajah

If language planning and policy (LPP) is about "deliberate efforts to influence the behavior of others with respect to the acquisition, structure, or functional allocations of their language codes" (Cooper, 1989, p. 45), ethnography might appear unrelated (if not contradictory) to this mission. While LPP largely works in a top-down fashion to shape the linguistic behavior of the community according to the imperatives of policy-makers, ethnography develops grounded theories about language as it is practiced in localized contexts. While LPP is largely concerned with the activities of specialists and policy-makers in defining language relationships from outside the community, ethnography is concerned with the community's own point of view about such matters. While LPP operates from the macro-social level of state and international institutions, ethnography focuses on the micro-level of interpersonal relationships, conversation, and everyday life. While LPP is deliberate and programmatic, ethnography unravels the largely unconscious "lived culture" of a community. In short, while LPP is about how things "ought to be," ethnography is about what "is."

Despite these differences, developments in scholarly discourse and the field of LPP itself point to the concerns of ethnography and LPP merging. These developments show that there are considerable benefits for LPP from adopting ethnographic methods to study languages and communities.

The Place of Ethnography in LPP

The human sciences in general are becoming increasingly sensitive to the ways social structures and institutions shape and are shaped by interpersonal relations in localized contexts. Giddens notes that "the study of day-to-day life is integral to analysis of the reproduction of institutionalized practices" (1984, p. 282). From an even more micro-social perspective, language and discourse are beginning to attain importance in the study of political and social structures. For example, language accomplishes hegemony by propagating partisan world-views and internalizing biased values. Therefore, ethnography has become useful for political scientists and policy-makers to understand the subtle play of power differences in interpersonal and local contexts (see Marcus & Fischer, 1986).

More importantly, the methodological crisis in LPP itself motivates an appreciation of ethnography in policy-making. The dominant *rational or positivist tradition* in LPP (see Ricento & Hornberger, 1996), which assumed that policies could be based on objective assessments of the needs, processes, and outcomes of language relationships, has fallen short. Considerations of language allegiance, linguistic identity, and linguistic attitudes are not necessarily rational, pragmatic, or objective. They are ideological. As such, language relationships are difficult to predict or manage. Since community needs and attitudes may be ambivalent, the processes of implementing policy can be multifarious, and the outcomes of policy surprising. It is understandable, therefore, that Cooper (1989) doubts the possibility of developing an all-encompassing model of LPP. He is prepared to consider how "sociologists have begun to build theories of smaller scope that apply to specific segments of society" (1989, p. 182). Developing knowledge on specific situations and communities is a necessary starting point for model-building. Ethnography, which is oriented toward developing hypotheses in context, can be of help in this regard.

Even more surprising is the realization that there is considerable policy formulation and institutionalization of linguistic practices at the other end of the policy spectrum – that is, local communities and contexts. In interpersonal and classroom relationships, marginalized subjects are resisting established policies, constructing alternative practices that exist parallel to the dominant policies and, sometimes, initiate changes that transform unequal relationships (see Canagarajah, 1999). Such realities point to incipient and emergent cases of "language planning from the bottom up" (the subtitle of Hornberger's 1996 book. It therefore behooves LPP scholars to listen to what ethnography reveals about life at the grass-roots level – the indistinct voices and acts of individuals in whose name policies are formulated.

Helen Moore (1996), in her analysis of recent Australian multi-cuturalist policies, critiques the rationalist assumptions in LPP for a more radical reason. She argues that policy documents are ideological discourses: that is, they make reality conform to them, rather than basing themselves on reality. She also critiques the progressivist assumptions in planning by showing that subsequent acts of policy are not necessarily closer approximations of reality, but reflect the changing ideological priorities of the status quo. To extend this argument to the geopolitical level, the Indian applied linguist Pattanayak (1988) argues that the dominant models of LPP assume monolingual norms typical of Western societies. He argues that postcolonial communities have to deviate from such models to consider radically polylingual norms as viable alternatives. Indian scholars have raised the possibility that the models developed in LPP are biased toward the communities of scholarship and power that formulate them (Khubchandani, 1997). Ethnography can help bring into focus atypical social and linguistic relationships in diverse geopolitical contexts. Developing policies informed by ethnography can counteract the unilateral hold of dominant paradigms and ideologies in LPP.

The Methods of Ethnography

To begin with the approaches adopted traditionally, the objective of ethnographers is to employ a first-hand, naturalistic, well-contextualized, hypotheses-generating, emic orientation to language practices. Let me explain each of the above: ethnographers expect to live for an extensive period of time in the community they are studying in order to capture first-hand its language patterns and attitudes. As much as possible, they try not to alter the "natural" flow of life and social relationships of the community, but understand how language works in everyday life. For this reason, they don't hastily isolate the variables or focus on them separately, but situate language practices in their fullest relevant contexts and capture them with all their complexity. Also, they try not to let their prior assumptions and scholarly dispositions interfere with their study; rather than confirming hypotheses they bring with them (as in other disciplines), they hope to *generate* hypotheses *through* the fieldwork experience. Though ethnographers are informed by the generalized patterns of language practices obtaining in other environments (*etic* view), they attempt to understand matters specifically in the way they are understood by community insiders (*emic* view). Hornberger (1988, pp. 4–11), in studying the prospects for the preservation of Quechua in the highland villages of Puno in Peru, provides a glimpse into the challenges for an ethnographer in entering a culturally alien community, giving up her comfort zone, correcting her biases, and "discovering" the people's values and thinking.

Researchers may employ a range of data-gathering methods, but *participant observation* remains the method of choice. Ethnographers attempt to enter into the flow of life of the community and experience how language relationships are lived out by the members. Detached observation (from the outside) may not provide valid insights into a community's ways with words. In actually living out a world-view, researchers gain insights from the inside – which are richer and deeper. To facilitate this perspective, ethnographers may supplement participant observation with surveys, questionnaires, and interviews. They may use audio- and video-taping, field notes, or digital media to "capture" data. They may analyze the data with quantitative or qualitative instruments. The multiplicity in the means and types of data gathered is important, as it permits them to cross-check (i.e., *triangulate*) their findings by playing off one kind of data against the other. Whatever means are used, ethnographers present a *thick description* of concrete details and narratives in their report, enabling readers to see language practices in all their contextuality and variability.

The traditional approaches above may be described as largely "descriptive" in their adoption of an objective and value-free orientation to the knowledge they produce. It is also assumed that the researcher's first-hand observation, sophisticated research instruments, and scholarly training will ensure an "authentic" representation of the language relationships in the community. But, as in other fields in social sciences (of which Moore's 1996 perspective on LPP is an example), the claim to objectivity has been questioned in ethnography. Hence the emergence of *critical ethnography* (Canagarajah, 1993; May, 1997). Critical approaches align themselves with the post-Enlightenment philosophical tradition in orienting to knowledge as non-foundational, socially constructed, and implicated in power differences. Contrasting with the relativistic tradition that perceives communities, languages, and cultures as different-but-equal, critical ethnography looks at them as positioned unequally in power relations. Furthermore, ethnographic descriptions are treated as being shaped by the interests of the researcher, the sponsors of the project, the audience of one's work, and the dominant power groups. Therefore, cultural representations are always somewhat partial and partisan. Furthermore, communities and cultures are treated as heterogeneous, conflictual, negotiated, and evolving, as distinct from unified, cohesive, fixed, and static (which characterizes traditional ethnographic descriptions). These orientations present new questions of validity and reliability. The pragmatic response has been to say that these concerns cannot be explained away, and that they must be frankly acknowledged and negotiated in the data. Therefore, critical ethnographers record in their data and address in their interpretation certain additional concerns that traditional ethnographers may not consider:

1 The way power differences between the researcher and inform-ants/subjects were negotiated (Chopra, 2001).
2 The researcher's own attitudes and biases toward the community and the ways they changed during the research process (Wright, 2001).
3 The influence of the researcher's activities and behavior on the community (Aikman, 1999).
4 The rationale for conflicts and inconsistencies in the community's representation of its language and culture (Stites, 2001).

Besides descriptive and critical approaches, there are other strands of ethnography. *Micro-ethnography* analyzes how talk constructs the very context that is treated as given (Garcez, 1997). This approach has been adopted for acquisition-planning studies, where the nego-tiation of competing codes by teachers and students reveals their co-construction of values and relationships (see Heller & Martin-Jones, 2001). *Ethnography of speaking* adopts an explicit cultural orientation to conversational interactions (Farah, 1997). *Sociolinguistic ethnography* is the term adopted by Monica Heller (1999) to focus on code choice as a means of bringing out the divergent values and relationships of competing languages. In these sub-fields, the basic ethnographic methods have been sharpened for specific research purposes and communicative domains.

Contributions of Ethnography

Ethnographic research can help in the different stages of language planning – that is, before, during, and after implementation. Before, it can provide crucial information to formulate relevant and effective policies: that is, the attitudes to competing languages and literacies in a community (Dyer & Choksi, 2001; Maddox, 2001); the aspirations and needs of the people (Jaffe, 1999; Resnick, 1993); the significance of language for identity and community (King, 2001). During implementation, ethnography may explore how different agencies and institutions function in promoting the policy (Freeman, 1996); specifically, it can bring out the tensions in the role of institutions at different levels of society, and the ensuing compromises in realizing the policy (Davis, 1994). After the implementation of a policy, ethnography may examine its consequences for the relevant communities and social groups (Papen, 2001; Stites, 2001); the ways in which what is on paper shapes everyday life and interpersonal relationships (Heller, 1999); the consistency with which it is implemented in diverse localities (as we see in the variable implementation of the Bilingual Education Act in the United States – see Freeman, 1996); and the fresh, unexpected problems a policy creates (Ramanathan, 1999; Schiffman, 2003). Ideally, then, ethnography can help in what we might consider a *language policy cycle* – providing feedback on the diverse stages of a policy. Such a research process would provide ongoing information to strengthen the implementation, bring about more effective results, or revise a policy. But the ideal situation, where ethnography accompanies all stages of the planning process, is realizable only with sufficient time and resources.

Ethnography can also help in the different *forms* of language planning. For example, in *status planning*, ethnography can suggest the importance competing languages should be given in different social domains in a multilingual nation-state (as Schiffman, 2003, does for Tamil in Singapore; Jaffe, 1999, for Corsican in France; and Davis, 1994, for foreign languages in Luxembourg). In *corpus planning*, ethnography can help a community understand its valuation of competing dialects and choose the variety most effective for schooling and other institutional purposes (as in King's 2001 comparison of "Unified Quichua" and "Authentic Quichua" in Ecuador; or in Heller's 1999 exploration of code mixing and local dialects in the French taught in Canada). Ethnography can also help in *acquisition planning*. It can help understand how language policies trickle down to classrooms (Freeman, 1996); the effectiveness of different pedagogies and curricula in accomplishing a policy (Hornberger, 1988); the role of schools in maintaining indigenous languages (Aikman, 1999) or in initiating language reversal (King, 2001); and the place of education in reproducing the social stratification of language groups (Heller, 1999; Ramanathan, 1999). Since ethnography is contextualized and holistic in approach, most studies straddle all these levels of planning. Besides, as many people have pointed out, acquisition is an important domain of consideration in status-oriented policies related to language maintenance or revitalization (see Hornberger, 1988). Similarly, corpus-related considerations (such as the diglossic varieties or regional dialects of a language) have implications for literacy and acquisition planning (see Heller, 1999; Schiffman, 2003).

Whatever the type or level of policy-making addressed, ethnography can bring out surprising findings about language relationships that elude those acting from outside the community. On the basis of their findings, ethnographers may offer recommendations that can make an important contribution to the formation or revision of language policies. I will illustrate the usefulness of insider knowledge below from some exemplary studies.

Jaffe (1999) reveals the paradoxical "unintended consequences" of the resistance policies of Corsican nationalists in France. Their policy has featured the following two strategies at different periods: (1) enforcing a strict separation from French (rejecting mixed forms of Corsican), and (2) preserving Corsican for in-group usage, while using French for public purposes (motivating the rejection of co-official status with French). But the first strategy adopts the discourse of purism. It prevents the development of Corsican as a suitable medium for contemporary purposes. The purist ideal also disempowers many vernacular forms of Corsican spoken in everyday contexts. The second strategy reduces the status of the language (as one used for only domestic purposes) and limits its currency. The resistance policy, therefore, becomes counter-productive. It produces new forms of linguistic alienation and insecurity among Corsican speakers. It also reduces the potency of Corsican to spread into other institutionalized functions.

However, even failed policy can have positive consequences. King (2001), in her research on the Saraguro community in the Ecuadorian Andes, finds the prospects for language revitalization of Quichua dismal. Local schools adopt a teacher-fronted and product-oriented literacy, failing to develop conversational fluency in the language. But King finds that the policy of trying to promote Quichua in schools has been "a valuable and worthwhile exercise" (2001, p. 188). Indigenous students learn that their language has the potential of being written and used for academic purposes. They acquire at least a limited amount of reading and writing knowledge of Quichua (perhaps for symbolic purposes). They also learn that Quichua enjoys an important status in their community. Therefore, though the direct expectations of the policy are not realized, there could be interesting side effects.

Schiffman (2003) makes a distinction between *overt* and *covert* policy. While the overt aspects are always motivated by the highest ideals, the covert policy may show ulterior motivations. After studying the prospects for maintaining Tamil in Singapore, Schiffman reveals that while the overt policy of the Singapore government appears to be egalitarian and pro-Tamil, its housing policy militates against the language policy, and has covert consequences. Encouraging integration by preventing the concentration of any single ethnic group in the same "estates," the housing policy works against the Tamils because they are prevented from enjoying the numerical strength or cohesiveness to use the language in social life. Schiffman also brings out covert policies at the micro-level of schooling and families. The official policy of providing mother-tongue education gets distorted, because students adopt the covert policy of studying Tamil only to gain entrance to the university by using their grades (and not to develop proficiency in the language). Such covert policies not only belie the good intentions of officials, they may also negate the small benefits achieved for the minority language by the overt policy.

Though Schiffman rejects an ideological reading of covert practices, in some cases they can function as a form of resistance against the unfair policies of the dominant groups. To give examples from the bilingual educational context, we can consider the collection of studies in Heller and Martin-Jones (2001). Researchers find that language use in the classroom defies policies that are largely monolingualist and purist. Teachers and students use unauthorized codes (usually the vernacular and other non-dominant languages) in surreptitious ways. While they use the authorized/dominant language for on-task and official sites, they use the unauthorized codes in unofficial and off-task contexts. I have labeled such contexts *hidden sites* or *safe houses* (Canagarajah, 1995, 1997). They provide a space for minority students (and sometimes teachers) to represent their preferred cultural identities, develop solidarity, and tap into local knowledge to facilitate their learning process. This strategy is an example of students and teachers exercising their agency to resist unfavorable policies. This may also be interpreted as an example of language planning from below. Students and teachers are initiating covert language-acquisition and communicative practices that counteract dominant policies. Such studies show that there is relative autonomy in the local contexts of society and schooling to negotiate policy decisions in one's favor. Ethnography is well suited to uncovering these subtle strategies of negotiation, resistance, and reconfiguration, suggesting the need to provide legitimate spaces in education for minority codes and discourses.

If such covert practices suggest tensions between policy and practice, ethnographers are also able to bring out conflicts between diverse social institutions in different levels of planning and implementation. Davis (1994) documents the pedagogical culture that militates against the policy recommendations of the state in Luxembourg. Though the government encouraged the use of Letzeburgesch in the mid-1980s by establishing it as the national language (to facilitate national and cultural cohesion, and to forestall the linguistic influences from immigrant workers), it now realizes that the shift from an industrial economy to an international banking economy spells out new language needs for the economic prospects of the local people. It is important for them to now be fluent in English, French, and German in order to vie for the opportunities available in the job market. However, a meritocracy-based educational system and teaching force find it difficult to break free from traditional pedagogies and practices. Teachers work on the assumption that students being prepared for different types of employment (and social classes) need to be given different types of education, paralleling greater or lesser linguistic and intellectual skills.

Sometimes the tensions are found within the community being served by the policy. Hornberger's (1988) findings of Quechua maintenance in Puno, Peru, paradoxically show a pedagogical success and yet policy failure. She finds that the new bilingual education project is successful in developing bilingualism in Spanish and Quechua (enabling indigenous children to maintain their language, become educationally successful, and develop pride in their identity). However, Quechua parents are not supportive of this project. They are influenced by the assumption that Quechua should be reserved for local domains of use (which can, therefore, be learnt at home) and Spanish for public domains (which should be learnt in schools). Hornberger finds that it is important to work from within the community in promoting positive language pedagogies, so that parents participate in educational changes, making their own contributions to the direction and implementation of the policy.

The power of community involvement in LPP is effectively brought out by Freeman (1996) in her study of Oyster Bilingual School in the

United States. The study additionally shows how the tensions between diverse levels of implementation, and the relative autonomy of local settings, can be exploited to serve the interests of minorities. The local Hispanic community reinterprets the Bilingual Educational Act in creative and radical ways to develop a more effective acquisition policy. While other schools adopt pedagogies such as transitional bilingualism or language-immersion programs which simply lead to English mono-lingualism among the minority Spanish-speaking students, Oyster develops an enrichment program that provides equal status for Spanish and English. Both English-speaking and Spanish-speaking students follow classes in both languages. This pedagogy provides scope not only for maintaining Spanish while acquiring English (for Spanish students) but, by asking dominant-community students to also learn Spanish, it provides dignity and affirmation for this minority language and equalizes the relationship between both groups. Freeman shows that the secret of the program's success is that local parents and teachers take an active role in planning this pedagogy. For Freeman, this is another example of language planning from below. The local com-munity members take over a federal policy and interpret it in their favor to give it radical new effects. However, the possibilities of local resistance and agency shouldn't be exaggerated. There are indica-tions that local efforts are not powerful enough to make deeper changes in the unequal relationship between English and Spanish. We see that while failing Spanish may not prevent any student from being promoted to the next class, failing English will definitely do so.

The Place of LPP in Ethnography

Before we conclude, we must acknowledge that the marriage between ethnography and language policy is not always harmonious. While ethnographic knowledge is useful for LPP – especially if it is trans-lated and adopted for LPP purposes, at a second remove from the original contexts of fieldwork – ethnographers have not been happy about being commissioned to carry out their research to directly serve the interests of policy-makers. Robinson-Pant (2001), asked by a Western NGO to develop a literacy policy that would help in the development of health among women in Nepal, discusses many ways in which her work cannot fit the interests of external agencies. She concludes, *"Designing and conducting* ethnographic research in a literacy policy context is far more problematic than *making use of* ethnographic findings from academic research projects for informing policy" (2001, p. 168; emphasis in original). She finds that the policy imperatives dictate a structure of questions that straitjacket the researcher, when the ethnographer wants the flexibility to pursue emerging hypotheses during the course of the research. There is also less space for reflexive exploration, enabling researchers to critique and revise their own assumptions; the policy focus requires them to be more objective. In terms of literacy, Robinson-Pant finds that she was expected to focus more on easily quantifiable *literacy events* rather than the more interpretive *literacy practices*. In other words, the researcher was expected to look for measurable data and not the more nebulous meanings and orientations of the community. Finally, at the stage of research reporting, the ethnographer has to write short/abstract accounts and not extended narratives of thick description.

A more complicated dilemma is posed by the relativism of ethnography (see Street, 2001, pp. 12–14). There is a bias in ethnography toward treating the views and interests of the community being researched as always right. Notions like "insider perspective" and "native point of view" can lead to a sympathy for (or even identification with) the views of the community. However, the community's perspective may be self-interested and partisan in a multilingual context, hampering inter-community relations. More importantly, the local community may adopt positions that go against the "enlightened" or "disciplined" positions of scholars and policy-makers. For example, though language maintenance in the interest of preserving linguistic ecology is a deeply held view of many linguists, some minority communities are not committed to preserving their language. They prefer to rise out of their marginalization by mastering the dominant codes – as in the case of Rabari nomads in India (Dyer & Choksi, 2001) and Quechua in Peru (Hornberger, 1988). Should the ethnographer simply validate these views in the interest of articulating the native perspective?

There are many ways in which critical ethnographers have attempted to move out of this limiting relativism. Geertz (1983) argues that the strength of ethnography lies in the rapprochement between *experience-near* and *experience-far* views: while ethnographers attempt to capture the experience-near view of the locals, they interpret it in light of the experience-far view they bring with them. The latter not only illuminates the insider perspective, but also provides a vantage-point for analysis and critique. Others point out that the "native point of view" can show the marks of domination. The ethnographers should, therefore, move beyond passively listening to the local informant and conduct a reflexive rethinking of their own and the informant's positions (Willis, 1977). The ethnographer can actively help the community think critically about their linguistic future, rights, and statuses – as Jaffe (1999) acknowledges about her relationship with Corsican nationalists. Ethnography can thus move closer toward policy discourse, enabling the researcher and the locals to interrogate conflicting viewpoints on language relationships from a macro-social perspective.

Conclusion

This chapter has explored the contribution ethnography can make to LPP by discovering and representing grounded, insider perspectives on linguistic needs and aspirations. Ethnography can also help assess the effectiveness of policies by showing their local realizations. Exemplary studies were reviewed to show the unique perspective provided by ethnography in uncovering the subtle tensions in policy and practice, different levels of planning/implementation, diverse social institutions, and between/within communities. Rather than being detrimental to policy, these tensions can also offer possibilities for local communities to negotiate or resist policies in their favor. While we saw some disciplinary tensions in the approaches of ethnography and LPP, I also articulated the way in which LPP is increasingly adopting a localized view of sociopolitical concerns, asking new questions and arriving at new answers. But this relationship works both ways. Just as LPP benefits from ethnography, ethnographers have themselves increasingly modified their approach of focusing exclusively on the local and the concrete (see Marcus & Fischer, 1986). Ethnographers are making efforts to integrate the global and historical in their research, moving directly toward policy and planning concerns.

Annotated Bibliography

Aikman, S. (1999). *Intercultural education and literacy: An ethnographic study of indigenous knowledge and learning in the Peruvian Amazon.* Amsterdam: John Benjamins.

This study focuses on the prospects for language maintenance among the Arakambut in Southern Peru. The nine-month-long ethnography attempts to understand the skepticism of this people about bilingual education, when neighboring indigenous communities are campaigning for it. The researcher finds that the intercultural education sponsored by the Spanish-language mission schools adopts a text-based curriculum and authoritarian pedagogy, putting off students who value oral/non-formal learning. As a defense against colonization, the Arakambut themselves keep the school domain separate from community. Aikman recommends community participation and a diversified pedagogical approach for effective language acquisition.

Davis, K. A. (1994). *Language planning in multilingual contexts: Policies, communities, and schools in Luxembourg.* Amsterdam: John Benjamins.
This book reports on a year-long ethnography on multilingualism in the industrial neighborhoods of Luxembourg. The study is unique in integrating considerations of economy in language policy (i.e., the linguistic changes dictated by the shift from an industrial to service economy). It provides an integrated perspective on various levels of planning and implementation: *intended policy* (what the government wants to accomplish); *implemented policy* (the actions taken to realize it); and *experienced policy* (the effects on individuals, families, and community values).

Heller, M. (1999). *Linguistic minorities and modernity: A sociolinguistic ethnography.* London: Longman.
This book is based on a study of a French school in Toronto – l'Ecole Champlain. Heller demonstrates the way identity and language politics at both the international and national levels get played out in the school setting. While French monolingualism and a Parisian standard dialect are its stated policy, the school faces challenges from alternative local dialects and bilingualism. Such tensions are resolved in off-center sites, where teachers and students adopt unauthorized practices. Bilingual middle-class students, who are adept at holding the stated and covert language policies in tension, succeed. But the ethnography adopts a chronological orientation and shows how the multilingual ethos of the international students gains prominence, with potential future policy changes.

Hornberger, N. (1988). *Bilingual education and language maintenance: A Southern Peruvian Quechua case.* Dordrecht: Foris.

This study is based on about 15 years of living intermittently in the region of Puno. The book is remarkable for showing the interconnections of status-planning and acquisition-planning issues, in relation to language-maintenance prospects for an indigenous community. Hornberger recommends providing more spaces for Quechua in institutional contexts to increase the community members' valuation of their language and motivate them to use it more frequently in their families. Such institutional promotion should lead to accessible and wide roles for both languages, which would ensure social mobility without linguistic bias. These changes will motivate the parents to be supportive of the school's success in developing proficiency in Quechua in addition to Spanish.

King, K. A. (2001). *Language revitalization processes and practices: Quichua in the Ecuadorian Andes*. Clevedon: Multilingual Matters.
On the basis of a year-long ethnography of two Quichua-speaking communities – Lagunas and Tambopamba – the author compares different approaches to language revitalization in light of the socio-economic factors influencing these communities. Since Lagunas is an urban community that has become mainstreamed into Spanish, the vernacular is an important marker of ethnic identity and vitality for the community members. But their everyday use of Quichua is not sufficient to sustain acquisition. Tambopamba, on the other hand, is a rural community which associates its way of life with identity. Therefore, the language is less central to maintaining ethnolinguistic vitality. Both communities are failed by the school, which adopts a teacher-fronted and product-oriented pedagogy. King calls for a multipronged, community-led, diversified pedagogy to aid language revitalization.

Street, B. (ed.) (2001). *Literacy and development: Ethnographic perspectives*. London: Routledge.
This collection of essays adopts an ethnographic approach to literacy policies that would aid development efforts in third world communities. The editor and many of the contributors wrestle honestly with the methodological tensions behind conducting ethnography in the service of policy agendas. The book is divided into two main sections. The first focuses on literacy pedagogies in cultural context, while the second explores the implications of local literacies for social development. Using currently popular literacy models – such as situated literacies, multiliteracies, and local literacies – the ethnographers throw new light on development plans in marginalized communities.

Discussion Questions

1 Considering the postmodern turn in research and the emergence of critical ethnography, what new problems does this research approach create for traditional concerns of validity and reliability? How can these questions be answered in critical ethnography?

2 Is it possible for a researcher to enter fieldwork with a commitment to reversing the decline or death of a minority language, raising its status, or providing an active place in education to help promote maintenance? What challenges would one face as an ethnographer in conducting research from this committed political position?

3 Can the same research lead to different, even contradictory, policy recommendations? Consider some of the studies reviewed in this chapter (or others you have read) to imagine alternative policy ramifications. How does one adjudicate between diverse interpretations?

4 Consider the relationship between micro- and macro-social realities. Are they as separate or conflicting as is usually assumed? How do these levels of analysis and social reality interact, cohere, and fuse in the specific policy-planning contexts you are interested in?

REFERENCES

Aikman, S. (1999). *Intercultural education and literacy: An ethnographic study of indigenous knowledge and learning in the Peruvian Amazon.* Amsterdam: John Benjamins.

Canagarajah, S. (1993). Critical ethnography of a Sri Lankan classroom: Ambiguities in opposition to reproduction through ESOL. *TESOL Quarterly, 27,* 601–26.

Canagarajah, S. (1995). Functions of code switching in the ESL classroom: Socialising bilingualism in Jaffna. *Journal of Multilingual and Multicultural Development, 16,* 173–96.

Canagarajah, S. (1997). Safe houses in the Contact Zone: Coping strategies of African American students in the academy. *College Composition and Communication, 48,* 173–96.

Canagarajah, S. (1999). *Resisting linguistic imperialism in English teaching.* Oxford: Oxford University Press.

Chopra, P. (2001). Betrayal and solidarity in ethnography on literacy: Revisiting research homework in a north Indian village. In B. Street (ed.), *Literacy and development: Ethnographic perspectives* (pp. 78–92). London: Routledge.

Cooper, R. L. (1989). *Language planning and social change*. Cambridge: Cambridge University Press.

Davis, K. A. (1994). *Language planning in multilingual contexts: Policies, communities, and schools in Luxembourg*. Amsterdam: John Benjamins.

Dyer, C. & Choksi, A. (2001). Literacy, schooling and development: Views of Rabari nomads, India. In B. Street (ed.), *Literacy and development: Ethnographic perspectives* (pp. 27–39). London: Routledge.

Farah, I. (1997). Ethnography of communication. In N. Hornberger & D. Corson (eds.), *Encyclopedia of language and education. Vol. 8: Research methods in language and education* (pp. 125–34). Dordrecht: Kluwer Academic.

Freeman, R. (1996). Dual-language planning at Oyster bilingual school: "It's much more than language." *TESOL Quarterly, 30*, 557–81.

Garcez, P. (1997). Mircroethnography. In N. Hornberger & D. Corson (eds.), *Encyclopedia of language and educatio.: Vol. 8: Research methods in language and education* (pp. 187–96). Dordrecht: Kluwer Academic.

Geertz, C. (1983). *Local knowledge: Further essays in interpretive anthropology*. New York: Basic Books.

Giddens, A. (1984). *The constitution of society: Outline of the theory of structuration*. Berkeley, CA: University of California Press.

Heller, M. (1999). *Linguistic minorities and modernity: A sociolinguistic ethnography*. London: Longman.

Heller, M. & Martin-Jones, M. (eds.) (2001). *Voices of authority: Education and linguistic difference*. Westport, CT: Ablex.

Hornberger, N. (1988). *Bilingual education and language maintenance: A Southern Peruvian Quechua case*. Dordrecht: Foris.

Hornberger, N. (ed.) (1996). *Indigenous literacies in the Americas: Language planning from the bottom up*. Berlin: Mouton.

Jaffe, A. (1999). *Ideologies in action: Language politics on Corsica*. Berlin: Mouton.

Khubchandani, L. M. (1997). *Revisualizing boundaries: A plurilingual ethos*. New Delhi: Sage.

King, K. A. (2001). *Language revitalization processes and practices: Quichua in the Ecuadorian Andes*. Clevedon: Multilingual Matters.

Maddox, B. (2001). Literacy and the market: The economic uses of literacy among the peasantry in north-west Bangladesh. In B. Street (ed.), *Literacy and development: Ethnographic perspectives* (pp. 137–51). London: Routledge.

Marcus, G. & Fischer, M. M. J. (1986). *Anthropology as cultural critique: An experimental moment in the human sciences*. Chicago: University of Chicago Press.

May, S. (1997). Critical ethnography. In N. Hornberger & D. Corson (eds.), *Encyclopedia of language and education. Vol. 8: Research methods in language and education* (pp. 197–206). Dordrecht: Kluwer Academic.

Moore, H. (1996). Language policies as virtual reality: Two Australian examples. *TESOL Quarterly, 30*, 473–98.

Papen, U. (2001). Literacy – your key to a better future? Literacy, reconciliation and development in the National Literacy Programme in Namibia. In

B. Street (ed.), *Literacy and development: Ethnographic perspectives* (pp. 40–60). London: Routledge.

Pattanayak, D. P. (1988) Monolingual myopia and the petals of the Indian lotus: Do many languages divide or unite a nation? In T. Skutnabb-Kangas & J. Cummins (eds.), *Minority education: From shame to struggle* (pp. 379–89). Clevedon: Multilingual Matters.

Ramanathan, V. (1999). "English is here to stay": A critical look at institutional and educational practices in India. *TESOL Quarterly, 33,* 211–32.

Resnick, M. (1993). ESL and language planning in Puerto Rico. *TESOL Quarterly, 27,* 259–73.

Ricento, T. & Hornberger, N. (1996). Unpeeling the onion: Language planning and policy and the ELT professional. *TESOL Quarterly, 30,* 401–27.

Robinson-Pant, A. (2001). Women's literacy and health: Can an ethnographic researcher find the links? In B. Street (ed.), *Literacy and development: Ethnographic perspectives* (pp. 152–70). London: Routledge.

Schiffman, H. (2003). Tongue-tied in Singapore: A language policy for Tamil? *Journal of Language, Identity, and Education, 2,* 105–26.

Stites, R. (2001). Household literacy environments as contexts for development in rural China. In B. Street (ed.), *Literacy and development: Ethnographic perspectives* (pp. 171–87). London: Routledge.

Street, B. (ed.) (2001). *Literacy and development: Ethnographic perspectives.* London: Routledge.

Willis, P. (1977). *Learning to labour: How working class kids get working class jobs.* Manchester: Saxon House.

Wright, M. (2001). More than just chanting: Multilingual literacies, ideology and teaching methodologies in rural Eritrea. In B. Street (ed.), *Literacy and development: Ethnographic perspectives* (pp. 61–77). London: Routledge.

CHAPTER TEN

Linguistic Analyses in Language Policies

Ruth Wodak

This chapter is concerned with linguistic (discourse-analytic) methods for analyzing texts debating, proposing, or criticizing language policies. Before elaborating on linguistic methods and methodologies, which allow systematic empirical research on aspects of language policies and the phenomena subjected to such policies, it is important to define what "language policies" or "language politics" are about.[1]

For this purpose, following Herbert Christ (1995, p. 75), I view *language policy* as every public influence on the communication radius of languages, the sum of those "top-down" and "bottom-up" political initiatives through which a particular language or languages is/are supported in their public validity, their functionality, and their dissemination. Like all policies it is subject to conflict and must regularly be reordered through constant discussion and debate (Christ, 1991, p. 55).

How does one study "policies"? Which research questions lead to or suggest which methodologies? Which genres are important in the study of language policies? Do we study documents proposing policies or implementing them; or do we focus on attitudes to languages and language policies, on people's experiences with language policies, on perceptions of official language policies, on the implementation in school books or curricula, on debates on such policies in the media or in television discussions? There are obviously many relevant research issues and a variety of genres and public spaces where a precise linguistic analysis of oral, visual, or written texts will provide differentiated knowledge on aspects of language politics/policies. Before providing some systematic details about specific genres and adequate modes of linguistic analysis, it is important to reflect on the status and functions a "text" has when analyzing (oral, written, or visual) policies through text and discourse analysis. Figure 10.1 illustrates very well that texts can be analyzed and treated as

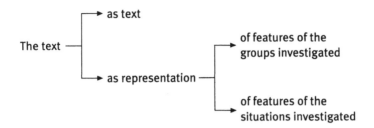

Figure 10.1   Functions of text material
Source: Titscher et al. (2000, p. 32)

representations of facts, realities, and policies; texts can also be used to elicit data, for example through questionnaires or interviews. The latter genres possess a double function: first, to elicit relevant information; second, as part of the interaction with the informants, as dialogue. And finally, texts serve metafunctions as well: to talk about language policies, debate them, question them, etc. In this latter case, we are able to analyze opinions, beliefs, and arguments on language policies.

Specific genres suggest specific methods of inquiry, that is, they might allow for several methodologies but can also exclude others. For example, a television debate could be investigated by conversation analysis, by rhetorical means, or on the foundation of argumentation theory. Functional systemic grammar (FSG) has not developed such precise tools as yet for the analysis of spontaneous interactions, but it does allow for more detailed linguistic information when applied to written or visual texts. Table 10.1 lists some of the linguistic methodologies or tools that could be used for specific genres. If several genres overlap or are connected (hybrid texts), multiple methodologies have to be applied (i.e., stories included in conversations; etc.).

I would like to propose a "multimethodical" approach to issues related to language policies/politics that integrates the analysis of different genres, different public spaces, different methods, and different perspectives or dimensions of the object under investigation (following the principles of "triangulation"). For reasons of space, I will have to neglect ethnographic methods (see chapter 9). I will also not be able to cover the theoretical aspects of the implied research questions (on European language policies), and refer readers to chapters 13 and 19 and to Wodak and de Cillia (2003). Thus, in the following, I will concentrate specifically on the linguistic analysis of focus groups, using the discourse-historical approach (see below).

Table 10.1 Genres and methods

Genres	Methods
Written texts:	Argumentation analysis, Functional Systemic Grammar, multimodal analysis
Oral texts: Speeches	Rhetoric, argumentation analysis, strategic analysis, linguistic pragmatics
Conversations	Conversation analysis, interactive sociolinguistics
Stories	Labov/Waltezkyian analysis, interactive sociolinguistics, narrative analysis
Visual texts:	Multimodal analysis, film analysis, semiotic analysis

Relevant Genres

Which genres are we dealing with when analyzing debates on language policies? These debates occur in very different settings. Politicians rarely mention language or language policies/politics in their speeches (see Wodak, 2003). However, written policy papers of various kinds (treaties, constitutions, proposals, declarations, etc.) contain statements on language policies.

In parliamentary debates, for example, policies and proposals are stated in a declarative mode; in the constitution, we are dealing with legal language; in speeches, politicians use persuasive rhetoric to convince their audience of certain measures, justify some, and reject others. Specific rhetorical tropes and figures are thus preferred, as well as strategies of argumentation, which are typical for political discourse. Finally, in spontaneous conversations in semi-private publics, pragmatic and linguistic rules of dialogues or conversations persist. Even more salient and significantly different linguistic features occur in emails, email lists, or internet forums. (I have not mentioned the specific national, minority, or majority language that is used in a specific text analysis; yet the choice of language has a huge impact on linguistic realizations.[2]

If we, on the other hand, experimentally elicit certain language data which relates to our topic "language policies/language politics," then we have to cope with interviews (semi-structured, narrative, standardized), questionnaires (with open and closed questions), focus groups (on video and on tape), tests, etc.

In contrast to other researchers in the humanities, cultural studies, or social sciences, linguists do not focus only on the contents of such texts, but view interviews, focus group discussions, etc. as communicative *interactions*. The whole interview, for example, has to be considered as one coherent text. Interviews consist of question-and-answer sequences; hence, not only are the answers of the interviewees to be analyzed, but also the interview as a certain type of conversation with features of this genre. The specific wording of the question implies certain modes of possible answers. The same is true for all the other standardized techniques.

Summary: Research Design and Implementation

Before elaborating the analysis of focus group discussions, I list the most important steps in investigating language policies (steps which are recursive) in order to embed the specific methodology in a broader research design (see Titscher et al., 2000, pp. 31ff):

1 Formulation of *research questions*.
2 *Ethnographic research*: interdisciplinary, historical, sociological, sociopolitical *research on the specific context* of the debates/conversations, policy papers, etc. – *pilot study*.
3 *Literature review*.
4 Formulation of *hypotheses: specification* of research questions.
5 *Operationalization of research questions*: important decisions about empirical methodologies have to be taken which seem adequate to operationalize the research questions. This is the point where the *data sampling* is decided upon, and certain methods of data sampling imply certain genres of text (see above). If possible, a *multimethodical approach* suggests itself: the same or similar phenomena are viewed from different perspectives. Such an approach allows for more differentiated results. Not only one but several dimensions of the object(s) under investigation could be analyzed, interpreted, understood, and hopefully

explained (see Weiss & Wodak, 2003; Wodak, 1996). Thus, quantitative and qualitative analyses complement each other.

6   Selection of *categories for the analysis of texts* reflecting certain methods of text analysis, the genre under investigation, the context and setting, and of course the research questions or hypotheses. For example, choosing the category of "inclusion/ exclusion" implies analyzing certain linguistic features and units, depending on the genre, etc.

7   Choice of *linguistic units* for the analysis of texts or discourses. These units are not independent of a theory of grammar or discourse/text theory (see table 10.1 above). A specific choice should be explicitly made on pragmatic grounds, because some linguistic methods and units are more *adequate* than others for the investigation of specific research questions (see Meyer, 2001; Titscher et al., 2000, pp. 226ff).

8   *Qualitative and possibly quantitative text analysis,* reflecting choices made in (5) and (6). The results might influence (1), (2), and (4), and require a rethinking of those items.

9   *Analysis and interpretation* of results in relationship to (1).

10 *Application of results and dissemination.*

The Discourse-Historical Approach

The *discourse-historical approach,* committed to critical discourse analysis (CDA), adheres to the sociophilosophical orientation of Critical Theory. CDA is not concerned with evaluating what is "right" or "wrong"; in my view (in contrast to some), it should try to make choices at each point in the research itself, and should make the object under investigation transparent. It should also justify theoretically why certain interpretations of discursive events seem more valid than others.

One methical way for critical discourse analysts to minimize the risk of being biased is to follow the principle of triangulation. Thus, one of the most salient distinguishing features of the discourse-historical approach is its endeavor to work with different approaches, multimethodically, and on the basis of a variety of empirical data as well as background information (e.g., Wodaket al, 1998, 1999).

In investigating historical, organizational, and political topics and texts, such as debates on language policies, the discourse-historical approach attempts to integrate a large quantity of available knowledge about the historical sources and the background of the social and political fields in which discursive "events" are embedded. Further, it analyzes the historical dimension of discursive actions by exploring the ways in which particular genres of discourse are subject to diachronic change (Kovács & Wodak, 2003; Wodak et al., 1990, 1994). Lastly, and most importantly, this is not only viewed as "information": at this point we integrate social theories to be able to explain the so-called context.

The notion of "discourse"

In accordance with other approaches devoted to CDA, the discourse-historical approach perceives both written and spoken language as a form of social practice (Fairclough & Wodak, 1997). A discourse is a way of signifying a particular domain of social practice from a particular perspective (Fairclough, 1995, p. 14). We assume a dialectical relationship between particular discursive practices and the specific fields of action (including situations, institutional frames, and social structures) in which they are embedded. The situational, institutional, and social settings shape and affect discourses, while discourses influence discursive as well as non-discursive social and political processes and actions. In other words, discourses as linguistic social practices can be seen as constituting non-discursive and discursive social practices and, at the same time, as being constituted by them.

In the following discussion I would like to make a distinction between "discourse" and "text," following Lemke's interesting approach (Lemke, 1995), further elaborated by Girnth (1996). *Discourse* can be understood as a complex bundle of simultaneous and sequential interrelated linguistic acts, which manifest themselves within and across the social fields of action as thematically interrelated semiotic, oral, or written tokens, very often as "texts," that belong to specific semiotic types, that is, genres (see Girnth, 1996). The most salient feature of the definition of a "discourse" is the macro-topic, like "language policies." Interdiscursivity can be detected when, for example, an argument (taken from the discourse on immigration restrictions) is used while arguing for other policies to combat unemployment. Each macro-topic allows for many sub-topics: "unemployment" thus covers sub-topics like "market," "trade unions," "social welfare," "global market," "hire

Fields of action				
Law-making political procedure	**Formation of public opinion and self-presentation**	**Party-internal development of an informed opinion**	**Political advertising, marketing, and propaganda**	**Political executive and administration**	**Political control**
		Genres		
• Laws • Bills • Amendments • Speeches and contributions of MPs • Regulations • Recommendations • Prescriptions • Guidelines, etc.	• Press releases • Press conferences • Interviews • Talk shows • Lectures and contributions to conferences • Articles, books • Commemorative speeches • Inaugural speeches, etc.	• Party programs, declarations, statements, and speeches of principle • Speeches on party conventions, etc.	• Election programs • Slogans, speeches in election campaigns • Announcements • Posters • Election brochures • Direct mailings • Fliers, etc.	• Decisions (approval/ rejection of applications for asylum) • Inaugural speeches • Coalition papers, speeches of ministers/heads • Governmental answers to parliamentary questions, etc.	• Declarations of opposition parties • Parliamentary questions • Speeches of MPs • Petitions for a referendum, press releases of the opposition parties, etc.

Discourse topic 1   Discourse topic 2   Discourse topic 3   Discourse topic 4   Discourse topic 5   Discourse topic 6

Figure 10.2 Selected dimensions of discourse as social practice
Source: Wodak & Meyer (2001)

and fire policies," and many more. Discourses are open and hybrid and not closed systems at all; new sub-topics can be created, and intertextuality and interdiscursivity allow for new fields of action. Discourses are realized in both genres and texts.

Texts can be conceived as materially durable products of linguistic actions (see Ehlich, 1983; Graefen, 1997, p. 26; Reisigl, 2000). A *genre* may be characterized, following Norman Fairclough, as the conventionalized, more or less schematically fixed use of language associated with a particular activity, as "a socially ratified way of using language in connection with a particular type of social activity" (Fairclough, 1995, p. 14).

Fields of action (Girnth, 1996) may be understood as segments of the respective societal "reality," which contribute to constituting and shaping the "frame" of discourse. The spatio-metaphorical distinction among different fields of action means a distinction among different functions or socially institutionalized aims of discursive practices. Thus, for example, in the area of political action, we distinguish between the functions of legislation, self-presentation, the manufacturing of public opinion, developing party-internal consent, advertising and vote-getting, governing as well as executing, and controlling as well as expressing (opposing) dissent (see figure 10.2). A discourse about a specific topic can find its starting point within one field of action and proceed through another one. Discourses and discourse topics "spread" to different fields and discourses. They cross between fields, overlap, refer to each other or are in some other way sociofunctionally linked with each other.

We can represent the relationship between fields of action, genres, and discourse topics with the example of the area of language policies below (see Wodak, 2001, p. 68). Our triangulatory approach is based on a concept of "context" which takes into account four levels. The first one is descriptive, while the other three are part of our theories dealing with context:

1 the immediate, language or text-internal co-text;
2 the intertextual and interdiscursive relationship between utterances, texts, genres, and discourses;
3 the extra-linguistic social or sociological variables and institutional frames of a specific "context of situation" (middle-range theories);
4 the broader sociopolitical and historical contexts, which the discursive practices are embedded in and related to (grand theories).

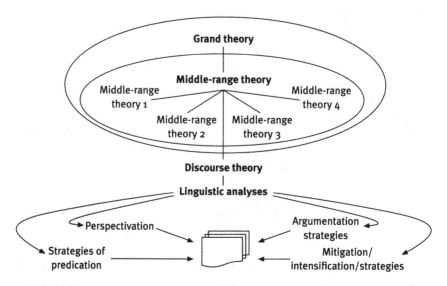

Figure 10.3   Levels of theories and linguistic analysis
Source: Wodak & Meyer (2001, p. 69)
See table 10.2 for details of the linguistic analysis.

See figure 10.3.

In our examples, I will make the sequential analysis transparent, following the categories of the discourse-historical approach.

The specific discourse-analytical approach is three-dimensional: after (1) establishing the specific *contents* or *topics* of a specific discourse, (2) the *discursive strategies* (including argumentation strategies) are investigated. Then (3), the *linguistic means* (as types) and the specific, context-dependent *linguistic realizations* (as tokens) are analyzed (see Reisigl & Wodak, 2001, pp. 44ff, for details).

Categories of analysis

In the following, I will describe some of the discourse-analytical tools useful in the analysis of discourses on language policies. There are several discursive elements and strategies which deserve special attention. We could orient ourselves to five simple but not at all randomly selected questions for the analysis of "Us" and "Them":

1 How are persons named and referred to linguistically?
2 What traits, characteristics, qualities, and features are attributed to them?
3 By means of what arguments and argumentation schemes do specific persons or social groups try to justify and legitimize the inclusion/exclusion of others?
4 From what perspective or point of view are these labels, attributions, and arguments expressed?
5 Are the respective utterances articulated overtly? Are they intensified or are they mitigated?

According to these questions, we are especially interested in five types of discursive strategies, which are all involved in positive self- and negative other-representation. These discursive strategies (and also others elaborated in Wodak et al., 1999) serve the justification or legitimization of inclusion/exclusion and of constructions of identities. By *strategy* we generally mean a (more or less intentional) plan of practices (including discursive practices) adopted to achieve a particular social, political, psychological, or linguistic goal. See table 10.2.

Debating Language Policies: Genres and Methods

"Nexus" of language policies: stating the problem

Let us start with a concrete example of research on language policies in the European Union. In many public spaces, debates on language policies have evolved. For example, the speeches of politicians in the member states deal with a number of issues related to European identities, where languages play a major role. European citizens discuss issues of language policy quite explicitly in a discussion forum on the EU website (www.europa.eu.int). Media (the press as well as television) report on statements of politicians, thus recontextualizing them in specific and salient ways. Finally, debates in national and the European parliaments on residence permits, migration, and asylum, as well as security policies, include numerous turns on language policies on national, regional, local, and transnational levels. Websites of grass-roots media or media in minority languages discuss these issues as well. Schools and other educational institutions propose

Table 10.2 Discursive strategies for positive self- and negative other-representation

Strategy	Objectives	Devices
Referential / nomination	Construction of in-groups and out-groups	Membership categorization Biological, naturalizing, and depersonalizing metaphors and metonymies Synecdoches (*pars pro toto, totum pro parte*)
Predication	Labeling social actors more or less positively or negatively, deprecatorily or appreciatively	Stereotypical, evaluative attributions of negative or positive traits Implicit and explicit predicates
Argumentation	Justification of positive or negative attributions	Topoi used to justify inclusion or exclusion, discrimination or preferential treatment
Perspectivation, framing, or discourse representation	Expressing involvement Positioning speaker's point of view	Reporting, description, narration, or quotation of events and utterances
Intensification, mitigation	Modifying the epistemic status of a proposition	Intensifying or mitigating the illocutionary force of utterances

textbooks for language learning; curricula have to adapt to new languages spoken in the respective countries. And most certainly, we could think of many other settings where debates on language policies occur, such as private contexts (families, relationships, etc.).

All these topical discourses overlap; they form a *nexus* on language policies (see Scollon & Scollon, 2004); or, to speak in Foucault's terms, we are confronted with a flow of discourses, which imposes certain constraints and regulations on our perceptions and actions (see Wodak, 2004).

A systematic analysis of the most important arguments for and against multilingual language policies (or for and against a lingua franca, such as English) would be a relevant research question. If we wanted to know which groups of European citizens think in what way(s) about such policies in the various member states, and in different professions, consistent proposals could be formulated, taking into account such views. Moreover, it is of relevance what the elites in politics, the media, and education suggest and how these suggestions coincide (or don't coincide) with the attitudes and opinions of ordinary citizens. In this chapter, I will restrict myself to the analysis of semi-public discussions in focus groups.

Multimethodical approach

Semi-public genres

After having analyzed official statements, it is important to investigate other public spaces and settings, where more spontaneous debates occur. On the one hand, television debates suggest themselves, because invited speakers tend to get involved in a debate; on the other hand, focus-group discussions could be set up to explore reception processes and to trigger certain topic-oriented discussions (see Benke & Wodak, 2003; de Cillia, Reisigl, & Wodak, 1999; Kovács & Wodak, 2003; Scollon, 2001). It should be emphasized that, although staged media discussions and experimental focus groups have some similarities, they have to be viewed as very different genres: a television debate is part of our daily life, while a focus group is set up as an experiment. In both cases, the moderator of the discussion is the most influential person because she or he determines the macro-topics and is allowed to interrupt and to start or end turns. Of course, depending on the specific media event, the rules can be more or less restrictive.

Discussions or debates are conversations or face-to-face interactions. The organization of conversation follows certain rules, which both conversation analysis and pragmatics have succeeded in describing and categorizing precisely over the last decades (see Schiffrin, 1994; Schiffrin, Tannen, & Hamilton, 2001). In such cases, the methods selected depend on the specific research question. In this example, the focus is on arguments pro and contra certain language policies.

Most importantly, linguists view the whole discussion or debate as one text. The single turns depend on each other, conflicts evolve throughout the development of the whole debate, and group dynamics play a decisive role. The first important step in analyzing such discussions or debates, after having transcribed the video or tape, is an attempt to lay out a semantic network. Such a semantic network

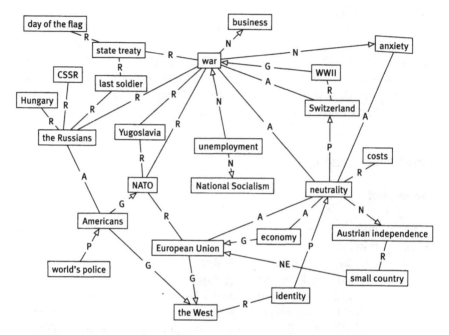

Figure 10.4 Semantic network of the family focus group, discussing "neutrality and NATO" in Austria, 1998
Source: Benke & Wodak (2003, p. 403)

heuristically grasps the flow of topics in such a conversation and the influence of certain speakers (see figure 10.4).

The semantic network describes the thematic connections that were made in the discussion of the focus group. While constructing the networks, we read the transcripts sequentially and observed various topics and their argumentative development. We used the text analysis program ATLAS.ti for the description. For each topic (of sufficient relevance and importance) identified, we introduced a new node and drew lines showing the discursive connections (links) between the existing topics. ATLAS.ti provides certain predefined relationships, but in principle, it is possible to define further relationships if necessary. When constructing the networks, we used the relationships offered, and in case of doubt – and for all other cases – the generic relationship. The following relationships were applied in the network:

- Symmetrical relationships A (for antagonism, where x is opposed to) and R (for relationships, where x is related to y, of the generic type).

- Asymmetric relationships N (for cause, where x is a cause of y), P (for property, where x is a property of y), G (for part of or kind of, where x is a part of or kind of y), and NE (for needs, where x needs y).

Such a diagram enables the researcher to formulate first hypotheses about the dynamics of the interaction and the flow of arguments. Of course, it would be possible to analyze a whole set of linguistic features. In our case, we restrict ourselves to the strategies listed above in table 10.2 by discerning macro- and sub-topics, important arguments, the co-construction of meanings, influential speakers, opposing positions, and the group dynamics. Such group discussions allow for testing the opinions on certain suggestions, quotations, or positions of the elite. For example, a quotation from a newspaper could be used as a triggering question. The participants of the group start debating the meanings of this quotation, while stating their own opinions.

Sequences sometimes contain co-constructions of certain concepts; that is, the participants co-construct the notion of "national identity" or "linguistic identity" together, as in the following example involving Slovenian-speaking Austrians, Carinthians, and Germans (M = male, F = female, MO = moderator).

F4:   [. . .] well for the first time I somehow: realized that Austria somehow is something different when I was in France for the first time then I was eighteen – and when I was working in a French family and: they then – / the first question was "are you German?" and I "no no I am Austrian" and the others "thank God" you know? – and then it somehow happened – "aha: thank God:" yes – just like that – see? – so. that / I / I can somehow only describe experiences in this way: umm – so. "well so there must be something" you know? – and umm I now simply think on my part / I mean it is / I live in this country and what now maybe makes me so: consciously Austrian after all is simply this – that I / it's not only politics and the culture which influence me in this country where I live but that I also try: to stick my oar in the politics and culture of this country and to get critically involved, you know?

MO: mhm

F4:   I don't know that is – now just a first somehow / I don't know / theoretical: definition for myself and I also have a lot of that – emotional stuff as well

MO: umm – okay

F5: My: my name is XXX ((name of F5)) – now comes the first now I think / yes some say what a kind of Carinthian one is. yes and what kind of Carinthian am I? right? am I: A Slovenian:-speaking Carinthian? well I would say – Slovenian / I am a Carinthian Slovene, right? – and then: / really a Slovenian-speaking Carinthian – but I also speak German, don't I? – only, you're already defining yourself this way

MO: why?

F5: right? – because – if someone says just Carinthian: one thinks that he can only speak: German "only" in inverted commas now

MO: mhm

[...]

F5: really and as to my being Austrian – umm – I'd say I am / well I like to be Austrian – I have been fed on it – since I was a small child one is taught that in primary school: "Austria this is my country dadada" well: that's because – really I am Austrian that's what I like to be it is completely natural for me – really.

MO: right – o / okay – if: – / yes?

M2: the more difficult this is the simpler the solution ((laughs)) as everything that:

F5: no

M2: you take in from the beginning comes into my mind and which is so complicated in the end ((laughs))

F5: yes. maybe / umm yes. I could add – umm – the idea of delimiting from Germany which: has been mentioned – I've never really thought about this problem in this way – well I'd say – the delimitation German not: – Germany that for me is further away – well Austria right. – it is interesting

M1: the delimitation is only / – it's / is only arbitrary or that is

F5: well well

M1: only an arbitrary delimitation: from Germany I'd say

MO: yes? – mhm

F5: well what I mean now in my mind well – mhm

M1: because I myself as: – / well because I see / I see Austria rather – so as a whole it is a political construction – nothing more – because I can't / for instance if I take the delimitation from Germany I can also: easily: include Bavaria in Austria can't I? I could also: add South Tyrol to Austria – but only: bec / well because of the: present borders this is not the case – but this doesn't intrinsically make any sense for me: why a border is in a certain place or if there is no border

MO: could one also say that Slovenia for example could also: be added to Austria?

M1: yes o / of course and also: I don't know

MO: – well in the same sense – / well because /

M1: well in this sense you can even include the whole of Kranska Gora to Austria, or Ljubljana – I think

MO: mhm

F1: I had at that time /

M1: because the / the thing surely not – the: / it's the regions that are so precious – for example Carinthia – I think – or / or Salzburg / or Upper Austria – I don't know or / or – umm – the / umm – umm – the area around Königsee is / belongs to Germany they belong so smoothly to Austria / umm – as maybe it is also the other way round –

M3: umm but there you have – you'll instantly have / umm I think a very big problem that's the problem of borders: principally the question is also: how did a border come about and how did they actually come into existence – I mean if you look at the history of Austria – then it happens like this doesn't it? Well in one place it separates in another it converges and meanders here and there and at the moment it is where we have it now

MO: mhm

M2: thus this is I think a very difficult question – umm if one wants to say what else one can – umm count as a part of Austria – I think one / one once: used to include umm the whole of Northern Italy to Austria down to Trieste – and: right now one doesn't you see well this for me is / this is a very – delicate story somehow that's how it seems to me.

This passage is an extract from a focus-group discussion recorded in Carinthia, one of the nine Austrian regions. Two participants explicitly express their perception/definition of Austria. F4 previously talked about the difficulties she had feeling primarily "Carinthian," although "rationally being of course . . . primarily an Austrian." She defines her Austrian identity in terms of delimitation from Germany (experience abroad, a topic which was discussed earlier in this group) and in terms of political and cultural socialization, and she introduces the element of active political participation as a constitutive component of her Austrian identity. Furthermore, she refers rather vaguely to the importance of "that emotional stuff." Modifying particles such as "somehow," "so," and "maybe" occur frequently, as do mitigating formulations, including verbs expressing beliefs and opinions, and hedges such as "like that," "I think," "I mean," "I don't know," which generally emphasize subjectivity and uncertainty of the speaker.

Participant F5 starts by clarifying her regional (Carinthian) identity. However, she is not at all sure whether she is primarily "Carinthian" or "Slovene," and finally decides on the order "Carinthian Slovene [. . .] and then [. . .] Slovenian-speaking Carinthian," a most interesting sequence from the point of view of language policies. She argues that bilingualism is an essential factor for her, as "just Carinthian" means that one "can only speak German." Here, the lexical or conceptual differentiation made between differing Carinthian identities, such as "Carinthian Slovenes," "Slovenian-speaking Carinthians," and "just Carinthians," is most relevant for the possibility of co-constructing a new definition. F5 defines her Austrian identity on the basis of emotional attachment and socialization through school. At the same time she denies that the distinction between Austria and Germany might be a problem for her, if she considered it rationally.

M1, taking this up and interpreting it literally, comments on the ostensible arbitrariness of the Austrian–German borders (*topoi* of history and definition) and claims that both Bavaria and South Tyrol could also be added to Austria. This sequence could be interpreted ironically as well; however, M1 does position himself in contrast to F5. The criteria for attributing definitions of borders or nation-states seem to be aspects of language use as well as historical roots and cultural characteristics.

Asked by MO (the moderator) whether this also applies to Slovenia, M1 agrees, but continues his argument by remarking that "it's the regions that are so precious," and offers another example which demonstrates the similarities between Austria and Germany ("the area around Königssee" could belong to Austria). (A frequent move in argumentation consists in using examples which can be generalized.) All in all, M1 appears to adhere to a cultural and linguistic national-ism, which he formulates rather cautiously (modified by mitigation strategies: use of particles, of the subjunctive, and of verbs of opinion and conjecture such as "I think," "I know").

At this point, a potential conflict, in particular because of the presence of the Slovenian-speaking Austrians, is prevented by interventions of other group members. M3 generalizes the issue of identity as a completely abstract "problem of borders." His whole statement is characterized by vagueness, which is a typical conflict-avoiding strategy: vagueness allows many readings and identifications. M2 finds the question as to what "one" may allocate to Austria and what not "very difficult." By using the impersonal "one," a predicational strategy, M2 attempts to bring the discussion to a more general level, thus defusing the "somehow very delicate story." This extract clearly shows how group members co-construct relevant concepts in focus-group discussions, such as national and ethnic identities. It also shows, however, that potentially controversial positions may be mitigated or even negotiated through group intervention. A potential conflict between the concept of state-based nationalism and a cultural or linguistic nationalism, which, *inter alia*, is propagated in the shape of regionalism, is prevented by group control. Linguistically, this passage is characterized by frequent use of mitigation strategies and many argumentative frames (*topoi*), such as *topoi* of definition, authority, history, etc. It is also obvious that a co-constructing process is underway, because no explicit "we" occurs in this extract (only M3 uses "we," which once refers to the discussion group and once to the Austrians), which points to the subjectivity of all positions and to possibly expected debates and compromises.

The method of analyzing focus-group discussions, although certainly tedious and time-consuming, thus presents us with very important data on opinion-making, media reception, and everyday life experiences. Group discussions, although non- representative on a statistical scale, display a microcosm of everyday life experiences that are very difficult to explore in less dynamic contexts or texts. The methods elaborated in this section can also be used while analyzing authentic conversations tape-recorded on the street or elsewhere.

Conclusions

The examples in this chapter illustrate the vast complexity of texts and discourses: each quotation can be analyzed in much more detailed ways, while taking specific research questions into account. The extensive fieldwork and discourse analysis involved, though time-consuming, allow us to understand and explain the latent and explicit meanings and functions of certain utterances. Through the integration of the context and important theoretical approaches from linguistics as well as from neighboring disciplines, we are able to interpret utterances in a much more differentiated way than by applying either quantitative methods, such as content analysis, or by focusing only on one linguistic unit without considering the structure of the whole text and the flow of argumentation.

The detailed analysis which could only be summarized here points to the ambivalence and to the "ideological dilemmas" to be found when debating language policies. More specifically, the co-construction of meanings and the recontextualization of arguments in different public spaces were emphasized. These important aspects of language policies and debates on language policies have to be taken into consideration not only by researchers but also by policy-makers. We hope that practitioners (teachers, politicians, social workers, etc.) will come to understand that, as Rudolf de Cillia suggests, "languages are far more than just media of communication . . . the mother tongue is the central symbol of individual and collective identity, a symbol which represents belonging to a certain ethnic group, to a certain language community" (de Cillia, 2002, p. 8).

Annotated Bibliography

Blommaert, J. & Verschueren, J. (1998). *Debating diversity: Analysing the discourse of tolerance*. London: Routledge.
The authors conducted data analysis of a large corpus of texts from newspapers, research reports, and government-sponsored anti-racism campaigns and training programs in Belgium. Although clear differences exist between the rhetoric of radical racist and nationalist groups and the rhetoric of politicians and government officials on immigration and immigrants in Belgium, the authors found remarkable similarities and consistencies in the underlying ideologies. This is a groundbreaking study in the analysis of immigration, racism, and nationalism in the Western world.

Santa, Ana, O. (2002). *Brown tide rising: Metaphors of Latinos in contemporary American public discourse*. Austin, TX: University of Texas Press.

This book applies the insights and methods from cognitive metaphor theory in the analysis of a large data set of articles from the *Los Angeles Times* and other media. Santa Ana found that negative portrayals of Latinos as invaders, outsiders, burdens, parasites, diseases, animals, and weeds in newspaper articles contributed to negative attitudes toward Latinos and to the passage of three anti-Latino referenda in California during the 1990s. This book is an excellent example of the use of triangulation of data in research concerning societal debates which involve language, race, and ethnicity.

Titscher, S., Wodak, R., Meyer, M., & Vetter, E. (2000). *Methods of text and discourse analysis*. London: Sage.
This book summarizes 14 different methodologies of text and discourse analysis. The best applications for each method are explained and examples are provided. This is a very useful book for linguists and social scientists analyzing discourses and texts for different means. Specifically, the choice of methods according to genre is also taken into account.

Wodak, R., de Cillia, R., Reisigl, M., & Liebhart, K. (1999). *The discursive construction of national identity*. Edinburgh: Edinburgh University Press. The discursive construction of national identities is studied through various genres (speeches, interviews, focus groups, media reports). In this way, the flow of arguments and topoi from one public space to another can be analyzed in detail. The methodology of the discourse-historical approach in CDA is precisely presented. The question of national and transnational language policies is thoroughly discussed.

Discussion Questions

1 What are the benefits of using focus groups in language-policy research? What are the possible drawbacks of this methodology?
2 Why would it be important to analyze different genres in different settings when studying language policies?
3 What are the implications of a more qualitative approach to studying language policies? Are the results obtained by such methodologies "representative"?

NOTES

I would like to thank my colleagues Rudolf de Cillia and Brigitta Busch for their important comments; moreover, I am very grateful to the Collegium Budapest, Budapest, for the opportunity of being invited to work there in September and December 2003, and to the Leverhulme Trust for granting me a visiting professorship to the University of East Anglia, Norwich, UK, in the spring term 2004 to finish this research. I would also like to thank the editor of the volume, Thomas Ricento, for his patience, comments, and support.

1　At this point, it must be stated that very few systematic overviews exist of the linguistic analysis of data related to language policies (see Blommaert & Verschueren, 1998; Busch, 2001a, 2001b, 2003; Clyne, 2003; de Cillia, 2003; Heller, 2003; Kettemann, de Cillia, & Haller, 2002; Wodak et al., 1998, 1999). Of course, the genres and linguistic data related to the topic of "language policies" are not different from other debates on other topics; thus the "tools" and methodologies described in the following books could all be used for the analysis of texts related to "language policies" as well: Fairclough (2003); Scollon and Scollon (2003); Titscher et al. (1998, 2000); Wodak and Meyer (2001, 2003).

2　For features of written genres in different languages, see Bellier (2002); Clyne (2003); Gruber et al. (2003).

REFERENCES

Bellier, I. (2002). European identity, institutions and languages in the context of the enlargement. *Journal of Language and Politics*, *1*, 85–114.

Benke, G. & Wodak, R. (2003). We are facing a new order in Europe: Neutrality versus NATO. In A. Kovács & R. Wodak (eds.), *NATO, neutrality and national identity: The case of Austria and Hungary* (pp. 281–310). Vienna: Böhlau.

Blommaert, J. & Verschueren, J. (1998). *Debating diversity: Analysing the discourse of tolerance*. London: Routledge.

Busch, B. (2001a). Slovenian in Carinthia: A sociolinguistic survey. In G. Extra & D. Gorter (eds.), *The other languages of Europe: Demographic, sociolinguistics, and educational perspectives* (pp. 119–37). Clevedon: Multilingual Matters.

Busch, B. (2001b). Grenzvermessungen: Sprachen und Medien in Zentral-, Südost- und Osteuropa. In B. Busch, B. Hipfl, & K. Robins, (eds.), *Bewegte Identitäten: Medien in transkulturellen Kontexten* (pp. 145–73). Klagenfurt/Celovec: Drava.

Busch, B. (2003). *Sprachen im Disput: Eine sprachenpolitische Studie zu Medien in multilingualen Gesellschaften*. Klagenfurt/Celovec: Drava.

Christ, H. (1991). *Fremdsprachenunterricht für das Jahr 2000*. Sprachenpolitische Betrachtungen zum Lehren und Lernen fremder Sprachen. Tübingen: Niemeyer.

Christ, H. (1995). Sprachenpolitische Perspektiven. In K.-R. Bausch, H. Christ, & H.-J. Krumm, *Handbuch Fremdsprachenunterricht. Vol. 3: Uberarbeitete und erweiterte Auflage* (revised edn) (pp. 75–81). Tübingen and Basel: Niemeyer.

Clyne, M. (2003). Towards inter-cultural communication in Europe without linguistic homogenization. In R. de Cillia, H. J. Krumm, & R. Wodak (eds.), *Die Kosten der Mehrsprachigkeit: Globalisierung und sprachliche Vielfalt/The Cost of Multilingualism: Globalisation and Linguistic Diversity* (pp. 39–48). Vienna: Austrian Academy of Sciences.

de Cillia, R. (2002). Fremdsprachenunterricht in Österreich nach 1945. In E. Lechner (ed.), *Formen und funktionen des fremdsprachenunterrichts im Europa des 20. Jahrhunderts* (Bildungsgeschichte und europäische Identität, vol. 3) (pp. 115–28). Frankfurt: Kohlhammer.

de Cillia, R. (2003). Grundlagen und Tendenzen der europäischen Sprachenpolitik. In M. Mokre, G. Weiss, & R. Bauböck (eds.), *Europas Identitäten: Mythen, Konflikte, Konstruktionen* (pp. 231–56). Frankfurt and New York: Campus.

de Cillia, R., Reisigl, M., & Wodak, R. (1999). The discursive construction of national identities. *Discourse and Society, 10*, 149–73.

Ehlich, K. (1983). Text und sprachliches Handeln: Die Entstehung von Texten aus dem Bedürfnis nach Überlieferung. In A. Assmann, J. Assmann, & C. Hardmeier (eds.), *Schrift und Gedächtnis* (Beiträge zur Archäologie der literarischen Kommunikation) (pp. 24–43). Munich: Fink.

Fairclough, N. (1995). *Critical discourse analysis: The critical study of language* (Language in Social Life Series). London: Longman.

Fairclough, N. (2003). *Analysing discourse: Text analysis for social research.* London: Routledge.

Fairclough, N. & Wodak, R. (1997). Critical discourse analysis. In T. A. van Dijk (ed.), *Introduction to discourse analysis* (pp. 258–84). London: Sage.

Girnth, H. (1996). Texte im politischen Diskurs: Ein Vorschlag zur diskursorientierten Beschreibung von Textsorten. *Muttersprache, 106*, 66–80.

Graefen, G. (1997). *Der wissenschaftliche Artikel: Textart und Textorganisation.* Frankfurt: Lang.

Gruber, H., Muntigl, P., Reisigl, M., Rheindorf, M. U., & Wetschanow, K. (2003). *Genre, Habitus und wissenschaftliches Schreiben.* Project report, Vienna University.

Heller, M. (ed.) (2003). *Linguistic minorities and modernity: A sociolinguistic ethnography.* London: Longman.

Kettemann, B., de Cillia, R., & Haller, M. (2002). Innovation im Fremdsprachenunterricht – am Beispiel der im Rahmen der Aktion "Europasiegel für innovative Sprachenprojekte" in Österreich von 1998–2000 eingereichten Projekte. Unpublished report, Universities of Vienna and Graz.

Kovács, A. & Wodak, R. (eds.) (2003). *NATO, neutrality and national identity: The case of Austria and Hungary.* Vienna: Böhlau.

Lemke, J. (1995). *Textual politics: Discourse and social dynamics*. London: Taylor and Francis.

Meyer, M. (2001). Between theory, method, and politics: Positioning of the approaches to CDA. In R. Wodak & M. Meyer (eds.), *Methods of critical discourse analysis* (pp. 14–31). London: Sage.

Reisigl, M. (2000). Literarische Texte als heuristische Quellen und kunstfertige Herausforderung für die sprachwissenschaftliche Analyse gesprochener Sprache – Eine Fallstudie am Beispiel von Friedrich Glauser. In O. Panagl & W. Weiss (eds.), *Dichtung und Politik* (pp. 237–319). Vienna: Böhlau.

Reisigl, M. & Wodak, R. (2001). *Discourse and Discrimination*. London: Routledge.

Schiffrin, D. (1994). *Approaches to discourse*. Oxford: Blackwell.

Schiffrin, D., Tannen, D., & Hamilton, H. (eds.) (2001). *The handbook of discourse analysis*. Oxford: Blackwell.

Scollon, R. (2001). *Mediated discourse: The nexus of practice*. London: Routledge.

Scollon, R. & Scollon, S. (2003). *Discourses in place: Language in the material world*. London: Routledge.

Scollon, R. & Scollon, S. (2004). *Nexus analysis: Discourse and the emerging internet*. London: Routledge.

Titscher, S., Wodak, R., Meyer, M., & Vetter, E. (1998). *Methoden der Textanalyse*. Wiesbaden: Westdeutscher Verlag.

Titscher, S., Wodak, R., Meyer, M., &Vetter, E. (2000). *Methods of text and discourse analysis*. London: Sage. (English translation of Titscher et al., 1998, revised edn.)

Weiss, G. & Wodak, R. (eds.) (2003). *Critical discourse analysis: Theory and interdisciplinarity*. Basingstoke: Palgrave Macmillan.

Wodak, R. (1996). *Disorders of discourse*. London: Longman.

Wodak, R. (2001). What CDA is about: A summary of its history, important concepts and its developments. In R. Wodak & M. Meyer (eds.), *Methods of critical discourse analysis* (pp. 1–13). London: Sage.

Wodak, R. (2003). Auf der Suche nach einer neuen Europäischen Identität. In R. de Cillia, H. J. Krumm, & R. Wodak (eds.), *DieKosten derMehrsprachigkeit: Globalisierung und sprachliche Vielfalt/The cost of multilingualism: globalisation and linguistic diversity* (pp. 125–34). Vienna: Austrian Academy of Sciences.

Wodak, R. (2004). Critical discourse analysis. In J. Seale (ed.), *Handbook of methods in the social sciences* (pp. 197–214). London: Sage.

Wodak, R. & de Cillia, R. (2003). Sprachliche Identitäten: Multikulturelles und multilinguales Erbe. Und welche Zukunft? In M. Csáky & P. Stachel (eds.), *Mehrdeutigkeit: Die Ambivalenz von Gedächtnis und Erinnerung* (pp. 153–77). Vienna: Passagen.

Wodak, R. & Meyer, M. (eds.) (2001). *Methods of critical discourse analysis*. London: Sage.

Wodak, R. & Meyer, M. (2003). *Métodos de análisis crítico del discurso*. Barcelona: Gedisa. (Spanish translation of Wodak and Meyer, 2001.)

Wodak, R., de Cillia, R., Reisigl, M., & Liebhart, K. (1999). *The discursive construction of national identity*. Edinburgh: Edinburgh University Press.

Wodak, R., Menz, F., Mitten, R., & Stern, F. (1994). *Die Sprachen der Vergangenheiten: Offentliches Gedenken in österreichischen und deutschen Medien*. Frankfurt: Suhrkamp.

Wodak, R., de Cillia, R., Reisigl, M., Liebhart, K., Hofstätter, K., & Kargl, M. (1998). *Zur diskursiven Konstruktion nationaler Identität*. Frankfurt: Suhrkamp.

Wodak, R., Pelikan, J., Nowak, P., Gruber, H., de Cillia, R., & Mitten, R. (1990). *Wir sind alle unschuldige Täter!* (Diskurshistorische Studien zum Nachkriegsantisemitismus). Frankfurt: Suhrkamp.

www.europa.eu.int

CHAPTER ELEVEN

Geolinguistic Analysis in Language Policy

Don Cartwright

Geolinguistics seeks to answer the questions "what, where, when, who and why" of language (van der Merwe, 1993, p. 23). Geolinguistic analysis involves the investigation of historical processes that have contributed to the development of current patterns of human contact and interaction between and among different cultural groups. It also involves the investigation of the patterns of movement of people and the concomitant shifts in regional ethnic composition. Field research will be conducted into language use in the local community to uncover and analyze places (domains) where a minority language is used or not used. Geolinguistic analysis operates on the premise that cultural domains are significant to the retention of ethnic identity, and as cultural space between ethnic groups erodes through domain sharing as opposed to domain exclusion, it is possible to anticipate demands for cultural protection. This protection may be sought through ratification of language rights and the expansion of domains for exclusive language use as a means of fortifying one (important) element of the group's eroding cultural identity (Veltman, 1977).

To investigate how a community identified by mother tongue could survive as a viable group, Giles, Bourhis, and Taylor (1977) developed a model that they designated "Structural Analysis of Ethnolinguistic Vitality." *Vitality* was defined as that which makes a group behave as a distinctive and active collective entity in inter-group situations. It was assumed that ethnolinguistic minorities that have little or no group vitality will eventually cease to exist as a distinctive society. The more vitality a linguistic group has, the greater the likelihood it will survive and develop as a collective entity even when it is in contact with a majority that has a different mother tongue. The structural variables that were considered to be most influential in assessing the vitality of ethnolinguistic groups were organized under three main headings:

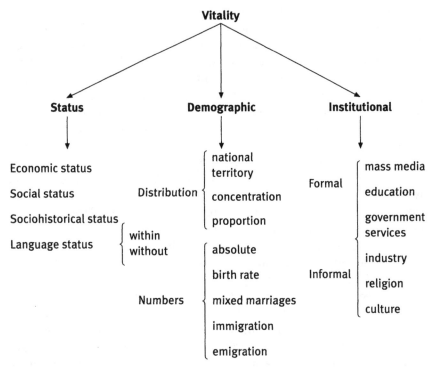

Figure 11.1 A taxonomy of the structural variables affecting ethnolinguistic vitality
Source: Giles et al. (1977, p. 305)

the status, demographic, and institutional factors (see figure 11.1). The authors maintained that the three structural variables interact to provide the context for understanding the vitality of ethnolinguistic groups. Status variables encompass elements of prestige of the minority, and the greater the status a linguistic group has in the context of inter-group interactions the more vitality it will have as a collective entity. The same may be said for a community that has positive demographic variables expressed through their numbers and their contiguous distribution throughout a geographical region. Institutional support for the group within the geographic area refers to the formal and informal areas in which members may use their mother tongue. Thus the vitality of a linguistic minority is assumed to be related directly to the degree that the language is used in various institutions (domains) such as government, church, school, and for services throughout the private sector.

In the field of geography, language studies did not figure prominently until a few scholars in the United States and Europe in the 1970s and 1980s began to collate their interests into the research of geolinguistics. At the outset, they emphasized the relationship between languages and their physical and human contexts by focusing on historical processes that contributed to the development of current patterns of human contact and interaction between and among different culture groups. These scholars focused on the sociospatial context of language use and language choice, measured language distribution and varieties, and identified the demographic characteristics of language groups, particularly on a local scale (Williams, 1984). Others who were interested in this evolving branch of human geography assessed the relative practical importance, usefulness, and availability of different languages from economic, psychological, political, and cultural perspectives (Ambrose & Williams, 1981; Breton, 1991; Williams, 1988). Hence practitioners of geolinguistic research attempt to go beyond the concept of distance, topography, or the built environment in the analysis of social structures and concomitant language use. These practitioners attempt to offer a more positive, practical appreciation of the role of geographic space, territory, and scale of analysis as additional elements that are employed in a more holistic, sociolinguistic approach to language communities (Williams, 1988).[1] An application of geolinguistic research, and its relevance to language policy, can be explored through two general examples: (1) a geographically peripheral and fragmented ethnolinguistic community, and (2) a more extensive and contiguous community.

Geographically Peripheral and Fragmented Communities

Until the end of the nineteenth century, the national space of a country consisted of separate, often isolated communities; hence the impact of a national culture upon these enclaves was limited. This was particularly evident in rural, peripheral societies, those that were geographically remote from the emerging political and economic core area of the nation. Examples can be found among the Celtic-speaking peoples of Britain, the Frisians of the Netherlands, and the Basques in the Iberian peninsula. By the late nineteenth and early twentieth centuries, however, a political theory emerged in the industrial societies of Europe that cultural and linguistic diversity threatened the unity of a nation. To counter this diversity, the dominant ethnic group adopted an assimilationist approach to national policy – politically, economically, and linguistically – by applying its resources, rewards, and symbolic power to influence directly the actions and interactions of people.

In the first half of the twentieth century many social scientists believed that diverse ethnic groups in advanced industrial states would, in time, be assimilated by the dominant culture of the state (Deutsch, 1953; Young, 1976). It is now recognized that many such groups have not lost their sense of identity; consequently, cultural pluralism prevails in most of the world. The dynamic of cultural pluralism now challenges the capability of statecraft to provide for all constituents through pluralistic policies and programs that will maximize social harmony. The demands from sub-state nationalities to influence such policy formation, and secure legislated rights and privileges, often reflect the importance of language to a minority, particularly when the language of the majority is dominant and considered to be a potential threat to the identity of that minority (Nelde, 1987) For a minority, language-planning legislation becomes a vital ingredient in the struggle to maintain ethnolinguistic vitality. An example of attempts to influence language policy in a situation of an eroding ethnolinguistic community can be taken from the efforts of Welsh speakers to sustain their heritage.

United Kingdom: the Welsh

Since the geographic situation of Wales is peripheral to the political and economic core area of the United Kingdom, the Welsh language in the nineteenth century enjoyed extensive usage in many domains beyond the home. As the assimilationist policy of the dominant English-speaking culture made inroads into these domains, the use of the Welsh language throughout the community contracted (Williams, 1980). Furthermore, minorities in multilingual states that are peripherally situated often fail to gain territorial control or influence over regional boundaries that have been penetrated by acculturating processes. The Basques and Catalans in Spain and the Bretons in France are similarly situated to the Welsh, and are considered to be territorially unprotected. They have become more accessible to the majority population of their state through the processes associated with time/space convergence (Janelle, 1973). Urbanization, industrialization, mass tourism, easy and rapid communication, and increased population mobility have developed rapidly since World War II. These processes have reduced the time that it takes to move and to interact over great distances, and increased the migration between the core area and the periphery. Television has also contributed to this by enhancing attraction to the dominant language. Time/space convergence has intensified the processes that are perceived to be culturally erosive to peripheral minorities in Spain, France, and the United Kingdom.

Some Welsh nationalists, who were concerned over the territorial shrinkage of the Welsh heartland, had used aggregate census data on monolingual Welsh speakers to foster a policy of territorial control by establishing formal boundaries, thereby creating a "Fortress Wales" against the encroachment of English. Such control would commence with private and community efforts, to be followed by a formal boundary demarcation. This would create an extensive, contiguous Welsh-speaking zone. Ambrose and Williams (1981) have argued against this policy. Through detailed, local area analysis (large-scale) of later census data, they and other Welsh scholars were able to demonstrate a geographical pattern of decline of a once strong Welsh-speaking heartland into a series of fragmented nuclei of Welsh-language use. Large-scale cartographic analysis identified a "zone of collapse" at the margins of these Welsh-speaking areas where English usage was replacing Welsh in households (Zelinsky & Williams, 1988). In the face of acculturating processes, the Welsh speakers had fewer and fewer institutional support agencies to draw upon for their ethnolinguistic vitality. Williams and his colleagues linked the data on language change with socioeconomic census data by incorporating educational, religious, cultural, and political variables as they related to language use. Later, these researchers were able to demonstrate through this form of analysis that, in districts where the Welsh schools had been established and where new, more positive attitudes to the nourishment of Welsh culture had developed, language decline showed a small but significant reversal. Williams and colleagues believed that the pattern of fragmentation and drift, and the outcome of their socioeconomic analysis, weakened the argument in favor of a uniformly designated territorial language region within which citizen rights and the primacy of Welsh could be specified and sanctioned. To be effective, the researchers argued, language planning must be functional rather than formal (as in "Fortress Wales"), and in concert with other reforms of the socioeconomic conditions that sustain communities. Thus, "planning policies, as well as being variable from one part of the region to another, must be adaptable at short notice in order to accommodate the suddenly changing fortunes of the language in any locality" (Ambrose & Williams, 1981, p. 6). Institutional support for minority-language use would be fostered in schools, churches, and chapels, and in public services in those areas identified as having a critical mass to justify such policies and programs. When feasible, magazines and newspapers published in Welsh would receive government support.

There have been advances in the revitalization of the Welsh language within the targeted domains; however, vigilance and language planning must be constant in the face of expanded economic opportunities within the European Union. There is a tendency for corporations that wish to exploit this huge market to view "lesser-used languages" as burdensome. This attitude in economic thinking views minority languages as extra costs to, and a drain upon, productivity. As Williams (2000) states, minority languages may be considered "a potentially complicating factor that might dissuade hesitant investors and reluctant relocators from siting any new activities in Wales" (Williams, 2000, p. 362).

In peripheral ethnolinguistic communities, the settlement pattern of population tends to be fragmented; hence, the nationalists' objectives are mainly to reinforce and entrench key domains in which the minority language exists. Language use is also fragmented, as residents frequently face the necessity of using the majority language beyond the home, particularly when the language of the majority is also the language of business and commerce. This can lead to a situation of *subtractive bilingualism*, where the mother tongue of the minority is gradually displaced in an increasing number of domains by the use of the majority language. The minority language becomes less and less significant as the majority language takes over daily patterns of contact and interaction. The younger members of the minority are particularly vulnerable, for they can become more mobile with their language skills and susceptible to exogamy. In a mixed marriage, language usage in the home may switch to the majority tongue, especially if the female spouse – the traditional carrier of the culture in the home – is from that group.

Extensive and Geographically Contiguous Ethnolinguistic Communities

Not all minority groups occupy peripheral locations within multilingual states. There are many examples of linguistic groups that are surrounded by a majority, as the Québécois in Canada, or in geographical juxtaposition, as the Walloons and Flemish in Belgium. Regardless of geographical location, Laponce (1987) believes that in a multilingual state a weak language will not enjoy the haven of independent status, and it is, therefore, in a constant struggle against a dominant language that has the erosive role of a lingua franca throughout the whole state. Even when granted official status within the multilingual state, if it does not attain supremacy in the public administration and the school system, the weak language will become merely symbolic.

To avoid assimilation, members of the minority must assert their ethnicity, an assertion that can manifest in demands for greater control of the ethnic region. This control can involve a partial or total exclusion of the majority language. The more geographically concentrated the minority language becomes, through territorial control behind a protective boundary, the less threatening is the majority language to the ethnolinguistic vitality of the minority community and to one's ethnic identity. The languages that will survive the multilingual environment, therefore, are those that are eventually protected by the state, for they will enjoy pre-eminence in national and international negotiations. Those least able to survive have only local cultural power and are without control of the government of either a state or a territory. To explore these developments, we can turn to the Flemish–Walloon conflict in Belgium.

Belgium: Flemish and Walloons

In Belgium, the Flemish in the north and Walloons in the south are highly homogeneous and regionally unilingual. The former are the majority in the country but struggled for decades to overcome a "minority status" because their language was considered to be culturally inferior to the French spoken by the Walloons. With ascendancy to independence in 1830, Walloons and the Francophones in Brussels controlled the Belgian government and the economy, and dominated cultural life; hence, upward social mobility became associated with the use of the French language even in Flanders. The Walloons also adhered to the theory that cultural and linguistic diversity threatened the unity of the nation. The struggle to achieve parity between the two linguistic groups was long and bitter; rights to use Flemish in secondary and post-secondary education, in administration, and in the criminal justice system in Flanders were enacted only gradually (Lorwin, 1972). The promotion of bilingual status for the whole of Belgium met with resistance from the Walloons, who resented having Flemish inflicted upon their region. In 1932, the effort was abandoned and unilingual regions were created behind an ethnolinguistic boundary, except for the capital and some small areas along the linguistic frontier that retained bilingual status (Baetens-Beardsmore, 1987).

The territorial limits were to have some flexibility to accommodate ethnic interaction; consequently, the language boundary was relatively permeable. If the population composition of an administrative unit changed from mainly unilingual to a mixture of Flemish and Walloon, an application to alter the unit from unilingual to bilingual would be entertained. Over the next 30 years, relations between the two language groups were tense as the Flemish continued to fear the encroachment of French upon their territory. This tension led to the official demarcation of Flanders and Wallonia in 1963 as permanently unilingual; a citizen's use of language beyond the home for services would be legally determined by his or her place of residence and not by the language spoken in the home or by personal preference. The capital, Brussels, remained an officially bilingual territory.

This legislation was the outcome of intense efforts by the Flemish to create a fully unilingual cultural realm in the north, and was the culmination of social, cultural, economic, and political tensions that had dominated relations between the two groups for over a century (McRae, 1986). Flemish nationalists had become as intransigent as the Walloons, who had traditionally opposed Flemish minority rights in the south. The separation of the two groups was fortified through the development and official sanction of institutional unilingualism. The Belgian government tried to maintain cultural linkages between Flanders and Wallonia, but the linkages have become weaker since the cultural trends of the 1960s and 1970s. Murphy (1993) found that manifestations of this division associated with the language boundary are the paucity of migrations between the two regions, and the few contacts by telephone between Flanders and Wallonia in comparison with intra-regional contacts or between either of the regions and Brussels.

The metropolitan area of Brussels, the capital, has evolved into an interesting geopolitical situation within Belgium. The capital is the only area that may be designated as a cultural transition zone, because of the opportunity for regular contact and interaction between the two major linguistic groups, for both residents and commuters, and because the 19 communes that constitute the metropolitan area are designated as officially bilingual. The city is situated, however, within the unilingual Flemish part of the country, and normal urban expansion into this territory has generated hostility. In spite of legislation in the 1960s that entrenched the limits of the Brussels–capital region, suburban growth has developed, particularly southward toward the linguistic boundary between Flanders and Wallonia. The Francophones of the capital have a preference for this suburban area, but Flemish nationalists fear urban growth in this direction will eventually reach the Wallonian sector. Hence, Brussels, rather than being a bilingual enclave within Flanders, will become a salient of the Wallonian cultural realm. This outcome is considered a potential territorial threat by Flemish nationalists (Witte, 1987). Relations between the two groups who inhabit small municipalities on the linguistic boundary across Belgium have been conditioned by this "battle of Brussels" (Murphy, 1988).

Throughout the 1980s, Brussels gained a regional council with an independent structure similar to those of Flanders and Wallonia. This has contributed to the formation of a distinctive regional context that has set the residents of the city apart, conceptually and functionally, from the inhabitants of the other two administrative units. There is the possibility of a distinct Brussels identity emerging among French and Dutch speakers alike, and this will generate an interactive situation that may contribute to intermarriage between the two groups (Murphy, 1991).

Various institutions have been established that are devoted to matters that concern the capital alone. Also, with the establishment of international bodies in the city, including the European parliament and attendant operations, Brussels has taken on an international aura that does not exist in other Belgian cities. In this environment, those who function in the two official languages may be considered to experience *additive bilingualism*, in which access to the other language brings no threat of replacement to the mother tongue. There is no loss of ethnolinguistic vitality to either community. This is in marked contrast to the experiences of the Flemish in Brussels prior to the 1960s. To an outsider, the fragmented nature of the Belgian state could appear as a precursor to dissolution, but the consensus is that the future existence of Belgium is not threatened. Nevertheless, differences between the Flemish and the Walloons will continue to be a constant source of internal friction.

The development of language regions in Belgium illustrates the application of two principles for policy formation: that of *territoriality* and that of *personality*. The principle of territoriality, under which an individual has the right to receive services in the language of the majority of the population in a given area, was appropriate in Belgium because there are clearly defined unilingual areas. The same applies to Switzerland. This provision of group rights allows a minority to sustain its territorial rights, within which it can continue to protect its language. These rights become anchored in unilingual institutions that are themselves anchored in geographical space (Laponce, 1987). Where the members of two language groups are not so concentrated, the principle of personality, according to which every person is free to obtain services in the language of his or her choice throughout a nation or designated area within a nation, usually prevails. South Africa is a good example of a nation under the principle of personality, though the principle is easily applied here because of the high proportion of the population that is competent in both English and Afrikaans. Brussels is an example of the application of the principle within a state (McRae, 1975).

Conclusion

The two plural societies discussed in this chapter have, at one time, through legislation or economic dominance, coerced the minorities to gradually integrate into the society of the majority. The assimilationist approach, at the outset, was to reduce conflict and competition in the nation and enhance cooperation and national unity. For the minority populations, who are, by definition, in a numerically or politically unbalanced situation, integrative processes were acculturating and inevitably assimilative. The domains in which these populations had cultural exclusiveness eroded, and mother-tongue usage beyond the home, and often within, gave way to the majority language. For Laponce (1987), this was an erosion of territory, for people who speak specific languages are like territories with restricted resources. The minority, through their representatives, had to find ways in which to protect their territories.

Nationalists from the small, fragmented ethnolinguistic communities will, in general, focus on strategic domains for exclusive minority-language usage. Their "resources" are too restricted to go beyond this strategy. Requests, or demands, will be made by a minority for improved language services in their mother tongue, and for exclusivity in domains that are considered vital to cultural survival, particularly in education. The costs of these services, however, must be shared by the whole society. When the members of the majority population fail to perceive the same acculturating and assimilating processes acting upon the smaller society, or if they believe the minority to be overreacting, competition and conflict can develop. How should political leaders, who decide to respond through a pluralist approach to the demands of the minority, proceed? Should they embark upon a program to educate the electorate thoroughly on the needs of the weaker ethnic group and the reasons for the accommodating policies and programs that are forthcoming? Or should they embrace gradualism, whereby policies are brought forth quietly and step by step, so that once they are fully in place the electorate has never been required to make a decision on whether it is for or against?

Within the larger, more contiguous ethnolinguistic communities, nationalists go beyond the entrenchment of minority-language domains alone, but seek to entrench their territorial boundaries as a form of fortification against invading majority languages. Language becomes the boundary, for it will re-establish the distance between minority and majority, or dominator and dominated in the case of Belgium. The exclusive use of the mother tongue throughout the society is the objective, thereby binding the members of the smaller or formerly dominated group more securely to the culture. Members of the once dominant group must now be prepared to alter the pattern of their language use in that society. They must be prepared to function under the principle of territoriality or change location. In Belgium, the decline in interaction across the linguistic boundary is symbolic of the distance that has emerged between the two ethnolinguistic communities in that country. The reduction in contact and interaction between ethnolinguistic groups in a plural society produces social distance that is considered a form of security by the leaders of a minority or linguistically weaker group. This in turn can reduce the knowledge and/or understanding of the "other" in society, since the loss of interaction curtails the opportunities to get to know members of the opposing community; a lack of empathy prevails. This is often referred to as *cognitive distance* between ethnic constituents in a plural society. Hence, reduced contact and interaction between the constituent societies also create a new demand on policy-makers to generate an acceptable form of national integration, to avoid a debilitating division in the country.

Annotated Bibliography

Breton, R.-L. (1991). *Geolinguistics: Language dynamics and ethnolinguistic geography*. Ottawa: University of Ottawa Press.
Languages are seldom static. Over time they evolve, and within the same language some forms evolve more quickly than others. Each form has its history and its geography. The geography of language forms has a well-established scientific tradition dating from the turn of the nineteenth century. The geography of language functions, however, is a developing study, and one to which this volume is a valuable contribution. The author develops a distinction between form and function at the outset, and follows with analysis of the various bondings a language can have to types of human groups – the ethnic nature of language. He also presents the theme that it is the society – the users of a language – that ultimately determines its dynamics. To study the dynamics, one must have recourse to some form of quantification, and this is developed as an important technical aspect of geolinguistics.

Gardner, N., Puigdevall i Serralvo, M., & Williams, C. H. (2000). Language revitalization in comparative context: Ireland, the Basque Country, and Catalonia. In C. H. Williams (ed.), *Language revitalization, policy and planning in Wales* (pp. 311–62). Cardiff: University of Wales Press.
Language planners have become more conscious of the value of drawing upon wide experience for policy and program development. The authors explain that most comparative studies that involved policy for the Welsh language were made with other Celtic lands, particularly Ireland and Brittany. This chapter is representative of the attempts by language-policy experts to draw from the wider experience of European nations, particularly Spain, in the field of language revitalization. The authors use this study to argue that the framers of Welsh language policy should rely less on the cliché of Celtic solidarity and turn, instead, to several of the proactive policies and programs that have developed in the Basque Country (Euskadi) and Catalonia. These proactive features demonstrate the value of a positive political element to language planning; the indispensable nature of institutional support systems, particularly in education; the need to integrate language planning with other forms of planning, particularly regional economic development; and the need for a thorough understanding of the economic imperative that structures language choice individually and collectively.

Laponce, J. A. (1987). *Languages and their territories*. Toronto: University of Toronto Press.
This book is rather dated, but it continues to set the standard for the exploration of bilingualism and the political issues that are generated by this phenomenon. The author begins with a study of how one learns a language and follows with a demonstration of the manner in which the brain resists bilingualism. He explores the theme that the impulse for unilingualism is related to the tendency to create unilingual territorial niches. Each language group, therefore, will strive to develop its exclusive territory. In opposition, the dominant language group in a plural society will attempt to force the minority into fewer and fewer minority-language domains. Laponce applies his theory to a number of multilingual societies and draws provocative conclusions.

Peeters, Y. J. D., & Williams, C. H. (eds.) (1993). *The cartographic representation of linguistic data* (Discussion Papers in Geolinguistics, Nos. 19–21). Stoke on Trent: Staffordshire University.
This publication is part of a series on geolinguistics that is produced at Staffordshire University in England. This issue contains nine selected presentations that were made at the Scientific Workshop in the Cartographic Representation of Linguistic Data sponsored by the European Centre of Ethnolinguistic Cartography in Brussels, Belgium. Through their contributions at the workshop, the authors seek to advance the conceptual and methodological development of geolinguistics. In addition to the conceptual and methodological themes, the authors apply geolinguistic analysis to South Africa, Hungary, Wales, and parts of Central Africa. The latter demonstrate the importance of providing accurate data in map form, and the related imperative that the evaluation and implications of these data must be fully understood by both map producers and map users.

Williams, C. H. (1993). *Called unto liberty: On language and nationalism*. Clevedon: Multilingual Matters.
The author has focused on the implications of language-related conflict and nationalist mobilization as expanding global issues. Interest groups are challenging the established state as they seek greater representation in international affairs and a diminution in threats to their cultural survival. These tensions are examined in this volume, and the appeals of national liberty are analyzed for those whose culture is challenged by structural and political changes in the global economy. Williams evaluates various themes of nationalism and cultural

identity, and then examines the manner in which language and nationalist political activity have interrelated in Wales and Quebec. He offers a set of scenarios as to how such interests are to be satisfied through applied public policy and social planning.

Discussion Questions

1 Discuss the queries presented in the conclusion of the chapter. When political leaders decide on a plural approach to the demands of a minority, should they:

(a) embark on a program to inform the population on the needs of the minority and the reasons for the accommodating policies and programs;

or

(b) operate under a plan of gradualism, whereby policies and programs are activated piece by piece without publicity or fanfare?

2 The lobby group U.S.English has endorsed an assimilationist policy for the plural society of the United States, and has started by promoting a change to the Constitution that would make English the official language of the country. Investigate the activities of this group. What successes have they had to date? Do they have a hidden agenda? Do they also operate at the state level of government, and if so with what success?

3 Assume you are a member of the municipal government of a small city in the southern United States near the international border. You are about to develop an annual budget on the basis of the size of the city's population and anticipated demands for services. There is a large Hispanic American portion of your population, and you know that many unilingual undocumented aliens could be attracted to your city to be near kin and kind. List the municipal services that could be affected by this unexpected increase in your population. What programs can you put in place to accommodate these demands? Are these programs likely to cause a backlash of annoyance among the permanent residents of your city?

4 The size of the Hispanic American population in California is increasing annually. With more representatives of that population being elected to the state legislature, it is reasonable to assume that a bill will be forthcoming to make Spanish and English official languages of California for all services, departments, and agencies

of the state government. What is your reaction to this potential legislation? What is the current size of the Hispanic American population in California?

NOTE

1 Space does not permit a detailed treatment of the growth and development of geolinguistics, but readers who wish to explore the evolution of research that has led to greater recognition of the contextual element of language and territory should consult the work of Colin Williams, a geographer at the University of Cardiff (Williams, 1980, 1984, 1988).

REFERENCES

Ambrose, J. E. & Williams, C. H. (1981). On the spatial definition of minority: Scale as an influence on the geolinguistic analysis of Welsh. In E. Haugen, J. D. McClure, & D. S. Thompson (eds.), *Minority languages today* (pp. 53–71). Edinburgh: Edinburgh University Press.

Baetens-Beardsmore, H. (1987). Language planning in Belgium. In L. Laforge (ed.), *Actes du Collogue International sur L'Amenagement Linguistiques, Ottawa, 25–29 mai, 1986* (pp. 105–13). Quebec: Presses de l'université Laval.

Breton, R.-L. (1991). *Geolinguistics: Language dynamics and ethnolinguistic geography*. Ottawa: University of Ottawa Press.

Deutsch, K. W. (1953). *Nationalism and social communication: An inquiry into the foundations of nationality*. Llandysul: Gomer Press.

Gardner, N., Puigdevall i Serralvo, M., & Williams, C. H. (2000). Language revitalization in comparative context: Ireland, the Basque Country, and Catalonia. In C. H. Williams (ed.), *Language revitalization, policy and planning in Wales* (pp. 311–62). Cardiff: University of Wales Press.

Giles, H., Bourhis, R., & Taylor, D. M. (1977). Towards a theory of language in ethnic group relations. In H. Giles (ed.), *Language, ethnicity and intergroup relations* (pp. 307–48). London: Academic Press.

Janelle, D. G. (1973). Measuring human extensibility in a shrinking world. *Journal of Geography, 72*, 8–15.

Laponce, J. A. (1987). *Languages and their territories*. Toronto: University of Toronto Press.

Lorwin, V. R. (1972). Linguistic pluralism and political tension in modern Belgium. In J. A. Fishman (ed.), *Advances in the sociology of language* (pp. 386–412). The Hague: Mouton.

McRae, K. D. (1975). The principle of territoriality and the principle of personality in multilingual states. *International Journal of the Sociology of Language, 4*, 33–53.

McRae, K. D. (1986). *Conflict and compromise in multilingual societies: Belgium.* Waterloo: Wilfred Laurier University Press.

Murphy, A. B. (1988). *The regional dynamics of language differentiation in Belgium* (Geography Research Paper no. 227). Chicago: University of Chicago Press.

Murphy, A. B. (1991). Regions as social constructs: The gap between theory and practice. *Progress in Human Geography, 15,* 22–35.

Murphy, A. B. (1993). Linguistic regionalism and the social construction of space in Belgium. *International Journal of the Sociology of Language, 104,* 49–64.

Nelde, P. H. (1987). Language contact means language conflict. *Journal of Multilingual and Multicultural Development, 8,* 3–42.

van der Merwe, I. J. (1993). A conceptual home for geolinguistics: Implications for language mapping in South Africa. In Y. J. D. Peeters & C. H. Williams (eds.), *The cartographic representation of linguistic data* (Discussion Papers in Geolinguistics, Nos. 19–21) (pp. 21–33). Stoke on Trent: Staffordshire University.

Veltman, C. (1977). The evolution of ethno-linguistic frontiers in the United States and Canada. *Social Science Journal, 14,* 47–58.

Williams, C. H. (1980). Language contact and language change in Wales, 1901–1971: A study in historical geolinguistics. *Welsh History Review, 10,* 207–38.

Williams, C. H. (1984). *On measurement and application in geolinguistics* (Discussion Papers in Geolinguistics, no. 8). Stoke on Trent: Staffordshire University.

Williams, C. H. (1988). *Language in geographic context.* Clevedon: Multilingual Matters.

Williams, C. H. (2000). Conclusion: Economic development and political responsibility. In C. H. Williams (ed.), *Language revitalization, policy and planning in Wales* (pp. 362–79). Cardiff: University of Wales Press.

Witte, E. (1987). Socio-political aspects: Bilingual Brussels as an indication of growing political tensions (1960–1985). In E. Witte & H. Baetens-Beardsmore (eds.), *The interdisciplinary study of urban bilingualism in Brussels* (pp. 47–74). Clevedon: Multilingual Matters.

Young, C. (1976). *The politics of cultural pluralism.* Madison, WI: University of Wisconsin Press.

Zelinsky, W. & Williams, C. H. (1988). The mapping of language in North America and the British Isles. *Progress in Human Geography, 12,* 337–68.

CHAPTER TWELVE

Psycho-Sociological Analysis in Language Policy

Colin Baker

Psycho-sociological research on language policy tends to derive from academic/theoretical propositions (e.g., language attitudes), bureaucratic and political needs (e.g., language census, language testing), and a newer strand relating to the aims and methodology of action research. This chapter covers these areas by discussing important terms and constructs, and then different styles of psycho-sociological language-policy research. The chapter finishes by briefly indicating the limitations of approaches to psycho-sociological research on language planning.

Frequent Constructs Used in Psycho-Sociological Research in Language Policy

Psycho-sociological research on language policy uses varying perspectives from within psychology and sociology. Four constructs will be briefly examined, illustrative of such varying traditions.

First, from social psychology there has been a continuous strand of research from the 1920s to the present on *language attitudes* (R. C. Gardner, 2002). In the life of a language, attitudes toward that language may be important in language revitalization and revival, as well as in language decay and death. Attitudes toward bilingual education, language laws, or immigrant languages may well affect the success of language-policy implementation. A survey of attitudes provides an indicator of current community thoughts and beliefs, preferences and desires. *Attitude surveys* provide social indicators of changing beliefs and the chances of success in policy implementation. In terms of minority languages, attitudes provide an imperfect barometer of the health of the language. A survey of attitudes to French in Canada, Spanish in the United States, and English in Japan might reveal the possibilities and problems of second languages within each country. As Lewis (1981) observed:

> Any policy for language, especially in the system of education, has to take account of the attitude of those likely to be affected. In the long run, no policy will succeed which does not do one of three things: conform to the expressed attitudes of those involved; persuade those who express negative attitudes about the rightness of the policy; or seek to remove the causes of the disagreement. In any case knowledge about attitudes is fundamental to the formulation of a policy as well as to success in its implementation.
>
> *(p. 262)*

The status, value, and importance of a language are often measured by attitudes at an individual level, or the common attitudes of a group or community may be elicited. At either level, the information may be important in attempting to represent democratically the "views of the people." *Opinion polls* may also aid in the understanding of social processes by revealing the relationship of attitudes to individual differences (e.g., age, gender, socioeconomic class) and contextual differences (e.g., indigenous/immigrant family, economics of community). The research, attitude scales, and attitude models of Robert Gardner (see R. C. Gardner, 1985a, 2002) have been particularly influential in this regard.

Second, the concept of *ethnolinguistic vitality* derives from a combination of social psychology and sociolinguistics (Bourhis, Giles, & Rosenthal, 1981; Giles & Coupland, 1991; Giles, Bourhis, & Taylor, 1977; Giles, Hewstone, & Ball, 1983; Giles, Noels, Ota, Ng, Gallois, Ryan et al., 2000). In an attempt to create a unified theoretical framework rather than a list of the many factors involved in (minority) language vitality, Giles et al. (1977) propose a three-factor model: (1) status factors (e.g., economic, historical); (2) demographic factors (e.g., raw numbers and density of speakers, birth rates and language reproduction in families); and (3) institutional support factors (e.g., representation of the group and its language in the media and education). These three factors combine to predict more or less minority-language vitality. Allard and Landry (1994) suggests that there are eight dimensions to ethnolinguistic vitality (an example of the results of a survey is given to illustrate each dimension):

1 Present vitality (e.g., "Spanish speakers are much more numerous than English speakers in this area").
2 Future vitality (e.g., "Spanish speakers will manage most of this area's businesses in the future").
3 Legitimate vitality (e.g., "In this area, local government services should be provided to Spanish speakers in Spanish").
4 Social models (e.g., "My peers attend cultural events in the Spanish language").
5 Belongingness (e.g., "I feel myself to be a Latino").
6 Valorization (e.g., "Students should have access to education through the medium of Spanish as well as English").
7 Efficacy (e.g., "I can be effective in my employment by speaking Spanish as well as English").
8 Goals (e.g., "I want to use Spanish in my future career").

Third, from sociolinguistics comes *language use* across various domains (e.g., in census and language-use surveys). Language-use surveys typically ask individuals to profile their varying language use across a long list of contexts and interlocutors (see Baker, 2001). For example, research may wish to investigate whether a bilingual's minority language is relegated to low-status functions in comparison with the more prestigious language. Such a profile may be a harbinger of language decline, even death. Ideally, language use is not just about contexts and interlocutors but also about the amount of quality time spent in different contexts (e.g., at work, home, religion, and leisure).

Domain use of a language relates to the concept of *diglossia* (Fishman, 1980), that is, a tendency toward the separate use of a bilingual's two languages for different functions (e.g., speaking Spanish at home and with relations; speaking English at school and with friends inside and outside school). The maintenance of domain boundaries between languages has been regarded as essential for minority-language survival (Fishman, 1980), although the Basques have challenged this notion, believing it relegates the minority language to low-status functions (N. Gardner, 2000).

Fourth, from psychometrics, educational measurement, management by performance indicators, and language planning, there is a plethora of research available on *language testing* (Spolsky, 1995). Language proficiency, or more accurately language performance (for definitional issues and limitations, see Baker, 2001), in understanding, speaking, reading, and writing one or more languages has often been either the focus of research or one of the variables used in research. Examples of language-performance research include English-language testing in the United States (Ovando, Collier, & Combs, 2003), Hebrew, Arabic, and English language testing in Israel (Shohamy, 2001), and National Curriculum testing of English in the United Kingdom (Baker, 1995, 2001) and of Irish in Ireland (Harris & Murtagh, 1999).

Styles in Psycho-Sociological Research on Language Policy

Both qualitative and quantitative traditions are well represented in psycho-sociological research on language policy. Indeed, a strength of language-policy research is that it is multimethod in approach, reflecting various ontological and epistemological ideologies, varying perspectives about individuals, groups, networks, and their interaction with contexts (e.g., determinist, positivist, subjectivist, naturalist, normative, interpretive, critical, feminist, politically activist, and interventionist approaches). This has led to a wide variety of research styles utilizing: questionnaires, structured interviews, focus groups, open-ended interviewing, meta-analysis, educational and psychometric testing, critical ethnography, action research, participant and nonparticipant observation, quasi-experiments, and evaluation techniques.

This section briefly illustrates psycho-sociological research on language policy with seven specific styles: language-attitude measurement, census surveys, language-use surveys, social network analysis, language-performance testing, the recent use of performance indicators and target setting, and action research.

Language attitudes

Various alternative methods exist for measuring language attitudes, of which *Likert*, the *Semantic Differential* technique, and the *Matched Guise* technique are examples (Baker, 1992; Garrett, Coupland, & Williams, 2003). Also, language attitudes may be gauged from document (content) analysis, structured or open-ended interviews, and autobiographies. The specific attitudes under investigation may include those toward language groups (e.g., Spanish speakers); toward a language itself; toward its features, uses, or cultural associations; toward learning a language; toward bilingual education as product or process; toward language provision; toward language policy; or toward language practices.

The Matched Guise technique is used to infer attitudes toward language varieties (e.g., Irish-accented English, "Miami Spanish," English Received Pronunciation). Evaluations of speakers of particular languages or dialects provide an indirect measure of language attitudes, especially in terms of status, prestige, and social preferences. Edwards (1977), for example, found different evaluations of Galway, Cork, Cavan, Dublin, and Donegal accents in Ireland. Differences were found on dimensions of competence, social attractiveness, and personal integrity. The Matched Guise approach to language attitudes is comprehensively reviewed in Garrett et al. (2003).

One of the most popular methods of attitude measurement is to produce an attitude scale composed of statements such as: "Spanish speakers should be offered bilingual education." Responses are typically measured on a five-point scale:

Strongly agree	Agree	Neither agree nor disagree	Disagree	Strongly disagree

Summation of scores across, for example, 10 to 20 statements produces one score per respondent, or sometimes scores on sub-scales. The Semantic Differential Technique is less popular for measuring attitudes but may sometimes tap the affective component as well as the cognitive component of attitudes. Meanings attached to a stimulus (e.g., "the Arabic language") can be profiled for an individual or, when calculated as an average, for a group. For example:

The Arabic language

	Very	Somewhat	Neither	Somewhat	Very	
Old fashioned						Modern
Easy						Difficult
Useful						Useless
Weak						Strong
Warm						Cold

Two components of language attitudes have been located by research and have become key terms in sociolinguistics: an *instrumental orientation* and an *integrative orientation*. Instrumental motivation reflects pragmatic, utilitarian motives. An instrumental attitude to a language is mostly self-oriented and individualistic. Instrumental attitudes to learning a second language or preserving a minority language might be, for example, for vocational reasons, status, achievement, personal success, self-enhancement, self-actualization, or basic security and survival. An example of an instrumental item from R. C. Gardner's (1985b) Attitude/Motivation Test Battery is: "Studying French can be important to me because I think it will someday be useful in getting a good job."

An integrative attitude to a language, on the other hand, is mostly social and interpersonal in orientation and represents a desire to be like representative members of the other language community. Thus an integrative attitude to a particular language may concern attachment to, or identification with, a language group and its cultural activities. An example of an integrative test item is as follows (from R. C. Gardner, 1985b): "Studying French can be important for me because it will allow me to meet and converse with more and varied people."

The instrumental–integrative orientation distinction has limitations (Ricento, 2005). For example, integrative and instrumental orientations can overlap and combine; an integrative orientation in minority-language contexts can imply assimilation into a majority-language culture; and an orientation may indicate desire but not action (e.g., interaction with the target language group).

Language attitudes appear to be helpful explanatory variables in language decay where minority languages are declining or in peril. In particular, the absence of strong integrative or instrumental attitudes may be linked to the absence of minority-language reproduction in the home. Negative attitudes to a minority language may be a prime cause of parents' not passing on the heritage language to a child. Also, minority-language production in school (e.g., by language lessons or content teaching in the minority language) is affected by the attitudes of children, teachers, administrators, and policy-makers. It often takes strong instrumental and/or integrative attitudes for students to learn a language successfully in school (R. C. Gardner, 2002).

Census data

Some countries have a long history of language questions in the census (e.g., Ireland from 1851; Canada from 1871; the United States from 1890), while other countries appear to have avoided inclusion of language questions in their census (e.g., England, France). A language question is included in an ever increasing number of censuses in the world (e.g., Australia, Hungary, Bolivia, and Venezuela). The linguistic detail and attempted precision from recent censuses in Venezuela (Oficina Central de Estadística e Informática, 1993) and Bolivia (CIPCA, 1995) are particularly noteworthy, and more sophisticated than those of Europe and North America (Baker & Jones, 1998).

One of the most impressive current language censuses (with major policy implications) derives from the 1992 census in Bolivia. A detailed map represents not only Aymara, Quechua, Guaraní, and Spanish but also many indigenous minority languages. Rather than just using simple coloring or shading, the map shows where there is language contact and bilingualism. This census language map also uses arrows to show the direction of language shift. For example, Portuguese is shown to be advancing in the extreme northwest of Bolivia. Spanish is generally advancing on Aymara, Quechua, Guaraní and the many indigenous languages with smaller populations, and the map shows specifically where this is occurring in a major way (CIPCA, 1995).

Another recent development has been the movement away from simple census language questions such as "Do you speak English? Yes/No." Questions recently tend to include not only oracy but also literacy, separating reading and writing. In the 2000 US census, questionnaires were made available in six languages: English, Spanish, Chinese, Tagalog, Vietnamese, and Korean. Language Assistance Guides were produced in 49 languages apart from English. Two questionnaires were used. A short questionnaire was sent to every household in the United States, requesting information on individuals (e.g., gender, race, ethnicity, home ownership, and age). A longer questionnaire was sent to about one in six of all US households. The longer version asked about ancestry, residence five years ago (migration), income, and education. It also included a question about home languages. Question 11 on the 2000 US census form was phrased as follows (see www.census.gov):

Question 11

   a. Does this person speak a language other than English at home?
      __ Yes
      __ No *Skip to 12*

b. What is this language?

....

(For example: Korean, Italian, Spanish, Vietnamese)

c. How well does this person speak English?
   __ Very well
   __ Well
   __ Not well
   __ Not at all

As an officially stated aim, US census data is made available to help states and counties benchmark and measure progress in meeting their objectives and legislatively mandated targets (e.g., in English-language spread among immigrants). Given the role of education in fostering English among US immigrants, such census data is directly relevant to educational policy-making.

Khubchandani (2001) and Baker (2001) detail the criticisms and limitations of language censuses. These include: ambiguous questions (e.g., not distinguishing between language ability and language use); aggregating a response across disparate domains; treating (possibly subconsciously) the language question as if it refers to image or identity (e.g., being Irish or Welsh); giving socially desirable or "postured" answers (e.g., to say one speaks English and speaks it well; also if a minority language is disparaged and of low status, a speaker of that language may claim not to speak the language); and non-response rates (e.g., those refusing to complete the questionnaire, too remote, or not located) making generalization about the population difficult.

Language-use surveys

Language-use surveys (sometimes called sociolinguistic surveys; see Baldauf, 2002) frequently use self-completed questionnaires or structured interviews to profile an individual's (and groups' such as teenagers, fluent speakers) use of language across domains (e.g., at home, school, work, mass media, religion, literacy). Such surveys are thus much more detailed and extensive about language use than the singular and simple questions on a census form.

A detailed and comprehensive example of a language-use question-naire derives from European Union-sponsored research. As part of a movement of Europeanization and European unity, the EU investigated language use among over 40 European indigenous-language minorities. The Euromosaic Project investigated the language vitality or otherwise of lesser-used languages in the EU (Nelde et al., 1996; Commission of the European Union DGXXII, 1998).

The surveys included official policies and legislation in language education; the situation of the language in teaching from pre-school level to university, adult, and continuing education; the provision of curricular material in the lesser-used languages; local movements that promote language in education; teacher training; the inspection and monitoring of language teaching; government acts, laws, and decrees governing language in education; plus pressure groups in education and language. It also surveyed language use in domains such as: literacy, mass media, local and central government, cultural festivals, computing, all types of music, advertising, labels on goods and packages, signage, medical care, families (especially in raising children), new marriages, religion, phoning, translation, dubbing, and subtitling. The social status of these different domains was also investigated.

An example of a language use survey question is: "What language is used in the home?"

	Almost always in Irish	Mostly in Irish	About equal in Irish and English	Mostly in English	Almost always in English
By the father	___	___	___	___	___
By the mother	___	___	___	___	___
Among the children	___	___	___	___	___

Language use in social networks

Language-use surveys provide individual-level analyses. Yet language use is essentially interactive and collective. Hence such surveys are complemented by analysis of *language life in groups and networks*. A social network comprises the sum of relationships its members have with each other. Social network analysis examines the structures and properties of different social networks (Milroy, 2001).

Social networks require individual-level language data that effectively limits the extent of network analysis to between 15 and 50 individuals, although larger samples can be explored. The calculation of density and multiplexity is of critical importance in the analysis of social networks. In a maximally dense and multiplex network, everyone will interact regularly with everyone else (density), and individuals will know one another across a range of language contexts/domains (multiplexity). When a social network is dense and multiplex ("close knit"), there is typically close conformity to norms of behavior in its membership (e.g., in always speaking the minority language with each other). Close networks increase the probability of solidarity and reciprocity, thus increasing the chances of the survival of a minority language within such networks. Where there is a loosening of close-knit ties over time, or a social network with relatively weak interpersonal links, this may be associated with language shift.

Social network analysis was employed in research conducted by the Commission of the European Union DGXXII (1998) in Ireland, Catalonia, Wales, and Friesland. Twenty people in each region were asked about whom they most frequently interact with, their relationships with these people, and the language used in these interactions. Three indices were calculated for the density of the Welsh social network: the overall network density, the density of Welsh speakers in the network, and the density of respondents' use of Welsh in the network. The Irish network analysis revealed the network size, average duration of acquaintance, network density, and density of Irish-language usage in networks.

The methodology for social network analysis typically involves the following procedures: (1) 20 people are asked the following questions about each person with whom they network; (2) the length of time that person has been known; (3) the connection with that person (e.g., work colleague, social friend, member of the nuclear or extended family); (4) which of the 20 people a person talks to in the minority language; (5) whether they speak that minority language to each person all the time or most of the time, equally in both languages, mostly in the majority language, or in the majority language all the time; and (6) whether that pattern has been consistent across time.

Language-performance testing

Language-performance testing is particularly exemplified in two areas: government or state testing for curriculum assessment purposes, and testing language proficiency for research purposes (see Brindley, 2002, for other perspectives). These two areas will be considered in turn.

Government/state language-performance testing

Shohamy (2001) provides an insightful analysis of the introduction into the curriculum of three *government/state language tests* in Israel: a reading comprehension test, an Arabic language test, and an English second-language test. She examines the intentions of the tests and the effects. While researchers are typically concerned about the technical reliability and validity of tests, Shohamy (2001) shows that curriculum policy-makers typically require high-stake tests to change what is taught (e.g., oracy rather than literacy) and how it is taught (teaching and learning methods, curriculum materials). The introduction of an Arabic-language test in schools "was capable of changing the whole domain of teaching Arabic, as the test content was in fact integrated into all the domains – curriculum, teaching and learning" (Shohamy, 2001, p. 73).

Similarly, a high-status test of English as a foreign language (EFL) in Israel became the determiner of classroom methodology: "The EFL test clearly triggered a tremendous impact on classroom activities, time allotment, content and methodology ... it became the de facto new curriculum, de facto new model of teaching methods and de facto new teaching material, which were very different from what was stated in the official curriculum" (Shohamy, 2001, p. 84).

Research using language-performance testing

Examples of the use of language tests in research are found in studies of the effectiveness of various forms of bilingual education (e.g., August & Hakuta, 1997; Ramirez, Yuen, & Ramey, 1991; Thomas & Collier, 2002). Lindholm-Leary's (2001) research on the effectiveness of dual-language schools is a particularly admirable example of such research. Her findings on such dual-language provision are based on a wealth of quality data from 20 schools.

Lindholm-Leary (2001) measured oral language proficiency, literacy, academic achievement, and attitudes, plus teacher and parent attitudes and classroom interactions. Students were tested bilingually in Spanish and English using the Language Assessment Scale (LAS) and the IDEA Proficiency Test (IPT). The LAS provides an overall picture of oral linguistic skills in English and Spanish, assessing the basic sounds of language (phonemic skills), vocabulary (referential skills), grammar (syntactic skills), and the ability to use the language (pragmatic skills). The IPT places students of seven oral language-proficiency levels (from beginning to mastery) and assists in the classification of students according to relative levels of bilingualism. Administered in both English and Spanish, the IPT measures four basic areas of oral language proficiency: vocabulary, comprehension, syntax, and verbal expression (see also Harris & Murtagh, 1999, for criterion-referenced testing of Irish-language listening and speaking competences based on linguistic theory).

Language-planning performance indicators/targets

It is important in language-policy-making and language planning to have clear aims and priorities. But broad aims can be the ruination of the best of intentions. Aims are often lofty aspirations toward which specific policies make varying degrees of progress. Language-policy aims can sometimes be well-intentioned wishes and hopes that do not relate to grounded activity or successful interventions. Broad-brush strategies seem rational because language policies can have much variety, but they may result in a lack of effective and cost-efficient policies and practices.

To remedy these shortcomings, the concept of *target language planning* has come into vogue (e.g., in Wales and the Basque Country). Target language planning involves (Baker, 2003): (1) a clear overall conceptualization of language planning (e.g., status, corpus, acquisition, and opportunity/incentive planning), and (2) the setting of realizable and sustainable targets that are (3) prioritized and (4) monitored for their completion, effectiveness, and outcomes. Examples of target planning are given below (adapted from Baker, 2003):

Examples of language acquisition-planning targets

1. By December 2008
100% of new parents to be provided with information about the benefits of early bilingualism.

2. By September 2008
The number of children in bilingual education at the elementary school level to have increased by 5% from a 2004 baseline.

Examples of opportunity/use language-planning targets

1. By September 2008
The numbers of students in vocational training through the minority language to have doubled against a 2004 baseline.

2. By March 2007
The number of workplaces operating bilingually to have increased by 10% against the 2003 survey baseline.

Examples of status language-planning targets

1. By December 2008
The number of public institutions with a bilingual customer interface to have risen from a 2004 baseline by 25%.

2. By December 2006
100% of road signposts to be bilingual

Examples of corpus language-planning targets

1. By December 2008
Specialized terminology dictionaries in the minority language to be available free on the World Wide Web.

2. By December 2005
Commencement of project to produce speech recognition software in the minority language.

Action research

The research methodology of performance indicators and target measurement is essentially top-down. Its model of language planning is usually about central initiatives and direction. In comparison, there are bottom-up approaches where language planning is driven more at grass-roots level, with local initiatives and interventions. In this vogue, one recent approach used in language-policy-making is action research (Cohen, Manion, & Morrison, 2000).

Action research aims to lead to an improvement in practice, usually within a unique context. Often collaborative, with the aim of evaluating a change in practice, action research aims to increase practical wisdom, situated knowledge, and insightful decision-making as well as enhancing current practice in an upward spiral of improvement. Rather than change being imposed from outside, or from research wisdom supplied by academics or bureaucrats, action research aims to give personal empowerment and emancipation by investing decision-making in practitioners and policy-makers. Action research works by a variety of qualitative and quantitative methods with the underlying principle of development occurring by a planned, systematic, and sustained relationship between research, reflection, and action. The methods of action research are derived from the widest portfolio of research techniques in psychology, sociology, anthropology, and other social sciences.

An example of action research derives from language planning in which interventions are concurrently researched and evaluated, not only to establish their impact, but to provide formative feedback to improve the intervention. For example, the Welsh Language Board (the government's language-planning agency in Wales: www.bwrdd-yr-iaith.org.uk) established an action-research project whereby midwives and health visitors were trained to inform parents about the many cultural, communication, cognitive, curriculum, character, and cash advantages of bringing up their children bilingually (Edwards & Newcombe, 2003). Such a project is about intergenerational language transmission and reproducing a minority language in families (Fishman, 1991).

A Critical Conclusion

Psycho-sociological research on language policy has received a series of criticisms that are general to human research, particularly the quantitative approach. At one level, there are ideologically based criticisms such as the following:

1 Research (e.g., on language use and language attitudes) cannot establish causal connections between variables.
2 Research is incapable of uncovering meaningful aspects of social action.
3 People's opinions are not contextualized and therefore are open to being misunderstood.
4 Such research assumes that human action is determined by external forces and neglects the role of human consciousness, intentions, and understandings as important sources of action.

5 Surveys in particular follow ritualistic methodological rules and lack imagination or depth of understanding.
6 Theoretical input is implicit rather than explicit.
7 Only the trivial and superficial is measured, and such research fails to penetrate the meanings and understandings of people who are sampled, but rather arranges answers to fit a conceptualization that is essentially that of the researcher.

There are also many technique-based criticisms that overlap with the ideological critique. Among these criticisms are the following:

1 Questions are ambiguous, sometimes leading, and have in-built social desirability or prestige biases in answers.
2 The questions themselves can create artificial opinions.
3 Little evidence is provided to establish the reliability or validity of research.
4 There is an over-reliance on single-item measurement.
5 The data provides a quick snapshot but no film of interaction and language life.
6 Samples are often small and unrepresentative.
7 The interviewer or researcher has an effect on responses.
8 The physical setting of the research and the "season" in which research is carried out affect responses.
9 Evidence is attenuated to simple categorization and a number system.
10 Ahistorical accounts of issues are presented.

Nevertheless, psycho-sociological language policy research has made key theoretical (e.g., ethnolinguistic vitality), programmatic (e.g., the attributes of effective bilingual education), and practical (e.g., action research on language transmission) contributions. Working within the limitations of extant research methodologies, such research has evolved key concepts (e.g., language attitudes) and made bridges between academia and government (e.g., census data) to supply meaningful and influential analyses to further language-policy-making.

Annotated Bibliography

CIPCA (Centro de Investigación y Promoción del Campesidado) (1995). *Bolivia plurilingüe: Guia para planifecadores y educadores*. La Paz: UNICEF.

This analysis of Bolivian language census data is outstanding for combining data analysis, informative maps, and analytical text, all of which both are informed by theory and inform policy-making.

Gardner, R. C. (1985). *Social psychology and second language learning.* London: Edward Arnold.
This book is a classic seeking to address the psycho-sociological origins of second-language acquisition. Using a quantitative approach, the book comprehensively reviews research and builds a theoretical framework, which is then tested by careful research for parsimony and power.

Garrett, P., Coupland, N., & Williams, A. (2003). *Investigating language attitudes: Social meanings of dialect, ethnicity and performance.* Cardiff: University of Wales Press.
This provides an up-to-date, international review of the literature on language attitudes. The commentary is critical but fair and balanced, with a strong analysis of methodological approaches. The Matched Guise technique is particularly favored and illustrated.

Lindholm-Leary, K. J. (2001). *Dual language education.* Clevedon: Multilingual Matters.
Using multiple educational, psychometric, and socio-psychological indices and large samples of students, Kathryn Lindholm-Leary provides robust and careful analyses revealing the success of dual-language schools in language development, educational effectiveness, and student and school achievement.

Shohamy, E. (2001). *The power of tests: A critical perspective on the uses of language tests.* Harlow: Pearson Education.
Elana Shohamy provides a well-rgued, erudite critical analysis of language testing that is internationally relevant. Using Israeli examples, she demonstrates that political change and top-down educational change are often achieved by language tests and testing.

Discussion Questions

1 What are the values and limitations of census data on languages? How does such data relate to language-policy-making?

2   In your experience, are changes in education language policy often driven by new language tests and testing? If so, who is controlling whom, and with what degree of success?

3   For one minority language, what attitudes exist toward that language among: (a) teenagers, (b) parents of newborn children, (c) educationalists, (d) politicians, and (e) the general public? Why are there differences in attitude among those groups?

4   Locate one social network of bilinguals (e.g., in a school). By asking questions about who speaks what language to whom, try to portray which language domains are used by each language, and what such a profile suggests for the future of each language.

5   What action research project would you initiate with a language in your region?

6   This chapter has illustrated different styles/tools of research. List the strengths and weaknesses of any two of these.

REFERENCES

Allard, R. & Landry, R. (1994). Subjective ethnolinguistic vitality: A comparison of two measures. *International Journal of the Sociology of Education, 108,* 117–44.

August, D. & Hakuta, K. (1997). *Improving schooling for language-minority children.* Washington, DC: National Academy Press.

Baker, C. (1992). *Attitudes and language.* Clevedon: Multilingual Matters.

Baker, C. (1995). Bilingual education and assessment. In B. M. Jones & P. Ghuman (eds.), *Bilingualism, education and identity* (pp. 130–58). Cardiff: University of Wales Press.

Baker, C. (2001). *Foundations of bilingual education and bilingualism* (3rd edn). Clevedon: Multilingual Matters.

Baker, C. (2003). Language planning: A grounded approach. In J.-M. Dewaele, A. Housen, & Li Wei (eds.), *Bilingualism: Beyond basic principles* (pp. 88–111). Clevedon: Multilingual Matters.

Baker, C. & Jones, S. P. (1998). *Encyclopedia of bilingualism and bilingual education.* Clevedon: Multilingual Matters.

Baldauf, R. B., Jr (2002). Methodologies for policy and planning. In R. Kaplan (ed.), *The Oxford handbook of applied linguistics* (pp. 391–403). New York: Oxford University Press.

Bourhis, R. Y., Giles, H., & Rosenthal, D. (1981). Notes on the construction of a "subjective vitality questionnaire" for ethnolinguistic groups. *Journal of Multilingual and Multicultural Development, 2,* 145–55.

Brindley, G. (2002). Issues in language assessment. In R. Kaplan (ed.), *The Oxford handbook of applied linguistics* (pp. 459–70). New York: Oxford University Press.

CIPCA (Centro de Investigación y Promoción del Campesidado) (1995). *Bolivia plurilingüe: Guia para planifecadores y educadores.* La Paz: UNICEF.

Cohen, L., Manion, L., & Morrison, K. (2000). *Research methods in education* (5th edn). London: Routledge.

Commission of the European Union DGXXII (1998). *Report submitted to the Commission of the European Union DGXXII: Education, Training, and Youth 31 May 1998: Developing policies to improve the conversion of language competence into language use among young adult groups* (Agreement 96-06-AUT-O145-00). Brussels: Commission of the European Union DGXXII.

Edwards, J. R. (1977). Students' reactions to Irish regional accents. *Language and Speech, 20,* 280–6.

Edwards, V. & Newcombe, L. P. (2003). *Evaluation of the efficiency and effectiveness of the Twf Project: Final report.* Cardiff: Welsh Language Board.

Nelde, P., Strubell, M., & Williams, G. (1996). *Euromosaic: The production and reproduction of the minority language groups in the European Union.* Luxembourg: Office for Official Publications of the European Communities.

Fishman, J. A. (1980). Bilingualism and biculturalism as individual and as societal phenomena. *Journal of Multilingual and Multicultural Development, 1,* 3–15.

Fishman, J. A. (1991). *Reversing language shift.* Clevedon: Multilingual Matters.

Gardner, N. (2000). *Basque in education in the Basque Autonomous Community.* Vitoria-Gasteiz: Eusko Jaurlaritzaren Argitalpen Zerbitzu Nagusia.

Gardner, R. C. (1985a). *Social psychology and second language learning.* London: Edward Arnold.

Gardner, R. C. (1985b). *The Attitude/Motivation Test Battery* (technical report). Canada: University of Western Ontario.

Gardner, R. C. (2002). Social psychological perspective on second language acquisition. In R. Kaplan (ed.), *The Oxford handbook of applied linguistics* (pp. 160–9). New York: Oxford University Press.

Garrett, P., Coupland, N., & Williams, A. (2003). *Investigating language attitudes: Social meanings of dialect, ethnicity and performance.* Cardiff: University of Wales Press.

Giles, H. & Coupland, N. (1991). *Language: Contexts and consequences.* Milton Keynes: Open University Press.

Giles, H., Bourhis R., & Taylor, D. (1977). Towards a theory of language in ethnic group relations. In H. Giles (ed.), *Language, ethnicity and intergroup relations* (pp. 307–48). London: Academic Press.

Giles, H., Hewstone, M., & Ball, P. (1983). Language attitudes in multilingual settings: Prologue with priorities. *Journal of Multilingual and Multicultural Development, 4,* 81–100.

Giles, H., Noels, K. A., Ota, H., Ng, S. H., Gallois, C., Ryan, E. B., et al. (2000). Age vitality across eleven nations. *Journal of Multilingual and Multicultural Development, 21,* 308–23.

Harris, J. & Murtagh, L. (1999). *Teaching and learning Irish in primary school: A review of research and development.* Dublin: Institiuid Teangeolaiochta Eireann.

Khubchandani, L. M. (2001). Linguistic census. In R. Mesthrie (ed.), *Concise encyclopedia of sociolinguistics* (pp. 648–50). Amsterdam: Elsevier Science.

Lewis, E. G. (1981). *Bilingualism and bilingual education.* Oxford: Pergamon Press.

Lindholm-Leary, K. J. (2001). *Dual language education.* Clevedon: Multilingual Matters.

Milroy, A. L. (2001). Social networks. In R. Mesthrie (ed.), *Concise encyclopedia of sociolinguistics* (pp. 370–6). Amsterdam: Elsevier Science.

Oficina Central de Estadística e Informática (1993). *Censo indígena de Venezuela 1992.* Caracas: Oficina Central de Estadística e Informática.

Ovando, C., Collier, V., & Combs, M. (2003). *Bilingual and ESL classrooms: Teaching in multicultural contexts* (3rd edn). New York: McGraw-Hill.

Ramirez, J. D., Yuen, S. D., & Ramey, D. R. (1991). *Final report: Longitudinal study of structured English immersion strategy: Early-exit and late-exit programs for language-minority children* (report submitted to the United States Department of Education). San Mateo, CA: Aguirre International.

Ricento, T. (2005). Considerations of identity in L2 learning. In E. Hinkel (ed.), *Handbook of research in second language learning and teaching* (pp. 895–911). Mahwah, NJ: Lawrence Erlbaum.

Shohamy, E. (2001). *The power of tests: A critical perspective on the uses of language tests.* Harlow: Pearson Education.

Spolsky, B. (1995). *Measured words: The development of objective language testing.* Oxford: Oxford University Press.

Thomas, W. P. & Collier, V. P. (2002). *A national study of school effectiveness for language minority students' long-term academic achievement* (final report). Washington, DC: Center for Research on Education, Diversity & Excellence.

PART III

Topical Areas in Language Policy

Topical Areas in Language Policy: An Overview

Thomas Ricento

In this part of the book, seven rather broad topics are dealt with by scholars who have made major contributions in each of the areas. The topics were chosen, in part, because they demonstrate the ways in which language (and language policy) is imbricated in all aspects of social identity and social change. Language is the medium by and through which individuals define and inhabit their own identities and, in the process, assess and ascribe the identities of others. It is often these differences in identities (whether achieved or ascribed) that lead to conflicts in which language may play an important role. The fact that there are between 6,000 and 8,000 oral languages and only about 200 states in the world means that most states are multilingual – and multicultural – to varying degrees. It is also the case that in most (but not all) states there is usually only one "national" language (official or not); this means that, by definition, those who command the national language(s) will tend to enjoy greater recognition and socioeconomic status than those who do not speak or write that language. If individuals or groups are barred access to the national language, and especially the standard "prestige" written variety, or if they are expected to assimilate into the dominant language and abandon their mother tongue (and cultural identities) without a realistic expectation of access to the political economy and the benefits it provides, there is the potential for conflict. Supporters of monolingualism in the national language will argue that all citizens and immigrants must abandon their "non-national" identities and conform to the expectations of the state; opponents of monolingualism will argue that citizenship should not depend on monolingualism in the national language, especially in cases in which other languages *could* be considered national languages, such as with Spanish in the US; further, opportunities for assimilating may be limited *because* of lack of opportunities to acquire oral fluency and/or literacy in the national language, and not because of an unwillingness to learn the national language. Frequently, other non-linguistic attributes, founded on racial, ethnic, religious, political, or other group-based characteristics, are invoked by dominant groups to explain the "failure" of minorities to integrate into the mainstream society. Here is where notions of identity, that is, "us" (good "insider" group) vs. "them" (bad "outsider" group), come into play. The valuation of groups changes over time, but at any given historical point there tends to be a socially constructed hierarchy from low to high, indexed to purported cultural (including linguistic and political) differences. Thus, a language is not the only (or even the central) factor informing conflicts around national identity; rather, it is an element which is invoked to assert the legitimacy of groups' claims in the assertion, or contestation, of power.

Given the roles that language(s) can play in the assertion, maintenance, and contestation of power and social arrangements, from local to national and supranational contexts, the question arises: how can different ethnolinguistic minority groups maintain their cultures and languages *if they so choose* while peacefully co-existing with the majority/ dominant group(s) within the modern, liberal state? Specifically, what solutions have been proposed by scholars and policy-makers and how likely is it that these solutions, or recommendations, will be accepted by states and the various interested parties?

One of the solutions to dealing with conflicts that may arise because of the existence of multilingualism within the current state system is proposed by advocates of language rights, variously referred to as minority language rights (MLR: Stephen May, chapter 14) and linguistic human rights (LHR: Tove Skutnabb-Kangas, chapter 15). Before considering the rationale for this approach, a case needs to be made as to why it is worthwhile, or even necessary, to be concerned about the fate of the languages (and cultures) of minority groups in the first place. Clearly, languages (and cultural groups) have come and gone since the first appearance of our human ancestors. Stephen May (chapter 14) lists four principal reasons why we should support MLR. First is the exponential decline and loss of many of the world's languages. May cites statistics from Krauss (1992, 1995), who predicts, on the basis of current trends, that between 20 percent and 50 percent of the world's estimated 6,800 languages (Grimes, 2000) will "die" by the end of the twenty-first century. May notes that "language decline and loss occur most often in bilingual or multilingual contexts in which a majority language – that is, a language with greater political power, privilege, and social prestige – comes to replace the range and functions of a minority language. The inevitable result is that speakers of the minority language 'shift' over time to speaking the majority language" (pp. 257–8). Beyond the loss of languages, May notes, are the social, economic, and political *consequences* for minority-language speakers of such shift and loss. The groups most affected (variously estimated at between 5,000 and 8,000, including 250 million to 300 million members of the world's indigenous peoples) tend to be those already marginalized and/or subordinated.

Second, the existence of "majority" and "minority" language hierarchies did not come about as a natural or even primarily linguistic process. Rather, May argues, languages, and the status attached to them, are the result of wider historical, social, and political forces. The development of standardized languages from a multitude of language varieties resulted from the politics of state-making. The ideal of one nation-state with one national language is a relatively recent phenomenon, arising from the French Revolution of 1789 and the advent of European nationalism. Thus, the concept of the nation-state as having one national language is not a natural or inevitable fact of human social organization. If anything, multilingualism (as was argued above) is the norm. Just as the choice and construction of a particular language variety as *the* national language were a deliberate political act, "so too was the process by which other language varieties were subsequently 'minoritized' or 'dialectalized' by and within these same nation-states" (May, p. 261). Rather than accept the dominant one-nation/one-language ideology as a given, with its many corollaries – for example, that multilingualism is a "threat" to the unity and stability of the state, that social mobility is enhanced by the abandonment of minority languages, that minority languages have little if any value, and so on – it behooves us to consider *how* languages became positioned as relatively "good, useful, valuable" or "bad, useless, valueless" within the state system.

Third, the belief that the replacement of the minority language with the "national" language will enhance social mobility creates the expectation among citizens that persons who maintain their minority languages are choosing to live in the past, since majority languages are viewed as "vehicles" of modernity while minority languages are viewed as "carriers" of identity. This dichotomizing of languages as having instrumental (majority-language) or identity (minority-language) functions is not only false but tends to perpetuate a negative and limited view of minority languages, and those who speak them.

The only "rational" choice available to speakers of minority languages, in this view, is to shift to the majority language (where this is an option), thus perpetuating and accelerating language shift to one of the roughly 300 languages that are likely to survive into the next century. Robert Phillipson (chapter 19) argues that in addition to putting pressure on national languages in Europe, the privileged status of English in most international organizations, scientific scholarship, and international banking and development helps perpetuate socioeconomic inequities between the "haves" and "have nots."

Finally, according to May, "the LHR research paradigm argues that minority languages, and their speakers, should be accorded at least some of the protections and institutional support that majority languages already enjoy" (p. 265) to enhance opportunities for civic participation from a position of greater equality. May, following the work of Kymlicka and others, does not argue that all languages be treated equally, or that speakers of all languages have equal rights claims. Rather, as he has argued elsewhere (e.g., May, 2001), only national minorities can make rights claims for "formal inclusion of their languages and cultures in the civic realm" (p. 266). While he supports the idea "that where there is a sufficient number of other-language speakers, these speakers should be allowed to use that language as part of the exercise of their individual rights as citizens," and to "cultivate and pursue unhindered their own historic cultural and linguistic practices in the private domain," May makes clear that "extending greater ethnolinguistic *democracy* to minority-language groups, via LHR, does not thus amount to an argument for ethno-linguistic *equality* for all such groups" (p. 266). Majority languages, according to May, will continue to dominate in most language domains; yet, formal (i.e., institutional) protection and support for national minority languages, along with active linguistic protection by the state for the unhindered maintenance of other languages "where numbers warrant," at the very least in the private domain, would go far toward slowing and perhaps reversing the loss of languages and reducing power differentials between languages in a given polity.

While May and Skutnabb-Kangas explore how a language-rights approach, with its focus on moral arguments and juridical frameworks, may help safeguard languages and domains for their use, Joshua Fishman (chapter 17) discusses the myriad ways by which language shift occurs despite, or even as a result of, deliberate attempts to forestall such shift. Fishman also argues that the absence of authoritative policy (a "no-policy policy") generally works in favor of the stronger party in many settings throughout the world. This is, of course, precisely why advocates of LHRs argue that state intervention on behalf of weaker parties is necessary, and why dominant groups, who wish to maintain their power, are reluctant to support such interventions. Yet there are domains in which the state plays an active, authoritative role in language planning and policy. Pre-eminent among these is the education sector (Christina Bratt Paulston and Kai Heidemann, chapter 16), especially public primary and secondary education, where choices are made by state and, in some contexts, local authorities about which language(s) and language varieties will be used as the medium of instruction, and which language(s) will be offered as foreign languages or languages of wider communication, among many other matters. As was noted previously, states generally recognize one, or sometimes two, languages as the "national" language(s) (whether officially or unofficially) and support this or these language(s) (to the exclusion of others) in national civic life, including the education system(s). This support in and of itself tends over time to promote language shift to the dominant language and loss of the minority language. Overall, the rate and degree of shift, according to Lieberson et al. (1975), varies depending on the relative status of the language minority group along four parameters: (1) indigenous superordinate; (2) migrant superordinate; (3) indigenous subordinate; and (4) migrant subordinate. The rate of mother-tongue loss among the first two groups, according to Lieberson et al., would be extremely slow, while shift and mother-tongue loss for the latter two groups would be expected to be much faster. Other factors that influence rate of language shift include: attitudes of groups toward language maintenance and cultural assimilation, lack of access or incentives to acquire the majority language, self-imposed or externally imposed boundary maintenance, and complementary functional distribution of other languages (Paulston and Heidemann, p. 297). Thus, while support of the national language in public education is an important means of promoting the linguistic and cultural assimilation of minorities (and shift to the national language), it alone does not determine the degree or rate of language shift in a society. It is also important to note that most of these discussions of language rights and language shift are about oral, not sign, languages. The situation with regard to sign languages is, if anything, even more complex and controversial since, as Timothy Reagan (chapter 18, p. 334) notes, "even the determination of what 'mother tongue' might mean in the case of the Deaf child is far from self-evident, and remains a matter of potential conflict."

Of course there are other ways that states, or agencies supported by the state, can influence the acquisition (or non-acquisition) of languages. One such way discussed by Paulston and Heidemann is standardization, the process by which a language comes to have a normative orthography, grammar, and lexicon. The decision on which variety of a language is chosen as the "standard" will have an impact on groups whose spoken variety is quite different from the written variety chosen. This occurred, for example, in Louisiana (US), where the Council for the Development of French in Louisiana had to choose between Cajun French, Haitian Creole, or International French as the written standard. Speakers of "non-standard" French in Louisiana, in learning the standard variety, come to believe that their variety is incorrect and inappropriate, and may have little incentive to acquire an imposed variety. Another example is provided by Skutnabb-Kangas (cited by Reagan, chapter 18, p. 333), who argues that recognized and sometimes standardized sign languages, such as American Sign Language, can become dominant and displace other Sign languages. Paulston and Heidemann describe another context in northern Italy, in which Ladin was used only as a spoken medium and attempts to create an artificial, common written variety were carefully avoided so as not to endanger the language. The authors also describe successful language-policy efforts to revitalize minority languages among the Maori in New Zealand and Basques in Spain and France. In the case of Basque in France, although the French state did not officially recognize the language, a small group of Basque parents organized a Basque language pre-school in the late 1960s, which expanded in the 1970s, largely through local resources and support. By the end of the 1970s enrollment had grown from 8 students to over 400, and by 1990 over a dozen schools were serving 830 students. By 2000, according to Paulston and Heidemann, "almost 2,000 students were enrolled in two dozen Basque-medium schools from pre-school to high-school level" (p. 304). While the situation of Basque in France is less favorable than that in Spain, the positive change in the learning of Basque in France demonstrates that grass-roots efforts at language revitalization can succeed, even in the absence of state support.

Jan Blommaert (chapter 13) argues that language policy should be seen as a niched activity, in which, for example, the role of certain actors (such as the state) is limited to specific domains, activities, and relationships, not general ones (p. 249). In other domains, different activities and relationships exist and will respond to different sets of norms and rules of language and communication produced by actors operating on different levels and scales. What the chapters in this part describe are the various domains in which actors influence and respond to different sets of norms and rules of language and communication.

REFERENCES

Grimes, B. (ed.) (2000). *Ethnologue: Languages of the world* (14th edn). Dallas, TX.: SIL.

Krauss, M. (1992). The world's languages in crisis. *Language, 68,* 4–10.

Krauss, M. (1995). Language loss in Alaska, the United States and the world: Frame of reference. *Alaska Humanities Forum, 6*(1), 2–5.

Lieberson, S., Dalto, G., & Johnston, M. E. (1975). The course of mother tongue diversity in nations. *American Journal of Sociology, 81,* 34–61.

May, S. (2001). *Language and minority rights: Ethnicity, nationalism and the politics of language.* London: Longman.

CHAPTER THIRTEEN

Language Policy and National Identity

Jan Blommaert

It is an unfortunate situation for social scientists, but the world is not neatly divided into monolingual states. Consequently, official administrative belonging – being a citizen of a state – is a poor indicator of sociolinguistic belonging, let alone of language behavior in general. The relationship between national *identity* and the language-oriented activities of the state is even less straightforward, if for nothing else because of the elusiveness of "identity." Whenever we talk about identity, we need to differentiate between "achieved" or "inhabited" identity – the identity people themselves articulate or claim – and "ascribed" or "attributed" identity – the identity given to someone by someone else. The two do not necessarily coincide, as will become clear further on, and matters are considerably complicated by this. This chapter will consequently have two aims: to clarify the general issues involved in the relationship between language policy and national identity, and to illustrate this relationship by means of an example.

The title "Language Policy and National Identity" presupposes the existence of each of the constituent terms and their collocations: "language," "policy" (language policy), and "national," "identity" (national identity). The overall collocation suggests that there is an effective relationship between language policy and national identity. I shall propose that there is one, but that it must be seen as an *ideological* relationship and as a *specific* one. I must start with basics, though: a reflection on the nation and the state.

Nation (and) State

It is a common feature of much academic writing in this field to use "nation" and "state" as near-synonymous terms. As soon as a state acquires sovereignty, it seems to acquire the label of "nation-state." This label, then, suggests that the "state" – a formal system of institutions – is also a "nation" – the result of *nationalism*, a very specific political and ideological process. Though at first glance commonsensical, the colloca- tion is by no means warranted as a default description of states. Empirically, there are a good number of states where a true nationalist project (as defined, e.g., by Hobsbawm, 1990) does not exist, or where, in fact, the "nation" is organized around *coercion* rather than around ideological *consent* and where, consequently, a term such as "statism" would be more appropriate. There is abundant evidence for this in my own field of study, Africa, and no doubt elsewhere as well. Second, nationalism does not require a state. Very often it emerges as a *reaction against* the state, and a good number of successful nationalisms were in fact anti-state nationalisms (as in Flanders–Belgium, Catalonia–Spain, Québec–Canada). The success of these nationalisms generated new state structures at the regional level, and thus transformed the nation- alist project into a statist one. So for sound analytic reasons, it is advisable to separate "nation" and "state," and consider the "nation- state" as one specific combination of the two, the existence of which needs to be empirically established, not posited *a priori*.

In the era of globalization, one also frequently encounters statements about the demise of the nation-state. It is argued, then, that con- temporary social processes, notably in the fields of labor and culture (including identity processes), develop in "transnational" networks no longer responding to "national" dynamics of labor division and identity categorization (see, e.g., Castells, 1998, for a discussion). This is partly true, but again we need to differentiate between the nation and the state. It may well be that a classic, modernist project of national- ism becomes far more difficult to accomplish under conditions of globalization, and that consequently, the traditional nation is on its way out. But that does not entail that the state is on its way out. If we follow Immanuel Wallerstein (1983, 2000), the contemporary (globalized) capitalist World System hinges on a complex of *inter-state* relations in which macro-scale labor divisions and value-allocations are organized unequally. We need not go into Wallerstein's argument in detail here, but we should note the way in which he emphasizes the active role of states in shaping and defining processes we now call globalization.[1] So under globalization the nation may be under pressure, but the state appears to do well.

But of course, the state does not remain untouched by globalization, and the notion of "state" itself suggests not only the internationally acknowledged existence of a "state" – like, for example, Somalia, Congo, or Sierra Leone – but also the effectiveness and autonomy of this state as a system of organizational and administrative apparatuses. This can by no means be taken for granted, and it is again a matter for investigation and not for positing. The examples given above – Somalia, Congo, and Sierra Leone – are "states" in the first sense of the term, but not in the second sense. Governments of these countries have hardly any effective control over their territories, and their capacity to enforce measures taken by the "state" over the totality of their territory is non-existent. All kinds of core "state" functions, ranging from organized (military and police) violence to education and medical services, are in effect performed by "non-state" agents such as rebel movements, international NGOs or international organizations such as UNHCR and UNICEF, local sub-state organizations, international businesses, and so on (Ferguson & Gupta, 2002). This is true not only for clear cases such as the ones given, but also for contemporary states in the center of the World System. Governments now share "state" power (e.g., in the fields of defense, economic, and monetary affairs) with international business, international organizations such as the European Union, the World Bank, NATO, regional or local autonomous governments (e.g., the states in the United States), and "civil society" organizations such as trade unions. The term "state" as a descriptor for "state activities" can thus technically pertain both to "sub-state" institutions, ranging from civil society organizations to regional and local governments, and to "super-state" institutions, such as business and other networks, the EU, NATO or the United Nations.

What does all this mean for our discussion here? It means that our object of investigation is in effect a rather narrow and highly specific category of cases: those countries where an effective state system manages to conduct nationalist policies through language policy. It also means that we should be careful with the term *national*: a national language policy may only seemingly be "national," that is, confined and specific to the territory of a single state, and effected exclusively by state actors. Actors and influences in the field of language policy can be manifold and involve both sub-state, state, and super-state actors in processes of considerable complexity (see the essays in Blommaert, 1999a).

In fact, one of the challenging new areas of research into language policies could precisely address the way in which language policies emerge out of an interplay of actors at very different levels, including, but not exclusive to, national governments. "National" language policies can be imposed by super-state forces, or these policies can be an effect of national governments seeking new international alliances with certain partners. The EU has a self-image of multilingualism, which it enforces through nationally ratified educational policies. The growing emphasis on the use of English in education in the peripheries of the World System, articulated in national language and educational policies in several countries, is based on an image of globalization as monocentric, with an English-dominant economic, financial, and political center. And the promotion of English in countries such as Congo and Mozambique, where English used to be a marginal linguistic commodity, is motivated by a desire of national governments to align themselves with the United States and international organizations such as the International Monetary Fund and the World Bank.

Finally, it also means that *national identity* seen in relation to *language* becomes a very problematic category. To this issue I now turn.

Language, Policy, and Identity

Let us recall some of the theses articulated in classic studies on nationalism: Anderson (1983), Gellner (1983), Greenfeld (1992), and Hobsbawm (1990). Interestingly, all these authors emphasize the importance of language in the process of nation-building. But it is a specific kind of language: the printed word circulating in mass quantities and stimulating the growth and dissemination of "standard national languages." In fact, print capitalism was central to the becoming of modernity – the historical phase in which the nation-state as we now know it was created (Bauman, 1991; Habermas, 1984, 1987; Latour, 1993). But print capitalism also became the instrument for the massification of specific *language ideologies*, and at this point I should introduce my main argument.

The notion of language ideologies grew out of Sapirian and Whorfian linguistic anthropology, and it stands for socially and culturally embedded *metalinguistic* conceptualizations of language and its forms of usage (Kroskrity, 2001; Silverstein, 1979; see the essays in Schieffelin, Woolard, & Kroskrity, 1998). Language users have conceptions of language and language use: conceptions of "quality," value, status, norms, functions, ownership, and so forth. These conceptions guide the communicative behavior of language users; they use language on the basis of the conceptions they have and so reproduce these conceptions. These are ideological constructs, and they are sites of power and authority. Language use is ideologically stratified and regimented, and the "best" language/language variety is distinguished from "less adaquate" varieties in every instance of use (Gal & Woolard, 2001; see the essays in Kroskrity, 2000). Thus, written language would be valued more highly than spoken language; standard more highly than dialect, specific expert registers more highly than general lay registers, and so forth.

The advent of print capitalism offered an instrument for the dissemination of language ideologies that attributed the highest prestige to an autonomous, structured, semantically transparent (written) language variety – an elite variety over which the educated (upper) middle classes had control, but which was now imposed on the whole of society as *the* (only) Language and opposed to the "jargons," "speech," "dialects," and other forms of "imprecise," "vulgar," or "confused" (oral) language of the less educated masses. It was the sort of Language that would be laid out in grammars and dictionaries and then offered normatively, as a collection of strict rules, in the emerging national education systems.

Bauman and Briggs (2003) trace this language ideology to Bacon and, more prominently, Locke. Locke developed a highly elitist view on language as something that needed to be decontextualized and "purified" as part of the program of rationalist and detached individualism, central to modernity. Language, in this sense, became detached from (oral folk) "tradition" – the vernacular stories and anecdotes told by the common people and perceived by Locke as anti-rational, emotional, chaotic. It became the "standard" language of modernity. But before that could happen, a second intervention was required, according to Bauman and Briggs (2003). The oral and folk tradition, rejected by Locke, was rescued by Herder and the Grimm brothers and elevated to the level of "national character." But "tradition" had been *rationalized*, so to speak: the tradition needed to become modulated by the kind of transparent, standard language promulgated by Locke. And it is the combination of tradition seen as national identity and rationalist perceptions of standard speech that offered the launching platform for national (standard) languages as we now know them: linguistic items with a name ("English," "German," "Zulu"), defined as a set of decontextualized rules and norms, and confined to *national* spaces within which they could become the emblems of national identity.[2]

Important is the way in which both the emergence and dissemination of "the language" as well as its relation to the state (i.e., a relation that is seen as symbolizing the state as a "nation") are *ideological* processes, that is, processes that need not in any significant way reflect what people in the nation actually use in the way of language. It is a sociolinguistic truism that societies are almost by necessity *multilingual*, in the sense that many varieties, genres, styles, and codes occur, despite self-perceptions of societal monolingualism. Societies do reflect and sustain the *sociolinguistic regime* in a country, that is, the relative hierarchies normatively maintained and the dominant ideas surrounding them. Such ideas would include ownership, membership, and authority: "this is *our* language," "we are Americans and speak English," "this language doesn't belong here," "he doesn't speak the language well."

Consequently, and following Silverstein (1998), we should distinguish between "linguistic communities" and "speech communities," where the former are groups professing adherence to the normatively constructed, ideologically articulated "standard" Language ("we speak English") and the latter are groups characterized by the actual use of specific speech forms (e.g., professional jargons, but also dialects and even "standard" varieties of languages). The two, as said earlier, are not isomorphic, and the distance between the sociolinguistically definable community and the linguistic-ideologically definable community reveals the degree of hegemony of the language ideologies, often resulting in blind spots for sociolinguistic phenomena. In my own case, Belgian-Flemish language laws compel me to deliver my academic courses monolingually "in Dutch," and Flanders is a region characterized by unshakable perceptions of Dutch monolingualism in public life (seen as a Flemish-nationalist victory over Belgian-Francophone imperialism). I do teach in Dutch – at least if "teaching" is reduced to my oral contribution to class performances. The bulk of my course materials, however, are in English and French, and my research output is likewise multilingual. So students who wish to take my courses are, in actual fact, subjected to a *multilingual* complex of communicative practices, despite a strong feeling that they study "in Dutch" and despite my university's (and my regional government's) emphasizing the Dutch-speaking character of academic life in Flanders.

Silverstein (1996) calls this phenomenon a "monoglot" ideology. It rests on an ideologically configured belief that a society is *in effect* monolingual – that monolingualism is a fact and not an ideological perception – coupled with a denial of practices that point toward factual multilingualism and linguistic diversity (Blommaert & Verschueren, 1998). The phenomenon rests on associations between "pure," standard language, membership of an ethnolinguistically defined "people," and a particular region occupied by these (ethnolinguistically homogeneous) people. This ideology has effects, and I shall discuss three crucial ones:

1   It *informs practical language regimes* in education and other crucial spheres of public life. Language policy is invariably based on linguistic ideologies, on images of "societally desirable" forms of language usage and of the "ideal" linguistic landscape of society, in turn often derived from larger sociopolitical ideologies. Thus, a monoglot ideology may not only deny the existence of linguistic diversity, it may also sustain practices that actually and effectively prohibit linguistic diversity in the public domain. Examples abound, and recently some scholars have qualified such practices as "linguicide" (Skutnabb-Kangas, 2000). In effect, much linguistically articulated nationalism constructs language policies aimed at *reducing* linguistic diversity in society, sometimes even while explicitly advocating societal multilingualism (see the essays in Blommaert, 1999a).

2   It also *produces and regulates identities*. The state often appears as the guardian of the monoglot idealization of the link "language–people–country," and thus offers (and often imposes by coercion) particular ascriptive ethnolinguistic identities for its citizens. This is a very widespread phenomenon: since this is Indonesia, people speak Bahasa Indonesia; since this is Tanzania, people speak Swahili; since this is Flanders, people speak Dutch; and so on. The processes by means of which this happens are intricate, manifold, and often also "automatic," that is, implicit and not spectacular, assuming the shape of what Foucault called "governmentality" (the network of measures aimed at regulating people's lives) and leading to what Bourdieu called "habitus," a set of naturalized predispositions that "automatically" guide our behavior and can thus be converted into "inhabited" identities. The most common and powerful ethnolinguistic identity promulgated by the state is that of "monolingual speaker of (one of) the national language(s)," assuming that people are intrinsically monolingual and that such monolingualism is an organic feature of being a citizen of that country. The state is thus very often the actor that sustains and elaborates the belief in the existence and value of "a Language" in the sense of language

names – Dutch, English, Chinese, Zulu. Initially, "national identity" is therefore almost invariably an *ascriptive* identity attributed by the state or state-affiliated institutions such as education systems, and it most often revolves around a monolingually imagined one-to-one relation between national-administrative belonging and language use. This may then lead to an *inhabited* identity in which people effectively adopt the ethnolinguistic-national identity as part of a broader repertoire of identities.

3 Finally, it also has had a tremendous *impact on scholarship*. The reified and stratified, monoglot image of "a language" has informed language description – the image of ethnolinguistically bounded and internally homogeneous communities characterized by a (pure, decontextualized, normative) language was projected onto languages spoken elsewhere in the world (Fabian, 1986; Irvine & Gal, 2000), and was later adopted by postcolonial governments as the model of "good" language (e.g., Blommaert, 1999b). Similarly, this same ideology informed much of linguistics and sociolinguistics, in which authors even today assume the existence of bounded, rule-governed, and reified "languages" as their units of study (see Blommaert, 1996; Hymes, 1996, for a critique).

All of this has a profound impact on our thinking on identity, of course. We have failed to see the fine shades of identity often articulated not by one monoglot "language," but by delicate and moment-to-moment evolving variation between *varieties* of language, including accents, registers, styles, and genres. As mentioned above, identity is best seen not as one item, but as a repertoire of different possible identities, each of which has a particular range or scope and function. In that sense, a term such as "national identity" is, as said above, best seen as a *specific* ascriptive label attached to people. In the best of cases it can occasionally be an "achieved," adopted identity of people, but always with restricted sociolinguistic functions, often related to interactions between individuals and the state (filling in administrative forms, responding to survey questions and opinion polls, or in my case, accounting for my teaching practices in my university). If taken as the dominant, overwhelming (single) identity of people, it does not help us much in understanding the multiple, often unpredictable and volatile identity work we effectively perform when we communicate.[3] In scholarly traditions based on such notions, it has led to rather simplistic associations between "a language" and "an identity," which again overlook (and render invisible) the multiplicity and complexity of identity-work on the ground (see, e.g., Myers-Scotton, 1993).

The Ideological Process Illustrated

I will now turn to an illustration of the processes discussed in the previous sections and provide an account of language policy in Tanzania (East Africa). My focus will be on demonstrating how the language-political process was primarily an ideological process. Space restrictions prevent me from engaging with the details of the sociolinguistic situation and the history of language policy; I will have to refer readers to Blommaert (1999b and references therein) for more detailed information and discussion. Tanzania, I should emphasize, qualifies as a state where language policy and national identity effectively occur as an issue: it was a nationalist state (at least during one phase of its existence) and language was explicitly thematized in this context.

The postcolonial Tanzanian (then still Tanganyikan) state was one of the first to declare an indigenous language, Swahili, the national language of the country. It also became an official language alongside the former colonial language, English. Despite the absence of any formal language planning, a lot of language-policy measures ensued from this. Swahili was immediately introduced as the medium of instruction in primary education, alongside English as the (inherited) medium of instruction in post-primary education. Swahili also instantaneously became the language of political life (Tanzanian leaders systematically used Swahili when addressing their constituencies, and the language of parliamentary proceedings was Swahili) and of the majority of the mass media, both radio and printed press. Literature in Swahili was actively encouraged.

The real boost for Swahili came when the state embarked on a massive campaign of nation-building in the mid-1960s. This nation-building campaign was an attempt toward establishing socialist hegemony, and Swahili was given a crucial role in this. The language was defined as the language of African-socialist ("*Ujamaa*") ideas and values, and the generalized spread of Swahili would be a measurable index of the spread of socialism across the population. In terms of national identity, the *mwananchi* ("citizen") of *Ujamaa*-Tanzania would be a socialist and an African, *and* a monolingual, Swahili-speaking individual. National identity in Tanzania was defined in political-ideological and linguistic terms, not in ethnic or other cultural terms.

In terms of what has been discussed in the previous sections, a few qualifications are in order here. First, the ideal situation envisaged by the architects of the nation-building campaign was monoglot. The campaign would be a success when the population would use *one language imbued with one set of ideological loads*: those of *Ujamaa*. "Homogeneism" was the target (Blommaert & Verschueren, 1998), and the spread of Swahili-and-*Ujamaa* would have to go hand in hand with the *disappearance* of other languages-and-ideologies. The first target, obviously, was English – the language of imperialism, capitalism, and oppression; but the same went for the local languages, which were seen as vehicles for traditional, pre-colonial cultures, as well as for "non-standard" varieties of Swahili (e.g., code-switching, urban varieties), which were sensed to indicate the incompleteness of the process of hegemony. The "better" and "purer" one's Swahili would be, the better a socialist Tanzanian patriot one would be. We have here a typical Herderian cocktail of one language–one culture–one territory as an ideal organization for society. Recall also Herder's adoption of the Lockean emphasis on "purified" language as the vehicle of true authenticity: African socialists would be authentic if and when their African language – the vehicle of their "values" – would be purified and standardized.

Second, not only was the conception of language as a vehicle for a specified (politically defined) set of ideological values a typical case of Herderian imagination (and thus an inherited ideology from colonial language descriptions), but the whole *operational* conception of language was that inherited from colonial predecessor regimes as well (in ways similar to those described by Irvine & Gal, 2000; cf. Blommaert, 1994). Swahili was standardized by academic experts and its main vehicle was (normative) literacy produced through formal education systems. Scholarly and political efforts concentrated on standardization, language "development and modernization," purism, and so forth; in short, on the construction of Swahili as a purified (Lockean) artifact of normativity focused on referential functions.

There was a model for such a degree of "full languageness": English. Throughout the history of postcolonial linguistics in Tanzania, scholars kept referring to English whenever they discussed the kind of level of "development and modernization" that needed to be attained for Swahili. English was perceived as the language of a leading world power with a flourishing economy, a fabulous cultural history, and world-wide prestige, and this was what a "real" language should stand for.[4] Pending the accomplishment of such "full languageness" for Swahili, English would *have* to be used in higher education in order to produce a class of top-notch intellectuals needed for specialized service to the country. Thus, while Swahili was spread to all corners of the country and was used in almost every aspect of everyday life, post-primary education remained (and still is) a domain where English was hegemonic.

Thirty years of concentrated efforts toward the goal set forth in the 1960s resulted in the generalized spread of Swahili. Sociolinguistically, Swahili and its varieties have become the identifying code of public activities throughout Tanzania. The campaign in that sense was exceptionally successful. But what did not happen was the ideological homogenization of the country. While Swahilization was manifestly a success, the monoglot ideal in which language, political ideology, and identity would be coterminous was a failure. Neither English nor local languages and "impure" varieties of Swahili disappeared, and in the eyes of the language planners, this meant that Tanzanians had still not fully become *Ujamaa*-socialists but still displayed adherences to bourgeois values (through English) and to pre-socialist modes of life (through local languages). And the spread of Swahili did not galvanize the hegemony of *Ujamaa*: the one-party system collapsed in the late 1980s and was replaced by a multiparty, liberal capitalist state-organization, which, ironically, adopted Swahili as its vehicle for nationwide communication.

What does this mean? It means, first, that there was a widening gap between the intended ascriptive identity constructed by language planners – the monolingual, Swahili-speaking, socialist Tanzanian – and the inhabited identities of the people. Swahili, as mentioned, was spread to almost every corner of the country, where it was adopted as part of the speech repertoires of the local people. They used it for specific purposes: interaction across ethnolinguistic boundaries, administrative contacts, and primary education. When doing so, they articulated an inhabited identity which aligned them with the projected ideal *mwananchi*. But they did more than that, of course. The language planners had been wrong in their totalizing conception of socialist hegemony and the use of Swahili. Politics, in reality, was one domain of language usage, and Swahili was absolutely dominant in that domain. But it was *only* one domain, and for other domains, people continued to use local languages or other newly emerged forms of communication (Msanjila, 1999). So to the extent that only *one* identity was envisaged, the campaign was a failure. Adopting a more realistic perspective in which people are seen as having a repertoire of (domain-bound) identities, the campaign was a success. The momentous sociolinguistic change induced by the generalized spread of Swahili offered people a collection of new opportunities for "inhabited," achieved identities, a richer and more diversified repertoire of identities. But only one ascribed identity was used to cover this repertoire: that of the *mwananchi*. It was hopelessly inadequate; the monoglot, Herderian ideology adopted in language policy created huge blind spots in assessing the true impact of the Swahilization campaign.

The Tanzanian state was, and is, part of the world. It was encapsulated in a dynamics from below – the persistent usage of local languages, the genesis of Swahili-based new urban varieties, accents in Swahili, and subcultural jargons and slangs – and one from above – the historical and world-wide dominance of monoglot ideologies and ideologies of linguistic purification, the market pressures for English, and so on. In its role as a switchboard between these different levels it adopted perhaps the worst possible language-political instrument, one that denied its insertion in the dynamics from below and above and stressed the autonomy of a particular space, that of the state. Its projected "ideal" identity for citizens could never work *in terms of the ideology that guided the process.*

Conclusion

The case of Tanzania may offer a lesson which other nation-building states may want to pay attention to. Singular projections of language onto national identity do not work any more. In a mature sociolinguistics, the state and its operations should be seen as part of what goes on in the sociopolitical and cultural field in a country. It results in *specific* domains, activities, and relationships, not (unless, perhaps, in totalitarian systems) in *general* ones. Apart from these specific domains, activities, and relationships, several others exist and will continue to exist, and they will respond to (sometimes very) different sets of norms and rules of language and communication produced by actors operating at different levels and scales. Language policy, consequently, should best be seen as a *niched* activity, and the same goes for its desired product, national identity. We can now identify it as a niched *ideological* activity, necessarily encapsulated in and interacting with many others, regardless of how dominant it may seem at first sight.

Annotated Bibliography

Bauman, R. & Briggs, C. L. (2003). *Voices of modernity: Language ideologies and the politics of inequality*. Cambridge: Cambridge University Press. This is a splendid discussion of the ideological developments from Bacon to Boas, which shaped our "modern" conception of language and which led to widespread politics of inequality.

Blommaert, J. (ed.) (1999). *Language ideological debates*. Berlin: Mouton. Starting from a historical and sociolinguistic angle, this book presents essays in which language ideologies are identified as crucial ingredients in political debates.

Blommaert, J. & Verschueren, J. (1998). *Debating diversity: Analysing the discourse of tolerance*. London: Routledge.
This book offers an analysis of how ethnocultural and ethnolinguistic diversity is discussed and conceptualized in the context of immigration in Belgium, and emphasizes tendencies toward "homogeneism," that is, the denial of diversity as a social ideal.

Castells, M. (1998). *End of the millennium* (2nd edn). Oxford: Blackwell. In the burgeoning field of globalization studies, this work by Castells still occupies a unique place, providing incisive analyses of interactions between states and global networks, and providing some of the basic lexicon for globalization studies.

Fabian, J. (1986). *Language and colonial power: The appropriation of Swahili in the former Belgian Congo 1880–1938*. New York: Cambridge University Press.
This book gives an excellent historical analysis of colonial language planning, demonstrating how a particular form of Swahili was manufactured by colonial authorities. This is a highly critical account of sociolinguistic processes.

Gal, S. & Woolard, K. A. (eds.) (2001). *Languages and publics: The making of authority*. Manchester: St Jerome.

This collection addresses the connection between language ideologies and forms of normativity and authority in language. It offers both historical and contemporary analyses.

Hobsbawm, E. (1990). *Nations and nationalism since 1780: Programme, myth, reality*. Cambridge: Cambridge University Press.
This classic treatment of the development of the European nation-state remains highly useful, if for nothing else because of its terminological precision.

Hymes, D. (1996). *Ethnography, linguistics, narrative inequality: Toward an understanding of voice*. London: Taylor and Francis.
This book fundamentally recasts our view of sociolinguistic processes, focusing on inequality rather than difference. The book is also one of Hymes's most eloquent statements on ethnographic method and methodology.

Kroskrity, P. (ed.) (2000). *Regimes of language*. Santa Fe: School of American Research Press.
Alongside Schieffelin et al. (1998), this is one of the standard references on language ideologies, where readers will find long and insightful papers on the development of "modern" language ideologies.

Rampton, B. (1995). *Crossing: Language and ethnicity among adolescents*. London: Longman.
Rampton documents the dynamics of identities in contemporary societies in his classic study of all kinds of language "mixing" and "crossing" among multiethnic youth in Britain. He discusses the implications of his findings for theory and practice, especially with relation to language teaching.

Schieffelin, B., Woolard, K., & Kroskrity, P. (eds.) (1998). *Language ideologies: Practice and theory*. New York: Oxford University Press.
A classic and groundbreaking collection on language ideologies, this offers both theoretical and empirical observations on a wide range of cases, and sketches the scope of research on language ideologies.

Wallerstein, I. (1983) *Historical capitalism*. London: Verso.
A standard reference for "World Systems analysis," with its emphasis on scales and processes of inequality in the interstate capitalist system of division of labor.

Discussion Questions

1 Given the niched activity of the state, are there any other "niches" that can be identified, in which other actors impose language-ideologically informed norms and rules and thus call for very different forms of sociolinguistic behavior?
2 Can you identify such other sociolinguistic regimes as "oppositional," that is, acting against state-imposed regimes?
3 Try to describe the kind of state-organized or state-oriented practices you find yourself in, and describe the linguistic norms and codes valid there.
4 Could you reflect on globalization processes (e.g., the world-wide spread of internet literacy) in terms of "niched" sociolinguistic activity?
5 Could you reflect on election campaigns in the same terms?

NOTES

1 This, one could note, invalidates the "TINA" argument (There Is No Alternative) about globalization, often used by politicians. Globalization is presented as a massive and impersonal force on which national governments have hardly any impact. See Giddens (1998) for an example.
2 This, then, became the classic "Herderian" triad *people–language–territory*. A "people" (*Volk*) is characterized by a "language" which is spread over a "territory." This Herderian image of ethnolinguistic-national community became one of the dominant language ideologies in the field of language policy. Note that Herder systematically used "*Volk*" in two ways: as the "ethnic" or ethnolinguistically defined people *and* as the "common" people, the *plebeian* section of society (Bauman & Briggs, 2003, p. 183). The site of national authenticity, consequently, was not among the intellectuals or the upper classes (often characterized by multilingual repertoires), but among the "common people," imagined by Herder as being monolingual. Note also that often, the territorial dimension is overlooked in commentaries on Herder, despite the fact that the nation-state as imagined by Herder was clearly a territorially bounded unit – the territory populated by the ethnolinguistically homogenous *Volk*.
3 Ben Rampton's work is exemplary in this respect. Rampton provides an analysis of the various ways in which ethnically mixed groups of young adolescents in Britain articulate identities, using each other's accents, elements from subcultural jargons such as that of reggae, imitations of teachers' speech styles, references to class-based codes, and so

forth (Rampton, 1995). This volatility – and the problematic nature of such volatility – are also manifest in cases where people become "deterritorialized." Asylum seekers, for instance, perform intricate identity-work through complex shifts in speech styles and varieties. The gaps are dramatic between people who by definition do not belong to any "national" sociolinguistic regime but whose life is spent migrating, and the "national" codes of official services in charge of refugees (Maryns & Blommaert, 2001).

4   Irvine and Gal (2000) call this process "iconization": the suggestion that qualities of language mirror qualities of societies.

REFERENCES

Anderson, B. (1983). *Imagined communities: Reflections on the origin and spread of nationalism*. London: Verso.

Bauman, R. & Briggs, C. L. (2003). *Voices of modernity: Language ideologies and the politics of inequality*. Cambridge: Cambridge University Press.

Bauman, Z. (1991). *Modernity and ambivalence*. Cambridge: Polity.

Blommaert, J. (1994). The metaphors of development and modernization in Tanzanian language policy and research. In R. Fardon & G. Furniss (eds.), *African languages, development and the state* (pp. 213–26). London: Routledge.

Blommaert, J. (1996). Language planning as a discourse on language and society: The linguistic ideology of a scholarly tradition. *Language Problems and Language Planning, 20*, 199–222.

Blommaert, J. (ed.) (1999a). *Language ideological debates*. Berlin: Mouton.

Blommaert, J. (1999b). *State ideology and language in Tanzania*. Cologne: Köppe.

Blommaert, J. & Verschueren, J. (1998). *Debating diversity: Analysing the discourse of tolerance*. London: Routledge.

Castells, M. (1998). *End of the millennium* (2nd edn). Oxford: Blackwell.

Fabian, J. (1986). *Language and colonial power: The appropriation of Swahili in the former Belgian Congo 1880–1938*. New York: Cambridge University Press.

Ferguson, J. & Gupta, A. (2002). Spatializing states: Toward an ethnography of neoliberal governmentality. *American Ethnologist, 29*, 981–1002.

Gal, S. & Woolard, K. A. (eds.) (2001). *Languages and publics: The making of authority*. Manchester: St Jerome.

Gellner, E. (1983). *Nations and nationalism*. London: Blackwell.

Giddens, A. (1998). *The third way: The renewal of social democracy*. Cambridge: Polity.

Greenfeld, L. (1992). *Nationalism: Five roads to modernity*. Cambridge, MA: Harvard University Press.

Habermas, J. (1984). *The theory of communicative action. Vol. I: Reason and the rationalization of society*. London: Heinemann.

Habermas, J. (1987). *The theory of communicative action. Vol. II: Lifeworld and system: A critique of functionalist reason.* London: Heinemann.

Hobsbawm, E. (1990). *Nations and nationalism since 1780: Programme, myth, reality.* Cambridge: Cambridge University Press.

Hymes, D. (1996). *Ethnography, linguistics, narrative inequality: Toward an understanding of voice.* London: Taylor and Francis.

Irvine, J. & Gal, S. (2000). Language ideology and linguistic differentiation. In P. Kroskrity (ed.), *Regimes of language* (pp. 35–83). Santa Fe: School of American Research Press.

Kroskrity, P. (ed.) (2000). *Regimes of language.* Santa Fe: School of American Research Press.

Kroskrity, P. (2001). Language ideologies. In J. Verschueren, J.-O. Östman, J. Blommaert, & C. Bulcaen (eds.), *Handbook of pragmatics 2001* (pp. 1–17). Amsterdam: John Benjamins.

Latour, B. (1993). *We have never been modern.* Cambridge, MA: Harvard University Press.

Maryns, K. & Blommaert, J. (2001). Stylistic and thematic shifting as a narrative resource: Assessing asylum seekers' repertoires. *Multingua, 20,* 61–84.

Msanjila, Y. (1999). The use of Kiswahili in rural areas and its implications for the future of ethnic languages in Tanzania. Doctoral dissertation, University of Dar es Salaam, Tanzania.

Myers-Scotton, C. (1993). *Social motivations for code-switching: Evidence from Africa.* Oxford: Clarendon Press.

Rampton, B. (1995). *Crossing: Language and ethnicity among adolescents.* London: Longman.

Schieffelin, B., Woolard, K., & Kroskrity, P. (eds.) (1998). *Language ideologies: Practice and theory.* New York: Oxford University Press.

Silverstein, M. (1979). Language structure and linguistic ideology. In P. Clyne, W. Hanks, & C. Hofbauer (eds.), *The elements: A parasession on linguistic units and levels* (pp. 193–247). Chicago: Chicago Linguistic Society.

Silverstein, M. (1996). Monoglot "standard" in America: Standardization and metaphors of linguistic hegemony. In D. Brenneis & R. Macaulay (eds.), *The matrix of language: Contemporary linguistic anthropology* (pp. 284–306). Boulder, CO: Westview Press.

Silverstein, M. (1998). Contemporary transformations of local linguistic communities. *Annual Review of Anthropology, 27,* 401–26.

Skutnabb-Kangas, T. (2000). *Linguistic genocide in education – or worldwide diversity and human rights?* Mahwah, NJ: Lawrence Erlbaum.

Wallerstein, I. (1983). *Historical capitalism.* London: Verso.

Wallerstein, I. (2000). *The essential Wallerstein.* New York: New Press.

CHAPTER FOURTEEN

Language Policy and Minority Rights

Stephen May

This chapter explores the interconnections between language policy (LP) and minority rights (MR). Minority rights may be described as the cultural, linguistic, and wider social and political rights attributable to minority-group members, usually, but not exclusively, within the context of nation-states. This definition is, in turn, based on the usual distinction between so-called minority and majority groups employed in the sociological and political literature; a distinction that is based not on numerical size, but on clearly observable differences among groups in relation to power, status, and entitlement.

The focus of the chapter is on the often complex and contested history surrounding the individual trajectories of LP and MR, with particular reference to the interconnections between LP and minority *language* rights. This focus will also highlight the importance of adopting a wider sociohistorical, sociocultural, and sociopolitical analysis of LP. In particular, ongoing questions surrounding the status, use, and power of minority languages in the modern world will be explored, along with the *material* implications of these questions for those minority-group members who continue to speak such languages.

A key reason why such a broader sociohistorical, sociopolitical research approach is necessary is because for much of its history, linguistics as an academic discipline has been preoccupied with idealist, abstracted approaches to the study of language. In short, language has too often been examined in isolation from the social and political conditions in which it is used (for useful critiques of linguistics along these lines, see Bourdieu, 1991; Mey, 1985). This ahistorical, apolitical approach to language has also been a feature of sociolinguistics, despite its emphasis on the social, and of many discussions of LP as well. The last is particularly surprising exactly because one might have reasonably expected any analysis of language policies and practices to engage critically with the wider social and political conditions – and, crucially, their historical antecedents – that have shaped them.

Early Language Policy

The tendency toward this "presentist" approach (May, 2003a) to LP was most evident in the early stages of formal LP development, in the 1960s–1970s. During this period, LP was seen by its proponents as a non-political, non-ideological, pragmatic, even technicist paradigm (for a useful overview, see Ricento, 2000). Its apparently simple and straightforward aim was to solve the immediate language problems of newly emergent postcolonial states in Africa, Asia, and the Middle East. Status language concerns at this time thus focused in particular on establishing stable diglossic language contexts in which majority languages (usually, ex-colonial languages, and most often English and French) were promoted as public languages of wider communication. If promoted at all, local languages – minority languages, in effect – were seen as being limited to private, familial language domains. While concern was often expressed for the ongoing maintenance of minority languages, the principal emphasis of LP at this time was on the establishment and promotion of "unifying" national languages in postcolonial contexts, along the lines of those in Western, developed contexts (see, e.g., Fishman, 1968; Rubin & Jernudd, 1971). What was not addressed by these early efforts at LP was the wider historical, social, and political issues attendant upon these processes, and the particular ideologies underpinning them. As Luke, McHoul, and Mey observe, while maintaining a "veneer of scientific objectivity" (something of great concern to early language planners), LP "tended to avoid directly addressing social and political matters within which language change, use and development, and indeed language planning itself, are embedded" (1990, pp. 26–7).

This omission was problematic for a number of reasons. First, it did not question or critique the very specific historical processes that had led to the hierarchizing of majority and minority languages, along with their speakers, in the first place. These processes are deeply imbricated with the politics of modern nationalism, and its emphasis on the establishment of national languages and public linguistic homogeneity as central, even essential, tenets of both modernization and Westernization (see below). Consequently, the normative ascendancy of national languages was simply assumed, even championed, by early advocates of LP, and all other languages were compared in relation to them.

Second, the notion of linguistic complementarity, so central to early language-planning attempts at establishing "stable diglossia," was itself highly problematic. Linguistic complementarity, as understood by early language planners, implied at least some degree of mutuality and reciprocity, along with a certain demarcation and boundedness between the majority and minority languages involved. Situations of so-called stable diglossia, however, are precisely *not* complementary in these respects. Rather, the normative ascendancy of national languages – and by extension, international languages such as English – specifically *militates against* the ongoing use, and even existence, of minority languages.

In other words, if majority languages are consistently constructed as languages of "wider communication" while minority languages are viewed as (merely) carriers of "tradition" or "historical identity," as was the case in early LP, it is not hard to see what might become of the latter. Minority languages will inevitably come to be viewed as delimited, perhaps even actively unhelpful languages – not only by others, but also often by the speakers of minority languages themselves. This helps to explain why speakers of minority languages have increasingly dispensed with their first language(s) in favor of speaking a majority language – a process of language shift or replacement that is a prominent concern of current sociolinguistic analysis. It is these wider concerns with the pejorative "positioning" of minority languages, and their speakers, that have led to the subsequent advocacy and development of minority language rights (MLR).

Language Shift and Loss

Advocacy of MLR arises out of four principal concerns. The first has to do with the consequent exponential decline and loss of many of the world's languages. Indeed, of the estimated 6,800 languages spoken in the world today (Grimes, 2000), it is predicted on present trends that between 20 percent and 50 percent will "die" by the end of the twenty-first century (Krauss, 1992, 1995). Language decline and loss occur most often in bilingual or multilingual contexts in which a majority language – that is, a language with greater political power, privilege, and social prestige – comes to replace the range and functions of a minority language. The inevitable result is that speakers of the minority language "shift" over time to speaking the majority language.

The process of language shift described here usually involves three broad stages. The first stage sees increasing pressure on minority-language speakers to speak the majority language, particularly in formal language domains, as seen most commonly in the "diglossic" language contexts discussed earlier. This stage is often precipitated and facilitated by the introduction of education in the majority language. It leads to the eventual decrease in the functions of the minority language, with the public or official functions of that language being the first to be replaced by the majority language. The second stage sees a period of bilingualism, in which both languages continue to be spoken concurrently. However, this stage is usually characterized by a decreasing number of minority-language speakers, especially among the younger generation, along with a decrease in the fluency of speakers as the minority language is spoken less, and employed in fewer and fewer language domains. The third and final stage – which may occur over the course of two or three generations, and sometimes less – sees the replacement of the minority language with the majority language. The minority language may be "remembered" by a residual group of language speakers, but it is no longer spoken as a wider language of communication (Baker & Prys Jones, 1998).

Of course, such language loss and language shift have always occurred; languages have risen and fallen, become obsolete, died, or adapted to changing circumstances in order to survive, throughout the course of human history, but never to this extent, and never before at such an exponential rate. Some sociolinguistic commentators have even described it as a form of "linguistic genocide" (Skutnabb-Kangas, 2000, and see chapter 15 in this volume). Such claims may seem overwrought and/or alarmist but they are supported by hard data. For example, a survey by the US-based Summer Institute of Linguistics, published in 1999, found that there were 51 languages with only one speaker left, 500 languages with fewer than 100 speakers, 1,500 languages with fewer than 1,000 speakers, and more than 3,000 languages with fewer than 10,000 speakers. The survey went on to reveal that as many as 5,000 of the world's 6,800 languages were spoken by fewer than 100,000 speakers each. It concluded, even more starkly, that 96 percent of the world's languages were spoken by only 4 percent of its people (Crystal, 1999).

These figures graphically reinforce an earlier suggestion made by Michael Krauss (1992, 1995) that, in addition to the 50 percent of languages that may die within the next century, a further 40 percent of languages are "threatened" or "endangered." Given the processes of language shift and decline just outlined, and the current parlous state of many minority languages, it is not hard to see why. Even some majority languages are no longer immune to such processes, not least because of the rise of English as a global language (Crystal, 1997a, 1997b). Thus, if Krauss is to be believed, as few as 600 languages (10 percent) will survive in the longer term; perhaps, he suggests, even as few as 300.

Where these concerns about language loss relate to MR more broadly is with respect to the social, economic, and political consequences for minority-language speakers of such shift and loss. Language loss – or linguistic genocide, as Skutnabb-Kangas (2000, chapter 15 in this volume) would have it[1] – almost always forms part of a wider pattern of social, cultural, and political displacement. We can see this clearly if we consider which groups are most affected by language loss – almost always minority groups which are (already) socially and politically marginalized and/or subordinated. These groups have been variously estimated at between 5,000 and 8,000 (Stavenhagen, 1992) and include within them the 250 million to 300 million members of the world's indigenous peoples (Tully, 1995), perhaps the most marginalized of all people groups. As Crawford (1994) notes, language death seldom occurs in communities of wealth and privilege, but rather to the dispossessed and disempowered. Moreover, linguistic dislocation for a particular community of speakers seldom, if ever, occurs in isolation from sociocultural and socioeconomic dislocation as well (Fishman, 1995).

Nationalism, Politics, and the Minoritization of Languages

And this brings us to the second principal concern that underlies the advocacy of MLR – why certain languages, and their speakers, have come to be "minoritized" in the first place. Advocates of MLR argue that the establishment of majority–minority language hierarchies is neither a natural process nor primarily even a linguistic one. Rather, it is a historically, socially, and politically constructed process (Hamel,

1997a, 1997b; May, 2000a, 2001, 2002, 2003a), and one that is deeply imbued in wider (unequal) power relations. Following from this, if languages, and the status attached to them, are the product of wider historical, social, and political forces, there is, in turn, nothing "natural" about the status and prestige attributed to particular majority languages and, conversely, the stigma that is often attached to minority languages, or to dialects.

There are two specific points at issue here. The first concerns what actually distinguishes a majority language from a minority language or a dialect. This distinction is not as straightforward as many assume. For example, the same language may be regarded as both a majority and a minority language, depending on the context. Thus Spanish is a majority language in Spain and many Latin American states, but a minority language in the United States. Even the term "language" itself indicates this process of construction, since what actually constitutes a language, as opposed to a dialect, for example, remains controversial (see Mühlhäusler, 1996; Romaine, 2000). Certainly, we cannot always distinguish easily between a language and a dialect on linguistic grounds, since some languages are mutually intelligible, while some dialects of the same language are not. The example often employed here is that of Norwegian, since it was regarded as a dialect of Danish until the end of Danish rule in 1814. However, it was only with the advent of Norwegian independence from Sweden in 1905 that Norwegian actually acquired the status of a separate language, albeit one that has since remained mutually intelligible with both Danish and Swedish. Contemporary examples can be seen in the former Czechoslovakia, with the (re)emergence in the early 1990s of distinct Czech and Slovak varieties in place of a previously common state language. In the former Yugoslavia, we are currently seeing a comparable (re)development of separate Serbian, Croatian, and Bosnian language varieties in place of Serbo-Croat, itself the artificial language product of the post-World War II Yugoslav Communist Federation.

What these examples clearly demonstrate is that languages are "created" out of the politics of state-making, not – as we often assume – the other way around (Billig, 1995). Independence for Norway and the break-up of the former Czechoslovakia and Yugoslavia have precipitated linguistic change, creating separate languages where previously none existed. The pivotal role of political context, particularly as it is worked out at the level of the nation-state, might also help to explain the scale of the projected language loss discussed earlier. One only has to look at the number of nation-states in the world today, at approximately 200, and the perhaps 300 or so languages that are projected to survive long-term, to make the connection.

And this brings us to the second key point at issue here: the central and ongoing influence of nation-state organization, and the politics of nationalism, to processes of national (and international) language formation and validation, along with the linguistic hierarchies attendant upon them. In this respect, the model of the linguistically homogeneous nation-state – the "ideal" linguistic model adopted in early LP efforts – is actually only a relatively recent historical phenomenon, arising from the French Revolution of 1789 and the subsequent development of European nationalism. Previous forms of political organization had not required this degree of linguistic uniformity. For example, empires were quite happy for the most part to leave unmolested the plethora of cultures and languages subsumed within them – as long as taxes were paid, all was well. Nonetheless, in the subsequent politics of European nationalism – which, of course, was also to spread throughout the world – the idea of a single, common "national" language (sometimes, albeit rarely, a number of national languages) quickly became the leitmotif of modern social and political organization.

How was this accomplished? Principally via the political machinery of these newly emergent European states, with mass education playing a central role (Anderson, 1991; Gellner, 1983). The process of selecting and establishing a common national language usually involved two key aspects: *legitimation* and *institutionalization* (May, 2001; Nelde, Strubell, & Williams, 1996). Legitimation is understood to mean here the formal recognition accorded to the language by the nation-state – usually, via "official" language status. Institutionalization, perhaps the more important dimension, refers to the process by which the language comes to be accepted, or "taken for granted," in a wide range of social, cultural, and linguistic domains or contexts, both formal and informal. Both elements, in combination, achieved not only the central requirement of nation-states – cultural and linguistic homogeneity – but also the allied and, seemingly, necessary banishment of "minority" languages and dialects to the private domain.

If the establishment, often retrospectively, of chosen "national" languages was therefore a deliberate and deliberative political act, it follows that so too was the process by which other language varieties were subsequently "minoritized" or "dialectalized" by and within these same nation-states. These latter language varieties were, in effect, *positioned* by these newly formed states as languages of lesser political worth and value. Consequently, national languages came to be associated with modernity and progress, while their less fortunate counterparts were associated (conveniently) with tradition and obsolescence. More often than not, the latter were also specifically constructed as obstacles to the political project of nation-building – as threats to the "unity" of the state – thus providing the raison d'être for the consistent derogation, diminution, and proscription of minority languages that have characterized the last three centuries of nationalism (see May, 2001, for a full overview). As Dorian summarizes it: "it is the concept of the nation-state coupled with its official standard language . . . that has in modern times posed the keenest threat to both the identities and the languages of small [minority] communities" (1998, p. 18). Coulmas observes, even more succinctly, that "the nation-state as it has evolved since the French Revolution is the natural enemy of minorities" (1998, p. 67).

Proponents of MLR argue that the emphasis on cultural and linguistic homogeneity within nation-states, and the attendant hierarchizing of languages, are thus neither inevitable nor inviolate – particularly in light of the historical recency of nation-states, and the related, often arbitrary and contrived, processes by which particular languages have been accorded "national" or "minority" status respectively. These arguments about the historical and geopolitical situatedness of national languages also apply at the supranational level. In particular, a number of prominent sociolinguistic commentators have argued that the burgeoning reach and influence of English as the current world language, or *lingua mundi*, is the result of equally constructed historical and political processes, most notably via the initial geopolitical influence of Britain and, subsequently, the United States (e.g., Pennycook, 1994, 1998; Phillipson, 1992, 2003).

As with the construction of national languages, the current ascendancy of English is also invariably linked with modernity and modernization, and the associated benefits which accrue to those who speak it. The result, MLR proponents argue, is to position other languages as having less "value" and "use" and, by extension, and more problematically, to delimit and delegitimize the social, cultural, and linguistic capital ascribed to "non-English speakers" – the phrase itself reflecting the normative ascendancy of English. The usual corollary to this position is that the social mobility of the minority-language speaker will be further enhanced if they dispense with any other (minority) languages.

Language Replacement and Social Mobility

A third principal concern of MLR is to critique the principle of "language replacement" that centrally underlies the social and political processes just outlined – that one should/must learn these languages *at the expense of* one's first language. Consequently, the promotion of cultural and linguistic homogeneity at the collective/public level has come to be associated with, and expressed by, individual monolingualism (see also Skutnabb-Kangas, chapter 15 in this volume). This amounts to a form of linguistic social Darwinism and also helps to explain why language shift, loss, or decline has become so prominent.

Central to these language replacement arguments is the idea that the individual social mobility of minority-language speakers will be enhanced as a result. Relatedly, minority-language advocates are consistently criticized for ghettoizing minority language communities within the confines of a language that does not have a wider use, thus actively constraining their social mobility (e.g., Barry, 2000; Brutt-Griffler, 2002; Schlesinger, 1992). Little wonder, such critics observe, that many within the linguistic minority itself choose to ignore the pleas of minority-language activists and instead "exit" the linguistic group by learning another (invariably, more dominant) language. We can broadly summarize the logic of this argument as follows (see May 2003b, 2004 for a fuller discussion.):

1 Majority languages are lauded for their "instrumental" value, while minority languages are accorded "sentimental" value, but are broadly constructed as obstacles to social mobility and progress.
2 Learning a majority language will thus provide individuals with greater economic and social mobility.
3 Learning a minority language, while (possibly) important for reasons of cultural continuity, delimits an individual's mobility; in its strongest terms, this might amount to actual "ghettoization."
4 If minority-language speakers are "sensible" they will opt for mobility and modernity via the majority language.
5 Whatever decision is made, the choice between opting for a majority or minority language is constructed as oppositional, even mutually exclusive.

These arguments appear to be highly persuasive. In response, however, MLR proponents argue that the presumptions and assumptions that equate linguistic mobility solely with majority languages are themselves extremely problematic. For a start, this position separates the instrumental and identity aspects of language. On this view, minority languages may be important for identity but have no instrumental value, while majority languages are construed as primarily instrumental with little or no identity value. We see this in the allied notions, evident in early LP attempts, of majority languages as "vehicles" of modernity, and minority languages as (merely) "carriers" of identity. However, it is clear that *all* language(s) embody and accomplish both identity and instrumental functions for those who speak them. Where particular languages – especially majority/minority languages – differ is in the degree to which they can accomplish each of these functions, and this in turn is dependent on the social and political (not linguistic) constraints within which they operate (Carens, 2000). Thus, in the case of minority languages, their instrumental value is often constrained by wider social and political processes that have resulted in the privileging of other language varieties in the public realm. Meanwhile, for majority languages, the identity characteristics of the language are clearly important for their speakers, but often become subsumed within and normalized by the instrumental functions that these languages fulfill. This is particularly apparent with respect to monolingual speakers of English, given the position of English as the current world language.

On this basis, MLR advocates argue that the limited instrumentality of particular minority languages at any given time need not always remain so. Indeed, if the minority position of a language is the specific product of wider historical and contemporary social and political relationships, changing these wider relationships positively with respect to a minority language should bring about both enhanced instrumentality for the language in question, and increased mobility for its speakers. We can see this occurring currently, for example, in Wales and Catalonia, with the emergence of these formerly subjugated languages into the public domain – particularly via, but by no means limited to, education (May, 2000b, 2002, 2003b).

Likewise, when majority-language speakers are made to realize that their own languages fulfil important identity functions for them, both as individuals and as a group, they may be slightly more reluctant to require minority-language speakers to dispense with theirs. Or to put it another way, if majority languages do provide their speakers with particular and often significant individual and collective forms of linguistic identity, as they clearly do, it seems unjust to deny these same benefits, out of court, to minority-language speakers.

And this brings us to the final principal concern of MLR – the legal protections that can potentially be developed in order to enhance the mobility of minority-language speakers while at the same time protecting their right to continue to speak a minority language, *if they so choose*. It is here that the influence of the linguistic human rights (LHR) paradigm is most prominent (see also Skutnabb-Kangas, chapter 15 in this volume).

Linguistic Human Rights

The LHR research paradigm argues that minority languages, and their speakers, should be accorded at least some of the protections and institutional support that majority languages already enjoy (e.g., Kontra, Skuttnabb-Kangas, Phillipson, & Várady, 1999; Skutnabb-Kangas, 2000, 2002; Skutnabb-Kangas & Phillipson, 1994). These arguments are also echoed in much of the academic legal discourse that has developed in recent years with respect to minority group rights more broadly (see Capotorti, 1979; de Varennes, 1996; Henrard, 2000; Thornberry, 1991, 2002). A central distinction in both discourses is one made between national minority groups and indigenous peoples on the one hand, and ethnic minority groups on the other. The former may be regarded as groups which are historically associated with a particular territory (i.e., they have not migrated to the territory from elsewhere) but because of conquest, confederation, or colonization are now regarded as minorities within that territory. The latter may be regarded as voluntary migrants and (involuntary) refugees living in a new national context (see Kymlicka, 1995; May, 2001; for further discussion).

Three key tenets of international law can be applied to the further development of LHR in relation to these two broad minority groupings. The first principle, which is widely accepted, is that it is not unreasonable to expect from national members some knowledge of the common public language(s) of the state. This is, of course, the central tenet underpinning the current public linguistic homogeneity of modern nation-states. However, LHR advocates assert that it is also possible to argue, on this basis, for the legitimation and institutionalization of the languages of national minorities within nation-states, according to them at least some of the benefits that national languages currently enjoy. LHR proponents qualify this by making it clear that the advocacy of such MLR is *not* the language replacement ideology in reverse – of replacing a majority language with a minority one. Rather, it is about questioning and contesting why the promotion of a majority (national) language should necessarily be at the expense of all others. By this, they argue, the linguistic exclusivity attendant upon the nationalist principle of cultural and linguistic homogeneity can be effectively challenged and contested.

A second principle is that in order to avoid language discrimination, it is important that where there is a sufficient number of other-language speakers, these speakers should be allowed to use that language as part of the exercise of their individual rights as citizens. That is, they should have the opportunity to use their first language if they so choose. As de Varennes argues, "the respect of the language principles of individuals, *where appropriate and reasonable*, flows from a fundamental right and is not some special concession or privileged treatment. Simply put, it is the right to be treated equally without discrimination, to which everyone is entitled" (1996, p. 117; my emphasis). Again, this principle can clearly be applied to minority-language speakers within particular nation-states.

The third principle arises directly from the previous one – how to determine exactly what is "appropriate and reasonable" with regard to individual language preferences. Following the prominent political theorist Will Kymlicka (1995), May (2001) has argued that only national minorities can demand as of right formal inclusion of their languages and cultures in the civic realm. However, this need not and should not preclude other ethnic minorities from being allowed at the very least to cultivate and pursue unhindered their own historic cultural and linguistic practices in the private domain. In other words, distinguishing between the rights of national and ethnic minorities still affords the latter far greater linguistic protection than many such groups currently enjoy – that is, active linguistic protection by the state for the unhindered maintenance of their first languages. This protection is applicable at the very least in the private domain and, "where numbers warrant," a principle again drawn from international law, potentially in the public domain as well.[2]

Extending greater ethnolinguistic *democracy* to minority-language groups, via LHR, does not thus amount to an argument for ethnolinguistic *equality* for all such groups. Similarly, a call for greater ethnolinguistic democracy clearly does not amount to asserting linguistic equivalence, in all domains, with dominant, majority languages. Majority languages will continue to dominate in most if not all language domains, since, as should be clear by now, that is the nature of their privileged sociohistorical, sociopolitical position(ing). Conversely, arguing that only national minorities can claim MLR, as of right, is not an argument for simply ignoring the claims of other ethnic groups (see May, 2001, for an extended discussion).

Conclusion and Caveats

These theoretical, policy, and legislative developments with respect to MLR have brought us a considerable way from early debates surrounding the formulation and implementation of LP. The subsequent development of the LHR paradigm has redirected attention to the underlying, often highly discriminatory processes that stigmatize and undermine minority languages and their speakers – not only linguistically, but also culturally, socially, economically, and politically. Accordingly, even when language rights are not the principal focus of attention, more recent research and policy in LP are increasingly having to address these concerns. Certainly, as Ricento (2000) observes, much of the "cutting edge research" in LP now deals directly with its limitations (May, 2001; Schiffman, 1996), as well as its potential for promoting social change (Freeman, 1998; Hornberger, 1998; May, 2001).

In both instances, the nationalist principle of cultural and linguistic homogeneity, and the language replacement ideology invariably attendant upon it, have been brought increasingly into question. The principal challenge that emerges from this critique is the need to rethink nation-states in more linguistically plural and inclusive ways. Such a process allows for the prospect of more representational multinational and multilingual states by directly contesting the historical inequalities that have seen minority languages, and their speakers, relegated to the social and political margins. For advocates of MLR, changing the language preferences of the state and civil society, or at least broadening them, would better reflect the cultural and linguistic demographics of most of today's multi-national and multilingual states. Not only this, it could significantly improve the life chances of those minority language individuals and groups who are presently disadvantaged in their access to and participation in public services, employment, and education, since linguistic consequences cannot be separated from socioeconomic and sociopolitical consequences, and vice versa. Likewise, changing "the rules of the game" that automatically presume an exclusive relationship between dominant languages, modernity, and mobility should make the process of maintaining minority languages a little easier.

Even so, it should also be clear that achieving a greater recognition and acceptance of minority languages, and their speakers, remains a formidable task, not least because of the extent of minority-language shift and loss already in train. The challenge for LP, and its academic analysis, is accordingly to dispense with the largely ahistorical, apolitical, and presentist approach that so dominated its origins in order to engage directly and critically with the wider social and political conditions – and, crucially, their historical antecedents – that have invariably framed and shaped such policies.

Annotated Bibliography

Blommaert, J. (ed.) (1990). *Language ideological debates*. Berlin: Mouton. This edited collection explores, via a range of widely different national contexts, the historical interconnections between language, political ideology, nationalism, and the subsequent influence on the implementation (and contestation) of LP and planning.

May, S. (2001). *Language and minority rights: Ethnicity, nationalism and the politics of language*. Harlow: Longman.
This interdisciplinary and critical analysis draws together for the first time sociological discussions of ethnicity and nationalism, and social and political theory discussions of MR, in order to explore their specific implications for MLR. The book develops a non-essentialist defense of MLR and includes in-depth discussion of key case studies from around the world.

Skutnabb-Kangas, T. (2000). *Linguistic genocide in education – or worldwide diversity and human rights?* Mahwah, NJ: Lawrence Erlbaum.
This gives a highly polemical and voluminous but also very accessible and informative overview of current processes of minority-language shift and loss, or what the author terms "linguistic genocide," and its obverse, MLR or LHR. The book is enhanced further by the large number of highly informative vignettes and exercises that are interspersed throughout the text.

Discussion Questions

1 What are the language varieties that are spoken within the borders of your own nation-state, and with which groups are they associated?

2 How are these language varieties, and their speakers, situated in relation to current emphases in language planning and policy (LPP)?

3 What is the balance among regional, national, and international languages in your LPP context? What arguments are used in relation to each and to what extent do you regard these arguments as valid?

4 Examine the history of LPP in your national context. What were its origins, and how has it changed over time?

5 In what ways, if at all, have the principles of MLR influenced discussions of LPP in your own context? How might they potentially do so?

NOTES

1 The term "linguistic genocide" is often viewed as highly problematic by skeptics of MLR – as too emotive and conspiratorial. Skutnabb-Kangas argues, in response, that terms such as "language death" and "language loss," which many of these skeptics prefer, have significant problems of their own – not least the notable absence of agency or responsibility. Language "loss" or "death" does not just happen, nor is it natural and/or inevitable. Rather, it is always socially, culturally, and politically situated within a wider nexus of (often highly unequal) power relations between, and within, language groups (see below).

2 Skutnabb-Kangas is generally more skeptical of the national–ethnic minority distinction, particularly given its potential to delimit the language entitlements of the latter. See Skutnabb-Kangas (2000).

REFERENCES

Anderson, B. (1991). *Imagined communities: Reflections on the origin and spread of nationalism* (rev. edn). London: Verso.

Baker, C. & Prys Jones, S. (eds.) (1998). *Encyclopedia of bilingualism and bilingual education*. Clevedon: Multilingual Matters.

Barry, B. (2000). *Culture and equality: An egalitarian critique of multiculturalism*. Cambridge, MA: Harvard University Press.

Billig, M. (1995). *Banal nationalism*. London: Sage.

Bourdieu, P. (1991). *Language and symbolic power*. Cambridge: Polity.

Brutt-Griffler, J. (2002). Class, ethnicity and language rights: An analysis of British colonial policy in Lesotho and Sri Lanka and some implications for language policy. *Journal of Language, Identity and Education*, 1(3), 207–34.

Capotorti, F. (1979). *Study on the rights of persons belonging to ethnic, religious and linguistic minorities*. New York: United Nations.

Carens, J. (2000). *Culture, citizenship and community: A contextual exploration of justice as evenhandedness*. Oxford: Oxford University Press.

Coulmas, F. (1998). Language rights: Interests of states, language groups and the individual. *Language Sciences, 20*, 63–72.

Crawford, J. (1994). Endangered Native American languages: What is to be done and why? *Journal of Navajo Education, 11*(3), 3–11.

Crystal, D. (1997a). *English as a global language*. Cambridge: Cambridge University Press.

Crystal, D. (1997b). *The Cambridge encyclopedia of language* (2nd edn). Cambridge: Cambridge University Press.

Crystal, D. (1999). The death of language. *Prospect*, November, 56–9.

de Varennes, F. (1996). *Language, minorities and human rights*. The Hague: Kluwer Law.

Dorian, N. (1998). Western language ideologies and small-language prospects. In L. Grenoble & L. Whaley (eds.), *Endangered languages: Language loss and community response* (pp. 3–21). Cambridge: Cambridge University Press.

Fishman, J. (1968). Sociolinguistics and the language problems of the developing countries. In J. Fishman, C. Ferguson, & J. Das Gupta (eds.), *Language problems of developing nations* (pp. 3–16). New York: John Wiley & Sons.

Fishman, J. (1995). Good conferences in a wicked world: On some worrisome problems in the study of language maintenance and language shift. In W. Fase, K. Jaspaert, & S. Kroon (eds.), *The state of minority languages: International perspectives on survival and decline* (pp. 395–403). Lisse: Swets and Zeitlinger.

Freeman, R. (1998). *Bilingual education and social change*. Clevedon: Multilingual Matters.

Gellner, E. (1983). *Nations and nationalism: New perspectives on the past*. Oxford: Blackwell.

Grimes, B. (ed.) (2000). *Ethnologue: Languages of the world* (14th edn). Dallas, TX.: SIL.

Hamel, R. (1997a). Introduction: Linguistic human rights in a sociolinguistic perspective. *International Journal of the Sociology of Language, 127*, 1–24.

Hamel, R. (1997b). Language conflict and language shift: A sociolinguistic framework for linguistic human rights. *International Journal of the Sociology of Language, 127*, 105–34.

Henrard, K. (2000). *Devising an adequate system of minority protection*. The Hague: Kluwer Law.

Hornberger, N. (1998). Language policy, language education, language rights: Indigenous, immigrant, and international perspectives. *Language in Society*, *27*, 439–58.

Kontra, M., Phillipson, R., Skutnabb-Kangas, T., & Várady, T. (eds.) (1999). *Language: A right and a resource. Approaching linguistic human rights*. Budapest: Central European University Press.

Krauss, M. (1992). The world's languages in crisis. *Language*, *68*, 4–10.

Krauss, M. (1995). Language loss in Alaska, the United States and the world: Frame of reference. *Alaska Humanities Forum*, *6*(1), 2–5.

Kymlicka, W. (1995). *Multicultural citizenship: A liberal theory of minority rights*. Oxford: Clarendon Press.

Luke, A., McHoul, A., & Mey, J. (1990). On the limits of language planning: Class, state and power. In R. Baldauf & A. Luke (eds.), *Language planning and education in Australia and the South Pacific* (pp. 25–44). Clevedon: Multilingual Matters.

May, S. (2000a). Uncommon languages: The challenges and possibilities of minority language rights. *Journal of Multilingual and Multicultural Development*, *21*, 366–85.

May, S. (2000b). Accommodating and resisting minority language policy: The case of Wales. *International Journal of Bilingual Education and Bilingualism*, *3*, 101–28.

May, S. (2001). *Language and minority rights: Ethnicity, nationalism and the politics of language*. London: Longman.

May, S. (2002). Developing greater ethnolinguistic democracy in Europe: Minority language policies, nation-states, and the question of tolerability. *Sociolinguistica*, *16*, 1–13.

May, S. (2003a). Misconceiving minority language rights: Implications for liberal political theory. In W. Kymlicka & A Patten (eds.), *Language rights and political theory* (pp. 123–52). Oxford: Oxford University Press.

May, S. (2003b). Rearticulating the case for minority language rights. *Current Issues in Language Planning*, *4*(2), 95–125.

May, S. (2004). Rethinking linguistic human rights: Answering questions of identity, essentialism and mobility. In D. Patrick & J. Freeland (eds.), *Language rights and language "survival": A sociolinguistic exploration* (pp. 35–53). Manchester: St Jerome.

Mey, J. (1985). *Whose language? A study in linguistic pragmatics*. Amsterdam: John Benjamins.

Mühlhäusler, P. (1996). *Linguistic ecology: Language change and linguistic imperialism in the Pacific region*. London: Routledge.

Nelde, P., Strubell, M., & Williams, G. (1996). *Euromosaic: The production and reproduction of the minority language groups in the European Union*. Luxembourg: Office for Official Publications of the European Communities.

Pennycook, A. (1994). *The cultural politics of English as an international language*. London: Longman.

Pennycook, A. (1998). *English and the discourses of colonialism*. London: Routledge.

Phillipson, R. (1992). *Linguistic imperialism*. Oxford: Oxford University Press.

Phillipson, R. (2003). *English-only Europe? Challenging language policy*. London: Routledge.

Ricento, T. (2000). Historical and theoretical perspectives in language policy and planning. In T. Ricento (ed.), *Ideology, politics and language policies: Focus on English* (pp. 9–24). Amsterdam: John Benjamins.

Romaine, S. (2000). *Language in society: An introduction to sociolinguistics* (2nd edn). Oxford: Oxford University Press.

Rubin, J. & Jernudd, B. (eds.) (1971). *Can language be planned? Sociolinguistic theory and practice for developing nations*. Hawaii: University of Hawaii Press.

Schiffman, H. (1996). *Linguistic culture and language policy*. London: Routledge.

Schlesinger, A. (1992). *The disuniting of America: Reflections on a multicultural society*. New York: W.W. Norton.

Skutnabb-Kangas, T. (2000). *Linguistic genocide in education – or worldwide diversity and human rights?* Mahwah, NJ: Lawrence Erlbaum.

Skutnabb-Kangas, T. (2002). Marvellous human rights rhetoric and grim realities: Language rights in education. *Journal of Language, Identity and Education*, I, 179–206.

Skutnabb-Kangas, T. & Phillipson, R. (1994). Linguistic human rights, past and present. In T. Skutnabb-Kangas & R. Phillipson (eds.), *Linguistic human rights: Overcoming linguistic discrimination* (pp. 71–110). Berlin: Mouton.

Stavenhagen, R. (1992). Universal human rights and the cultures of indigenous peoples and other ethnic groups: The critical frontier of the 1990s. In A. Eide & B. Hagtvet (eds.), *Human rights in perspective* (pp. 135–51). Oxford: Blackwell.

Thornberry, P. (1991). *International law and the rights of minorities*. Oxford: Clarendon Press.

Thornberry, P. (2002). Minority and indigenous rights at "the end of history." *Ethnicities*, 2, 515–37.

Tully, J. (1995). *Strange multiplicity: Constitutionalism in an age of diversity*. Cambridge: Cambridge University Press.

CHAPTER FIFTEEN

Language Policy and Linguistic Human Rights

Tove Skutnabb-Kangas

Language policy can be defined in dozens of ways, as the introduction and several other chapters in this book show. Linguistic human rights (LHRs) combine language rights (LRs) with human rights (HRs). LHRs are those (and only those) LRs that, first, are necessary to fulfill people's basic needs and for them to live a dignified life, and, second, that therefore are so basic, so fundamental, that no state (or individual or group) is supposed to violate them. There are many LRs which are not LHRs. It would, for instance, be nice if everybody could, even in civil court cases, have a judge and witnesses who speak (or sign) this person's language, regardless of how few users this language has. Today it is in most cases only a linguistic *human* right to be informed of the charge against oneself in criminal cases in a language one understands (i.e., not necessarily the mother tongue); everything else may be a *language* right that people may or may not have, depending on the country and language; in the best cases, interpreters paid for by the state are used. Likewise, it would be nice if the following demands were to be met:

> All language communities are entitled to have at their disposal all the human and material resources necessary to ensure that their language is present to the extent they desire at all levels of education within their territory: properly trained teachers, appropriate teaching methods, text books, finance, buildings and equipment, traditional and innovative technology.
>
> *(Universal Declaration of Linguistic Rights (draft), 1996)*

But these demands are completely unrealistic and cannot be considered part of LHRs.[1] At the moment, only a few dozen language communities in the world have these kinds of rights; consider that there are some

6,500–7,000 spoken languages and perhaps an equal number of sign languages in the world.[2]

Two kinds of interest in LHRs can be distinguished. One is "the expressive interest in language as a marker of identity," the other an "instrumental interest in language as a means of communication" (Rubio-Marín, 2003, p. 56; these correspond fairly close to what Skutnabb-Kangas & Phillipson [e.g., 1994] have called "necessary" and "enrichment-oriented" rights). The *expressive* (or non-instrumental) language claims "aim at ensuring a person's capacity to enjoy a secure linguistic environment in her/his mother tongue and a linguistic group's fair chance of cultural self-reproduction." (Rubio-Marín, 2003, p. 56). It is only these rights that Rubio-Marín (professor of constitutional law in Seville) calls "language rights in a strict sense" (p. 56); that is, these could be seen as LHRs. The *instrumental* language claims "aim at ensuring that language is not an obstacle to the effective enjoyment of rights with a linguistic dimension, to the meaningful participation in public institutions and democratic process, and to the enjoyment of social and economic opportunities that require linguistic skills" (p. 56).

So far, it is far from clear what should and what should not be considered LHRs, and there are lively debates about the topic. One of the difficulties is that the issue is multidisciplinary. Often HRs lawyers know little about language, at least initially. Often language specialists know little about legal matters. Some sociolinguists, sociologists, educationists, political scientists, etc. may be more knowledgeable about the power relations necessarily involved in all language-policy matters, but are still too little informed about HRs law and sometimes even languages. Negative debates ensue when instrumentalists claim that those interested in the expressive aspects exclude the more instrumental, communication-oriented aspects (e.g., unequal class- or gender-based access to formal language or to international languages). The debates in the *Journal of Language, Identity and Education* (1(3), 2002; 3(2), 2004) are an example of this old division being reinvented again. The same debates were held over both integration of minorities (are they more interested in their languages or in jobs?) and indigenous claims (identity or autonomy, land rights) in the 1960s and 1970s. Most groups are interested in both types of rights, expressive and instrumental, and often one is a prerequisite for the other, with both being alternately causal and dependent variables. Many of us work with both aspects, and see them as complementary, not mutually exclusive.

In this short chapter, I shall first ask what kind of LHRs international and regional HRs covenants and declarations contain (or do not contain), and then discuss educational LHRs and the lack of them. Next follows a listing of some dichotomies often used when discussingLRs, and a clarification of where LHRs might stand in relation to them if proper integration (of minorities, and of the whole society), rather than forced assimilation, is one of the goals in language policy. Finally, some tentative conclusions are drawn.

Language in Human Rights

Language is one of the most important of those human characteristics on the basis of which people are not supposed to be discriminated against. Others are gender, "race," and religion. Still, language often disappears in the educational paragraphs of binding HRs instruments. One example: the paragraph on education (Article 26) in the Universal Declaration of Human Rights (1948) does not refer to language at all. The main thrust of the paragraph is to ensure free universal education (and even this right is violated in dozens of countries, as the United Nations Special Rapporteur on the Right to Education, HRs lawyer Katarina Tomaševski, states in many of her reports (see www. right-to-education.org/content). There are references to the "full development of the human personality" and the right of parents to "choose the kind of education that shall be given to their children," but this does not include the right to choose the language in which this education is given. Educational LHRs, especially the right to mother-tongue-medium education, are among the most important rights for any minority. Without them, a minority whose children attend school usually cannot reproduce itself as a minority. It cannot integrate but is forced to assimilate.

Binding educational clauses of HRs instruments have more opt-outs, modifications, alternatives, etc. than other Articles. One example is the UN Declaration on the Rights of Persons Belonging to National or Ethnic, Religious and Linguistic Minorities (1992; emphases added: *"obligating"* and positive measures in italics, "**opt-outs**" in bold):

1.1. States *shall protect* the existence and the national or ethnic, cultural, religious and linguistic identity of minorities within their respective territories, and *shall encourage* conditions for the *promotion* of that identity.

1.2. States *shall adopt* appropriate legislative *and other* measures *to achieve those ends.*

1.3. States **should** take **appropriate** measures so that, **wherever possible**, persons belonging to minorities have **adequate** opportunities to learn their mother tongue **or** to have instruction in their mother tongue.

The Council of Europe's Framework Convention for the Protection of National Minorities, and The European Charter for Regional or Minority Languages, both in force since 1998, also have many of these modifications, alternatives and opt-outs.[3] The Framework Convention's education Article reads as follows:

> In areas inhabited by persons belonging to national minorities traditionally or in substantial numbers, *if there is sufficient demand*, the parties shall *endeavour* to ensure, *as far as possible* and *within the framework of their education systems*, that persons belonging to those minorities have *adequate* opportunities for being taught in the minority language *or* for receiving instruction in this language. (emphases added)

Of course there are real problems in writing binding formulations that are sensitive to local conditions. Still, it is clear that the opt-outs and alternatives in the Charter and the Convention permit reluctant states to meet the requirements in a minimalist way which they can legitimize by claiming that a provision was not "possible" or "appropriate," or that numbers were not "sufficient" or did not "justify" a provision, or that it "allowed" the minority to organize teaching of their language as a subject, at their own cost. This means that minority languages and sometimes even their speakers *might*, "*as far as possible*" and "*within the framework of* [the State's] *education systems*," get some vaguely defined rights, "*appropriate measures*," or "*adequate opportunities*," but only "*if there is sufficient demand*" and "*substantial numbers*" or "*pupils who so wish in a number considered sufficient*" or "*if the number of users of a regional or minority language justifies it.*" The Articles covering medium of education are so heavily qualified that the minority is completely at the mercy of the state. Other regions of the world normally have even fewer general instruments pertaining specifically to minority languages or speakers of minority languages (see May, chapter 14 in this volume, for a discussion of minority rights), even if a few specific named languages may have extensive rights (like French in Canada).

Still, the HRs system should protect people in the globalization process rather than giving market forces free range. HRs, especially economic and social rights, are, according to HRs lawyer Katarina Tomaševski (1996, p. 104), to act as *correctives to the free market*. The first international HRs treaty abolished slavery. Prohibiting slavery implied that *people* were not supposed to be treated as market commodities. The International Labor Organization (ILO) has added that *labor* should not be treated as a commodity. But price tags are to be removed from other areas too. Tomaševski claims (p. 104) that "The purpose of international human rights law is . . . to overrule the law of supply and demand and remove price tags from people and from necessities for their survival." These necessities for survival thus include not only basic food and housing (which would come under economic and social rights), but also basics for the sustenance of a dignified life, including basic civil, political, *and cultural* rights. It should, therefore, be in accordance with the spirit of HRs to grant people full LHRs.

Educational Linguistic Human Rights and Lack of Them

Without binding educational LHRs most minorities have to accept subtractive education through the medium of a dominant/majority language. In subtractive language learning, a new (dominant/ majority) language is learned at the cost of the mother tongue, which is displaced, leading to a diglossic situation,[4] and often the replacement of the mother tongue. Assimilationist subtractive education is genocidal. Educational systems and mass media are (the most) important direct agents in linguistic and cultural genocide. Behind them are the world's economic, techno-military, and political systems.

When people hear the term "genocide" about languages and education, they often react by exclaiming: "The term is too strong." The UN International Convention on the Prevention and Punishment of the Crime of Genocide (E793) (1948) has five definitions of genocide. Two of them fit today's indigenous and minority education: Article II(e), *"forcibly transferring children of the group to another group,"* and Article II(b), *"causing serious bodily or mental harm to members of the group"* (emphases added). There is also a specific definition of linguistic genocide in Article III(1) from the Final Draft of the Convention – this Article was voted down by 16 states and is thus not part of the Convention: *"Prohibiting the use of the language of the group in daily intercourse or in schools, or the printing and circulation of publications in the language of the group."* Some examples from various studies follow. All of them show either the forcible transfer of children from a linguistic group to another linguistic group, or serious mental harm caused to children through submersion education. Pirjo Janulf (1998) showed in a longitudinal study that of those Finnish immigrant minority members in Sweden who had had Swedish-medium education, not one spoke any Finnish to their own children. Even if they themselves might not have forgotten their Finnish completely, their children were certainly forcibly transferred to the majority group, at least linguistically. Edward Williams's study from Zambia and Malawi, with 1,500 students in grades 1–7, showed that large numbers of Zambian pupils (who had all their education in English) "have very weak or zero reading competence in two languages" (1998, p. 62). The Malawi children (taught in local languages during the first four years, with English as a subject) had slightly better test results in the English language than the Zambian students. Williams's conclusion is: "there is a clear risk that the policy of using English as a vehicular language may contribute to stunting, rather than promoting, academic and cognitive growth" (pp. 63–4). This fits the UN genocide definition of "causing mental harm." In Zubeida Desai's (2001) study, Xhosa-speaking grade 4 and grade 7 learners in South Africa were given a set of pictures, which they had to put in the right order and then describe, in both Xhosa and English. In Desai's words, it showed "the rich vocabulary children have when they express themselves in Xhosa and the poor vocabulary they have when they express themselves in English" (p. 321). Kathleen Heugh's (2000) country-wide longitudinal statistical study of final exam results for "Black" students in South Africa showed that the percentage of "Black" students who passed their exams went down every time the number of years spent learning through the medium of the mother tongues decreased. Anne Lowell and Brian Devlin's article describing the "miscommunication between Aboriginal students and their non-Aboriginal teachers in a bilingual school" clearly demonstrated that "even by late primary school, children often did not comprehend classroom instructions in English" (1999, p. 137). Communication breakdowns occurred frequently between children and their non-Aboriginal teachers (p. 138), with the result that "the extent of miscommunication severely inhibited the children's education when English was the language of instruction and interaction" (p. 137).

Conclusions and recommendations: "the use of a language of instruction in which the children do not have sufficient competence is the greatest barrier to successful classroom learning for Aboriginal children" (p. 156).

Katherine Zozula and Simon's (1985) report "Keewatin perspective on bilingual education" tells about Canadian Inuit "students who are neither fluent nor literate in either language" and presents statistics showing that the students "end up at only Grade 4 level of achievement after 9 years of schooling" (quoted in Martin, 2000b, p. 3; see also Martin, 2000a). The Canadian Royal Commission on Aboriginal Peoples (1996) Report notes that "submersion strategies which neither respect the child's first language nor help them gain fluency in the second language may result in impaired fluency in both languages" (quoted in Martin, 2000b, p. 15). The Canadian Nunavut Language Policy Conference in March 1998 stated that "in some individuals, neither language is firmly anchored" (quoted in Martin, 2000b, p. 23). Mick Mallon and Alexina Kublu (1998) claim that "a significant number of young people are not fully fluent in their languages" and many students "remain apathetic, often with minimal skills in both languages" (quoted in Martin, 2000b, p. 27). In a Canadian report, Kitikmeot (1998) struggles to prevent the death of Inuktitut, and shows that "teenagers cannot converse fluently with their grandparents" (quoted in Martin, 2000b, p. 31).

Many studies on Deaf students (Branson & Miller, 2002; Jokinen, 2000; Lane, 1992; etc.) show that assimilationist submersion education, where Deaf students are taught orally only and sign languages have no place in the curriculum, often causes mental harm, including serious prevention or delay of cognitive growth potential. And so we could go on. In sum, what does subtractive teaching do? It is genocidal, according to the UN Genocide Convention's definitions of genocide. It replaces mother tongues and kills languages. It prevents the attainment of profound literacy. It prevents students from gaining the knowledge and skills that would correspond to their innate capacities and would be needed for socioeconomic mobility and democratic participation. It wastes resources.

All these students (and their parents and communities) need LHRs as one of the necessary (but not sufficient) measures to stop linguistic genocide. Linguistic diversity (LD) seems to many researchers (not to speak of politicians, or "ordinary people") to be messy. Even respected scholars like political theorists Will Kymlicka and Alan Patten seem to accept that things are "complicated by linguistic diversity" (Patten &

Kymlicka, 2003, p. 3), or that LD is "one of the most important obstacles to building a stronger sense of European citizenship" (p. 9), or that LD is a "problem" (p. 9). These are not just unfortunate slips: Kymlicka and Patten (2003) repeat these prejudices about LD as an obstacle (p. 6) and add new ones (see later). Labeling LD as a complication, obstacle, or problem is denying and lamenting facts – just like claiming that having two legs and five fingers is more complicated than having one. With very few exceptions, the world's countries *are* multilingual, and, in Debi Pattanayak's words, "One language is an impractical proposition for a multilingual country" (1988, p. 382). LD is the normal state of life on our planet. To me, the complication, obstacle, or problem is not LD but attitudes which I have discussed as monolingual reductionism (e.g., 2000, pp. 238–48).

Other misconceptions that abound even among solid scholars are that minorities are somehow reluctant ("unable or unwilling," Kymlicka & Patten, 2003, p. 12) to learn the majority/dominant language, and become ghettoized (p. 12), so that "even the second and third generations of immigrant groups will live and work predominantly in their ancestral language, with only minimal or non-existent command of the state language" (Patten & Kymlicka, 2003, p. 8; the same sentence in Kymlicka & Patten, 2003, p. 6). It seems that not forcing them to "linguistic integration" (which seems to mean assimilation, with "standardized public education in a common language" [Kymlicka & Patten, 2003, p. 12]) "serves to separate citizens into distinct and mutually antagonistic groups" (p. 12). Thus granting minorities a right to mother-tongue-medium (MTM) education would, according to this type of theorizing, be a veritable disaster, both to the minorities themselves and to the whole society.

These claims are in most cases not true, but they have been part of the assimilationist myths leading to linguistic and cultural genocide instead of LHRs. Educational LHRs include both the right to have the basic education mainly through the medium of the mother tongue, *and* the right to learn the official/dominant language well. These two are not contradictory: quite the opposite. In additive learning situations, high levels of majority-language skills are added to high levels of mother-tongue skills. Arlene Stairs's (1994) study shows that "in schools which support initial learning of Inuttitut, and whose Grade 3 and Grade 4 pupils are strong writers in Inuttitut, the results in written English are also the highest" (quoted in Martin, 2000b, p. 60; see also Stairs, 1988). The Alaska Yu'piq teacher Nancy Sharp (1994) compares:

when Yu'piq children are taught through the medium of English, they are treated by "White" teachers as handicapped, and they do not achieve; when they are taught through the medium of Yu'piq, they are "excellent writers, smart happy students" (quoted in Martin, 2000b, p. 62; see also Lipka with Mohatt & the Ciulistet Group, 1998). Many books show in detail how additive teaching that respects educational and other LHRs can be organized.[5]

There is also some support in several soft law documents (see below for this concept). The Hague Recommendations Regarding the Education Rights of National Minorities, from the OSCE (Organization for Security and Cooperation) High Commissioner on National Minorities (1996), recommend MTM education for minorities at all levels, including secondary education. This includes bilingual teachers in the dominant language as a second language (Articles 11–13). The Explanatory Note has the following to say about submersion education: "Submersion-type approaches whereby the curriculum is taught exclusively through the medium of the State language and minority children are entirely integrated into classes with children of the majority are not in line with international standards" (OSCE High Commissioner on National Minorities, 1996, p. 5). This means that most indigenous and minority education – which is submersion – is not in line with international HRs standards.

Some politicians might agree with this, and many claim that they want to organize better education, but the counter-argument usually is: "Surely sustainable education that leads to profound literacy, creativity, and high levels of multilingualism for the student, and to maintenance of the world's languages, cannot be possible? Or economically viable?" A good example here is Papua New Guinea, a fairly small country, with a population of around 5 million. It has the highest number of languages in the world: over 850. According to David Klaus from the World Bank (2003), as of 2002, 470 languages are used as the media of education in pre-school and the first two grades. Some of the results are as follows (Klaus, 2003): children become literate more quickly and easily. They learn English more quickly and easily than their siblings did under the old English-medium system. Children, including girls, stay in school. Grade 6 exams in the three provinces that started MTM teaching in 1993 had much higher results than in provinces which still teach through the medium of English from day one. It is perfectly possible to organize education so that it does not participate in committing linguistic genocide.

Human Rights Dichotomies

Many of the fears that prevent states from guaranteeing LHRs originate from claims about LD preventing the integration of a state through a common language. One type of language-policy goal (linguistic assimilation of minorities) is said to further this integration. First we need to define the concepts of integration and assimilation, to see whether a language policy denying LHRs really leads to integration.[6]

Assimilation can be defined as: (1) disappearance of distinctive features, that is, objectively the loss of specific elements of material and non-material culture and subjectively the loss of the feeling of belonging to a particular ethnic group; and (2) simultaneously, objectively, adoption of traits belonging to another culture, which replace those of the former culture, accompanied by the subjective feeling of belonging to the second culture. *Integration* is the formation of a series of common features in an ethnically heterogeneous group. Assimilation is subtractive, whereas integration is additive. In terms of the education of indigenous and minority children, these concepts can be defined in the following way. In *subtractive teaching*, minority children are taught through the medium of a dominant language, which replaces their mother tongue. They learn the dominant language at the cost of the mother tongue. In *additive teaching*, minority children are taught through the medium of the mother tongue, with good teaching of the dominant language as a second language. Additive teaching makes them high-level bilingual or multilingual. They learn other languages in addition to their own language and learn them all well. We can use the concepts of subtractive and additive for another definition of assimilation or integration: *assimilation* is enforced subtractive "learning" of another (dominant) culture by a (dominated) group. Assimilation means being transferred to another group. *Integration* is characterized by voluntary mutual additive "learning" of other cultures. Integration means a choice of inclusive group membership(s). In terms of both these definitions, it is clear that most state attitudes toward indigenous peoples and minorities are still in a phase where assimilation/integration are discussed only in terms of what happens and is envisaged in relation to the indigenous peoples/ minorities, whereas very little happens in relation to the dominant population, which is not asked or envisaged to change. If real integration rather than assimilation is the goal in both education and language policy in general, what kind of LHRs are needed and can contribute?

When discussing HRs one often comes across several pairs of dichotomies. In the following, we look at these dichotomies to determine which rights are necessary so that indigenous peoples and minorities do not need to assimilate but can participate in mutual integration. Some of these dichotomies are as follows:

- negative versus positive rights;
- toleration-oriented versus promotion-oriented rights;
- individual versus collective rights;
- territorial versus personal rights;
- rights in "hard law" versus "soft law."

Negative rights have been defined by Max van der Stoel (1999, p. 8) as "the right to non-discrimination in the enjoyment of human rights," whereas positive rights have to do with "the right to the maintenance and development of identity through the freedom to practise or use those special and unique aspects of their minority life – typically culture, religion, and language." Negative rights must

> ensure that minorities receive all of the other protections without regard to their ethnic, national, or religious status; they thus enjoy a number of linguistic rights that all persons in the state enjoy, such as freedom of expression and the right in criminal proceedings to be informed of the charge against them in a language they understand, if necessary through an interpreter provided free of charge.
>
> *(van der Stoel, 1999, p. 8)*

Positive rights are those

> encompassing affirmative obligations beyond non-discrimination . . . [These] include a number of rights pertinent to minorities simply by virtue of their minority status, such as the right to use their language. This pillar is necessary because a pure non-discrimination norm could have the effect of forcing people belonging to minorities to adhere to a majority language, effectively denying them their rights to identity.
>
> *(van der Stoel, 1999, pp. 8–9)*

Many political scientists seem to think that it is only (large) national minorities that should have their languages promoted by the state, that is, have positive rights, whereas small national minorities and small indigenous peoples and, especially, immigrant minorities cannot expect more than toleration-oriented negative rights. On the other hand, toleration and non-discrimination, understood in liberal terms of the state not interfering on behalf of a group's special characteristics (like religion), does not work in relation to language. A state has to choose some language(s) as the language(s) of administration, courts, education, possibly the media, etc., and this necessarily privileges some language(s) (see Rubio-Marín, 2003). My claim is that, for proper integration, positive *promotion-oriented rights* are necessary. Negative toleration-oriented rights are not sufficient and may lead to forced assimilation.

The following dichotomy is about individual versus collective rights. The HRs regime of the League of Nations between the two "world" wars contained many collective rights; in principle most minority rights should be collective rights (see May, chapter 14 in this volume). In the United Nations regime after 1945, it was claimed that no collective rights were necessary since every person was protected as an individual, by individual rights. To simplify somewhat, Western countries have largely opposed collective rights and African countries have supported many of them, while Asian countries have been so divided on the issue that it has been one of the major hurdles preventing an acceptance of regional Asian HRs instruments. My second claim is that, for proper integration, *both individual and collective rights* are necessary. One or the other type alone is not sufficient. It is not a question of either/or, but both/and.

The next claim is that for proper integration, *both territorial and personal rights* are necessary. Territorial rights (if you live in a certain territory, e.g., a "German" or "Italian" canton in Switzerland, you have a right to services in that language only, regardless of what your mother tongue is) are of good service only to minorities who have a traditional territory and live within its borders. Personal rights (you have a right in your personal capacity, regardless of where you live) are more important for the Deaf, the Roma, immigrant minorities, and other non-territorial minorities. These rights are also vital for dispersed people in diaspora outside the group's territory.

The last claim is that, for proper integration, *both traditional "hard law" rights* (rights included in covenants, conventions, charters, etc. that are binding on the state that has ratified them) *and "soft law" rights* ("rights" in declarations, recommendations, etc., and Supreme court decisions that start forming precedents but are nevertheless not binding) are necessary. Most hard law instruments reflect the phases directly after World War II, or the main decolonisation phase. They do not address present challenges.

Various groups can be placed in a hierarchical order relative to how good their HRs protection is. The descending order is as follows:

1 Linguistic majorities/dominant-language speakers versus minority/dominated-language speakers:
   (a) national (autochthonous) minorities;
   (b) indigenous peoples;
   (c) immigrant minorities;
   (d) refugee minorities.
2 Speakers of oral languages versus users of sign languages.

Speakers of oral languages have many more rights than users of sign languages (even if users of sign languages have some rights as a handicap group). An example is the European Charter for Regional or Minority Languages (Council of Europe, 1998a): no state has ratified it for any sign languages, only spoken languages, even if the definitions of "regional or minority languages" for the purposes of the Charter would have allowed it. This is fatal, because the European Charter in its Educational Article 8 might grant a group at least some educational rights.

Conclusion

LHRs might be one way of:

- preventing linguistic genocide;
- promoting integration and defending people against forced assimilation;
- promoting positive state policies toward minority languages;
- promoting the maintenance of the world's LD;
- promoting conflict prevention; promoting self-determination.

Should we be optimistic? Professor Rodolfo Stavenhagen (1995, pp. 76–7) says the following:

> Too often, policies of national integration, of national cultural development, actually imply a policy of ethnocide, that is, the willful destruction of cultural groups. The cultural development of peoples, whether minorities or majorities, must be considered within the

framework of the right of peoples to self-determination, which by accepted international standards is the fundamental human right, in the absence of which all other human rights cannot really be enjoyed. Governments fear that if minority peoples hold the right to self-determination in the sense of a right to full political independence, then existing States might break up. State interests thus are still more powerful at the present time than the human rights of peoples.

Creativity, invention, investment, multilingualism, and additive teaching belong together. Creativity and new ideas are the main assets (cultural capital) in a knowledge society, and a prerequisite for humankind to adapt to change and to find solutions to the catastrophes of our own making. In an *industrial society*, the main products are *commodities*. Those who control access to raw materials and own the other prerequisites and means of production are those who do well. In a *knowledge or information society*, the main products are *knowledge and ideas*. Those who have access to diverse knowledges, diverse information, diverse ideas – that is, creativity – are those who do well. In knowledge societies, uniformity is a handicap. Some uniformity might have promoted aspects of industrialization. In postindustrial knowledge societies, uniformity will be a definite handicap.

We can describe the relationship between creativity, innovation, investment – results of additive teaching and multilingualism – as follows: creativity precedes innovation, also in commodity production. Investment follows creativity. Multilingualism may enhance creativity. High-level multilinguals as a group have done better than corresponding monolinguals on tests measuring several aspects of "intelligence," creativity, divergent thinking, cognitive flexibility, etc.[7] And finally, additive teaching can lead to high-level multilingualism. Countries should promote LHRs not only because of ethical concerns but indeed in their own interest.

Annotated Bibliography

de Varennes, F. (1996). *Language, minorities and human rights*. The Hague: Kluwer Law.
So far this is the most complete reference work on language and law. Written by a lawyer, it includes provisions of close to 100 international, multilateral, and bilateral instruments involving LRs, as

well as the constitutional provisions dealing with language from 140 countries.

Kontra, M., Phillipson, R., Skutnabb-Kangas, T., & Várady, T. (eds.) (1999). *Language: A right and a resource. Approaching linguistic human rights*. Budapest: Central European University Press.
This multidisciplinary book, with contributions from sociolinguists, lawyers, economists, media researchers, and linguists, tries to clarify concepts within LHRs, comparing and applying them across national borders. There are several Eastern European examples.

Kymlicka, W. & Patten, A. (eds.) (2003). *Language rights and political theory*. Oxford: Oxford University Press.
This collection of articles by political scientists, most in a liberal tradition, highlights the empirical constraints and normative complexities of language policy and rights, identifying the challenges presented by LD to political theory.

May, S. (2001). *Language and minority rights: Ethnicity, nationalism, and the politics of language*. London: Longman.
This is a thorough presentation by a multidisciplinary sociologist of the relationships between the issues in the title of the book. It draws together debates on language from the sociology of language, ethnicity and nationalism, sociolinguistics, social and political theory, education, history, and law, presenting cross-national contexts and examples.

Skutnabb-Kangas, T. (2000). *Linguistic genocide in education – or worldwide diversity and human rights?* Mahwah, NJ: Lawrence Erlbaum.
This 818-page text synthesizes theoretical concerns and empirical investigations from LHRs, multilingual and minority education, language ecology and threatened languages, the relationship between biodiversity and LD, and the impact of unequal power relationships on ethnicity, linguistic and cultural competence, and identities.

Skutnabb-Kangas, T. & Phillipson, R. (eds.) (1994). *Linguistic human rights: Overcoming linguistic discrimination*. Berlin: Mouton.
This book describes what LHRs are, who enjoys them and who is deprived of them, and why, and analyzes the LRs of indigenous peoples and minorities both generally and in North and Latin America, several European countries, the former USSR, India, Kurdistan, and

Australia. A substantial appendix contains extracts from selected documents covering LRs.

Thornberry, P. (1997). Minority rights. In Academy of European Law (ed.), *Collected courses of the Academy of European Law. Vol. VI, book 2* (pp. 307–90). The Hague: Kluwer Law.
This is a thorough presentation and discussion of contemporary minority rights.

Discussion Questions

1 Think of your own life. First, draw up a list of those LRs which you think should belong to LHRs. Which LRs have been (or should have been) absolutely necessary for you to live a dignified life and to satisfy your basic needs? Do this in groups and compare your lists. Make sure that there are at least some linguistic-minority representatives in your group. Where do you agree, and where do you have differences? Have all of you had basic LHRs? If not, analyze the reasons.

2 Look at the opt-out formulations and modifications in the Council of Europe's instruments. Choose a country you are interested in and know something about, and find its country report on the web for each instrument, and the corresponding monitoring committee's reports. See how the education articles have been interpreted and reported. Do the monitoring committees (which mostly consist of lawyers) know enough about education? What could you teach them?

3 Organize a discussion, simulating the first court case (which is currently being prepared), testing whether a specific child's or group's majority-language-medium education fulfills the criteria for genocide. Find a relevant case you know in the neighborhood schools. Play both lawyers and expert witnesses from both sides (one party arguing that it is a question of genocide, the other that it is not). How would you argue? What additional knowledge would you need in order to be able to argue the case? Where can you find it?

4 Have you yourself participated in committing linguistic genocide in education? Discuss!

5 If "it is perfectly possible to organize education so that it does not participate in committing linguistic genocide," why is it not done?

Compare the short-term and long-term costs of both alternatives. Use two neighborhood schools' budgets as a starting point, one with dominant-language-medium submersion programs, one with late-exit transitional programs. Look at statistics about the long-term consequences. (You might want to look at Thomas and Collier, 2002.) What kind of data would you need to be able to get a full picture? François Grin, economist of language (www.geneve.ch/sred/collaborateurs/pagesperso/d-h/ grinfrancois/francoisgrin_eng.html), is a good source for theories and applications in the area.

NOTES

A big hug of thanks to Kelly Lynne Graham for the most thorough editing I have ever experienced.

1 See Skutnabb-Kangas (2000, pp. 541–8) for a presentation and critical assessment of the draft Universal Declaration of Linguistic Rights.
2 See the ethnologue at www.sil.org/ethnologue for a listing of languages, and Skutnabb-Kangas (2000, ch. 1) for the unreliability of the statistics.
3 See http://conventions.coe.int/treaty/EN/cadreprincipal.htm for updates.
4 "Diglossia" means functional differentiation of languages; for example, one at home and the neighborhood, another one in school and with authorities.
5 See the homepages of Jim Crawford (http://ourworld.compuserve.com/ homepages/JWCRAWFORD) and Jim Cummins (www.iteachilearn.com/ cummins/index.htm), and the bibliographies at www.terralingua.org, for literature; see also Skutnabb-Kangas (1995).
6 The definitions of integration and assimilation are from Skutnabb-Kangas (2000: see pp. 123–34 for discussion).
7 For an overview, see Cummins (2001).

REFERENCES

Branson, J. & Miller, D. (2002). *Damned for their difference: The cultural construction of deaf people as disabled*. Washington, DC: Gallaudet University Press.

Council of Europe (1998a). The European Charter for Regional or Minority Languages. Retrieved April 19, 2004, from http://conventions.coe.int/treaty/ EN/cadreprincipal.htm.

Council of Europe (1998b). Framework Convention for the Protection of National Minorities. Retrieved April 19, 2004, from http://conventions.coe.int/ treaty/EN/cadreprincipal.htm.

Cummins, J. (2001). *Negotiating identities: Education for empowerment in a diverse society*. Los Angeles: California Association for Bilingual Education.

Desai, Z. (2001). Multilingualism in South Africa with particular reference to the role of African languages in education. *International Review of Education*, 47(3–4), 323–39.

Heugh, K. (2000). *The case against bilingual and multilingual education in South Africa* (PRAESA Occasional Papers No. 6). Cape Town: University of Cape Town.

Janulf, P. (1998). *Kommer finskan i Sverige att fortleva? En studie av språkkunskaper och språkanvändning hos andragenerationens sverigefinnar i Botkyrka och hos finlandssvenskar i Åbo (Will Finnish survive in Sweden? A study of language skills and language use among second-generation Sweden Finns in Botkyrka, Sweden, and Finland Swedes in Åbo, Finland)* (Acta Universitatis Stockholmiensis, Studia Fennica Stockholmiensia 7). Stockholm: Almqvist & Wiksell.

Jokinen, M. (2000). The linguistic human rights of sign language users. In R. Phillipson (ed.), *Rights to language: Equity, power and education* (pp. 203–13). Mahwah, NJ: Lawrence Erlbaum.

Klaus, D. (2003). The use of indigenous languages in early basic education in Papua New Guinea: A model for elsewhere? *Language and Education*, 17(2), 105–11.

Kymlicka, W. & Patten, A. (2003). Language rights and political theory. *Annual Review of Applied Linguistics*, 23, 3–21.

Lane, H. (1992). *The mask of benevolence: Disabling the deaf community*. New York: Alfred Knopf.

Lipka, J., with Mohatt, G. W. & the Ciulistet Group (1998). *Transforming the culture of schools: Yup'ik Eskimo examples*. Mahwah, NJ: Lawrence Erlbaum.

Lowell, A. & Devlin, B. (1999). Miscommunication between Aboriginal students and their non-Aboriginal teachers in a bilingual school. In S. May (ed.), *Indigenous community-based education* (pp. 137–59). Clevedon: Multilingual Matters.

Martin, I. (2000a). Aajjiqatigiingniq: Language of instruction research paper. A report to the government of Nunavut. Unpublished manuscript, Department of Education, Nunavut. imartin@glendon.yorku.ca.

Martin, I. (2000b). Sources and issues: A backgrounder to the discussion paper on language of instruction in Nunavut schools. Unpublished manuscript, Department of Education, Nunavut. imartin@glendon.yorku.ca.

OSCE High Commissioner on National Minorities (1996). *The Hague Recommendations Regarding the Education Rights of National Minorities*. Retrieved April 19, 2004, from www.osce.org/hcnm.

Pattanayak, D. P. (1988). Monolingual myopia and the petals of the Indian lotus: Do many language divide or unite a nation? In T. Skutnabb-Kangas & J. Cummins (eds.), *Minority education: From shame to struggle* (pp. 379–89). Clevedon: Multilingual Matters.

Patten, A. & Kymlicka, W. (2003). Introduction. Language rights and political theory: Context, issues, and approaches. In A. Patten & W. Kymlicka (eds.), *Language rights and political theory* (pp. 1–10). Oxford: Oxford University Press.

Rubio-Marín, R. (2003). Language rights: Exploring the competing rationales. In W. Kymlicka & A. Patten (eds.), *Language rights and political theory* (pp. 52–79). Oxford: Oxford University Press.

Skutnabb-Kangas, T. (ed.) (1995). *Multilingualism for all.* Lisse: Swets & Zeitlinger.

Skutnabb-Kangas, T. (2000). *Linguistic genocide in education – or worldwide diversity and human rights?* Mahwah, NJ: Lawrence Erlbaum.

Skutnabb-Kangas, T. & Phillipson, R. (1994). Linguistic human rights, past and present. In T. Skutnabb-Kangas & R. Phillipson (eds.), *Linguistic human rights: Overcoming linguistic discrimination* (pp. 71–110). Berlin: Mouton.

Stairs, A. (1988). Beyond cultural inclusion: An Inuit example of indigenous education development. In T. Skutnabb-Kangas & J. Cummins (eds.), *Minority education: From shame to struggle* (pp. 308–27). Clevedon: Multilingual Matters.

Stavenhagen, R. (1995). Cultural rights and universal human rights. In A. Eide, C. Krause, & A. Rosas (eds.), *Economic, social and cultural rights: A textbook* (pp. 63–77). Dordrecht: Martinus Nijhoff.

Thomas, W. P. & Collier, V. P. (2002). *A national study of school effectiveness for language minority students' long term academic achievement.* George Mason University, VA: Center for Research on Education, Diversity & Excellence (CREDE). Retrieved April 19, 2004, from www.crede.ucsc.edu/research/llaa/1.1_final.html.

Tomaševski, K. (1996). International prospects for the future of the welfare state. In *Reconceptualizing the welfare state* (pp. 100–117). Copenhagen: The Danish Centre for Human Rights.

UN Declaration on the Rights of Persons Belonging to National or Ethnic, Religious and Linguistic Minorities (1992). Retrieved April 19, 2004, from www.unhchr.ch/html/menu6/2/fs18.htm#ANNEXI.

UN International Convention on the Prevention and Punishment of the Crime of Genocide (E793) (1948). Retrieved April 19, 2004, from www.hrweb.org/legal/genocide.html.

Universal Declaration of Linguistic Rights (draft) (1996). Article 25. Retrieved April 19, 2004, from www.unesco.org/most/lnngo11.htm

Universal Declaration of Human Rights (1948). Article 26. Retrieved April 19, 2004, from www.un.org/Overview/rights.html.

van der Stoel, M. (1999). *Report on the linguistic rights of persons belonging to national minorities in the OSCE area* and *Annex: Replies from OSCE participating states.* The Hague: OSCE High Commissioner on National Minorities.

Williams, E. (1998). *Investigating bilingual literacy: Evidence from Malawi and Zambia* (Education Research No. 24). London: Department for International Development.

www.right-to-education.org/content

CHAPTER SIXTEEN

Language Policies and the Education of Linguistic Minorities

Christina Bratt Paulston and Kai Heidemann

By way of introduction, a definition and delimitation of the two main concepts of the title as used in this chapter are called for, as they are given many and various meanings.

Educational language policies, probably best seen as a subset of language policy/language planning (LPLP), will be considered primarily at the national level and so will exclude private schools and the practices of individual linguistic groups. Also excluded for reasons of space is any discussion of literacy, bilingual education, the signing Deaf, and teacher training, as well as testing and textbook and materials writing, although they all form a significant part of educational policies for linguistic minorities.

Language planning as "deliberate efforts to influence the behaviour of others with respect to the acquisition, structure, and functional allocations of their language codes" (Cooper, 1989, p. 45) is one frequently cited definition. Hornberger (1994) takes it further in an attempt to integrate two decades of LPLP scholarship in one coherent framework (see table 16.1).

Spolsky, on the other hand, simplifies language policy to three components:

> a useful first step is to distinguish between the three components of the language policy of a speech community: its language practices – the habitual pattern of selecting among the varieties that make up its linguistic repertoire; its language beliefs or ideology – the beliefs about language and language use; and any specific efforts to modify or influence that practice by any kind of language intervention, planning or management.

> *(2004, p. 5)*

Table 16.1 Language-planning goals: an integrative framework

Approaches	Policy planning (on form)	Cultivation planning (on function)
Types	Goals	Goals
Status planning (about uses of language)	Standardization status Officialization Nationalization Proscription	Revival Maintenance Interlingual communication: International Intranational Spread
Acquisition planning (about users of language)	Group Education/school Literature Religion Mass media Work	Reacquisition Maintenance Foreign language/ second language Shift
Corpus planning (about language)	Standardization: Corpus Auxiliary code Graphization	Modernization: Lexical Stylistic Renovation: Purification Reform Stylistic simplification Terminology unification

Source: Based on Cooper (1989); Ferguson (1968); Haugen (1983); Kloss (1968); Nahir (1984); Neustupný (1974); Stewart (1968).

For the purposes of this chapter, *acquisition planning* or *language management* will do equally well in thinking about educational language policies. *Linguistic minorities* do not yet have a generally accepted definition, either at the international or at the European level (Henrard, 2003, p. 9), even though there are ordinances and charters by the European Union involving linguistic minorities. *Minority* refers to quantitative differences only, but as several writers (Giordan, 1992; Paulston, 1994; Vilfan, 1993) have pointed out, the most salient characteristics of most minorities is that of a superordinate–subordinate status relationship with the majority within a polity. As Vilfan discusses, it is more correct to speak of privileged or dominant and non-privileged or non-dominant ethnic groups. Dominance, or its lack, depends "upon numerous circumstances, for instance, social structure, the dispersion of social groups, the electoral system, historical traditions, and the respective prestige of the 'historic nations' involved" (Vilfan, 1993, p. 6). To this should be added some further comments cited by Henrard. The size of the population group plays a legitimate role in determining the specific demands that a minority can make on the state (Deschênes, 1986, p. 269). As concerns the notion of dominance, "it is evident that non-dominance does not necessarily imply being subordinate or oppressed. This tends to support the view that in a plural society the various ethnic, religious and linguistic groups may be considered minorities. Actually none of the population groups in such a society may find themselves in a dominant position (Thornberry, 1991, p. 169)" (Henrard, 2003, p. 10).

The notion of linguistic minorities in this framework then refers to the prolonged contact of ethnic groups within a modern nation-state or polity. The main linguistic outcomes of such contact are language maintenance, bilingualism, or language shift, and an understanding of these phenomena and the social conditions under which they occur is a prerequisite to understanding educational language policies which seek to regulate the interactions of ethnic groups within a country.

Viewpoint

The education of linguistic minorities can of course be studied from many different viewpoints. A fruitful and complementary viewpoint to the one from which this chapter is written is that of Heller and Martin-Jones (2001), who see classrooms in multilingual settings as significant sites for the production and reproduction of cultural identity and social inequality. Education is evoked as a primary site wherein inequality is reproduced as well as challenged.

However, in this chapter we look particularly at the language policies that attempt to deal with the problems of linguistic minorities. As classroom practices represent an implementation of policies (explicit and implicit) rather than the policies themselves (if language management indeed is at all possible, as both Spolsky, 2004, and Wright, 2004, wonder aloud), we take another approach.

The major viewpoint from which this chapter is written is that we can begin to understand the problems of the schooling of linguistic non-dominant minorities only when we see such schooling as the result of certain societal factors rather than as the cause of certain behaviors of children. Most research on bilingual education and the like treat the educational programs as the independent or causal variable – as the factor that solely accounts for certain subsequent results. The many studies that have attempted to assess students' reading achievements by standardized test scores, where the independent variable is the language (mother tongue or L2) used as medium of instruction, are examples of this approach. We believe the programs should rather be seen as intervening variables, as factors modifying the effects of ethnic relations on reading scores. The social backgrounds the children bring to school, the support efforts available to them, the life chances beckoning, and their sense of self, to mention just a few, have ultimately more to do with children's educational success (or lack of). This is also the case for children monolingual in the national language, but it becomes especially marked with linguistic minorities, and so we gain better insights if we consider the programs as intervening – or contextual – variables, whether in formal research designs or in our conceptualization of the issues concerning educational language policies.

It is our contention that we can best do so within a framework of comparative ethnic relations that attempts to account for the socio-historical, cultural, and economic-political factors which lead to certain forms of the education of linguistic minorities.

Language Maintenance and Shift: Social Variables

Some much-abbreviated points follow about social conditions that contribute to language maintenance or shift. The main point is simply that ethnic groups within a modern nation-state, given opportunity and incentive, typically shift to the language of the dominant group. The proviso is important; without access to learn the new language and without motivation, primarily in the form of source of income or prestige, language learning is not salient and the old language is maintained. One of the primary factors in accounting for the subsequent course of mother-tongue diversity, to use Lieberson's phrase, lies in the origin of the contact situation (Lieberson, Dalto, & Johnston, 1975; Schermerhorn, 1970). Voluntary migration, especially of individuals and families, results in the most rapid shift; annexation and colonization, where entire groups are brought into a nation with their social institutions of marriage and kinship, religious and other belief and value systems, still in situ and more or less intact, tend to result in much slower shift, if any.

It should also be emphasized that all these generalizations are based on analyses at the level of nation-states as the basic polity. The development of minority nationalism and the changing international order (Keating & McGarry, 2001) are too recent to allow definite statements, but it seems more than likely that regional nationalism, such as in Catalunya, contributes significantly to language maintenance.

Lieberson et al. claim that "the course of race and ethnic relations will be different in settings where the subordinate group is indigenous as opposed to those where the migrant populations are subordinate" (1975, p. 53). They consider four groups: (1) indigenous superordinate, (2) migrant superordinate, (3) indigenous subordinate, and (4) migrant subordinate. They find it unlikely that much, if any, mother-tongue shift will occur among the first two groups: "Almost certainly a group enjoying both political and economic dominance will be in a position to ensure that its linguistic position is being maintained. Bilingualism may occur, but this is not the same as mother-tongue shift. At the very most, one can normally expect only an extremely slow rate of mother-tongue change among such groups" (1975, p. 53).

Subordinate groups that are indigenous at the time of contact, through either colonization or annexation, are unlikely to change rapidly. Migrant subordinate groups are the only groups likely to show rapid rates of mother-tongue shift, and in the so-called great immigration countries of Australia, Canada, and the United States, the norm is a three- or four-generation shift. In contrast, within the United States, with access to the same educational institution of public schooling, the indigenous subordinate groups have changed at a much slower rate. In Louisiana, purchased over 200 years ago from France (in 1803), French is an official language along with English, and as we write this, the new governor – the first woman governor ever in that state – is being sworn in using both languages, with French reflecting her Cajun (from Acadia, now Nova Scotia) background.

The mechanism of language shift is bilingualism, often but not necessarily with exogamy, where parent(s) speak(s) the original language with the grandparents and the new language with the children. The mechanism of bilingualism holds in all cases of group shifts, although the rate of shift will vary.

Schermerhorn sees three major causal factors as determining the nature of the relationship between ethnic groups and the process of integration into the environing society. The first refers to the origin of the contact situation between the subordinate and dominant groups, such as annexation, migration, and colonization; the second to the degree of enclosure (institutional separation or segmentation) of the subordinate group from the society-wide network of institutions and associations; and the third to the degree of control exercised by the dominant group over access to scarce resources by subordinate groups in a given society.

Although most ethnic groups within a nation, given access and incentive, do shift language, they will vary in their degree of ethnic culture maintenance and in their rate of shift. They also vary in their degree of ethnic pride or ethnic stubbornness – Edward Spicer's "the enduring peoples of the world" (Castile & Kushner, 1981, p. xv) – even after they have shifted language and become socially incorporated into a nation. Groups also vary in group adhesion, and there is wide intra-group variation in members' attitude toward language maintenance and cultural assimilation. Where shift does not take place, the three major factors or reasons are (besides lack of access and incentive): self-imposed boundary maintenance, externally imposed boundary maintenance, and complementary functional distribution of the languages.

Self-imposed boundary maintenance (Barth, 1969) serves to keep the group apart, usually for reasons of religion, through the mechanism of a different language and sometimes dress. The Amish (Pennsylvania Dutch, really German) and the orthodox Jewish Hassidim (Yiddish) are examples.

Externally imposed boundaries are an example of Schermerhorn's degree of enclosure, and are usually in the form of a group's being denied access to goods and services, especially jobs. The African communities on the homelands under apartheid are an example. Geographic isolation is also a form of external boundary that contributes to language maintenance, as the many tribes in the Amazon jungle attest to.

Functional distribution of the languages is a diglossic-like situation where the two languages exist in complementary functional distribution. Each language has its specified purpose and domain and the one language is inappropriate in the other situation, as with Modern Standard Arabic and the mother tongue in the Maghreb.

The final possible consequence is prolonged group bilingualism, as with Catalonia and the Basque lands, or national official bi-/

multilingualism with mostly monolingual speakers, as in Switzerland or Belgium. This brief chapter is not the place for a discussion of bilingualism, but we would speculate in passing that much of it is due to regional nationalism.[1]

Common Language Policies for the Education of Minorities

What follows is a discussion of some of the most common language policies at the national level enacted with regard to the education of linguistic minorities. The underlying motivational factors vary considerably, from outright state control and assimilation (e.g., the so-called Unz initiative in the California referendum, which effectively outlawed bilingual education) to general human rights and good will to one's neighbors (as in the recent choice of an additional nine national languages in the Republic of South Africa [RSA]). It is invariably to the social context one needs to look to understand such policies, whatever one's linguistic ideologies are, and there are very few generalizations that do not carry exceptions. But no language policy is likely to be successful in the long run if it goes counter to the existing sociocultural forces acting on the local contextual situations.

Although we have organized the discussion by language policies, it is readily seen that these policies overlap and criss-cross in an imbricated pattern, and the same case study could appear under different headings. Of Richard Ruiz's (1984) frequently cited three basic orientations to language – language as problem, language as right, and language as resource – one would expect, at least in Utopia, that language policies for children should deal primarily with language rights and resources. Instead, Turi points out that the fundamental goal of all legislation about language is to resolve the linguistic problems that stem from the conflicts and inequalities among languages used within the same territory, by legally establishing and determining the status and use of the languages concerned (1994, p. 111). The following discussion is written, and should be understood, from the perspective that we, with UNESCO, take it as "axiomatic that the best medium for teaching a child is his mother tongue." However, that paragraph ends with the much more rarely cited "it is not always possible to use the mother tongue in school and, even when possible, some factors may impede or condition its use" (UNESCO, 1953, p. 11).

Language Choice

Language choice is one of the major language problems. Choice of national language (or avoidance of such a choice – the United States does not have a national or official language de jure although some 20 states do) has implications for education because the national language most of the time becomes at least one of the mediums of education. The end of apartheid in the RSA was begun in 1979 with riots in Soweto, a suburb of Johannesburg, by the students over the introduction of Afrikaans, one of the two official languages, into the curriculum. Similarly, the Latvian parliament passed a law (February, 2004) to introduce the only national language, Latvian, into all public school curricula, and the streets of Riga filled with thousands of protesting Russian-speaking Latvian inhabitants. We say "similarly" because on the surface both situations involved a new language policy, by the politically dominant group, to introduce the national language into the curriculum. In fact, the situational contexts were vastly different. In South Africa, it was not so much the language that the black (sic, following Mesthrie, 2002, p. 4) students rebelled against as the hated symbolism of apartheid in the language of their oppressors. The new South Africa of 1994 and 1996 now has 11 official languages (English, Afrikaans, and nine indigenous, mostly Bantu, languages), all of which are planned as mediums of instruction (Deprez & du Plessis, 2000; Mesthrie, 2002). However, the clear preference of the black population for their children is not their mother tongue, but English, mostly for reasons of perceived upward social mobility.

In Latvia, the driving force behind the language legislation is fear of impending language shift to Russian and the loss and death of the Latvian language forever. Latvian is truly a small language. It has barely 2 million speakers and a territory shared with almost the same number of Russian speakers (from the Soviet days), most of whom are monolingual in Russian, while most Latvians are bilingual in Latvian and Russian – a classic scenario for language shift, where the bilingual population shifts to the language of the monolingual majority. But this scenario was changed overnight with independence in 1991, as the majority, the Latvians, were able to enforce language legislation in order to protect their language. The more control, the more enclosure, the more likely such language policies are to result in conflict and contestation. In addition, the minority-language policies of the

European Union (Latvia became a member in 2004) are likely to support the Russian speakers' demands (Bernier, 2001), and no one can predict the future consequences with accuracy.

Clearly, the language policies concerning national language choice may look similar in the RSA and Latvia, but they represent in fact very different situations, and the attempts to rectify them vary. What remains the same, as Turi puts it, is that "major language legislation in the area of language policy is evidence, within certain political contexts, of contracts, conflicts and inequalities among the languages used within the same territory" (1994, p. 111).

Another language choice concerns that of alphabet or writing system, which, again, on the surface may seem just an esoteric choice for language specialists to make, but in fact is highly political. Fierman's (1991) study of language policies in Uzbekistan outlines some of the implications of such choices for social identity, protection of elite status, and national development. The Chinese communists, who well understood how learning the elaborate Chinese character-writing system favored the upper strata of society, have for decades suggested various reforms such as pin-yin. In the end, they settled for simplified characters, their national identity and historical past being unimaginable without characters.

A third language choice directly concerns medium of instruction. Yards of bookshelves are filled with books on bilingual education, immersion programs, heritage language programs, and the like. Colin Baker's (2001) *Foundations of bilingual education and bilingualism* is a very good place to begin exploring this topic and its literature.

Harlech-Jones, in his study of language policies in Namibia after independence in 1990 from the control of the RSA (like the new South Africa, Namibia chose English), is indubitably right when he says "Education is thus a directly political activity, regarded and utilized by decision-makers as a major instrument of social policy" (1990, p. 68). This is especially so when the national language is not the medium of education.

In the United States, many of the language policies fought out in the courts took as precedent the Civil Rights Act of 1964, a major hallmark of social policy. The 1974 *Lau v. Nichols* Supreme Court decision, which basically agreed that language minorities that did not understand English did not receive equal educational opportunities, is still in effect at the federal level, but voters in three states – California, Arizona, and Massachusetts – have approved referenda on this, which severely restrict or curtail primarily Spanish as a medium of instruction.[2]

The increased integration of the EU at the supranational level and the de-emphasis on nationalism have simultaneously brought about an increased concern for autochthonous language minorities. In particular, the European Charter for Regional and Minority Languages as developed by the Council of Europe in 1992 represents an established set of provisions for such recognition and support. The Charter represents a marked historical shift in the political discourse regarding indigenous minority languages in European education systems (Wright, 2000), although the efficacy of the Charter beyond the symbolic level remains to be established.

However, there are other organizations, and the combined influence of the Organization for Security and Cooperation (OSCE) High Commissioner on National Minorities, the Council of Europe, and the European Union together carry considerable force, especially on the candidatures of new nations in the process of accession to the EU and NATO, as both Bernier (2001) and Ozolins (2003) document, if from very different perspectives. The "moving goal posts" (Ozolins, 2003) are going in the direction of increased language-minority rights.

Clearly, the United States and the European Union demonstrate two markedly different approaches to ethnic minorities within national borders.

Standardization

Linguists refer to a standard language as one which has a normative orthography, grammar, and dictionary, arrived at through processes of selection, codification, expansion, and acceptance of some linguistic variety or other (Haugen, 1966). Children learn very early in their schooling that there is a "correct" way to say something, and other ways either do not exist (" 'ain't' is not a word") or are "wrong." Few parents can argue successfully against a teacher's dictum (luckily "ain't" was in the dictionary), and so many children learn early on in school that their home language is not acceptable to the teacher and the school. This problem permeates all public schooling all over the world, but it becomes especially troublesome in mother-tongue teaching of a standard language where the children speak a marked areal dialect, frequently the case with linguistic minorities. The result is not the intended outcome, but accounts of such failures are hard to come by in the literature.

Becky Brown (1993) reports on one such case in "The social consequences of writing Louisiana French." The Louisiana State Legislature declared French an official language of the state in 1968 (the same year as the Bilingual Education Act and a time of social awareness), and it established the Council for the Development of French in Louisiana (CODIFIL). The problem was which French to develop: Cajun French, Haitian Creole, or International French, the standard prestige variety. As Brown notes, "On the one hand are the lawmakers, searching for a prestige norm; on the other are the local community members, learning that their mother tongue is incorrect and inappropriate" (1993, p. 92). It is a very real problem, repeated in many parts of the world (see Heller & Martin-Jones, 2001, and their notion of "legitimate" language).

Egger and Lardschneider McLean report on an unusual solution of this problem from the Ladin Valley of South Tyrol in northern Italy. The school system is trilingual in German, Italian, and Ladin (not to be confused with Judeo-Spanish Ladino), and represents a political compromise between "two opposing sociopolitical tendencies, one that favored German as the primary medium of instruction and one that favored Italian" (2001, p. 65). The result was an officially supported and successful program. The really interesting aspect for our purpose is the unusual approach taken by the schools to the vernacular, Ladin. It is only used as a spoken medium,[3] and any attempts to standardize the many dialects (typical of mountain valley areas everywhere) into "a creation of an artificial, common variety" have been carefully avoided as unnecessary and perceived as a danger to the language. The Ladin Valley schools elegantly avoided the entire "legitimate language" problem by not adopting a standard, written form. It works just fine.

Promotion of Minority Languages

Historically, language policies in Europe have been characterized by a relative intolerance for minority languages and national multilingualism more generally (Wright, 2000). However, in Norway the character of Saami-language policy following World War II began to change quite considerably, and today Saami-language provisions within Norway can be regarded as one of the more progressive indigenous-language-policy settings across the globe (as can the language provisions of New Zealand). Particularly since the early 1990s, Saami has gained significant representation within the context of public schooling and is recognized as a legitimate medium across the curriculum (Todal, 2003). These educational provisions have specifically included the creation of Saami-language curriculum materials and textbooks at the primary, secondary, and tertiary levels, as well as the development of teacher training programs at the Saami College in Kautokeino.

While it may be premature to consider the extent to which Saami-language policy in Norway has reinvigorated the sociolinguistic vitality of the language, it represents nonetheless a significant change in the national political perspective regarding minority-language use in Norwegian public education. Writing about the mechanisms which have influenced this policy change, Jon Todal cites an interrelationship between regional political mobilization and international indigenous rights organizations, which helped facilitate "a new attitude towards conflict solving on the part of the [Norwegian] authorities" (2003, p. 191).

We also see, more frequently than the promotion of minority languages, their actual demotion in favor of (sometimes forced, sometimes sought) assimilation of ethnic minorities and promotion of the national language(s). California, Arizona, and Massachusetts represent such cases through their recent referenda.

Revitalization Efforts

Language revitalization refers to new-found vigor in a language already in use (and so differs from language revival, the rebirth of a dead language), often as a result of attempts to stop language shift and death. The New Zealand government has long carried out energetic revitalization programs for Maori, the indigenous language (Benton, 1981, 2001; May, 2001; Spolsky, 2003).

Probably more successful are revitalization efforts carried out not by the majority government but by the minority itself. The Basque Country and the Ikastola represent one such case. The significant impact of collective community action to revitalize a minority language within an educational context is illustrated by the *ikastola* movement in the Basque region of France. While the Basque language has co-official status with Spanish within the Autonomous Basque Community of Spain (Euskadi), as well as some territorial recognition in the Spanish province of Navarra, Basque is not officially recognized and only minimally supported by the French state. Within the relative cultural conservatism that has long characterized minority-language policy in

France (see Wright, 2000), a small group of Basque parents organized a Basque language pre-school in the late 1960s. A decade later the small group became an organization called "Seaksa," literally meaning seed. In 1969–70 Seaksa began coordinating a few community-based Basque-language primary schools, based on the model of similar schools that had long been rather clandestinely run across the border in the Basque region of Spain during much of the Franco era. With no provisions from the French state, the initial schools, known as *ikastolak* (the plural form of *ikastola*), were being run on a combination of local resources garnered from fund-raising activities, ranging from rock concerts to recycling bottles, and the benevolent labor of parents who cooked meals and cleaned classrooms. By the close of the 1970s, enrollment had grown from 8 students to over 400, with a middle school being added in 1980. This growth in student numbers coincided with an increased commitment and participation across other communities. By 1990 over a dozen schools were serving an enrollment that had doubled over the decade to 830. In 1994, collective community action paid off when the French state recognized the *ikastola* system under a national contract of association with the public education system, and agreed to provide for teacher salaries on a par with those of other national public school teachers. Throughout the 1990s the growth continued, and by the year 2000, almost 2,000 students were enrolled in two dozen Basque-medium schools from pre-school to high-school level.

While the quantitative situation of Basque language loss within southwestern France remains rather dismal in relation to the environment of relative maintenance across the border in Spain (see Oyharçabal, 1999, pp. 33–53), there can be no doubt that attitudes toward the language are altering, and with this comes the potential for change. The increased enrollment of children from non-Basque families within the *ikastolak* is just one example of the growth of the more positive attitudes people in the region are adopting toward the same language that not so long ago was considered "vulgar" and "backwards."

Conclusion

In this chapter we have explored the more important language policies for linguistic minorities, and the sociocultural and politico-economic conditions which characterize their educational settings.

Throughout, we have emphasized a framework of comparative ethnic relations and pointed toward numerous case studies. Our aim has been to contextualize the relations of power and inequality that characterize the landscape of language planning within education, in order to (re)emphasize that a language policy is never simply and only about language.

Annotated Bibliography

Heller, M. & Martin-Jones, M. (eds.) (2001). *Voices of authority: Education and linguistic difference.* Westport, CT: Ablex.
The central question of this edited volume asks how social order is reproduced as well as challenged through the sociolinguistic practices of actors within educational systems. The authors operationalize the question by presenting a comparative approach that examines multiple multilingual contexts, including postcolonial and neocolonial sites in the developing countries, as well as the situations of migrant, indigenous, and regional language minorities within postindustrial nations. The goal is to look at the relationship between education, cultural identity, and social inequality within multilingual settings.

Ogbu, J. (1990). Minority education in comparative perspective. *Journal of Negro Education, 59,* 45–57.
In this seminal article Ogbu provides a theoretical framework for understanding why some minority students do better than others in public schools. He develops a general typology for examining US minority groups as either "autonomous" (e.g., Amish in Pennsylvania), "immigrant" (e.g., East Asians in California), or "involuntary/caste-like" (e.g., African American and Native American communities). The conceptual categories help provide insight into the social, cultural, historical, and politico-economic conditions that characterize a minority in relation to the majority group. This is subsequently related to how and why different minority groups have different experiences within public education.

Spolsky, B. D. (ed.) (1999). *Concise encyclopedia of educational linguistics.* Oxford: Elsevier.
This 877-page volume covers just about every imaginable topic in the field of language and education and includes a name and subject

index. It is a very good place to begin thinking about term papers, class presentations, and theses, to find topical references as well as, of course, just to look up facts.

Spolsky, B. D. (2004). *Language policy.* Cambridge: Cambridge University Press.
In this new introduction to the field, Bernard Spolsky explores many debates at the forefront of language policy: ideas of correctness and bad language; bilingualism and multilingualism; language death and efforts to preserve endangered languages; language choice as a human and civil right; and language education policy. Through looking at the language practices, beliefs, and management of social groups from families to supranational organizations, he develops a theory of modern national-language policy and the major forces controlling it, such as the demands for efficient communication, the pressure for national identity, the attractions of (and resistance to) English as a global language, and the growing concern for human and civil rights as they impinge on language. Two central questions asked are how to recognize language policies, and whether or not language can be managed at all.

Tollefson, J. (ed.) (2002). *Language policies in education: Critical issues.* Mahwah, NJ: Lawrence Erlbaum.
This volume of collected works utilizes the lens of critical theory to comparatively explore the relationship between language policies and inequalities based largely in contexts of class, nationality, region, and ethnicity. In particular, Tollefson has assembled a collection which problematizes language planning in education around four main themes. These include: multilingualism and the nation-state; socio-political conflict; identity; and language ideology. By employing an international and comparative presentation of case studies, the text provides insight into the local, national, and transnational forces affecting contemporary and historical trends in educational language policies.

Wright, S. (2004). *Language policy and language planning: From nationalism to globalization.* New York: Palgrave.
This is a comprehensive book, covering not only language learning imposed by economic and political agendas but also language choices freely entered into for reasons of social mobility, economic advantage, or group identity. The first part of the book reviews the development and role of standard languages in the construction of national

communities and identities. The second part examines the linguistic accommodation of groups in contact, major lingua francas, and the case of international English. The third section explores reactions to nationalisms and globalization, with some attention to language rights.

Discussion Questions

1 In an exploration of educational language policies, what is the significance of using a comparative analysis?
2 Compare and contrast language policies in Latvia and South Africa. What social and historical variables seem most similar, and what seem most different? How might these conditions influence the education of linguistic minorities?
3 What are the major factors influencing language shift? What is the significance of this process for education?
4 What are the sociopolitical dimensions and consequences of language standardization?
5 Can a school contribute to the revitalization of a minority language? What sociocultural and politico-economic variables need to be involved?

NOTES

1 See Paulston (1994) for a discussion of language maintenance and shift.
2 Much of the argument of the English-only movement is at the level of H. L. Mencken's "If English was good enough for Jesus, it is good enough for you" (but see González, 2000, for serious criticism of the Official English Movement).
3 This is not to be confused with the fact that Ladin in its various dialects has been written.

REFERENCES

Baker, C. (2001). *Foundations of bilingual education and bilingualism*. Clevedon: Multilingual Matters.
Barth, F. (1969). *Ethnic groups and boundaries: The social organization of culture difference*. Boston: Little, Brown.

Benton, R. A. (1981). *The flight of the Amokura: Oceanic languages and formal education in the South Pacific*. Wellington: New Zealand Council for Educational Research.

Benton, R. A. (2001). Balancing tradition and modernity: A natural approach to Maori language revitalization in a New Zealand secondary school. In D. Christian & F. Genessee (eds.), *Bilingual education* (pp. 95–108). Arlington, VA: TESOL.

Bernier, J. (2001). Nationalism in transition: Nationalizing impulses and international counter-weights in Latvia and Estonia. In M. Keating & J. McGarry (eds.), *Minority nationalism and the changing international order* (pp. 342–62). New York: Oxford University Press.

Brown, B. (1993). The social consequences of writing Louisiana French. *Language in Society*, 22, 67–101.

Castile, G. P. & Kushner, G. (1981). *Persistent peoples*. Tucson, AZ: University of Arizona Press.

Cooper, R. L. (1989). *Language planning and social change*. Cambridge: Cambridge University Press.

Deprez, K. & du Plessis, T. (eds.) (2000). *Multilingualism and government*. Pretoria: Van Schaik.

Deschênes, J. (1986). Qu'est-çe qu'une minorité? *Les Cahiers de Droit*, 255–91.

Egger, K. & Lardschneider McLean, M. (2001). Trilingual schools in the Ladin Valleys of South Tyrol, Italy. In D. Christian & F. Genessee (eds.), *Bilingual education* (pp. 57–67). Arlington, VA: TESOL.

Ferguson, C. A. (1968). Language development. In J. Fishman, C. A. Ferguson, & J. Das Gupta (eds.), *Language problems of developing nations* (pp. 27–35). New York: John Wiley & Sons.

Fierman, W. (1991). *Language planning and national development: The Uzbek experience*. Berlin: Mouton.

Giordan, H. (1992). *Les minorités en Europe: Droits linguistiques et droits de l'homme*. Paris: Kimé.

González, R. D. (ed.) (2000). *Language ideologies: Critical perspectives on the official English movement. Vols 1 and 2*. Mahwah, NJ: Lawrence Erlbaum.

Harlech-Jones, B. (1990). *You taught me language: The implementation of English as a medium of instruction in Namibia*. Cape Town: Oxford University Press.

Haugen, E. (1966). *Language conflict and language planning: The case of modern Norwegian*. Cambridge, MA: Harvard University Press.

Haugen, E. (1983). The implementation of corpus planning: Theory and practice. In J. Cobarrubias & J. Fishman (eds.), *Progress in language planning: International perspectives* (pp. 269–90). Berlin: Mouton.

Heller, M. & Martin-Jones, M. (2001). Introduction: Symbolic domination, education, and linguistic difference. In M. Heller & M. Martin-Jones (eds.), *Voices of authority: Education and linguistic difference* (pp. 1–28). Westport, CT: Ablex.

Henrard, K. (2003). Language rights in education: The international framework. In P. Cuvelier, T. du Plessis, & L. Teck (eds.), *Multilingualism, education, and social integration* (pp. 9–22). Pretoria: Van Schaik.

Hornberger, N. H. (1994). Literacy and language planning. *Language and Education, 8*, 75–86.

Keating, M. & McGarry, J. (eds.) (2001). *Minority nationalism and the changing international order*. New York: Oxford University Press.

Kloss, H. (1968). *Research possibilities on group bilingualism: A report*. Quebec: International Center for Research on Bilingualism.

Lieberson, S., Dalto, G., & Johnston, M. E. (1975). The course of mother tongue diversity in nations. *American Journal of Sociology, 81*, 34–61.

May, S. (2001). *Language and minority rights: Ethnicity, nationalism, and the policies of language*. London: Longman.

Mesthrie, R. (2002). *Language in South Africa*. Cambridge: Cambridge University Press.

Nahir, M. (1984). Language planning goals: A classification. *Language Problems and Language Planning, 8*, 294–327.

Neustupný, J. V. (1974). Basic types of treatments of language problems. In J. Fishman (ed.), *Advances in language planning* (pp. 37–48). The Hague: Mouton.

Oyharçabal, B. (1999). Droits linguistique et langue Basque: Diversité des approaches. In C. Clairis, D. Costaouec, & J. B. Coyos (eds.), *Langues et cultures regionale de France: Etat des lieux, enseignement, politiques* (pp. 33–53). Paris: L' Harmattan.

Ozolins, U. (2003). The impact of European accession upon language policy in the Baltic states. *Language Policy, 2*, 217–38.

Paulston, C. B. (1994). *Linguistic minorities in multilingual settings*. Amsterdam: John Benjamins.

Ruiz, R. (1984) Orientations in language planning. *NABE Journal, 8*, 15–34.

Schermerhorn, R. A. (1970). *Comparative ethnic relations*. New York: Random House.

Spolsky, B. D. (2003). Reassessing Maori regeneration. *Language in Society, 32*, 553–78.

Spolsky, B. D. (2004). *Language policy*. Cambridge: Cambridge University Press.

Stewart, W. (1968). A sociolinguistic typology for describing national multilingualism. In J. Fishman (ed.), *Readings in the sociology of language* (pp. 531–45). The Hague: Mouton.

Thornberry, P. (1991). *International law and the rights of minorities*. Oxford: Clarendon Press.

Todal, J. (2003). The Sámi school system in Norway and international cooperation. *Comparative Education, 39*, 185–92.

Turi, J.-G. (1994). Typology of language legislation. In T. Skutnabb-Kangas & R. Phillipson (eds.), *Linguistic human rights: Overcoming linguistic discrimination* (pp. 111–19). Berlin: Mouton.

UNESCO. (1953). *The use of vernacular languages in education.* Paris: UNESCO.

Vilfan, S. (ed.) (1993). *Ethnic groups and language rights.* Aldershot: Dartmouth Publishing.

Wright, S. (2000). *Community and communication: The role of language in nation-state building and European integration.* Clevedon: Multilingual Matters.

Wright, S. (2004). *Language policy and language planning: From nationalism to globalization.* New York: Palgrave.

CHAPTER SEVENTEEN

Language Policy and Language Shift

Joshua A. Fishman

"Language policy" denotes the authoritative allocation of resources to language in general and to the written/printed language in particular. Every natural language is traditionally associated with a community of users. The decisions of that community's language authorities concerning proposed changes or improvements in the community's language (including decisions not to change or improve) are arrived at and implemented in accord with the community's norms governing the "culture of authoritative decision-making" more generally. Authoritative decision-making concerning language (particularly written/printed and formal spoken language) has been practiced for centuries, if not millennia, throughout the world. Nevertheless, during the past century, it has primarily been a concern among later-developing communities in the Americas, Europe, Africa, Asia, and Oceania. Within those communities language planning frequently co-occurs with educational planning, industrial planning, agricultural planning, culture planning, identity planning, and other aspects of authoritatively directed community modernization.

Language Authorities

Language authorities are normally linked to the political authorities of the communities upon whom the implementation of language policy ultimately depends. The language authorities may run the gamut from "language academies" (viz., France, Spain, Israel) or "language boards" (viz., Hausa in Nigeria) and "language committees" (e.g., for Indonesian during the World War I Japanese occupation), through to ad hoc groups of writers, educators, dictionary compilers, or clergy, and even individual arbiters or experts (e.g., at the *New York Times*, where decisions must be made on how to pronounce, spell, and hyphenate foreign names in the news). None of the above necessarily need to wield physical force or economic sanctions in order to operate effectively. Some authorities may have only the power of moral suasion (e.g., the annual color-terminology board of the American fashion industry or the Committee on Updating the *Diagnostic and Statistical Manual of Mental Disorders* of the American Psychological Association). Presumably, the use of idiosyncratic, passé, or inaccurate terms is sufficiently intrapunitive to keep the language usage of most members of professional groups "in line." However, there are other authorities (or their political sponsors) that dispense very severe sanctions or rewards, even involving life and death themselves (e.g., in connection with the decision in the 1930s to prohibit the revision of the Ukrainian orthography that had been completed and approved in the late 1920s: Hornjatkevyc, 1993).

This brief reference to sanctions in language policy implies that enforcement flows directly from the nature of the power link that language authorities have at their disposal. Various intermediate positions between extreme enforcement and mild enforcement also exist; for example, the academy's nomenclature decisions may be binding only upon the government per se (e.g., in Israel, where school textbooks can be adopted only if they carry the Education Department's approval and where that department, being a government agency, is required by law to implement the Hebrew Academy's lexical and orthographic recommendations). In some settings, the academy regularly polls the community of users in order to determine, for example, which of several alternative changes in modern Swedish (e.g., in connection with neologisms) would be more acceptable either to the public as a whole or to specific occupational groups in particular. Some authorities provide a generous transition period during which time teachers, editors, and proofreaders can learn the newly recommended usage; others unilaterally set an early target date and inflict serious penalties upon all who do not meet it (as was the case with Ataturk's revisions and innovations in Turkey, in the 1920s: Landau, 1993). The culture of sanctions with respect to language policy implementations reflects the general culture of sanctions within any particular society. There is absolutely no ground for suspecting all language-policy implementation of being either draconian or mind-numbing. No planning culture is democratic in all other respects but authoritarian only in connection with language policy.

Status Planning

The initiation of federal support for bilingual education in the United States in 1968 and its many reappropriations since then are instances of language policy. The policy required that the various non-English languages spoken by large numbers of non-English-speaking or limited-English-speaking immigrant children be given the status of *co-languages of instruction*, in publicly funded education, for a limited number of years. Since the American federal government does not conduct schools of its own, the most that it could do to implement this new status was to offer grants to compensate states whose interest in providing co-languages of instruction met the competitive strictures of the Federal Department of Education. In this case the "authority" for language policy was split between the federal government, on the one hand, and the state government and even other more local governmental units (e.g., school district), on the other hand.

The few prior or subsequent occasions on which support for languages other than English in public education was federally permitted or supported in the United States also focused on "status planning." Note, however, that there was no federal or state requirement that schools introduce bilingual education. Indeed, the US Supreme Court's *Meyer v. Nebraska* (1923) decision, which denied South Dakota's right to prohibit schools and teachers from giving instruction in any foreign language other than English, was an important instance of language-policy planning. It may be an exaggeration to refer to that decision, as some have, as the Magna Carta of language rights in the United States, but it definitely reserved the right of deciding school language matters to the parents and teachers themselves, and took such curricular language-policy decisions out of governmental jurisdiction. The various more recent state prohibitions on utilizing any languages other than English in the provision of state benefits or services (other than in language-instruction per se) have not been tested in the US Supreme Court. However, many Amerindian nations have "treaty rights" that enable them to conduct their own tribal schools fully or partially in their own languages (McCarty, 2002). Accordingly, some are even willing to forego governmental support of education so that their own language policy may triumph over that of the state(s) that surround(s) them. Most educational issues that involve Amerindians are commonly settled in the state courts, but many are sent on to higher federal courts for adjudication. There are still many such cases that have been indefinitely postponed at one level or another, particularly those that are in any way connected with contested land claims.

However, most of the non-English-language speakers in the United States are either immigrants or the children of immigrants and as such have no treaty rights to protect their language-planning autonomy. Immigrant languages world-wide (or, more precisely, "immigration-marked languages") are always low on the "power totem pole," with two exceptions. One is related to numbers (English was also originally an immigrant language in the United States, Australia, and South Africa); the other to colonization rather than to immigration as usually defined. Immigrants do not overpower the pre-existing power structure; colonizers do just that. Colonialism has, of course imposed a small number of European languages, particularly English, Spanish, and French, on every continent. The English tide is receding slowly (Fishman, 1996); the French one more slowly (except in the Maghreb, where its replacement by Arabic has been precipitous); the Spanish one hardly at all, although indigenous languages have been declared co-official in a few instances (viz., Guarani in Paraguay, and Quechua/Quichua in Peru, Ecuador, and Bolivia). A byproduct of the sheer power of colonizers to extirpate and decimate languages is not only the planned displacement and replacement of local language but even the rise of new languages altogether on the colonial base (viz., Afrikaans, Papiamento, Tok Pisin, and a variety of pidgins and creoles). None of these, whether conquest or immigration derived, is now marked as an immigrant language.

However, by and large, immigrant languages are bereft of power and are at the mercy of languages and authorities that are far stronger than they. Not even as linguistically permissive an authoritative body as the European Union, with its 20 official languages (as of 2004) and its view that all indigenous European languages are, "in principle," really equally "children of Europe," has made any effort whatsoever to extend any rights or courtesies to that continent's manifold immigrant languages. The status of those languages is one of permissive tolerance, under normal circumstances, and more overt governmental use is normally reserved for life-threatening or special commemorative or emergency occasions. Bilingual education is transitional or return-migration oriented and in other than extremely local affairs, the American precedent (court-ordered) of offering bilingual ballots to facilitate voting by non-English-reading minorities, immigrant or indigenous, is *not* followed. Nevertheless, in a few instances immigrant minorities have established their own internal language-policy authorities, on a completely voluntary basis in the United States (e.g., for Yiddish, Romani, and several Soviet minority languages, such as Ukrainian and Belarus, before "perestroika").

In most instances where corpus planning (see next section) for immigrant languages is of interest, usually within small literary circles and in ethnic community schools, the spelling, grammar, and nomenclature rules and regulations of their "old world" homeland language authorities are followed. In a very few cases, the establishment of bilingual education leads to host-government initiatives to develop spelling, grammar, and nomenclature rules for classroom reading in immigrant languages that were not used for purposes of literacy in their home countries (viz., Haitian Creole, Vernacular Arabic, Cape Verdian, etc.). Since bilingual education under federal governmental funding is officially transitional, the creation of such short-term literacies is much more a passing phase than in the cases of the similar efforts by missionaries to spread Christianity or Islam via translating the Bible or the Koran into languages in which no prior literacy has existed. It is noteworthy that even in the best of circumstances, when corpus planning is engaged in for an indigenous population, it may, nevertheless, mask a language-shift rather than a language-maintenance agenda.

The Hidden Status-Planning Agenda

Status planning (pertaining to the *societal functions* that will be authoritatively recognized for a specific language) is also aided and abetted by corpus planning (pertaining to various desiderata of the language per se, such as technological nomenclatures, writing systems, spelling guides, style books, dictionaries, grammars, punctuation rules, etc.). Corpus planning and status planning are often referred to as "two sides of the same [language planning] coin" (Fishman, 2004), but any such implied unavoidable co-occurrence, desirable though it may be theoretically, is neither required nor commonly available in practice. Actually, language policy is most frequently a constant "catch-up" operation between the two sides of its "coin." Obviously, it is unwise for a language to attain new statuses (e.g., in government, the courts, higher education, the military, etc.) without having an adequate corpus by which the topics relevant to such statuses can be readily, accurately, and felicitously expressed. It is similarly undesirable for corpuses to be endlessly extended and modernized without attaining the relevant statuses for which they were intended. Since status planning is the more difficult and contested of the two, it is not uncommon to find it trailing somewhat (although not too much) behind its counterpart in the entire process. There is, indeed, much evidence from modernization settings throughout the world that corpus planning is the first to be entered into, particularly where status-competitors confront one other. Particularly where the power differences between two or more languages are great, it may prove far easier for the weaker of the two to obtain outside authoritative permission to convene a corpus-planning conference than to convene one dealing openly and obviously with politically prohibited or contested statuses.[1]

But, just as power-statuses can be denied and outlawed, so even corpus planning itself can be manipulated in order to undercut the very language on whose behalf it is ostensibly being engaged in. Corpus planning for *Einbau* (making one language out of two structurally very similar ones: see Fishman, 2004) sets the stage for an eventual takeover of language B by language A via the engineering of interlingual proximity. The vital discriminanda of language B can be done away with by changing its writing system to that of language A, as was the case when the Soviet Union required almost all of its minority languages to be written in Cyrillic, rather than in their own traditional native scripts. New words entering language A may be required to be the same as those newly entering language B (e.g., from 1938 on, after many decades of a wrenching and expensive *Nynorsk* vs. *Ryksmal* struggle in Norway, via the creation of yet another variety of the language: [language C] *Samnorsk*) (Ager, 2003). This represented an attempt to require even well-established words dealing with politically sensitive or culturally crucial issues to be the same in both languages. Suffice it to say that corpus planning too, for all of its apparent political innocence, can and often does make some contribution to the authoritative support for guided language shift.

There are also alternative directions within corpus planning, some of which tend to lead weaker languages into more contact or earlier interaction with their surrounding stronger neighbors than is advisable for their own longevity. Corpus policies that stress *Westernization* of technological or scientific terms instead of *uniqueness, vernacularity* (i.e., recognizing for written purposes the popular "street terms" that are already in informal use and that are largely derived from contact with tourism and outside media or products) instead of *classicization* (the classical linguistic component that is closest to one's own independent "great tradition"), *regionalization* (using neighboring great powers as corpus-planning models) instead of pursuing *"purity,"* all have shift tendencies that are rarely realized at the time such corpus-planning decisions are made. Pursuing *Einbau* interaction with and similarity to far stronger cognate languages, versus *Ausbau* (i.e., building the language away from an overpowering and structurally very similar neighbor, relative to which it is often perceived as a dialect rather than as a really autonomous language: Fishman, 1993), is another such self-weakening choice, ultimately leading toward shift rather than toward maintenance. The guiding direction of corpus planning, both within and on behalf of threatened languages, often changes track, pari passu with political and economic change in the A and/or B communities. Westernization goals can also be transmitted via regionally more proximate intermediaries (e.g., Chinese Putonghua for the Mongols, Russian for the Rusyns, and Swahili for peoples deep in the hinterland of Tanzania or Uganda). Such influences wax and wane; 180 degree reversals are not at all unknown. For example, Moldovan has been viewed as a regional dialect of Romanian, before World War II; as a separate language fully independent from Romanian and written in Cyrillic, under Soviet domination and up until the collapse of Communism; as separate from but clearly related to Romanian and, like it, written in a Latin-type script, during the early years of in-dependent Moldova; and, finally, at the moment, again as no more than a spoken variant of Romanian and, therefore, having written Romanian as its literary form. This peregrination fully reflects the extent to which corpus planning too is politically encumbered. This is why corpus planning and also status planning often involve as much unplanning and replanning as planning per se, but in each case it can be used for language shift (Clyne, 1997).

Language Shift

Language shift often occurs under governmental auspices, although direct authoritative sponsorship does not always obtain. Language spread from area A to area B may be due to the economic differences between the two settings. Such differences inevitably lead to cross-border migrations, even when both governments are decidedly opposed to such crossings. The US–Mexico border is a good example of the foregoing circumstances involving a constantly northbound stream of populations, followed by the diffusion southward of goods, electronic communications, and consumption practices, not to mention culture-bound behaviors. The fact that there is no policy requiring the shift from Spanish to English as a result of such migration (or the shift from English to Spanish as a result of the much smaller return-migration) does not in any way affect the shifts that occur. Indeed, the absence of authoritative policy always works in favor of the stronger party and gives rise to a "no-policy policy" in many settings throughout the world. The stronger establishment distributes its rewards in accord with its own interests, values, and goals, all of which are supported by its own authorities. Such "no-policy policies" and their consequences must be rendered visible and conscious (as, e.g., the French in Quebec have done, even though there were few, if any, anti-French or pro-English laws on the books at the time) if they are to be successfully confronted, opposed, and changed. However, the truth remains that *most language shift of formal and written language is caused or consciously facilitated* (i.e., by conquest or other major dislocations of the status quo), rather than that "just happens." Indeed, many languages today are so fragile and weakened that even "friendly language planning" can topple them by implying that even the diminishing band of native speakers do not really know how to read, write or speak their own mother tongue correctly or effectively. The stronger party may engage in either *intra-polity* or *inter-polity* actions, including both explicit and implicit language-planning decisions, to disrupt the ongoing customary culture and economy of the situationally weaker language.

Intra-Polity Actions

American Indians have been exposed to forced removal (on a group basis) and the attendant destruction of traditional conventions, inter-locutors, and reward mechanisms on which language maintenance depends and by means of which it is intergenerationally continued. Treaty rights have been unilaterally abrogated, as was also true in the case of the Waitangi Treaty signed by the surrendering Maoris in New Zealand, whose expectations of public support to "maintain their treasures," language among them, were immediately and then constantly dashed. The "reluctance" of Norwegian, Swedish, and Finnish authorities to exclude most indigenous areas and settlements from European commercial exploitation and competition (or, conversely, to foster indigenous industries and occupations along self-governing lines) has prompted many residents to give up the constant struggle for autonomy and to leave for "off-reservation" cities, where they encounter the sharp break with home languages and traditions that full and rapid immersion in life there entails. This has also been the main problem within nearly all aboriginal Australian, Latin American, and African communities, regardless of whether or not they are ethnically related to the central authorities of the local polities involved. The latter have already undergone transculturation and translinguification a generation or more ago (viz., Mestizos in Mexico, Peru, Bolivia, Ecuador, and much of Central America) and often consider these processes, in retrospect, to be a blessing rather than an abomination for their latecomer kin.

The Mayan (Zapatista) antipathies toward the "central authorities" in Mexico are of this nature, as are the Quechua/Shining Path resistance in Peru, Tibetan resistance in China, and the long-festering Chechyn resistance in the Russian Caucuses area. They represent the latest attempts to resist a process which began with the industrial, commercial, and agricultural revolutions that transformed most of Western Europe half a millennium ago at the expense of such regional languages as Irish, Welsh, and Scottish, not to mention most of the regional languages of Spain and France. Both capitalism and communism were equally opposed to "non-state-building" local languages, as was the Catholic church.

Inter-Polity Processes

When we need to consider world-wide modernization, as we now do, it is difficult to differentiate between intra-polity and inter-polity causes on any hard-and-fast basis. It was only the ethnolinguistic basis of organization of the Eastern Orthodox and Eastern Catholic ("Uniate") churches in most of Eastern and Southern Europe, and the overriding influence of Johann Gottfried Herder, that avoided a similar deracination there and led to the failure of the Pan-movements around German and Russian that were espoused there by the multiethnic and multilingual Austro-Hungarian and Czarist empires. Although local (initially sub-state) languages and identities were abused by "state-building" authorities everywhere, fewer were pushed to the edge of the virtual extinctions in which the West has long taken pride.

Nevertheless, once we leave the Orthodox and Herderian combination behind, as we do in almost all of Asia, Africa, and the Pacific, we find that the combination of zealous Islam and triumphalist Westernization has often had a regional impact, much as Catholicism and the Industrial Revolution had had earlier in the West. The Arabization of North Africa (replacing French but by no means liberating Berber or Woloff) and the Anglophone dominance in parts of South and East Asia (viz., the consideration being given by both Japan and Korea to declaring English as a co-national language, a status similar to the one it had in the former British colonies of India and Singapore) are instructive instances of external and internal interactions in promoting language shift. The continuing lingering and "official" or "co-official" dominance of English in the Philippines and in New Guinea should also be noted. Each of the above mentioned countries has utilized authoritative language-planning measures on behalf of English and, therefore, has not only fostered language shift toward English for speakers of various local languages, but has also fostered wildly unrealistic rising aspirations among the lower middle classes aspiring to share in the English-related successes of their local elites.

The Special Language-Shift Role of Education

More than most other authoritative specialists, the authorities of the educational system are deeply implicated in planned language shift. Like other agencies of government, education is focused on the formal, written language. Because education is generally obligatory, it focuses on the young, and its sway not only continues uninterrupted for many years among those who "stay with it," but is oriented toward future gains that may last for additional untold years. This combination of factors renders education a very useful and highly irreversible language-shift mechanism for statuses that are literacy related. The usual postmodern critique – that language planning disregards the truly mixed and spontaneous nature of current media-influenced, tourism-influenced, youth-culture-influenced speech – misses the boat completely in connection with formal and educated language (oral and written).

It is the latter forms of communication that are of governmental authoritative concern, and education is the agency that carries that concern for a number of years in each child's life, into every corner of the country on an obligatory basis. Schools may or may not adopt a transitional conciliatory attitude toward "recognizing the language of the child" (e.g., in the Bilbao area of the Basque country, where the San Sebastian/Donostia standard is replaced in the earliest grades by the transitional use of a school variety based on the local spoken dialect), but this too is no more than a passing phase, intended to ease the child into institutional life and into dialect shift toward acceptance of the true institutional variety. Furthermore, the same is true whether it is a local, regional, or national language that is employed for literacy-based education. It is a variety necessarily removed from the ongoing chaotic nature of everyday speech, particularly that of the poor, the young, and the unschooled. This is also the variety that becomes mythologically embroidered and that comes to play the foremost symbolic role in national functioning and in national identity. Those who are exposed to it longest and most intensively cannot hope but to shift to it, increasingly, in their adult and after-school lives. Indeed it may become the lingua franca among school leavers and graduates and, ultimately, the mother tongue of a new generation.

There are, of course, some international provisions and agreements (in Europe) for safeguarding local and other minority cultures and their languages. However, none of them is binding, enforced by sanctions, and required for membership in the most important international bodies. None of them applies also to local dialects (which leaves much "wiggle room" as to where the dialect/language boundary should be drawn), or to the languages of immigrants. This leaves "as many as 200 [language varieties], spoken by nearly 100 million people in western and central Europe and in the Baltic states" alone (Dandridge, 1997, p. 3), without even the lukewarm protection that these agreements provide. Furthermore, these agreements pertaining to sub-national languages apply almost entirely to elementary education, little attention being paid to secondary education, while college or university education is almost entirely outside of their purview. All of this leaves the prospect of much language shift in Europe's future, both consciously and unconsciously related to drawing minority speech communities (including dialects of the "national" language) ever more tightly into the orbit of modernization and globalization. The same process may be expected on all other continents as they too head in the same developmental direction, not only belatedly but also less "profitably" than was the case earlier. The establishment of minority-medium schools (even universities) can have little impact upon this process, other than to draw it out. Even central authorities, with secure national borders and the ability to keep the flow of other-language products in check, certainly relative to the abilities of minorities that lack any authoritative power of their own, are beginning to feel the pressure. Proposals to conduct secondary and higher education entirely, or virtually so, in English have lately been entertained by the Netherlands, Denmark, and Finland, not to mention Japan, Korea, Singapore, and India, as well as most other former British and American colonies (Fishman, Conrad, & Rubal-Lopez, 1996).

The Pro-English "Conspiracy"

The above discussion is formulated mostly in terms of *intra*-national authoritative language-planning policies, even though, admittedly, these too can have international consequences when conducted by world powers such as the United States, Britain, France, etc. However, the entire discussion has been raised one notch higher, to that of a conspiratorial *inter*national level (Phillipson, 1992). What Phillipson suspects (without quite proving it) is that the British Council and the (American-based) Teachers of English to Speakers of Other Languages (TESOL) have successfully conspired to support the teaching of English abroad, largely in former British and American colonies, in order to surreptitiously further the foreign policy and economic ascendancy of their own respective countries (in addition to and under the "cover" of their avowed educational goals). Furthermore, these agencies supported the use of textbooks from their home countries that subtly fostered their own ways of life (consumer culture) and thereby further undercut indigenous cultures and lifestyles. Most linguists and language teachers have rejected the conspiratorial charge, but the consequential charge of responsibility for actually attaining language and culture shift still remains unaddressed. The conspiracy charge is the more dramatic of the two (something akin to a newly unearthed "Protocols of the Elders of English"), but it is the consequential charge which is the more important. There are so many other strong ties that bind former colonies to their erstwhile colonizer powers – economic, industrial, commercial, political, educational, etc. – that it is almost impossible to tease out the independent role of the language planning engaged in by the two agencies that Phillipson has placed in the spotlight. It is also noteworthy that some of the countries that have come to emphasize continuous, strong, and early concentration on English in education have been distinctly anti-Western in their orientations – for example, Cuba (Corona & Garcia, 1996) and Saudi Arabia (Al-Haq Al-Abed & Smadi, 1996) – and have used English in order to more expeditiously influence and oppose the West, that is, to push their own agendas through English, rather than to be influenced by the agendas of the "conspiratorial imperialists."

It may be more reasonable to consider the Phillipsonian argument as somewhat different than the inadvertent language-shift policies and consequences that we have already considered above. The globalization of material and non-material culture in the twentieth and twenty-first centuries has undoubtedly favored English, but it has also done so in the Francophone world, in the Hispanophone world, the Arabophone world, the Slavophone world, and the Sinophone world (not to mention the many worlds of secondary globalizers, such as the Hausaphone, the Swahiliphone, the Lusophone, the Niponophone, etc.), which serve their respective client cultures as indirect purveyors of English and modernization. Furthermore, to a smaller degree, the same Westernization process as Phillipson decries is also taking place under the auspices of their respective secondary languages of secondary power, many of which have been engaged in planned relinguification (and even re-ethnicization) for decades or even longer. Their substantial local successes are not due to English alone, by any means, but, rather, are due to the same larger, more primary forces that even the spread of English is subjected to.

Rather than entertaining either conspiracy theories or Anglo-linguistic causality aspersions, we may look back upon several pre-modernization massive language-shift phenomena for an overall perspective on the linguistic role in past translinguification and transethnification eras that transpired well before globalization. These involved the Anglification of the North American continent, the Arabization of the Maghreb, the Russification of Siberia and the Caucuses, the Hispanization and Lusoization of Latin America, and the Sinoization of the entire Chinese interior. All of these major changes occurred under authoritative sponsorship and had widespread (although incompletely so) and fairly irreversible language-shift consequences. The fact that most of the foregoing involve conquest scenarios (whereas the globalization process rarely does) still does not make it impossible to find some common threads between the two. The major such thread may be the *severe dislocation from indigenous, self-regulated social change* – whether this dislocation is planned or unplanned – that both scenarios entail, as well as the nullification of prior authorities, in language as in culture more generally.

Planned versus Unplanned Shift

In view of the major language-shift processes now going on throughout the world, it is not irrelevant to ask how much of this shift is planned. It is not possible to answer that question with any great degree of accuracy because little if any precise cultural accounting is done in connection with globalization. However, my own impression is that (distinctly unlike the "conquest cases" mentioned previously) globalization involves considerable "non-Phillipsonian" planning. Since we are dealing, first and foremost, with formal and written language use in the most power-related status-roles, we are also dealing with change in language use via courses, pedagogical materials, academic certification and degrees, seminars, conferences, official record-keeping, official correspondence with and by governmental agencies, and various other pursuits that are visible to the authorities and, therefore, more controllable and directable than the transfer of powers (with a total loss of control) that so often obtains in the conquest case. Language planning, both corpus and status, is quintessentially of the "top-down" variety, the "top" being the very same personnel most actively involved – actually or referentially – in most globalization efforts as well.

Conclusion

Any tool can be used for good or for evil, to build or to destroy. So it is also with language planning, which is most commonly used to advance the status or the corpus of a particular language or group of languages. Nevertheless, in a highly interactive world, the "good" that is achieved for one language may cause damage or problems to others, consciously or unconsciously, purposely or accidentally. Language decline, language shift, and language death are no longer objects of politically correct language planning, but these deleterious consequences are every bit as alive and as destructive today as they have ever been throughout the long history of language planning. Even as beneficent and as desirable an activity as "education" has been put to use for hidden negative purposes, such as the disruption of local traditions, legal systems, religion, and authoritative structures. Given the foregoing, it is only natural that the world's greatest (and at this time, only) superpower should have impacted on both the language functions and the social structures (not to mention the very longevity) of languages large and small all over the world. The fact that the United States does not usually have an overtly proactive language policy toward specific other languages does not mean that such a "no-policy policy" does not strongly foster the spread of English for power functions in non-English mother-tongue countries both in the Americas and elsewhere, or that the languages of the world are not being flooded with English terms, expressions, comics, and songs via publications, television, and radio everywhere. The United States may not mean to do so, and it may not actually be involved in a conspiracy (as some would claim) to kill off the world's languages, but the consequences may very well be the same, regardless of whatever its conscious motivation may be. This is all the more likely to be the case within the borders of the United States, where not a single immigrant tongue has reached a self-sustaining level (not even Spanish in our own days) in over 200 years. If such an outcome is ever to be realized then a proactively positive and consciously implemented language policy will be called for. The only questions in that regard are (1) whether that goal (the regreening of languages other than Englishes in the US) is really desired by the decision-makers of the country, and (2) whether it isn't already too late for most American languages to bring such a rescue mission to fruition.

Annotated Bibliography

Al-Haq Al-Abed, F. & Smadi, O. (1996). The status of English in the Kingdom of Saudi Arabia (KSA) from 1940–1990. In J. A. Fishman, A. W. Conrad, & A. Rubal-Lopez (eds.), *Post-imperial English: Status change in former British and American colonies, 1940–1990* (pp. 457–84). Berlin: Mouton.
This chapter is a suitable point from which to re-examine the charge that English abroad is fostered for the explicit purposes of advancing

American goals. What alternative to English is there for the world-wide spread of Islam?

Clyne, M. (ed.) (1997). *Undoing and redoing language planning*. Berlin: Mouton.
This volume is outstanding for coming to grips with the cyclical and oppositional nature of language planning, regardless of its goals at any particular time.

Corona, D. & Garcia, O. (1996). English in Cuba: From imperial design to imperative need. In J. A. Fishman, A. W. Conrad. & A. Rubal-Lopez (eds.), *Post-imperial English: Status change in former British and American colonies, 1940–1990* (pp. 85–112). Berlin: Mouton.
This chapter forces us once again to recognize that there are anti-American authorities that are insisting on requiring their citizens to attain mastery in English in order to counter, rather than to foster, America's interests throughout the world (and particularly in the New World).

Fishman, J. A. (ed.) (1993). *The earliest stage of language planning*. Berlin: Mouton.
This book illustrates how language planning, of the earliest and most rudimentary type, nevertheless attracts authorities (mostly teachers, writers, professors, and clergy) to its banners and, when successful, adopts easily realizable goals that will permit them to reconvene frequently and establish a permanent "center."

Fishman, J. A. (1996). Summary and interpretation: Post-imperial English, 1940–1990. In J. A. Fishman, A. W. Conrad, & A. Rubal-Lopez (eds.), *Post-imperial English: Status change in Former British and American colonies, 1940–1990* (pp. 623–40). Berlin: Mouton.
This provides an empirical test of the hypothesis that there are strong forces advancing the world-wide spread of English other than those controlled by and at the service of the United States.

Fishman, J. A. (2004). Ethnicity and supra-ethnicity in corpus planning: The hidden status agenda in corpus planning. *Nations and Nationalism 10*, 79–94.
This article illustrates the various directions that language planning can take when accentuating one's uniqueness and separateness, on the one hand, or one's relatedness and involvement with others, on the

other hand. Many language planning authorities attempt to pursue both directions simultaneously (impossible though this may seem to be) or in tandem, which leads them to a zig-zaggy policy (such as the U.S. Federal Government's policies for Amerindians.)

Discussion Questions

1 Would a centralized language-planning agency be useful to the United States. Why? Why not?
2 Why and how can "no policy" turn out to be a language policy in its own right?
3 In what ways were language policies in the United States and in Soviet Russia similar or opposite to each other?
4 Why don't any of the major English mother-tongue countries have English language academies?
5 Usually, corpus-planning policy is concerned with vocabulary. Can you identify cases in which it was concerned with writing-system reform and grammatical change as well?
6 Which type of language planning is more difficult in each of the following: (a) to strengthen or to weaken a language, and (b) corpus planning or status planning?

NOTE

1 See, for example, with the weaker language italicized: Spanish vs. *Catalan* (Marti i Castell, 1993); the Dutch vs. *Indonesian* case (Moeliano, 1993); or the English vs. *Tok Pisin* case (Wurm, 1993); among many others that could be cited.

REFERENCES

Ager, S. (2003). Norwegian (Norsk). Omniglot: A guide to writing systems. Retrieved February 26, 2004, from www.omniglot.com/writing/Norwegian. htm.

Al-Haq Al-Abed, F. & Smadi, O. (1996). The status of English in the Kingdom of Saudi Arabia (KSA) from 1940–1990. In J. A. Fishman, A. W. Conrad, & A. Rubal-Lopez (eds.), *Post-imperial English: Status change in former British and American colonies, 1940–1990* (pp. 457–84). Berlin: Mouton.

Clyne, M. (ed.) (1997). *Undoing and redoing language planning*. Berlin: Mouton.

Corona, D. & Garcia, O. (1996). English in Cuba: From imperial design to imperative need. In J. A. Fishman, A. W. Conrad, & A. Rubal-Lopez (eds.), *Post-imperial English: Status change in former British and American colonies, 1940–1990* (pp. 85–112). Berlin: Mouton.

Dandridge, B. (1997). Protecting minority languages proves a challenge for EU officials. *European Dialogue, 2*, 1–3.

Fishman, J. A. (ed.) (1993). *The earliest stage of language planning: The "first congress" phenomenon*. Berlin: Mouton.

Fishman, J. A. (1996). Summary and interpretation: Post-imperial English, 1940–1990. In J. A. Fishman, A. W. Conrad, & A. Rubal-Lopez (eds.), *Post-imperial English: Status change in former British and American colonies, 1940–1990* (pp. 623–40). Berlin: Mouton.

Fishman, J. A. (2004). Ethnicity and supra-ethnicity in corpus planning: The hidden status agenda in corpus planning. *Nations and Nationalism, 10*, 79–94.

Fishman, J. A., Conrad, A. W., & Rubal-Lopez, A. (eds.) (1996). *Post-imperial English: Status change in former British and American colonies, 1940–1990*. Berlin: Mouton.

Hornjatkevyc, A. (1993). The 1928 Ukrainian orthography. In J. A. Fishman (ed.), *The earliest stage of language planning: The "first congress" phenomenon* (pp. 293–304). Berlin: Mouton.

Landau, J. (1993). The first Turkish language congress. In J. A. Fishman (ed.), *The earliest stage of language planning: The "first congress" phenomenon* (pp. 271–92). Berlin: Mouton.

Marti i Castell, J. (1993). The first international Catalan language congress. In J. A. Fishman (ed.), *The earliest stage of language planning: The "first congress" phenomenon* (pp. 47–68). Berlin: Mouton.

McCarty, T. (2002). *A place to be Navaho: Rough Rock and the struggle for self-determination in indigenous schooling*. Mahwah, NJ: Lawrence Erlbaum.

Moeliano, A. (1993). The first efforts to promote and develop Indonesian. In J. A. Fishman (ed.), *The earliest stage of language planning: The "first congress" phenomenon* (pp. 129–42). Berlin: Mouton.

Phillipson, R. (1992). *Linguistic imperialism*. Oxford: Oxford University Press.

Wurm, S. (1993). The first congress for Tok Pisin in 1973. In J. A. Fishman (ed.), *The earliest stage of language planning: The "first congress" phenomenon* (pp. 257–70). Berlin: Mouton.

CHAPTER EIGHTEEN

Language Policy and Sign Languages

Timothy Reagan

This chapter will address issues and developments related to language planning and language policies for sign languages. There is something rather unusual about writing about sign languages: unlike discussing other languages, one is almost inevitably obligated to first establish the case for sign language constituting a "legitimate" kind of human language. This said, it is not only well established, but almost universally recognized by linguistics, that sign languages are fully and completely human languages, meeting every reasonable criterion that we might apply to describe language (see Fromkin, 2000; Valli & Lucas, 2000, pp. 2–15). Nevertheless, the picture is considerably more complex and complicated than this might suggest. Not all "signing" is "sign language," and the diversity among sign languages is significant. Thus, before moving to the central topic of this chapter, language planning and language policies for sign languages, we do need to delineate the different kinds of sign languages that exist, and indeed co-exist, in various settings.

The Diversity of Sign Languages

The diversity of sign languages actually refers to a number of different, and significant, kinds of diversity. First, there are large numbers of sign languages that are natural sign languages used by Deaf people in different settings around the world. Although these different natural sign languages share certain generic features (such as their gestural and visual nature, their use of space for linguistic purposes, etc.), and while some sign languages are genetically related to others (that is, there are sign language families just as there are spoken language families),[1] these languages are nevertheless distinct languages in their own right. Many of these natural sign languages have been studied by linguists; among these are not only American Sign Language (ASL), but also Australian Sign Language, British Sign Language, Danish Sign Language, Dutch Sign Language, French Sign Language, German Sign Language, Hong Kong Sign Language, Indo-Pakistani Sign Language, Israeli Sign Language, Italian Sign Language, Russian Sign Language, South African Sign Language, Swedish Sign Language, Taiwanese Sign Language, and Venezuelan Sign Language; and this is far from an exhaustive list. Indeed, although impressive in its own right, this list is but the proverbial "tip of the iceberg," since most natural sign languages (like most spoken languages) remain unstudied. Skutnabb-Kangas has reminded us that "there probably are something between 6,500 and 10,000 spoken (oral) languages in the world, and a number of sign languages which can be equally large" (2000, p. 30).

The numbers of natural sign languages are but one sense in which we can talk about sign-language diversity, however. The second way in which diversity enters the picture is with respect to the diversity present *within* particular natural sign languages. In the case of ASL, for instance, we know that there is not only extensive lexical diversity related to region of the country, but also diversity related to age, gender, and ethnicity (see Lucas, Bayley, & Valli, 2001). A far more extreme case is provided by South African Sign Language (SASL). SASL, at least in part as a consequence of the social and educational policies of the apartheid regime, is characterized by extensive lexical variation coupled with an underlying syntactic unity. As Penn and Reagan have noted,

> Of the 2500 lexical items collected under the auspices of the SASLRP [South African Sign Language Research Programme] for the dictionary of SASL, only 2% of all of the words represented had a single, common sign across all the different deaf groups, and roughly 10% of the words have as few as one or two signed variants . . . On average, six variants per word were found and the range went as high as eleven variants [for a single word].
>
> *(Penn & Reagan, 2001, p. 55)*

Indeed, the situation is so complex that sign-language linguists concerned with SASL actually engaged in arguments about whether it is a single sign language or a related collection of different sign languages (see Aarons & Akach, 2002; Branson & Miller, 2002, pp. 244–5).

The third sort of diversity that plays a role in understanding sign language is not so much in terms of sign language as with respect to "signing." The distinction between "sign language" and "signing" is in fact a very significant one. Up to this point, we have been concerned only with natural sign languages – the sign languages that emerge and are used in communities of Deaf people for intra-group communication. The Deaf, however, do not live apart from the hearing: rather, they are integrated into the hearing world in a number of ways and on a number of different levels. The vast majority of Deaf people have hearing parents, and the vast majority of Deaf people will have hearing children. In addition, the Deaf need to have access to at least some other hearing people in order to function socially and economically. While the children of Deaf people may well learn their parents' sign language as a native language, most parents of Deaf children and other hearing people who are in contact with the Deaf will generally not learn the natural sign language. Instead, they will learn to sign using what is in essence a contact sign language – that is, a sign language that has elements of both the natural sign language and the surrounding spoken language (see Lucas & Valli, 1989, 1991, 1992). Such contact languages, originally labeled "pidgin sign," are in fact the primary kind of sign language used in hearing–Deaf communicative interchanges. These contact languages, like natural sign languages, are the result of normal linguistic development, and their emergence parallels that of spoken contact languages. Finally, there have been efforts to design "manual sign codes" to represent spoken languages (see Bornstein, 1990; Reagan, 1995). These manual sign codes are simply efforts to represent a spoken language in a gestural or visual modality – comparable, really, to writing a spoken language. Manual sign codes were developed in educational settings as a way of providing Deaf children with access to spoken language. In the US case, for instance, the most popular of these manual sign codes is Signing Exact English (SEE-II) (Gustason & Zawolkow, 1993); in Britain, the Paget-Gorman system essentially served the same purpose, albeit on a somewhat less sophisticated level (see Paget, 1951). It is important to note that manual sign codes are just that: codes to represent language, not language in and of themselves (see Reagan, 1995, 2001a). The actual educational value of such manual sign codes is somewhat debatable, but to a fluent signer, the codes are often perceived as slow, awkward, and confusing.

Language Planning and Language Policy for Sign Languages

With this background in mind, we can now turn to a discussion of language-planning and language-policy efforts related to sign languages. Sign languages have been the focus of both status-planning and corpus-planning efforts in recent years, not only in the United States, but in a variety of other nations as well (see Covington, 1976; Deuchar, 1980; Erting, 1978; Nash, 1987; Nover, 1995; Ramsey, 1989; Reagan, 2001a; Reagan & Penn, 1997; Woodward, 1973). Although each individual effort is of course unique, there are nevertheless a number of common themes that emerge in language-planning efforts concerned with sign languages around the globe. We will examine here, first, efforts at status planning, and then efforts at corpus planning.

Status planning

Status-planning efforts, as Kaplan and Baldauf have argued, "can be defined as those aspects of language planning which reflect primarily social issues and concerns and hence are external to the language(s) being planned. The two status issues which make up the model are *language selection* and *language implementation*" (1997, p. 30, emphasis in original). In the context of sign languages, language selection generally refers to the official recognition of a natural sign language, while language implementation primarily refers to the use of (or the banning of) sign language in educational settings, and, to some extent, in legal and medical settings. In the United States, efforts to officially recognize ASL have taken place predominantly at the state level; to date, approximately 35 of the 50 states have passed legislation granting legal status to ASL, and efforts are underway in several other states to pass similar legislation.[2] It is important to note that such legislation, and similar national legislation that was approved, for instance, in Sweden in 1981 (see Wallin, 1994), does *not* entail the recognition of a sign language as an "official" language; rather, it is simply concerned with placing "on the record," as it were, the fact that the sign language is indeed a "real" language, and, in some cases, articulates the specific language rights of users of sign languages. The same is true, interestingly enough, in the World Federation of the Deaf's "Call for Recognition of Sign Languages," which seeks the recognition of sign languages as "indigenous languages" and emphasizes the linguistic rights of Deaf people as members of linguistic minority groups (see Reagan, 2001a, pp. 178–80). The only instance in which "official" status has been considered for a natural sign language is in the case of South Africa. In the post-apartheid era, as the new constitution was being drafted, serious discussions took place about whether SASL should be accorded the status of an "official" language (Reagan, 2002). Although the new constitution does include a section on the rights of users of SASL, as well as a recognition of the status and importance of SASL, it does not actually include SASL as one of South Africa's official languages (though a total of 11 languages are granted that status) (see Reagan, 2001b; Webb, 2002).

Status planning related to sign languages also takes place extensively in educational institutions, especially in schools for the Deaf, where the historic tensions between "oralists" (who generally reject the use of signing) and "manualists" (who advocate the use of signing, although sometimes of a manual sign code rather than a natural sign language) are often played out as language policy debates (see Baynton, 1996; Reagan, 1989; Weisel, 1998; Winefield, 1987). The other educational context in which status debates about sign language occur is with respect to the study of sign language as a "foreign" language – an ongoing concern in both secondary and tertiary institutions in the United States, and one which is likely to take place in other national settings as well in the years ahead (see Reagan, 2000; Wilcox & Wilcox, 1997).

Discussions and debates about the status of sign languages are generally seen as positive developments, both by the Deaf and by advocates for and supporters of the Deaf. However, while such discussions do have a great deal of positive potential, it is important to note that they are not without risks as well. As Skutnabb-Kangas has argued,

> Now when some of the Sign languages slowly start getting some recognition, rights and visibility, others are being replaced (and killed) by . . . recognised, sometimes standardised Sign languages and – surprise surprise – by subtractive spreading of American Sign Language . . . Just like the dominant dialects became "languages," and dominant official languages displace and replace other languages nationally, in each country where the Deaf start organising, usually only one Sign language becomes recognised. Hearing people, sometimes Sign language teachers but often teachers with no knowledge of any Sign languages, in most cases dominate these linguicist processes.
>
> *(Skutnabb-Kangas, 2000, p. 227)*

Perhaps the single most important aspect of status planning with respect to sign languages has been the growing concern with the language rights of sign-language users, and it may also be in this arena that the greatest work remains to be done. Minority-language rights are a very controversial matter in settings around the world, in spite of public proclamations to the contrary, and the question of minority-language rights for the Deaf is an especially complex and difficult one – not only because of issues of language rights per se, it should be noted, but rather, because the vast majority of Deaf people have hearing parents. Thus, even the determination of what "mother tongue" might mean in the case of the Deaf child is far from self-evident, and remains a matter of potential conflict (see Jokinen, 2000; Muzsnai, 1999; Skutnabb-Kangas, 1994).

Corpus planning

Corpus-planning efforts, according to Kaplan and Baldauf,

> can be defined as those aspects of language planning which are primarily linguistic and hence internal to language. Some of these aspects related to language are: (a) orthographic innovation, including design, harmonization, change of script, and spelling reform; (b) pronunciation; (c) changes in language structure; (d) vocabulary expansion; (e) simplification of registers; (f) style; and (g) the preparation of language material.
>
> *(1997, p. 38)*

In the case of sign languages, corpus-planning efforts fall into five broad categories: lexicography, lexical creation and expansion, textbook production, the creation of manual sign codes, and the development of orthographic systems for representing sign languages. Each of the categories is discussed briefly below.

Lexicography for sign languages has made tremendous strides in recent years (see Armstrong, 2003a, 2003b). The earliest dictionaries of sign languages were generally little more than collections of drawings or pictures of signs, usually in alphabetical word order based on the dominant spoken language. In many instances, these "dictionaries" did not even rely on native informants as sources, but rather were based on hearing professionals' ideas about how particular words ought to be signed. Although "dictionaries" of this sort still abound, there are also a number of quite good sign-language dictionaries based on very solid linguistic research. Among the best are Tennant and Brown's *The American Sign Language handshape dictionary* (1998), Johnston's *AUSLAN dictionary* (1989) for Australian Sign Language, and Brien's *Dictionary of British Sign Language/English* (1992). Perhaps most impressive is the *Multimedia dictionary of American Sign Language*, which utilizes computer technology to provide a far more useful kind of dictionary for sign-language learners and users (see Wilcox, 2003).

Lexical creation and expansion in natural sign languages take place in five ways: through the compounding of existing signs, through borrowing, through various morphological processes, through the invention of new signs, and through semantic expansion (Reagan, 1990, pp. 257–8). Compounding occurs when two existing signs are put together to create a new sign with distinctive semantic content. This process, which is quite common in spoken languages (as in English, "breakfast" from "break" + "fast"), has been documented in ASL, French Sign Language, and Israeli Sign Language, and almost certainly exists in most natural sign languages. Examples in ASL include SPACESHIP[3] (SPACE + SHIP), SMOG (SMOKE + FOG), and DECODER (TELEVISION + CAPTION); in Israeli Sign Language, we find LIBRARY (BOOK + EXCHANGE) and CAFÉ (COFFEE + SIT). Natural sign languages meet new lexical needs by borrowing from other languages, both spoken and signed (see Brentari, 2001). Sign languages commonly borrow terminology from spoken languages, generally through finger-spelled loan signs (finger-spelled terms which undergo processes of structural and formational change and become standard signs). ASL examples of such finger-spelled loan signs include #OR,[4] #TOY, #DOG, #EARLY, and #TOAST; British Sign Language examples include #QUARTER, #ENGLAND, and #ANSWER. Some sign languages also utilize "initialized" signs (that is, signs that have embedded in them the first letter of the word they represent). Initialized signs allow the creation of groups of related signs based on a single common sign: for instance, in ASL, the signs FAMILY, GROUP, ASSOCIATION, and TEAM are distinguished only by the letter used in the handshape formation. Sign languages also increasingly borrow signs from other sign languages; most often, ASL is the source sign language because of its relatively large and technically well-developed lexicon, although ASL also borrows from other sign languages (this has been especially true in recent years with respect to the names of countries of foreign place names, as in GERMANY, JAPAN, KOREA, CHINA, and so on).[5] In ASL two morphological processes are sometimes used to create new signs. The first results in what can be termed a "derivational sign"; here, for instance, one begins with a verb and by changing the nature of the movement, a corresponding noun is created. Thus, the verb BLOW-DRY-HAIR, when made with a short, repeated action, becomes the noun for BLOW-DRYER. The second morphological process that is used is to combine classifier morphemes, as in using the classifier for "a large flat object" together with the classifier for "a two-legged person" to form the sign HANG-GLIDING. Technical signs are often created to meet user needs, especially in educational settings. Such signs are especially common in such areas as computer science, medicine, engineering, and so on. In the ASL case, the National Technical Institute of the Deaf and Gallaudet University have been important contributors to the creation of new lexical items. Finally, semantic expansion occurs when an existing sign takes on new or additional meanings. In ASL, for example, the sign FULL has also come to mean "fed up," while in British Sign Language the sign ENOUGH performs the same function. Also in British Sign Language, the sign for PULL-THINGS-OFF-A-WALL has undergone semantic expansion, and is now used to entail any sort of decorating or redecorating.

Textbook production has been an important arena of corpus planning for sign languages. The first sign-language textbooks consisted of not much more than vocabulary lists, with little (if any) information about the syntax and structure of natural sign language. In fact, it is clear that sign-language teaching was focused primarily on teaching hearing students to communicate in some sort of contact sign language with the Deaf, and so, in a very real sense, students were not studying a natural sign language at all. Recent efforts in the United States to develop textbooks, curricula, and qualified teachers for ASL have made important strides in correcting this, and there are now a number of quite good textbooks that are, in reality as well as in name, textbooks of ASL. Examples of these include not only the well-known "Green Books" series written by Cokely and Baker-Shenk (1980a, 1980b, 1981a, 1981b; see also Baker-Shenk & Cokely, 1980), but also the more recent contributions of Humphries and Padden (1992), Humphries, Padden, and O'Rourke (1994), Shelly and Schneck (1998), and Stewart (1998).

The creation and use of manual sign codes for spoken language is the fourth type of corpus planning involving sign languages. Although the development of manual sign codes is an international phenomenon, the emergence and educational implementation of manual sign codes have taken place primarily in the United States. The first manual sign code to be developed in the United States was created in the mid-1960s, and provided the foundation for what was eventually to become Seeing Essential English (SEE-I). Beginning in January, 1969, groups of Deaf and hearing people started meeting in Southern California to develop signs and guidelines for Seeing Essential English. As Gustason and Woodward recount, "a working committee of five [was] elected. Sign classes were taught by these five, and dittoed papers with written descriptions of each sign were utilized in these classes. The papers were mailed to interested persons" (1973, p. v). Disagreements and differences of opinion about certain features of manual signing led to the breakup of this original group in 1971, however, and as a consequence SEE-I now co-exists with both Signing Exact English (SEE-II) and Linguistics of Visual English (LOVE) (see Ramsey, 1989; Schein, 1984, pp. 66–7; Wilbur, 1979, pp. 204–5). A further addition to the array of artificial manual sign codes in the United States has been Signed English, designed for use with pre-school children, which shares a number of the general characteristics of SEE-I and its progeny while attempting to remain relatively simple syntactically, semantically, and structurally (see Bornstein et al., 1975, pp. 295–6). This growing diversity of manual sign codes has even been the subject of humor in the Deaf community, as can be seen in the ASL play *Sign Me Alice*, written by the Deaf playwright Gilbert Eastman (1974) and loosely based on *My Fair Lady*.

Despite the differences among them, the various American manual sign codes are similar in terms of both their philosophical underpinnings and their guiding structural principles. For example, all of the different artificial systems utilize at least some signs borrowed from ASL (though not necessarily with the same semantic space as that identified with the sign in ASL). The different manual sign codes operate with radically different morphological principles than does ASL, and all require the use of various prefixes and suffixes to convey specific English syntactic information. Further, all of the different manual sign codes not only allow the use of finger-spelling, but also employ widespread initialization, though again, the actual parameters within which such linguistic behaviors are appropriate vary among the different manual code systems. Finally, word order in the different sign codes is always, as a matter of principle, the same as that found in English. These features taken together make clear the fundamental objective of the creators of the various manual sign codes: to represent English in a visual/manual modality. Although undoubtedly widely accepted as a legitimate goal by both teachers of the Deaf and hearing parents of Deaf children (see Ramsey, 1989, pp. 143–54), such an objective is at best highly questionable from a linguistic perspective. The problem here is that the manual sign codes, in essence, seek to represent the lexical items of an oral/aural language in a gestural/visual linguistic context. The result is a type of signed communication that is, in essence, "neither fish nor fowl." Manual sign codes tend to be both awkward and confusing, and often entail violations of the structural and morphological rules and norms of ASL. As Padden and Humphries argue, the efforts to devise manual sign codes, "however well-intentioned, rest on the pervasive belief that signed languages are essentially 'incomplete' systems and amenable to modification for educational purposes. They ignore the fact that individual signs, like words, are inseparable parts of a larger grammatical system" (1988, p. 64). Further, as Nover has pointed out:

> In the United States, there exist seven manual codes of English none of which express the real, authentic perspective of the Deaf community. These were developed and implemented by those who lacked knowledge and expertise in general linguistics, the linguistics and sociolinguistics of American Sign Language, or language planning processes . . . these invented, *ad hoc* codes have inadequate bases in the systematic conventions for representing manually either oral or written English, yet are widely recognized by English-only educators for instructional purposes . . . Research . . . indicates that these language development and planning processes do not take into account the expressions of the Deaf community.
>
> *(Nover, 1995, p. 128)*

The final sort of corpus planning involving sign languages consists of the efforts to develop orthographic systems for representing such languages in written form. These "sign-writing systems" have become increasingly common and viable in recent years as a consequence of developments in computer science. Such efforts, although interesting (see Hutchins et al., 1990; Papaspyrou & Zienert, 1990; Prillwitz & Zienert, 1990), have not thus far gained much support from the signing community, which universally uses the surrounding hearing community's written language as its own. Nevertheless, these efforts are useful in the linguistic descriptions of sign languages, and may have a great deal of potential for both dictionaries and sign-language textbooks.

Conclusion

Language planning as an applied sociolinguistic activity can function either as a tool for empowerment and liberation or as a means of oppression and domination (Reagan, 2002). This is the case, in part, because language-planning and language-policy activities often involve both implicit and explicit goals and objectives. As Robert Cooper has noted,

> That language planning should serve so many covert goals is not surprising. Language is the fundamental institution of society, not only because it is the first institution experienced by the individual but also because all other institutions are built upon its regulatory patterns . . . To plan language is to plan society. A satisfactory theory of language planning, therefore, awaits a satisfactory theory of social change.
>
> *(Cooper, 1989, p. 182)*

Further, and closely related to the presence of both implicit and explicit goals and objectives in language planning and language policy, is the fundamentally ideological nature of such activities. As Tollefson has explained,

> Language policy is a form of disciplinary power. Its success depends in part upon the ability of the state to structure into the institutions of society the differentiation of individuals into "insiders" and "outsiders" . . . To a large degree, this occurs through the close association between language and nationalism. By making language a mechanism for the expression of nationalism, the state can manipulate feelings of security and belonging . . . the state uses language policy to discipline and control its workers by establishing language-based limitations on education, employment, and political participation. This is one sense in which language policy is inherently ideological.
>
> *(Tollefson, 1991, pp. 207–8)*

The case of language planning for sign languages provides powerful and compelling support for this view, as we have seen. In terms of both status and corpus planning, language-planning activities involving sign languages offer examples of group empowerment as well as of continued domination and oppression. We see this, for instance, in the nature and objectives of attempts to have sign languages "recognized" – and, of course, in how such "recognition" differs from the selection of a language as "official." Perhaps most clearly, we can see this fundamental tension in the development of manual sign codes for use in Deaf education. Such efforts provide us with an interesting case in which language-planning activities have promoted both an explicit agenda (i.e., the teaching of English to Deaf children) and an implicit agenda (i.e., the devaluation of natural sign languages and continued hearing hegemony in Deaf education) (see Ramsey, 1989; Reagan, 1995). What are at issue in such activities, ultimately, are fundamentally questions of power – as, indeed, are all matters of language planning and language policy.

Annotated Bibliography

Baynton, D. (1996). *Forbidden signs: American culture and the campaign against sign language.* Chicago: University of Chicago Press.
This book provides an historical overview of the debate between the "oralists" and "manualists" in Deaf education during the nineteenth and early twentieth centuries.

Lane, H., Hoffmeister, R., & Bahan, B. (1996). *A journey into the DEAF-WORLD.* San Diego: DawnSign Press.
DEAF-WORLD is the sign used in ASL for the cultural and linguistic world of the Deaf. This is a powerful and compelling introduction to that world, which includes a number of chapters dealing with ASL, bilingual education for Deaf children, language, and literacy as they relate to Deaf students, as well as to the cultural world of the Deaf.

Valli, C. & Lucas, C. (2000). *Linguistics of American Sign Language: An introduction* (3rd edn). Washington, DC: Gallaudet University Press.
This is the most reader-friendly introduction to the linguistics of ASL; it includes a variety of supplemental readings related to the linguistic study of ASL. Although not essential, it is helpful if the reader is already familiar with the basics of signing and sign language.

Discussion Questions

1   How do the nature and structure of sign language, as presented in this chapter, differ from your assumptions and expectations?

To what extent do you believe that natural sign languages are indeed full and complete examples of "human language"? What reservations about this claim do you have? Why?

2   The community of users of natural sign languages is unusual, in that most members of the community (approximately 90 percent) learn their language not from parents, but rather from peers (often in residential school settings, such as schools for the Deaf). What are the implications of this fact for language policies related to sign languages?

3   The practice of mainstreaming students with special needs, and more recently moves toward "inclusive education," have been perceived by some Deaf people as a threat to the continuity and even survival of the Deaf cultural and linguistic community. What are the implications of such social and educational practices for language policy?

4   In recent years, there have been debates in many settings in the United States about whether students (both in high school and university) ought to be allowed to study ASL in place of a "foreign" language. What sort of language policy would you advocate to help to address this controversial matter?

5   What should the role of hearing educators of the Deaf be with respect to status planning and corpus planning for sign languages? What should the role of hearing parents of Deaf children be? What role should be played by the adult Deaf community in such decisions?

6   How does the creation of a manual sign code differ from the creation of an orthography for a previously unwritten language? Why is this difference important?

NOTES

1   See Woll, Sutton-Spence, and Elton (2001) for a discussion of the historical relationships among sign languages.

2   There is a Model ASL Bill promoted by the National Association of the Deaf and the American Sign Language Teachers Association, available at www.nad.org/infocenter/infortogo/asl/modelASLbill.html.

3   I have followed the common practice of indicating a particular sign by writing its English meaning in capital letters (e.g., BOY). It should be noted that many signs require multiple English words to represent a single sign; in these instances, the English words are joined by hyphens to indicate that although there are several English words used to express the meaning of the sign, there is only a single sign (e.g., I-ASK-YOU).

4 The # indicates that the sign is a finger-spelled loan sign.
5 These signs have replaced earlier ASL signs which had offensive, and often racist, connotations.

REFERENCES

Aarons, D. & Akach, P. (2002). South African Sign Language: One language or many? In R. Mesthrie (ed.), *Language in South Africa* (pp. 127–47). Cambridge: Cambridge University Press.

Armstrong, D. (ed.) (2003a). Special issue on dictionaries and lexicography. Part I: General issues in lexicography. (Special issue). *Sign Language Studies*, 3(3).

Armstrong, D. (ed.) (2003b). Special issue on dictionaries and lexicography. Part II: The development of national sign language dictionaries. (Special issue). *Sign Language Studies*, 3(4).

Baker-Shenk, C. & Cokely, D. (1980). *American Sign Language: A teacher's resource text on grammar and culture.* Washington, DC: Gallaudet University Press.

Baynton, D. (1996). *Forbidden signs: American culture and the campaign against sign language.* Chicago: University of Chicago Press.

Bornstein, H. (ed.) (1990). *Manual communication: Implications for education.* Washington, DC: Gallaudet University Press.

Bornstein, H., Hamilton, L., Saulnier, K., & Roy, H. (eds.) (1975). *The Signed English dictionary for preschool and elementary levels.* Washington, DC: Gallaudet College Press.

Branson, J. & Miller, D. (2002). *Damned for their difference: The cultural construction of deaf people as disabled.* Washington, DC: Gallaudet University Press.

Brentari, D. (ed.) (2001). *Foreign vocabulary in sign languages: A cross-linguistic investigation of word formation.* Mahwah, NJ: Lawrence Erlbaum.

Brien, D. (ed.) (1992). *Dictionary of British Sign Language/English.* London: Faber and Faber.

Cokely, D. & Baker-Shenk, C. (1980a). *American Sign Language: A student's text, Units 1–9.* Washington, DC: Gallaudet University Press.

Cokely, D. & Baker-Shenk, C. (1980b). *American Sign Language: A teacher's resource text on curriculum, methods, and evaluation.* Washington, DC: Gallaudet University Press.

Cokely, D. & Baker-Shenk, C. (1981a). *American Sign Language: A student's text, Units 10–18.* Washington, DC: Gallaudet University Press.

Cokely, D. & Baker-Shenk, C. (1981b). *American Sign Language: A student's text, Units 19–27.* Washington, DC: Gallaudet University Press.

Cooper, R. (1989). *Language planning and social change.* Cambridge: Cambridge University Press.

Covington, V. (1976). Problems for a sign language planning agency. *International Journal of the Sociology of Language, 11,* 85–106.

Deuchar, M. (1980). Language planning and treatment of BSL: Problems for research. In I. Ahlgren & B. Bergman (eds.), *Papers from the First International Symposium on Sign Language Research* (pp. 109–19). Stockholm: Swedish National Association of the Deaf.

Eastman, G. (1974). *Sign me Alice: A play in sign language.* Washington, DC: Gallaudet College Bookstore.

Erting, C. (1978). Language policy and deaf ethnicity in the United States. *Sign Language Studies, 19,* 139–52.

Fromkin, V. (2000). On the uniqueness of language. In K. Emmorey & H. Lane (eds.), *The signs of language revisited: An anthology to honor Ursula Bellugi and Edward Klima* (pp. 533–47). Mahwah, NJ: Lawrence Erlbaum.

Gustason, G. & Woodward, J. (eds.) (1973). *Recent developments in manual English.* Washington, DC: Department of Education, Gallaudet College.

Gustason, G. & Zawolkow, E. (1993). *Signing exact English.* Los Alamitos, CA: Modern Signs Press.

Humphries, T. & Padden, C. (1992). *Learning American Sign Language.* Englewood Cliffs, NJ: Prentice-Hall.

Humphries, T., Padden, C., & O'Rourke, T. (1994). *A basic course in American Sign Language* (2nd edn). Silver Spring, MD: T. J. Publishers.

Hutchins, S., Poizner, H., McIntire, M., & Newkirk, D. (1990). Implications for sign research of a computerized written form of ASL. In W. Edmondson & F. Karlsson (eds.), *SLR '87: Papers from the Fourth International Symposium on Sign Language Research* (pp. 255–68). Hamburg: Signum.

Johnston, T. (1989). *AUSLAN dictionary: A dictionary of the sign language of the Australian deaf community.* Petersham: Deafness Resources, Australia.

Jokinen, M. (2000). The linguistic human rights of sign language users. In R. Phillipson (ed.), *Rights to language: Equity, power, and education* (pp. 203–13). Mahwah, NJ: Lawrence Erlbaum.

Kaplan, R. & Baldauf, R. (1997). *Language planning: From practice to theory.* Clevedon: Multilingual Matters.

Lucas, C. & Valli, C. (1989). Language contact in the American Deaf community. In C. Lucas (ed.), *The sociolinguistics of the deaf community* (pp. 11–40). San Diego, CA: Academic Press.

Lucas, C. & Valli, C. (1991). ASL or contact signing: Issues of judgement. *Language in Society, 20,* 201–16.

Lucas, C. & Valli, C. (1992). *Language contact in the American deaf community.* San Diego, CA: Academic Press.

Lucas, C., Bayley, R., & Valli, C. (2001). *Sociolinguistic variation in American Sign Language.* Washington, DC: Gallaudet University Press.

Muzsnai, I. (1999). The recognition of sign language: A threat or the way to a solution? In M. Kontra, R. Phillipson, T. Skutnabb-Kangas, & T. Várady (eds.), *Language: A right and a resource. Approaching linguistic human rights* (pp. 279–96). Budapest: Central European University Press.

Nash, J. (1987). Policy and practice in the American Sign Language community. *International Journal of the Sociology of Language, 68,* 7–22.

Nover, S. (1995). Politics and language: American Sign Language and English in deaf education. In C. Lucas (ed.), *Sociolinguistics in deaf communities* (pp. 109–63). Washington, DC: Gallaudet University Press.

Padden, C. & Humphries, T. (1988). *Deaf in America: Voices from a culture.* Cambridge, MA: Harvard University Press.

Paget, R. (1951). *The new sign language.* London: Welcome Foundation.

Papaspyrou, C. & Zienert, H. (1990). The syncWRITER computer programme. In S. Prillwitz & T. Vollhaber (eds.), *Sign language research and application: Proceedings of the International Congress* (pp. 275–93). Hamburg: Signum.

Penn, C. & Reagan, T. (2001). Linguistic, social and cultural perspectives on sign language in South Africa. In E. Ridge, S. Makoni, & S. Ridge (eds.), *Freedom and discipline: Essays in applied linguistics from Southern Africa* (pp. 49–65). New Delhi: Bahri.

Prillwitz, S. & Zienert, H. (1990). Hamburg notation system for sign language: Development of a sign writing with computer application. In S. Prillwitz & T. Vollhaber (eds.), *Current trends in European sign language research* (pp. 355–79). Hamburg: Signum.

Ramsey, C. (1989). Language planning in deaf education. In C. Lucas (ed.), *The sociolinguistics of the deaf community* (pp. 123–46). New York: Academic Press.

Reagan, T. (1989). Nineteenth-century conceptions of deafness: Implications for contemporary educational practice. *Educational Theory, 39,* 39–46.

Reagan, T. (1990). The development and reform of sign languages. In I. Fodor & C. Hagège (eds.), *Language reform: History and future. Vol. 5* (pp. 253–67). Hamburg: Buske.

Reagan, T. (1995). Neither easy to understand nor pleasing to see: The development of manual sign codes. *Language Problems and Language Planning, 19,* 133–50.

Reagan, T. (2000). But does it *count?* Reflections on "signing" as a foreign language. *Northeast Conference on the Teaching of Foreign Languages Review, 48,* 16–26.

Reagan, T. (2001a). Language planning and policy. In. C. Lucas (ed.), *The sociolinguistics of sign languages* (pp. 145–80). Cambridge: Cambridge University Press.

Reagan, T. (2001b). The promotion of linguistic diversity in multilingual settings: Policy and reality in post-apartheid South Africa. *Language Problems and Language Planning, 25,* 51–72.

Reagan, T. (2002). Language planning and language policy: Past, present and future. In R. Mesthrie (ed.), *Language in South Africa* (pp. 419–33). Cambridge: Cambridge University Press.

Reagan, T. & Penn, C. (1997). Language policy, South African Sign Language, and the deaf: Social and educational implications. *Southern African Journal of Applied Language Studies, 5,* 1–13.

Schein, J. (1984). *Speaking the language of sign: The art and science of signing*. New York: Doubleday.

Shelly, S. & Schneck, J. (1998). *The complete idiot's guide to learning sign language*. New York: Alpha Books.

Skutnabb-Kangas, T. (1994). Linguistic human rights: A prerequisite for bilingualism. In I. Ahlgren & K. Hyltenstam (eds.), *Bilingualism in deaf education* (pp. 139–59). Hamburg: Signum.

Skutnabb-Kangas, T. (2000). *Linguistic genocide in education – or worldwide diversity and human rights?* Mahwah, NJ: Lawrence Erlbaum.

Stewart, D. (1998). *American Sign Language: The easy way*. Hauppauge, NY: Barron's.

Tennant, R. & Brown, M. G. (1998). *The American Sign Language handshape dictionary*. Washington, DC: Gallaudet University Press.

Tollefson, J. (1991). *Planning language, planning inequality: Language policy in the community*. London: Longman.

Valli, C. & Lucas, C. (2000). *Linguistics of American Sign Language: An introduction* (3rd edn). Washington, DC: Gallaudet University Press.

Wallin, L. (1994). The study of sign language in society. In C. Erting, R. Johnson, D. Smith, & B. Snyder (eds.), *The deaf way: Perspectives from the International Conference on Deaf Culture* (pp. 318–30). Washington, DC: Gallaudet University Press.

Webb, V. (2002). *Language in South Africa: The role of language in national transformation, reconstruction, and development*. Amsterdam: John Benjamins.

Weisel, A. (1998). *Issues unresolved: New perspectives on language and deaf education*. Washington, DC: Gallaudet University Press.

Wilbur, R. (1979). *American Sign Language and sign systems*. Baltimore, MD: University Park Press.

Wilcox, S. (2003). The multimedia dictionary of American Sign Language: Learning lessons about language, technology, and business. *Sign Language Studies, 3*, 379–92.

Wilcox, S. & Wilcox, P. (1997). *Learning to see: Teaching American Sign Language as a second language* (2nd edn). Washington, DC: Gallaudet University Press.

Winefield, R. (1987). *Never the twain shall meet: Alexander Graham Bell, Edward Miner Gallaudet – The communications debate*. Washington, DC: Gallaudet University Press.

Woll, B., Sutton-Spence, R., & Elton, F. (2001). Multilingualism: The global approach to sign languages. In C. Lucas (ed.), *The sociolinguistics of sign languages* (pp. 8–32). Cambridge: Cambridge University Press.

Woodward, J. (1973). Manual English: A problem in language standardization and planning. In G. Gustason & J. Woodward (eds.), *Recent developments in manual English* (pp. 1–12). Washington, DC: Department of Education, Gallaudet College.

CHAPTER NINETEEN

Language Policy and Linguistic Imperialism

Robert Phillipson

> The most serious problem for the European Union is that it has so many languages, this preventing real integration and development of the Union.
>
> *The ambassador of the United States to*
> *Denmark, Mr Elton, 1997*

> The Union shall respect cultural, religious and linguistic diversity.
>
> *Charter of Fundamental Rights of*
> *the European Union, Article 22, 2000*

The concept of linguistic imperialism resonates with the historical fact of empires as sociopolitical structures that have risen and fallen over three millennia, and with the analytical exploration of the role of language in the empires that dominated the world scene in recent centuries. The current strength of English, French, Portuguese, and Spanish globally reflects the policies that have entrenched use of these languages in colonially occupied territories. The fate of German in Africa and Asia was sealed by German defeat in 1918. Likewise the defeat of Japan in 1945 reversed the impact in several Asian states of Japanese as a language of empire. The demise of Dutch in Indonesia and its decline in southern Africa also flag a reduction of the political power of speakers of Dutch and Afrikaans. The collapse of Soviet communism has constrained the use of Russian in central Asia and severely limited its use in Eastern Europe. Similar patterns of change are affecting other languages of former empires, such as Danish in Greenland and Iceland. World-wide, there is great fluidity and dynamism in the way hierarchies of language are being adjusted. Language policy is torn between top-down pressures to maintain the position of national languages, and bottom-up pressures to secure linguistic diversity and the implementation of language rights. Impacting on both of these trends is the ever-increasing use of English world-wide. The power associated with English also affects the fate of other languages that have been widely used in international relations, in particular French.

I shall confine myself to exploring linguistic imperialism in the contemporary expansion of English. I shall focus on developments globally, and language policy trends in Europe, which are illuminating because the European Union is officially committed to multilingualism and linguistic diversity, while integrally involved in processes of globalization that are symbiotically linked to English. There is an unresolved tension between many languages being used in running EU affairs and in member states, and the momentum propelling English forward. Related to this is the question of whether the United States is establishing a global empire, different in kind from earlier empires, and if so, what implications follow for language policy. Assessing the adequacy of our theoretical tools for addressing the multiple roles of English and its impact on local language ecologies is needed because of the increasingly rich documentation of languages world-wide. This includes numerous books on English as a "world" language: recent titles include Block and Cameron (2002), Brutt-Griffler (2002; see Phillipson, 2004), Jenkins (2003), and Maier (2003), as well as synthesizing volumes such as Maurais and Morris's *Languages in a globalising world* (2003).

From Imperial via Post-Imperial to Neo-Imperial

My book on linguistic imperialism (Phillipson, 1992) explores how English has retained its dominant role in former colonies and its pivotal role in North–South relations, and the way language pedagogy has consolidated a hierarchy of languages, invariably with English at the top. Some of the strengths and limitations of my approach have been insightfully reviewed (Canagarajah, 1999; Pennycook, 2001). In the article "English in the new world order: variations on a theme of linguistic imperialism and 'world' English," in *Ideology, politics, and language policies: Focus on English* (Ricento, 2000), I reviewed three books, one of which – Fishman, Conrad, and Rubal-Lopez's *Post-imperial English: Status change in former British and American colonies, 1940–1990* – has a wealth of empirical description of the functions of English in many contexts. "Post-imperial" is, however, a very general label, and I concur with Görlach in a review of the book (1997, p. 218) that "the methods underlying the statements on 'post-imperial' are not sufficiently defined. If we combine this with the lack of reliable statistics on which arguments are based we see how much thinking, and empirical research, is still needed."

The 29 contributors to Fishman et al.'s volume were specifically asked to assess whether linguistic imperialism, in the sense in which I have used the term, was in force in the country studies they were responsible for. They all address the issue, but none attempts to refine the concept or to see whether there might be more powerful or precise ways of coming to grips with theorizing the dominance of English. It is only Fishman, in his introductory and closing comments, who, as well as tabulating the degree of "anglification" in each state, speculates on English being "reconceptualized, from being an imperialist tool to being a multinational tool . . . English may need to be re-examined precisely from the point of view of being post-imperial (. . . in the sense of not directly serving purely Anglo-American territorial, economic, or cultural expansion) without being post-capitalist in any way" (Fishman et al., 1996, p. 8). Corporate activities, which are global, in tandem with the World Bank, the IMF, the World Trade Organization, the United Nations, NATO, and regional economic blocs, have made the locus of power more diffuse than in earlier, nation-state imperialism and neo-colonialism. In constituting and controlling the current world "order," English plays a central role, but not one that is isomorphic with the interests of a single state.

Görlach's comment on statistics refers to the absence of reliable data on users of English as a second or foreign language.[1] The same methodological weakness is bewailed in profiling "Francophonie," since most of the statistics on competence in French world-wide are unreliable, if not fraudulent, because they use woolly or no definitions of competence (Chaudenson, 2003). However, improved figures for users of English are less significant than identifying which functions English serves, and whether English has the sharpest beak in a pecking order of languages.

Critical sociolinguistics faces a major challenge in teasing out and theorizing how globalization dovetails with Americanization and Englishization. Linguistic imperialism entails unequal exchange and unequal communicative rights between people or groups defined in terms of their competence in specific languages, with unequal benefits as a result, in a system that legitimates and naturalizes such exploitation. Linguistic imperialism was manifestly a feature of the way nation-states privileged one language, and often sought actively to eradicate others, forcing their speakers to shift to the dominant language. It was also a feature of colonial empires, with a deeper degree of linguistic penetration in settler countries (e.g., Canada) than exploitation and extraction colonies (e.g., India, Nigeria). Some of the complexities of colonial policies toward English and local languages are being unearthed (Brutt-Griffler, 2002; Pennycook, 1998), but such studies in no way conflict with the hierarchical world of English linguistic imperialism, even if their authors interpret matters differently (Phillipson, 2004). Seeing English from the point of view of both demand and supply is explored in a study of Hong Kong past and present that seeks to go beyond seeing English as an addictive, enfeebling imposition, analogous to opium, preferring the image of English as ginseng, costly, varied, somewhat bitter, but enabling (Li, 2002).

Language policies continued largely unchanged into the postcolonial age, as a result of which it is speakers of the former colonial languages who are the dominant group in such states. Postcolonial education systems, particularly due to the influence of the World Bank in recent decades, have tended to give priority to the former colonial language and a marginal status to local languages.

But just as there has never been a close fit between linguistic groups and the states they found themselves in, languages in the globalizing world are no respecters of state borders. Technology permits the instant exchange of financial, commercial, and cultural information in ever more complex networks. The global economy is run from "global cities" that manage the "internationalization of capital, production, services, and culture" (Yeung, 2000, p. 24). Thus Hong Kong, Seoul, Singapore, and Tokyo are global in the same way as Frankfurt, London, and New York, whereas Delhi and Shanghai are not, since their functions are essentially local ones.

Dominant groups in the military, political, economic, and cultural worlds network with similar groups elsewhere to run a global economy that continues to widen the gulf between haves and have-nots, as unambiguously documented by a World Bank insider (Stiglitz, 2002). Constantly recurring military, economic, and political crises reveal that the system is chronically unable to deliver to the whole world's population peace, stability, and a quality of life that lives up to human rights norms. "Free" trade liberalism supports the strong against the week. This might be remedied by a shift to fair trade, but successive WTO meetings from Seattle to Cancun reveal little will on the part of the haves, the United States and EU in particular, to move in that direction. Equitable conditions are also needed in our language ecologies, national and international. In both democracies and more repressive systems, particular languages are given more support than others. In most international fora, English is privileged, and attention is seldom paid to ensuring the equality of speakers from different language backgrounds. Is it fair that some should be able to communicate, negotiate, trade, and be culturally productive in their mother tongue, whereas others have to use a second or foreign language? Is it fair that the United States and United Kingdom can avoid investing substantially in foreign-language education, whereas virtually all other education systems are obliged to in order to access the global economy and cultural industries? Such inequity is largely unrecorded and unquantified, since the structural and ideological underpinning of global linguistic hegemony tends to be regarded as legitimate, despite the massive economic and cultural advantages this gives the English-speaking world.

For example, scientific scholarship is increasingly an English-only domain in international communication (journals, reference works, textbooks, conferences, networking), which has a knock-on effect nationally (language shift to English, particularly at the graduate level; funding needed for training, or for translation) and internationally (paradigms from the Anglo-American world being favored, marginalization of non-native speakers at conferences). In the journal *Discourse & Society*, *8*(3), an editorial entitled "The imperialism of English" (van Dijk, 1997) notes that English increasingly intrudes on territory occupied earlier by other languages: "The language barrier has become a more general scholarly and cultural barrier . . . The main obstacle to linguistic diversity, also in scholarship, however, is the arrogance of linguistic power in Anglophone countries, and especially the USA" (p. 292).

In several continental European countries, there is major concern about the impact of English on national languages. Thus studies were commissioned in each of the Nordic countries to assess whether domain loss is occurring in Danish, Finnish, Icelandic, Norwegian, and Swedish, in business, the media, and other fields, as well as in science. Provisional results have been published in each of the relevant languages (those who only read English possibly need reminding that good work is in fact published in other languages). They confirm that there is a serious problem, hence a need for more proactive language-policy formation. The overall picture has been presented in Swedish, in a popularizing form, complete with a 15-page English summary (Höglin, 2002). As this is a far from precise or correct translation from a Swedish source text, it ironically confirms the existence and nature of the problem of inequity in international communication.

It goes without saying that many factors contribute to the current dominance of English. They can be broadly grouped as structural (the interlocking of English with the global economy, finance, and the military-industrial complex; British and American promotion of English; investment in the teaching of English in education systems) and ideological (imagery of English created through the media, popular and elite culture, connotations of success, necessity, etc.).[3] The policy-makers of the Bush II administration regard it as their right and duty to impose American values globally.[4]

The unilateralism of the Bush II government represents a break with the more multilateral policies of the Clinton administration, to the point where many scholars talk of an American empire, of the United States as hegemon. Language is subordinate to economic and military policies, as noted by the historian Erik Hobsbawm (in *Le Monde Diplomatique*) in June 2003, soon after the occupation of Iraq: "Although the US retains some political advantages, it has thrown most of them out of the window in the past 18 months. There are the minor assets of American culture's domination of world culture, and of the English language. But the major asset for imperial projects at the moment is military" (p. 2). Language policy is essential to this mission, as formulated in an article in *Foreign Policy* by David Rothkopf, director of the Kissinger Institute, in 1997:

> It is in the economic and political interest of the United States to ensure that if the world is moving toward a common language, it be English; that if the world is moving toward common telecommun-ications, safety, and quality standards, they be American; and that if common values are being developed, they be values with which Americans are comfortable. These are not idle aspirations. English is linking the worlc
>
> (*p. 45*)

Gradual processes of Americanization gathered speed throughout the twentieth century, and have been marketed in recent years as globalization:

> "Globalization" serves as a password, a watchword, while in effect it is the legitimatory mask of a policy aiming to universalize particular interests and the particular tradition of the economically and politically dominant powers, above all the United States, and to extend to the entire world the economic and cultural model that favors these powers

most, while simultaneously presenting it as a norm, a requirement, and a fatality, a universal destiny, in such a manner as to obtain adherence or at the least, universal resignation.

(Bourdieu, 2001, p. 84)

This analysis reveals how the hegemonic power imposes or induces acceptance of its dominion.

In their book *Empire*, Hardt and Negri (2000) draw together many threads from political, economic and cultural theory, and philosophy, and astutely unravel the role of communication in global social trends, and how language constitutes our universe:

> The great industrial and financial powers thus produce not only commodities but also subjectivities. They produce agentic subjectivities within the biopolitical[5] context: they produce needs, social relations, bodies and minds – which is to say, they produce producers. In the biopolitical sphere, life is made to work for production and production is made to work for life.
>
> (p. 32)

> One site where we should locate the biopolitical production of order is in the immaterial nexuses of the production of language, communication, and the symbolic that are developed by the communications industries. The development of communications networks has an organic relationship to the emergence of the new world order – it is, in other words, effect and cause, product and producer. Communication not only expresses but also organizes the movement of globalization. It organizes the movement by multiplying and structuring interconnections through networks. It expresses the movement and controls the sense and direction of the imaginary that runs throughout these communicative connections ... This is why the communications industries have assumed such a central position. They not only organize production on a new scale and impose a new structure adequate to global space, but also make its justification immanent. Power, as it produces, organizes; as it organizes, it speaks and expresses itself as authority. Language, as it communicates, produces commodities but moreover produces subjectivities, puts them in relation, and orders them. The communications industries integrate the imaginary and the symbolic within the biopolitical fabric, not merely putting them at the service of power but actually integrating them into its very functioning.
>
> (Hardt & Negri, 2000, pp. 32–3)

These authors explain why it has been so important for the corporate world to dominate not only the media but also education, which is increasingly run to service the economy, and produce consumers rather than critical citizens (Monbiot, 2000). In the teaching and marketing of "communication skills," a shift from linguistic imperialism to communicative imperialism can be seen: "Language becomes a global product available in different local flavours . . . The dissemination of 'global' communicative norms and genres, like the dissemination of international languages, involves a one-way flow of expert knowledge from dominant to subaltern cultures" (Cameron, 2002, p. 70). The modern focus on communication skills, defined by "experts," entails the dissemination of American ways of speaking. Globalization is extending these world-wide, often without their ethnocentricity being perceived. The forms of communication, genres, and styles of the dominant consumerist culture have the willing but possibly unwitting support of teachers of English and "communication."

Many continental Europeans appreciate that if the shift to English and Anglo-American norms is allowed to continue unchecked, cultural vitality and diversity will suffer, as a result of contemporary linguistic imperialism. In government policy documents produced in Sweden in 2002 and Denmark in 2003 on how to strengthen the national language in view of the increasing importance of English, the declared goal is to cultivate "parallel" linguistic competence.[6] This would mean that Swedes and Danes active in business, politics, higher education, science, and the media are able to function equally well in the national language and in English. It would ensure that domain loss and linguistic hierarchization are counteracted, through ensuring resource allocation to the language that now risks marginalization, despite having had an unchallenged status nationally in recent centuries, and through fostering awareness of the need to provide conditions for languages other than English to thrive.

These proposed measures indicate clearly that states which traditionally have had a laissez-faire approach to language policy are involved in status planning for national and international languages. France also promulgated a law in 1994 to counter an increasing use of English. What is problematical is that many of the pressures involved lie beyond the control of the nation-state, which may therefore be addressing symptoms rather than causes. It is likely that increasing European integration strengthens the forces of globalization, Americanization, and Englishization rather than constraining them.

The recognition of English as a threat to the languages and cultures of member states is beginning to influence the formulation and synchronization of language policy at the supranational level. During the 1990s, EU policy-making moved into the areas of education, language, and culture. The Commission document *Promoting language learning and linguistic diversity: An action plan 2004–2006*, of August, 2003, is designed to curb an excessive focus on English in education systems and the wider society. It states (pp. 4, 8): "learning one lingua franca alone is not enough... English alone is not enough... In non-anglophone countries recent trends to provide teaching in English may have unforeseen consequences on the vitality of the national language." The policy statement, which it is now up to member states to react to, advocates life-long foreign-language learning, including two foreign languages in the primary school. It strives to bring language policy higher up on national agendas, and to raise awareness of linguistic diversity. It endorses the notion of an inclusive "language-friendly environment."

It is impossible to predict what impact, if any, this document will have. In a complex, evolving scene, with fuzzy dividing lines between supranational and national interests and languages, it is difficult to gauge how significant the ritual support of multilingualism in many EU official texts is, and how far policies that can counteract English-ization will be pursued. There are skeptics: "No-one is fooled by fiery declarations in favour of multilingualism, which is nothing but a smoke screen for the spread of English" (Chaudenson, 2003, p. 297). De Swaan regards English as "the lingua franca" of the EU (an eminently falsifiable statement – there are several lingua francas), and claims that in the EU "the more languages, the more English" (2001, pp. 144, 147).[7]

To understand whether the EU can control, convert, or resist the major pressures behind an increased use of English requires some historical analysis. The economic and political unification of Europe has followed two mutually reinforcing agendas: to establish forms of interdependence that would render military aggression impossible, and to position America as the pre-eminent force globally. The Marshall Plan was conditional on the integration of European economies. As Europeanization intensifies (80 percent of legislation in member states entails implementing decisions already made at the supranational EU level), communication between the citizens and representatives of European states and between national bureaucracies and the EU Commission increases; hence the focus in EU funding on strengthening foreign-language learning, and the provision of language services in EU institutions. These are in principle committed to the equality of 20 official and working languages (as of 2004), buttressed by translation and interpretation services that employ literally thousands of translators and about 750 interpreters per working day, at an average of 55 meetings. Official documents are promulgated in each language, with equal legal validity, and in theory there is no source text of which the others are translations. However, it is arguable that in some in-house EU activities, and in business, science, politics, the media, and education in European civil society, English is taking over to the point where other languages are on a fast track to second-class status. In the initial decades of the EU, French was *primus inter pares*, but since the accession of the United Kingdom, Ireland, and Denmark in 1973, there has been a progressive shift to English. Two-thirds of EU drafts are now written in English, a figure that is rising by 2 percent per annum. In negotiations with new member states, which brought in nine additional languages in 2004, English was in effect the sole language in use.[8]

The shift from French to English (which the French and Belgian governments are trying to counteract) signals a shift in power from French thought processes and influence to Anglo-American ones that reflect many of the contemporary trends in globalization. There is undoubtedly now linguicist favoring of competent users of English, whether as a first or second language. It is explicitly seen by some as symptomatic of linguistic imperialism.

The Germans have, because of the Nazi experience, been reluctant to be seen to promote their language energetically, despite the fact that a quarter of EU citizens have German as a mother tongue, and Germany foots a disproportionately large part of the EU bill. But bodies such as the Verein Deutscher Sprache (German Language Association) are concerned about whether German will retain its national pre-eminence. It accuses elites in Germany of facilitating Americanization and failing for decades to support German (Gawlitta & Vilmar, 2002, a volume that begins with an article entitled "Sprachimperialismus: Analyse; Widerstand" ["Linguistic imperialism: Analysis, resistance"]).

By contrast, Germany was accused of linguistic imperialism during the Finnish presidency of the EU in 1999. Germany boycotted informal ministerial meetings in Finland because interpretation into and from German was not provided. The Finns accused the Germans of linguistic imperialism because they insisted on the same rights as speakers of other "big" European languages. The diplomatic crisis was solved by the Finns caving in to German pressure without matters of principle or language rights being clarified. The Finns failed to appreciate that French and German insistence on the equality of the official languages of the EU is in the interest of speakers of "small" EU languages like Finnish (Kelletat, 2001, p. 37). This study of the coverage of this crisis in the Finnish and German media concludes that the Americanization of Finland has reached the point where a Finnish prime minister, despite personal multilingualism, was in effect pressing for a single-language regime at EU meetings, an English-only solution, on the model of the European Central Bank in Frankfurt. Advocacy of this conflates globalization, Europeanization, and Englishization under the guise of "pragmatism."[9] Such a change of policy would represent a volte-face in EU activities.

The equality of EU languages is a reality at meetings at the highest levels and in the massive output of legally binding documents from Brussels and Strasbourg. But the issue of linguistic hierarchies that exist *de facto* is so politically sensitive that it has never been squarely addressed. As the president of the group of French members of the European Parliament puts it, it is "an explosive topic in Europe."[10] The Spanish foreign secretary, Ana Palacio, implies this when writing in *El País* on December 16, 2002, after the Copenhagen EU summit, which was primarily concerned with reaching agreement on terms for the accession of new member states. At the concluding press conference with heads of state from the existing and potential states, the monolingual banner headline behind the politicians read "One Europe." Palacio wrote:

> The motto "One Europe," solely in English, requires a reflection. Even though Copenhagen did not face the question of languages, this is one of the pending subjects that sooner rather than later must be debated for the very survival and viability of this project of Europe with a world vocation. Within it, Spanish, one of the official UN languages, spoken by more than 400 million people in more than 20 countries, must take on the place it is entitled to.

She did not write what that "place" should be. This is not surprising, since little effort has gone into devising criteria that might guide more equitable language policies (but see Phillipson, 2003, chapter 5). The EU is a novel political construction. Hitherto its language policies have represented those of the nation-state writ large at the supranational level, plus uncritical acceptance of a globalization agenda that has no overt language policy. Multilingualism is an EU mantra, but EU institutions reflect complex processes of reaching consensus among diverse national groups and the developments in the economic, political, military, and cultural spheres that privilege English. Proactive language-policy formation has yet to address how the changing communicative needs of European citizens and states can strengthen the cultural and linguistic diversity that has characterized Europe hitherto.

Conclusion

Even when the term "linguistic imperialism" is used in a loose sense, as in the examples above, or not at all, as in the case of the Spanish minister, what is being referred to is inequality, absence of a level linguistic playing-field, unfair privileging of the use of one language and those who use it more easily, the uncritical acceptance of English having a "natural" right to be the default language, and a blind belief in English as a "lingua franca" of Europe, as though this somehow detaches the language from Americanization and inequality.

Linguistic imperialism dovetails with communicative, cultural, educational, and scientific imperialism in a rapidly evolving world in which corporate-led globalization is seeking to impose or induce a neo-imperial world order. There are major unresolved tensions between national and international languages (English being both for some people), and in reconciling participation in the global economy with maintaining national sovereignty, linguistic diversity, and personal freedoms. We may be moving in the direction of global linguistic apartheid of the kind that the first prime minister of independent India, Nehru, warned against, the emergence of an English-knowing caste at the summit of national or international society. But as Americanization is so pervasive, English is expanding in bottom-up processes as well as top-down ones, and in oppositional ways that seek the creation of a more just world order as an alternative to the current world disorder.

Annotated Bibliography

Canagarajah, S. (1999). *Resisting linguistic imperialism in English teaching*. Oxford: Oxford University Press.
This gives a theoretically subtle critique of Western analyses of language dominance and educational inappropriateness, which builds

on a rich empirical grounding of critical pedagogy in Sri Lanka and documents how English can be appropriated.

Fishman, J. A., Conrad, A. W., & Rubal-Lopez, A. (eds.) (1996). *Post-imperial English: Status change in former British and American colonies, 1940–1990*. Berlin: Mouton.
This compilation of empirical studies has substantial sections on countries in the American and British spheres of influence and the EU, as well as general articles. There is some inconsistency in the way contributors analyze linguistic imperialism and the way the editors distance themselves from the concept and its application.

Jenkins, J. (2003). *World Englishes. A resource book for students*. London: Routledge.
This wide-ranging set of readings and questions brings together analyses of the forms and functions of world Englishes, the historical development of English, current debates, and aspects of power, ownership, and norms for an international language.

Maurais, J. & Morris, M. A. (eds.) (2003). *Languages in a globalising world*. New York: Cambridge University Press.
This is an anthology of 21 articles, some dealing with general aspects of global linguistic ordering and language policy, some with the major regions of the world, others with specific widely used languages. Of particular relevance for the hegemony of English is Hamel on Mercosur countries in South America.

Mühlhäusler, P. (1996). *Linguistic ecology: Language change and linguistic imperialism in the Pacific region*. London: Routledge.
This book covers the region with a great deal of linguistic and cultural detail from pre-colonial times, through Europeanization (the impact of literacy, creoles, language shift, policy) to future prospects for the maintenance of diversity.

Phillipson, R. (2003). *English-only Europe? Challenging language policy*. London: Routledge.
This is a book for the general reader, with chapters on the risks of laissez-faire language policies; European languages: families, nations, empires, states; global trends impacting on European language policy; languages in EU institutions; toward equitable communication; and recommendations for action on language policies.

Discussion Questions

1 Can Englishization be seen as independent of globalization and Americanization? You might consider assessing whether the literature on world Englishes achieves this.

2 Are there ways of counteracting inequality in international communication that avoid privileging fluent users of English?

3 If it is possible that monolinguals will miss out in the future, whereas multilinguals will thrive, is aiming at parallel linguistic competence a valid and realistic educational and social goal?

4 Consider whether the developments occurring in Europe are being experienced in other contexts, such as the Americas, Africa, or Asia.

5 If globalization is intrinsically neither good nor evil, just as all languages are, what language policies should be adopted so as to maintain a balanced language ecology?

6 Can you think of a better term than "linguistic imperialism" for the role that English plays in the current phase of globalization?

NOTES

1 In Pennycook's table 3.2, "Frameworks for the understanding of the global role of English" (2001, p. 59), he states that a linguistic imperialism analysis entails that one should "teach English sparingly." Not so: one should teach English additively, as in Canagarajah's approach to resisting English linguistic imperialism. See also a range of views on linguistic imperialism and the global role of English in Seidlhofer (2003).

2 Skutnabb-Kangas (2000, pp. 37–46) contrasts such figures.

3 For elaboration see Phillipson (2003, ch. 3).

4 See Brzezinski (1997), reported in the *Wilderness Publications*, www.copvcia.com, accessed January 9, 2003. (Condoleezza Rice: "The rest of the world is best served by the USA pursuing its own interests because American values are universal." See www.newamericancentury.org.)

5 Biopower, following Foucault, is seen as "a form of power that regulates social life from its interior, following it, interpreting it, absorbing it, and rearticulating it. Power can achieve an effective command over the entire life of the population only when it becomes an integral, vital function that every individual embraces and reactivates of his or her own accord. . . . what is at stake in power is the production and reproduction of life itself." (Hardt & Negri, 2000, pp. 23–4).

6 Little is available on these policies in languages other than Swedish and Danish. Try internet searching under such key words as Denmark, Sweden, Ministry of Culture, language policy, sprogpolitik, språkpolitik.

7 For a critical review of de Swaan's book, see Phillipson (2004).
8 For details of language in EU institutions, see Phillipson (2003, ch. 4).
9 The Finnish government is seen as convinced that Finnish membership of the EU is primarily a matter of Finland's benefiting maximally from the economic dimension of globalization and Europeanization. On Finland as a success story economically while retaining strong cultural and linguistic traditions, see Phillipson (2003, p. 83).
10 Pierre Lequiller, Compte rendu no. 48, Délégation pour l'Union Européenne, June 11, 2003.

REFERENCES

Block, D. & Cameron, D. (eds.) (2002). *Globalization and language teaching*. London: Routledge.

Bourdieu, P. (2001). *Contre-feux 2: Pour un mouvement social européen (Counter fire 2: For a European social movement)*. Paris: Raisons d'agir.

Brutt-Griffler, J. (2002). *World English: A study of its development*. Clevedon: Multilingual Matters.

Brzezinski, Z. (1997). *The grand chessboard: American primacy and its geostrategic imperatives*. New York: Basic Books.

Cameron, D. (2002). Globalization and the teaching of "communication skills." In D. Block & D. Cameron (eds.), *Globalization and language teaching* (pp. 67–82). London: Routledge.

Canagarajah, S. (1999). *Resisting linguistic imperialism in English teaching*. Oxford: Oxford University Press.

Chaudenson, R. (2003). Geolinguistics, geopolitics, geostrategy: The case for French. In J. Maurais & M. A. Morris (eds.), *Languages in a globalising world* (pp. 291–7). New York: Cambridge University Press.

Commission of the European Communities. (2003). *COM (2003) 449 Final. Communication from the Commission to the Council, the European Parliament, the Economic and Social Committee and the Committee of the Regions. Promoting language learning and linguistic diversity: An action plan 2004–2006*. Brussels. Retrieved January 4, 2004, from http://europa.eu.int/comm/education/doc/official/keydoc/keydoc_en.html.

de Swaan, A. (2001). *Words of the world: The global language system*. Cambridge: Polity.

Fishman, J. A., Conrad, A. W., & Rubal-Lopez, A. (eds.) (1996). *Post-imperial English: Status change in former British and American colonies, 1940–1990*. Berlin: Mouton.

Gawlitta, K. & Vilmar, F. (eds.) (2002). *"Deutsch nix wichtig?" Engagement für die deutsche Sprache ("German unimportant?" Commitment for the German language)*. Paderborn: IFB.

Görlach, M. (1997). Review of *Post-imperial English: Status change in former British and American colonies, 1940–1990*. *Sociolinguistica, 11*, 215–18.

Hardt, M. & Negri, A. (2000). *Empire.* Cambridge, MA: Harvard University Press.

Hobsbawm, E. (2003). United States: Wider still and wider. *Le Monde Diplomatique,* 1–2.

Höglin, R. (2002). *Engelska språket som hot och tillgång i Norden (The English language as threat or opportunity in the Nordic countries).* Copenhagen: Nordiska Ministerrådet.

Jenkins, J. (2003). *World Englishes: A resource book for students.* London: Routledge.

Kelletat, A. F. (2001). *Deutschland: Finnland 6:0. Saksa: Suomi 6:0. Vol. 4.* Tampere: University of Tampere, Deutsche Studien.

Li, D. (2002). Hong Kong parents' preference for English-medium education: Passive victims of imperialism or active agents of pragmatism? In A. Fitzpatrick (ed.), *Englishes in Asia: Communication, identity, power and education* (pp. 29–61). Melbourne: Language Australia.

Maier, C. (ed.) (2003). *The politics of English as a world language: New horizons in postcolonial cultural studies* (Cross/Cultures 65 ASNEL papers 7). Amsterdam: Rodopi.

Maurais, J. & Morris, M. A. (eds.) (2003). *Languages in a globalising world.* New York: Cambridge University Press.

Monbiot, G. (2000). *Captive state: The corporate takeover of Britain.* London: Macmillan.

Mühlhäusler, P. (1996). *Linguistic ecology: Language change and linguistic imperialism in the Pacific region.* London: Routledge.

Pennycook, A. (1998). *English and the discourses of colonialism.* London: Routledge.

Pennycook, A. (2001). *Critical applied linguistics: A critical introduction.* Mahwah, NJ: Lawrence Erlbaum.

Phillipson, R. (1992). *Linguistic imperialism.* Oxford: Oxford University Press.

Phillipson, R. (2003). *English-only Europe? Challenging language policy.* London: Routledge.

Phillipson, R. (2004). English in globalization: Three approaches. Review article, books by de Swaan, Block and Cameron, and Brutt-Griffler. *Journal of Language, Identity, and Education,* 3, 73–84.

Ricento, T. (ed.) (2000). *Ideology, politics, and language policies: Focus on English.* Amsterdam: John Benjamins.

Rothkopf, D. (1997). In praise of cultural imperialism? *Foreign Policy,* 107, 38–53.

Seidlhofer, B. (ed.) (2003). *Controversies in applied linguistics.* Oxford: Oxford University Press.

Skutnabb-Kangas, T. (2000). *Linguistic genocide in education – or worldwide diversity and human rights?* Mahwah, NJ: Lawrence Erlbaum.

Stiglitz, J. (2002). *Globalization and its discontents.* New York: W. W. Norton.

van Dijk, T. A. (1997). Editorial: The imperialism of English. *Discourse & Society,* 8(3), 291–2.

Yeung, Y-m. (2000). *Globalization and networked societies: Urban–regional change in Pacific Asia.* Honolulu: University of Hawai'i Press.

Index

CPSIA information can be obtained
at www.ICGtesting.com
Printed in the USA
JSHW040458271222
35263JS00002B/39